PRAISE FOR
Yellow Bird

"Remarkable . . . [Sierra Crane] Murdoch resists easy portraiture (Indians as pitiful or pathetic or damaged) and blind compassion (Indians as noble sufferers or keepers of special knowledge). Joan Didion once wrote that writers are always selling someone out. But Murdoch doesn't sell out Yellow Bird or the people of Fort Berthold, and she doesn't gloss over their problems either. Rather, she finds a way to balance her journalistic curiosity with respect for these complicated people. . . . [The book's] strength derives not from vast panoramas but from an intimate gaze. . . . I've long felt that Native communities are perceived (by Native and non-Native people alike) as places *in* America but not *of* America. Murdoch troubles this false separation and helps us understand Yellow Bird and Clarke, and by extension Native and non-Native lives, as deeply intertwined. . . . Yellow Bird's fanatical but dignified search brought closure to Clarke's family and change to Fort Berthold. In her telling of the story, Murdoch brings the same fanaticism and dignity to the search for and meaning of modern Native America."

—DAVID TREUER, *The New York Times Book Review*

"A great true-crime story . . . Lissa Yellow Bird is one of the most fascinating characters I've ever read about—and she's a real person. . . . It's Yellow Bird's incremental fight that makes the book addictive, full of twists and turns and surprising choices. . . . Murdoch reports the hell out of it, digging up text messages and conversations and business dealings and shifts in tribal power. She also gets deep into personal relationships and reveals their richness from all sides. It's a remarkable accomplishment."

—*Los Angeles Times*

"Journalist and first-time author Sierra Crane Murdoch follows an Arikara woman named Lissa Yellow Bird who is determined to solve the mystery of a missing white oil worker on the North Dakota reservation where her family lives. The book offers a gripping narrative of Yellow Bird's obsession with the case, but it's also about the harsh history of the land where the man vanished, how it was flooded and remade, first by an uncaring federal government and then again by industry. *Yellow Bird* teaches us that some things aren't random at all—that a crime, and its resolution, can be a product of a time and a place, and a history bringing together the people involved."

—*Outside*

"A deep and vivid portrait . . . As she describes Yellow Bird's efforts, Murdoch also does her own excavating, trying to uncover the connections between the region's settler colonial history and its ongoing human disappearances. The result is an illuminating book that draws a complex portrait of Yellow Bird as well as of life in Fort Berthold during the boom and the historical context of the region's disappearances. . . . Her prose is lucid and lyrical, alternately calling to mind nonfiction writers like Ian Frazier and novelists like Marilynne Robinson. . . . Murdoch turns her attention not only to what is gone, but to a woman who is still there, and in doing so, has produced a masterful book."

—*High Country News*

"The centerpiece of the work is a grisly crime, yes—one made more compelling by the window through which it is viewed: a Native woman named Lissa Yellow Bird, who is determined to get to the bottom of the disappearance of a white oil worker, Kristopher Clarke, on the reservation. But it's essential reading not because of the journey to get to the truth behind the crime—rather because it's a nuanced, careful exploration of a Native community and the impact of generational trauma and violence on a family. . . . The resulting work is a tome where every word is weighted with meaning, where the prose is careful, exacting, and lovely; it's a deeply reported portrait of a Native woman and the lingering effects of systemic trauma on a nation of people, threaded with crucial historical context."

—*Mother Jones*

"A powerful portrayal of an unusual sleuth whose dogged pursuit of a missing person inquiry led to justice. . . . Murdoch deepens her narrative with a searing look at the deficiencies of law and order on Native American land, corruption, and the abrogation of responsibility by the federal government. Admirers of David Grann's *Killers of the Flower Moon* will be drawn to this complex crime story with similar themes and settings."

—*Publishers Weekly* (starred review)

"A story that expertly blends true crime, environmental drama, and family saga. For a first nonfiction work, Murdoch has outdone herself by telling the story in a beautifully narrative way. . . . Required reading for all fans of true crime."

—*Library Journal* (starred review)

"Few people gave Kristopher Clarke's disappearance much thought until Lissa Yellow Bird, a member of the Mandan, Hidatsa, and Arikara Nation based on the Fort Berthold Reservation, made it her cause. . . . Thanks to Yellow Bird's tireless search, the truth eventually emerged—with poor Clarke considered a 'truly innocent victim' in an endlessly elaborate con game. An impressive debut that serves as an eye-opening view of both the oil economy and Native American affairs."

—*Kirkus Reviews*

"This book will tear your heart out. I don't know a more complicated, original protagonist in literature than Lissa Yellow Bird, or a more dogged reporter in American journalism than Sierra Crane Murdoch. At the center of this extraordinary story is a murder mystery, which unfolds within the ongoing travesty of the Bakken oil boom, which takes place within the unending dispossession of Native Americans. The Fort Berthold Indian Reservation, in North Dakota, has a stomach-turning history, and life there today as dramatized here is a haunted, unforgettable struggle, full of courage and beautifully drawn characters."

—WILLIAM FINNEGAN, author of *Barbarian Days*

"Sierra Crane Murdoch has written a deft, compelling account of an oil field murder and the remarkable woman who made it her business to solve it. Like the best true crime books, *Yellow Bird* is about much more than an act of violence. Murdoch's careful reporting delves into the long legacies of greed and exploitation on the reservation and the oil patch, and also the moments of connection and transcendence that chip away at those systems of power. I can't stop thinking and talking about this book."

—RACHEL MONROE, author of *Savage Appetites*

"In *Yellow Bird*, oilfield meets reservation, and readers meet a true-to-life Native sleuth unlike any in literature. Sierra Crane Murdoch takes a modest, ignored sort of American life and renders it large, with a murder mystery driving the action. . . . An empathetic, attentive account by a talented writer and listener."

—TED CONOVER, author of *Newjack: Guarding Sing Sing*

"This book is a detective story, and a good one, that tells what happens when rootless greed collides with rooted culture. But it's also a classic slice of American history and a tale of resilience in the face of remarkable trauma. Sierra Crane Murdoch is a patient, careful, and hence brilliant chronicler of this moment in time, a new voice who will add much to our literature in the years ahead."

—BILL MCKIBBEN, author of
Falter: Has the Human Game Begun to Play Itself Out?

Yellow Bird

Yellow Bird

*Oil, Murder,
and a Woman's
Search for Justice
in Indian Country*

Sierra Crane Murdoch

RANDOM HOUSE | NEW YORK

2021 Random House Trade Paperback Edition

Copyright © 2020 by Sierra Crane Murdoch

All rights reserved.

Published in the United States by Random House, an imprint and division of
Penguin Random House LLC, New York.

RANDOM HOUSE and the HOUSE colophon are registered trademarks of
Penguin Random House LLC.

Originally published in hardcover in the United States by Random House,
an imprint and division of Penguin Random House LLC, in 2020.

Portions of this work were originally published in different form in
High Country News and in the electronic versions of *The Atlantic* (theatlantic.com)
and *The New Yorker* (newyorker.com). Photograph on page 361 by
Kalen Goodluck used by permission of Kalen Goodluck.

LIBRARY OF CONGRESS CATALOGING-IN-PUBLICATION DATA
Names: Murdoch, Sierra Crane, author.
Title: Yellow Bird: oil, murder, and a woman's search for justice in
Indian country / by Sierra Crane Murdoch.
Description: First edition. | New York : Random House, [2020]
Identifiers: LCCN 2019022833 (print) | LCCN 2019022834 (ebook) |
ISBN 9780399589171 (trade paperback) | ISBN 9780399589164 (ebook)
Subjects: LCSH: Yellow Bird, Lissa. | Clarke, Kristopher. | Missing persons—
Investigation—North Dakota—Fort Berthold Indian Reservation. |
Criminal investigation—United States—Citizen participation. |
Oil industry workers—North Dakota—Fort Berthold Indian Reservation. |
Three Affiliated Tribes of the Fort Berthold Reservation, North Dakota. |
Fort Berthold Indian Reservation (N.D.)—Social conditions.
Classification: LCC HV6762.U5 M78 2020 (print) | LCC HV6762.U5 (ebook) |
DDC 364.152/3092—dc23
LC record available at https://lccn.loc.gov/2019022833
LC ebook record available at https://lccn.loc.gov/2019022834

From The New York Times. © 2020 The New York Times Company.
All rights reserved. Used under license.

Printed in the United States of America on acid-free paper

randomhousebooks.com

2 3 4 5 6 7 8 9

Book design by Susan Turner

For my family

Every day they had to look at the land, from horizon to horizon,
and every day the loss was with them; it was the dead unburied,
and the mourning of the lost going on forever.

—LESLIE MARMON SILKO

Let's say he knows we need someone
to admire, and says a hero is a person
who blunders into an open cave,
and that it takes courage to blunder.

—STEPHEN DUNN

Contents

Yellow Bird

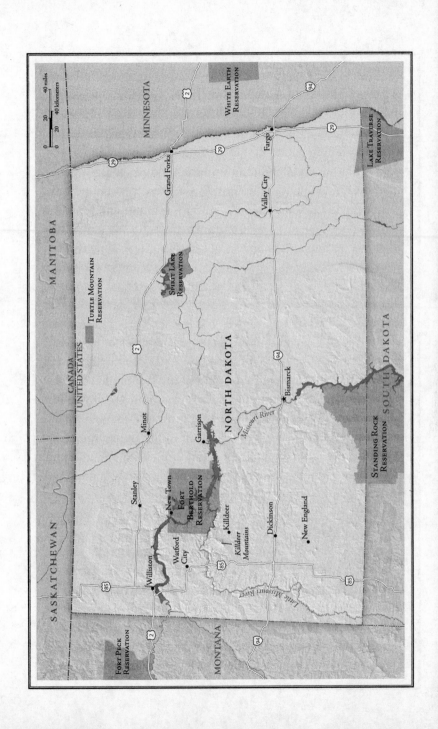

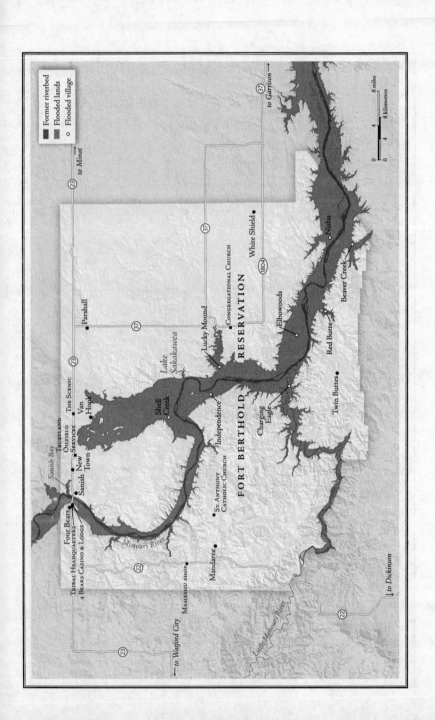

Prologue

Fort Berthold Indian Reservation, North Dakota

A MAN ONCE TOLD ME A STORY OF HOW HE DUG UP THE BONES OF HIS RELA-tives and held them in his hands. He is an old man now; then, he was young. He said he took the job because there were no others on the reservation and because the work was easier if a man did not think too hard about whose bones he was handling.

The reburials began in the summertime, in 1952, after the ground had thawed and the grass hung heavy with wood ticks. There were sixteen men, he said, two of them Native, and a foreman from Louisiana. The foreman did not seem to care, or perhaps he did not notice, when some of the men were careless with the bones and posed with them in various positions. The young man cared but did not say anything. He went on with his work. He placed the fragments in pine boxes, nailed the boxes shut, marked them with the names to which the bones apparently belonged.

The work lasted two summers, but the young man stayed just one and then enlisted in the Marines. His father, who had died the year before, was among the first laid in the new churchyard on the grasslands that rose from the Missouri River to the east edge of the reservation.

The other families had left their villages by this time. In winter, when the river froze, the Army Corps of Engineers lifted houses onto pallets and pulled them over the ice. There would not be time to move all of the houses; nor would there be time to dig every grave. People would tell stories of heading for the bluffs, turning now and then to watch the water rise, though it did not happen quite like this. When the Garrison Dam was finished, the river came up slowly into the creases of the valley's palm, filling first the ditches and furrowed fields, and then climbing steps and spilling onto floors.

The churches were among the last structures to be moved, and it is said that the bells rang all the way to their new locations. Sunday services continued for a time, though they were poorly attended after the flood claimed the only roads on the reservation crossing the river, and after the people scattered on higher ground. One day, the young man returned to find his church emptied and the concrete grave markers grown over like stumps. People came now and then to carve their names in the church walls or to lay cigarettes and flowers on the graves of their relatives, but only at funerals did the living outnumber the dead. It would not take long for the prairie to claim the church, for wind to unhook the battens and shatter windows, and for rodents to make homes in the floors and walls. This became the nature of the reservation. A person could come home and find things taken or worn out. It was something you got used to, the inevitability of loss. The lake that rose in the river's place was a shrine to this loss, to the things that had been and could be lost. Things pried from their foundations. Swept away with wood and bones. Pressed against the dam. Buried in the silt.

PART I

Boom

The Brightest Yellow Bird

Lissa Yellow Bird cannot explain why she went looking for Kristopher Clarke. The first time I asked her the question, she paused as if I had caught her by surprise, and then she said, "I guess I never really thought about it before." For someone so insatiably curious about the world, she is remarkably uncurious about herself. She is less interested in why she has done something than in the fact of having done it. Once, she asked me in reply if the answer even mattered. People tended to wonder all kinds of things about her: Why did she have five children with five different men? Why had she become an addict and then a drug dealer when she was capable of anything else?

Lissa stands five feet and four inches tall, moonfaced and strong-shouldered, a belly protruding over hard, slender legs. Her teeth are white and perfectly straight. Her hair is lush and dark. She has a long nose, full lips, and brows that arch like crescents above her eyes. When I met Lissa, she was forty-six years old and looked about her age—though, given the manner in which she lives, one might expect her to look older. She has a habit of going days without sleep, of sleeping upright in chairs. She rarely cooks, subsisting largely on avocados, tuna, croissants, mangoes, and candied nuts, and smokes like a fish takes water into its gills. She often loses things, particularly her lighters. One night, I watched as Lissa searched for one, nearly gutting her kitchen, until she gave up, bent over the countertop, and lit her cigarette with the toaster.

She is a member of the Mandan, Hidatsa, and Arikara Nation, an assembly of "Three Affiliated Tribes" who once farmed the bottomlands of the Missouri River and now call a patch of upland prairie in western North Dakota their home. The Fort Berthold Indian Reservation is three times the area of Los Angeles. The tribe has more than sixteen thousand members. Like a majority of these members, Lissa has not lived on Fort Berthold in some time, but she keeps in her possession an official document establishing her tribal citizenship:

Arikara Blood Quantum: 23/64
Mandan Blood Quantum: 1/4
Hidatsa Blood Quantum: 3/16
Sioux (Standing Rock) Blood Quantum: 1/8

Total Quantum This Tribe: 51/64
Total Quantum All Tribes: 59/64

"What's the other 5/64ths?" I once asked.

"I don't know," Lissa replied, "but somebody fucked up."

It was a joke. As far as she knew, at least two fathers of her children were white, and if anyone had fucked up her blood quantum, Lissa thought, it was the United States government. The fractions were controversial and arbitrary, assigned to her great-grandparents in the 1930s by the Bureau of Indian Affairs to determine how many individuals belonged to the tribe and how much federal assistance the tribe thus deserved. One could be a whole Indian, a fraction of an Indian, or no Indian. The idea was that a person's Indian-ness could be defined solely by race. It was the Bureau's way of applying order to the mess it had made, though to Lissa the fractions had always seemed superficial. In reality, she believed, there was no clear order to her life. She had worked as a prison guard, bartender, stripper, sex worker, advocate in tribal court, carpenter, bondsman, laundry attendant, and welder. She studied corrections and law enforcement at the University of North Dakota, where she graduated from the criminal justice program, though rather than working for the police, she spent much of her adult life evading them. She was arrested six times, charged twice for possessing meth "with intent to deliver," and given two concurrent prison sentences—ten and five years—two years of which she served. When Kristopher Clarke went missing in 2012, Lissa was on parole. Her interest in his disappearance may have seemed misplaced were it not for the fact that it made as much sense as every other random interest she had taken in her lifetime.

Lissa was born on June 13, 1968, to Irene* Yellow Bird and Leroy Chase, both members of the MHA Nation. Leroy had joined the Air Force and was not present for her birth, nor was he present for the rest of her life except on a rare phone call. Irene's mother, Madeleine, was Catholic and, since Irene was twenty-one and unmarried, arranged for a relative to take Lissa. The arrangement lasted seven months before Irene, swayed by the new radicalism of the era, decided she would not be shamed into giving up her daughter and asked for Lissa back.

It was her mother whom Lissa would later blame for the patternlessness of her life—her mother's ambition, to be exact. After they reunited, Irene dedicated herself to academic pursuits. They left North Dakota for California, where Irene enrolled again in school, then returned to North Dakota, then left for Wisconsin, where Irene pursued another degree before returning, again, to North Dakota, where she served for a while as the only Native American professor in the state. The longest Lissa and her mother remained anywhere was

* Five first names in this book are pseudonyms: Irene, Madeleine, Paul, Candace, and Caitlin.

three years, when they lived in Bismarck, a few hours south of the reservation. They moved to the city in 1972, when Lissa was four years old, into an apartment with a single bedroom where Lissa kept a pet fish. One day, the fish died, and Irene flushed it down the toilet. Lissa could not forgive her mother for this. It seemed unfair to her that something living, which she had loved, should end up in the sewer. Her sensitivity exasperated Irene, who supposed her daughter had wanted a full burial, with a procession and drums and star quilts draped over a casket. She supposed her daughter even wanted a priest. Lissa had acquired certain habits in church, such as fashioning bowls out of paper and placing them around the apartment. "Alms for the poor!" she called when anyone came to visit. Sometimes the visitors were her mother's white, wealthier friends, but often they were family. "Alms for the poor!" she called nonetheless, shaking her bowls piously, until one day her mother had enough and scolded, "Lissa, we are the poor."

Lissa had always been like this, Irene later told me—a fanatic with a bleeding heart, giving weight to weightless things. I supposed it was a kind way of explaining her daughter's passionate tendencies, since Shauna, Lissa's own daughter, explained them to me differently. "My mom is an addict," Shauna said. She meant this in the broadest sense.

Shauna is the oldest of her mother's five children, only nineteen years younger than Lissa, a generational closeness that pressed her up against her mother's faults and made her feel them more acutely than her siblings. When Lissa started smoking crack, Shauna was eight years old. Six years later, Lissa turned to meth. But even in the years before she got high, Lissa, Shauna believed, had been prone to obsession.

Among the first of these obsessions Shauna recalled were plants. When she was in preschool, her mother had discovered an interest in growing things, and after that they kept all kinds of plants—leafy, tropical, sun-starved plants spilling from the windows of their apartment in Grand Forks, where Lissa attended college, as well as trays of vegetable starts Lissa grew from seed, though they never had any space for a garden. After that, her mother's obsessions came in all forms, sudden and indiscriminate, but each one Lissa had taken on with the faith and focus of a zealot. For a while, it had been music— Lissa taught herself to play piano—before she purchased a camera and became an ardent documentarian.

If these obsessions sounded like hobbies, Shauna insisted they were not. It had never been enough for her mother to take an interest in something. Rather, Lissa was set on being the best at everything she did. The best drug dealer. The most dogged bondswoman. The eventual leader of each organization she joined. After Lissa emerged from prison sober, she still found plenty of things to obsess about and, in fact, it seemed that sobriety intensified her fixations. According to Shauna, the only difference between the things that occupied her mother when she was sober and the things that made her high was that Lissa often abandoned the sober things with the same swiftness and ease with which they came to her. In one of their many moves, they had left the plants behind. This was one thing Shauna expected as a child, that whatever life they were living at one moment would last only so long. Always they had kept moving, from hotels to shelters, from apartments they rented to the houses of friends, and from the papery walls of all the places they lived, her mother had hatched, again and again, changed and yet the same.

And so when Lissa first told Shauna about the oil worker who was missing—and how she planned on finding him—Shauna assumed this obsession would also pass. She thought it would last weeks or months until the young man was found. She did not think it would go on for years. "I don't know what it was about that boy," Shauna would say, but Kristopher Clarke was different.

IT WAS BECAUSE OF CLARKE that I encountered Lissa. I was a journalist reporting on the mystery of his disappearance, which, by the time I met her in 2014, mostly had been solved. On February 22, 2012, Clarke had gone missing from the Fort Berthold Indian Reservation.

He was twenty-nine years old at the time, white, from Washington State. North Dakota was booming with oil development, and Fort Berthold was in the center of the oil fields. Clarke worked for a trucking company based in a remote southern district of the reservation where most of the wells were being drilled. He was a "pusher," in the lingo of the industry: Among other things, he arranged contracts to haul water to drilling sites, where the water was mixed with chemical additives and shot down holes to "frack" the wells. On the morning he went missing, Clarke was spotted at the trucking company offices. Several people who spoke to him said he was leaving that day to visit his grandfather in Oregon, but no one saw Clarke again. In February 2014, after he had been missing two years, I came across some news about a break in his case: There had been arrests and, soon afterward, a confession. The alleged perpetrators were awaiting trial, but while prosecutors believed Clarke had been murdered, they lacked one thing that would prove their case: They could not find his body.

The story caught my eye because I was familiar with the reservation from which Clarke disappeared. Since 2011, I had been going there myself to report on the oil boom that was transforming the tribal community. One of the ways I had seen the place change was a rise in crime, a new pervasiveness of violence due to an influx of non-Native workers over whom the MHA Nation had no criminal jurisdiction. That was why I took an interest in Clarke: I had some understanding of the legal topography into which he disappeared, and I suspected his case might be a window into the darker realities of the boom.

On the morning of November 4, 2014, I dropped by the tribal newspaper offices, where the editor, a woman I knew, suggested I interview Lissa, who at that moment happened to be out searching for Clarke's body. The editor arranged for us to meet that night.

The offices were in a clapboard house perched on the west shore of Lake Sakakawea, a reservoir that flooded the center of the reservation in 1954 after the federal government built a dam on the Missouri River. It was dusk when I arrived, a cold wind sweeping off the surface of the lake. I climbed a set of steps, knocked, and the editor answered. She led me past an office furnished with a space heater, a coffee maker, and a crystal lamp into an airy room strewn with proofs and cardboard boxes, where she instructed me to wait. An hour passed. I began to shiver. Then, at last, the door opened, and Lissa entered.

Her face was luminous with cold, her hair flecked with ice. She wore a sweatshirt, long underwear, hiking boots, reading glasses, and a Bluetooth device affixed to her right ear. She did not shake my hand or say hello but spoke as if we had seen each other just that morning. Only when she caught me glancing at her long underwear did it seem to occur to her that we had never met. She explained that she had been searching for Clarke "down at the river" and sunk in a pit of mud.

She had been looking for him since the summer of 2012, when a relative sent her a Facebook message posted by Clarke's mother. The mother, Jill Williams, was pleading for information regarding the whereabouts of her son. By that time, Clarke, or "KC," as Jill called him, had been missing for three months. Investigators found his pickup truck parked on a street in Williston, about an hour west of the reservation, but no other clues had turned up. Lissa thought she could help. Since 2008, she had been living five hours east of Fort Berthold, in Fargo, but many of her relatives lived on the reservation, and she often visited them there. Lissa sensed that Jill, who lived with her husband in Washington State and was unfamiliar with Fort Berthold, had no idea where to begin. So she wrote to Jill, offering to ask around about her son.

Lissa had a ready laugh, I noticed, the bearing of a woman who derives entertainment from the absurdities of the world. Her speech was rushed and giddy, her legs kicked beneath her chair, and her hands were in flight, touching pens and cigarettes and the Bluetooth earpiece and darting in her lap. She did not seem nervous. Rather, she seemed so intent on telling the story that she had lost track of her own body. Only in her expressions did she retain full control. She laughed when I became confused, smiled when I looked surprised. Once, when I interrupted her with a question, she stared at me, stone-faced and abruptly still, as if the question were stupid and the answer too obvious to say. I stopped asking questions, and as I listened, it occurred to me that Lissa knew far more about Clarke's disappearance than the editor had let on. Lissa was not just searching for his body. She had done much more than that. If she had not exactly solved the case, I suspected that she had, at least, influenced its outcome. It seemed possible to me that because of Lissa, everything had come to light.

She must have mistaken my quiet for disbelief, because after we had spoken for more than hour, she said, in a flicker of self-consciousness, "It's all in my files. I kept everything." If I wanted, she added, I could visit her in Fargo, and she would give me her documents.

The following spring, I flew to Fargo, as I would many times after that. Lissa would pick me up at the airport, and when we arrived at her apartment, she would brew a pot of coffee no matter the time of night. In the morning, before she left for the welding shop where she worked, she would open her computer so that I could spend the day sifting through files, through emails, text messages, photographs, and audio recordings, which I copied to my laptop. There were hundreds of these files, spanning three years, some thousands of pages long. In the evening, Lissa would fix tuna sandwiches, and we would scroll together through the documents. We did this every day for weeks, often until after midnight. I don't know why she trusted me, and I don't think she knows, either. Once, she said, "You just kind of showed up, and then you kept coming back."

It was over those weeks, and then over years, that I pieced together this story, beginning with a note Lissa composed to Jill Williams on June 2, 2012:

> *Hi to KC's mom! I am a member of the Three Affiliated Tribes which head-*
> *quarters in New Town, North Dakota. My family, which consists of most*
> *of the reservation, mostly live on Fort Berthold. . . . That is federal land*
> *and there are many hoops to jump in order to get information or get the ball*

rolling on an investigation. . . . I have many connections there and would like to help you if you need me to. . . . I'm sorry to hear about your boy. I'm a mother too. My prayers are with you.

LISSA'S LIFE AT THE TIME of KC's disappearance had entered a period of rare stability. It had been four years since her release from the Dakota Women's Correctional and Rehabilitation Center in New England, North Dakota, where she served two years after she had been caught twice with large quantities of meth. Her first charge carried a mandatory minimum of five years in prison; the second, ten years, since she was arrested near a school. Lissa refused to snitch on her fellow dealers—she would not bargain with prosecutors—so it had come as a surprise to her when she was notified of her early release on account of her good behavior. On April 4, 2008, she was transferred to a halfway house, Centre, Inc., in Fargo, where she spent ten more months in state custody before she was granted parole.

The city of Fargo is on the west bank of the Red River, which flows north along the border of North Dakota and Minnesota and empties into Lake Winnipeg in Manitoba. The land around it is vast and treeless, the otherwise fertile remnant of a glacial lake bottom, but the city center is small, cozy, made up of old wooden houses, brick-and-mortar shops, and streets shaded by maples and oaks. Lissa requested placement there to be closer to her sons, who had lived with her uncle since her arrests. She did not want to displace the boys again. After her release from the halfway house on February 10, 2009, she moved into an apartment on Ninth Avenue Circle, on the bottom floor of a three-story building inhabited by families from war-torn countries.

It had not been easy to find a place. From the halfway house, Lissa had called all over the city until at last, a landlord told her that, yes, there were openings, and no, it did not matter that she was a felon, though the credit check cost forty dollars. She sent the money. The landlord never replied. When she called again from the halfway house, the landlord informed her that she was sorry—she could not accept a felon.

Then, one night, as Lissa rode from the halfway house to the church where she attended addiction recovery meetings, her driver offered to call a friend who managed some apartments. The property manager agreed to meet with Lissa, and on a Monday evening, Lissa caught a ride to the west side of the city. She brought a copy of her criminal record. The manager refused to see it. "I already know," she said, and told Lissa she could have the place. The next day, Lissa waited at her uncle's house for her youngest son, Micah, to return from school, and together they drove to the apartment. It was small and dark, with three bedrooms, the windows level with the ground so that snow piled against them, and with a sliding glass door that opened from the living room onto a patio. The walls and ceilings were painted white, and the floors, except for in the kitchen, were carpeted. It felt cozy inside, like a fort made of blankets, padded from the noise of the outer world. Lissa and Micah used their clothes for pillows, lying side by side on the floor of the bedroom nearest the kitchen, and fell asleep as lights from out on the cul-de-sac played across the ceiling.

For many nights, they slept like this, curled together on the floor. Lissa called Micah her "baby," though he was nine years old and had grown in their years apart. He was roughly the height of her shoulders, now, with sleepy eyes and prominent ears and a dark, thick mat of hair. He was the sort of boy older women stopped on the street to admire. On Thursday nights, Lissa brought him to her addiction recovery meetings at the church, where Micah was polite, a keen listener. He liked hearing the stories people told, and when it was his turn to speak, he liked to stand and say, "My name is Micah, and I've been sober my whole life." The program, called The Red Road to Wellbriety, was modeled after Alcoholics Anonymous but emphasized Indigenous ways of cultural healing. Founded in the nineties, the Wellbriety movement held that the twelve steps bandied in recovery programs were circular, that humans healed in cycles, and that one should acknowledge—in the words of movement founders—"the roots of addiction," the "sociopolitical causes without removing an individual's need to do the hard work it takes to heal."

The ideas made sense to Lissa immediately; and when, after only her second gathering, the leader of the group announced he was leaving town, Lissa led the meetings. The other attendees seemed to like when she brought Micah along, and some men even asked Micah to be their "sponsor," the person they turned to whenever they were having a hard time. Micah did not have a phone, so the men rode their bicycles to the apartment or called Lissa and requested to speak with him. They often asked Micah about their own children: What did they like to do for fun? What gifts would they like for Christmas? One man who had not visited his kids in years worried they did not want to see him. "Give them a call," Micah advised. "They can't hate you for making an effort." On other occasions, the men asked him about women. Micah had no romantic experience of his own, but his answers seemed to satisfy the men. "He's just so simple," they told Lissa when they met for meetings. This was a rule of their recovery group—*keep things simple.*

Of her children, Lissa felt closest to Micah. In 2002, when he was two years old, a train hauling farm fertilizer had derailed in Minot, the city east of the reservation, and released a cloud of anhydrous ammonia gas into the neighborhood where they lived. Micah's lungs had been severely damaged. He spent his childhood in and out of hospitals, where doctors insisted he would not live past the age of twelve. Lissa supposed their mutual desperation had cinched them to each other, and it was not long after her release from the halfway house that they resumed their positions as mother and son.

It was not as easy with her other children. CJ, seventeen, moved into the apartment soon after Micah did, but Obadiah, ten, took more time. Obie did not want to leave Lissa's uncle, Dennis, who was the closest he had come to having a father since his own went to prison a year after he was born. "Grandpa," the boys called Dennis—a term of respect for elder relatives—and, indeed, Dennis had done a good job with them, Lissa thought, taking them to wrestling practice and tending to their religious instruction. Obie had become attached. "I'm going to sleep at Grandpa's tonight," he said whenever his mother stopped by Dennis's in the evenings. Lissa did not argue with him. If Micah was her caregiver, Obie was her "warlord." He was always lighting fires at the same time he was putting them out. Of all her children, Obie most reminded Lissa of herself.

In March, winter cloaked the city in dim light. Obie moved into the apartment. At six each morning, Lissa left the boys at Dennis's and went to work at a laundry downtown, where she stuffed hospital sheets into washing machines and fed them into giant pressers. The work was simple. Lissa moved fast and resented anyone who slowed her down. If a machine broke, she fixed it herself, having no patience for the maintenance man who was rarely there when she needed him. He was usually outside, smoking cigarettes with another woman who worked at the laundry. Lissa held particular contempt for the kind of person who never paid attention, and her temper flared. One day, when a wheel fell off a machine and knocked her in the face, and her boss, Bruce, asked what was wrong, she laid into him: "What's wrong? This fucking machine and your fucking five-star maintenance guy who's out there sucking ass to get with a married woman." Bruce often invited Lissa to funk shows in the bars around Fargo, but she declined. After the incident, Bruce took to winking at her, saying, "Well, you know, Lissa. Five-star."

In the evenings, Lissa furnished the apartment. She added beds, a dining table, and a desk. She bought a computer and, in the living room, hung a clock. One weekend, she drove to Minot, where she had kept her belongings in a storage unit while in prison. The door to the unit had been pushed in, letting in years of rain and snow. She discarded most things except for two couches and several plastic crates containing medical records, police reports, letters, and court transcripts.

She focused on each day as if a routine life—billing accounts, file transfers, doctor appointments, school enrollment—might accumulate into an opaque wall dividing the present from her past. The truth was that her release from prison had come so unexpectedly that at first Lissa believed she had not deserved to get out. She had been prepared to serve her entire sentence and had practiced thinking in geologic terms: "Like, the dinosaurs," she said. If life was just a fleck on the timeline of the universe, then her sentence was too brief to appear. This had made it easier to shrug off the time she already lost—ten years to addiction, what were ten more? Not until she boarded the prison van to Fargo had her sense of time shrunk again, and not until she saw her sons had it become clear to her how long—two years— she had been away. After she moved into the apartment on Ninth Avenue Circle, she purchased a smartphone on which she shot videos of her sons. In one, the camera panned around a bedroom where Micah and Obie were playing a video game. Lissa told them to look at the camera, but neither listened. The video would seem sad, grasping across a distance, and indeed Lissa would admit that it was not until spring, weeks after Obie and CJ joined her in the apartment, that the familiarity she once had felt with them returned.

One day in late March, a storm blanketed the city in snow, and Lissa came home to find the refrigerator empty. The grocery store was not far, a few blocks south where the city's outer neighborhoods gave way to warehouses and big-box stores, but Lissa worried her car would not make it. It was a blue Ford hatchback she had bought for $500. One door barely opened, and when it did, it would not shut. The first time Lissa pressed the gas, the engine had belched a cloud of blue smoke. She suspected her sons were embarrassed by the car but did not want to hurt her by saying so. They were cautious around her, watchful, she noticed, as if they might startle her back into addiction. When Lissa said she was going to the store, they put on their jackets and followed her into the storm.

The snow was blowing hard, collecting in icy drifts. Where the cul-de-sac met Ninth Avenue, a plow had left a bank as high as their front bumper. "I don't know about this," CJ said, but the car kicked as it crested the bank, the snow giving way beneath them. Then it happened again: At a traffic light, they came across a pickup spinning its wheels, teetering on a higher bank of snow. "I don't know about this," CJ repeated, but when the light turned green, the car crept forward, and—as if lifted by an invisible palm—moved effortlessly over the bank.

The car would not last long after the storm, but Lissa and her boys would tell the story for years. "Shit, that was like the little car that could," they would say. It was one thing they would all remember from the year Lissa got out: the car coughing blue smoke, a door banging open and never-quite-shut, but mother and sons floating on through the white, as feathery and invulnerable as the snow.

That same March, Lissa's daughter Shauna moved in as well from Minot, where she had been living with her children. She had been sixteen when she had her first child; her second came two years later, on the day of her mother's last arrest; and when Lissa got out of the halfway house, Shauna—twenty-one-years-old—had given birth to her third. She was single, having escaped an abusive relationship with the baby's father, which ended when she was nine months pregnant in an incident for which they had both been charged with assault. He was convicted, her charges dismissed, but they lingered on her record. Shauna had found herself broke and unemployed, and when her mother suggested she move to Fargo, she agreed. If anyone knew how to start life over, her mother did, Shauna thought. That winter and spring, Shauna shared a bedroom in her mother's apartment with her kids, and when Lissa returned from the laundry each afternoon, Shauna went looking for work. After many rejections, she found a job tracking fraud for a major financial institution. She rented her own place. As soon as she moved out, her younger sister, Lindsay, who was nineteen, moved in. Lindsay had been raised by her father in Bakersfield, California, and that spring, for the first time, Lissa lived near all five of her children at once.

In appearance, Shauna took after her mother. They were roughly the same height, with sharp cheekbones, dark eyes, and milky-coffee skin. Shauna's nose was different, small and upturned, but her face was as round. They had similar habits. "My mom and sister are like the same person," Obie observed, by which he meant they were confident, opinionated, and shared a fondness for television crime shows. But in other ways they were distinct—so distinct that some relatives claimed they were nothing alike. Irene, with whom Shauna spent much of her childhood, was sharply attuned to the differences. Where Lissa had refused to wear anything but T-shirts and jeans and had made a habit of turning her stockings into ribbons, Shauna had let her grandmother clothe her in floral vests and take her to get her nails done. Shauna smiled like her grandmother—lips pursed, eyes electric. Appearances mattered to Shauna in a way they had rarely mattered to Lissa.

It was Shauna who suggested they make a trip to the reservation. More than a year had passed since her last visit—longer for her mother. Shauna was the only one of her siblings who had ever lived on the reservation, and she had no desire to do so again. An "urban Indian" she called herself, suckled on the amenities of the city, but if ever asked where she was from, Shauna always replied, "Up on the rez." The Yellow Bird family was from White Shield, a town in a southeast "segment" of Fort Berthold. Most of their relatives had left the reservation for school or work, but some uncles and cousins remained, as did Irene's own mother, Madeleine, who was approaching ninety years of age. Every July, the family gathered in White Shield for a reunion on the weekend of the segment's powwow, when many people who had left came home from far-flung cities and reservations. Shauna wanted to go. Lissa was less sure. "I'll think about it," she said, but Shauna would insist.

To SAY THE YELLOW BIRDS were from White Shield is not exactly true. To be more accurate, they were from the bottomlands of the Missouri River, where their ancestors farmed for more than four centuries before White Shield came into existence. If the Yellow Birds identified with any one tribe, it was with the Arikara—the Ree, as white settlers called them; or Sáhniš, as they call themselves, meaning, in their own language, "the people." The Arikara belonged to a family of tribes that lived on the eastern Great Plains. Around the fifteenth century, they separated from the Pawnee and pushed north, settling in a string of villages that spanned the Missouri from the southern to northern border of present-day South Dakota. In the 1700s, twenty thousand Arikara lived in these villages. They grew a variety of crops, which they traded with other tribes for meat, hide, fur, and horses, but their most valuable yield was corn. According to the Arikara genesis story, it was At'ná, or Mother Corn, who led the people from their resting place underground to the surface of the earth, where, after enduring many obstacles, they made a home on the Missouri River.

How the Arikara found their way to White Shield was less a matter of mythology than survival. By the late 1700s, European settlement to the east had pushed Sioux bands west, and the Arikara became ancillary recipients of the colonizers' violence. The Sioux frequently attacked, forcing the tribe to consolidate into larger villages, and after these attacks and a smallpox epidemic reduced the tribe to 2,500 people in 1780, the Arikara moved north. When Meriwether Lewis and William Clark encountered them in 1804, they were living at the confluence of the Missouri and Grand rivers, by the southern border of what would become North Dakota. They stayed barely two decades. In 1823, fur traders led by a brigadier general, William Ashley, entered a village and attempted to seduce women. One trader was killed; the next day, Arikara warriors killed twelve others. In retaliation, the U.S. Army attacked with more than a thousand soldiers and Sioux warriors. The Arikara fled, living as nomads, and then moved north, again, to the Knife River, where they settled near a Mandan village and a trading outpost called Fort Clark. In 1837, a steamship arrived at the fort bearing passengers infected with smallpox. Half the Arikara died of smallpox, while the Mandan fared worse—nine in ten succumbed. The hundred Mandan who survived moved north to a bend in the Missouri, where they formed a new village with the Hidatsa called Like-a-Fishhook. In 1862, the Arikara joined them there.

By then, the Arikara, Mandan, and Hidatsa had signed a treaty with the United States drawing the boundaries of a reservation—west of the Missouri, north of the Heart, east of the Powder rivers, south of the Canada border—containing more than twelve million acres. According to the terms of the 1851 Fort Laramie Treaty, which five other tribes including the Sioux signed, the tribes would "make an effective and lasting peace" with neighboring tribes and white settlers. In exchange, the U.S. pledged to protect each tribe "against the commission of all depredations by the people of the said United States" and provide annuities—food, material, and tools necessary to the tribes' survival while confined to reservations. But even after the treaty was signed, white settlers continued to encroach on Sioux territory. The Sioux, in an effort to undermine good relations between the three tribes and the U.S. government, attacked more frequently, destroying crops, burning homes, and pillaging resources. The Arikara were trapped on their reservation, unable to hunt, and in 1867, when U.S. officials requested assistance for military campaigns against the Sioux, a chief named Son-of-the-Star sent more than a hundred Arikara men to serve as scouts for the army. Some of these men served under General George Armstrong Custer in the Battle of the Little Bighorn.

Son-of-the-Star had a son named Sitting Bear, who had a daughter named Fannie Bear, who had a daughter named Jessie Everett, who had a daughter named Madeleine Young Bird. Madeleine would marry a man named Willard Yellow Bird, who was the son of Charles Yellow Bird, whose father was called Old Man Yellow Bird.

In 1870, nineteen years after the Three Affiliated Tribes signed the Fort Laramie Treaty, the U.S. government violated the treaty by shrinking the reservation, claiming eight of the twelve million acres. The government took land for a railroad by executive order in 1880 and, in 1891, divided the remaining land into 160-acre parcels, which it "allotted" to a head of each Indian household; and eighty- and forty-acre parcels, assigned to each woman and child. The purpose of allotment, apart from acquiring land for white settlers—what land the government did not allot, it sold—was to replace communalism with individualism. In 1887, Congress had applied the policy to tribes nationwide by passing the General Allotment Act, whose architect, Henry Dawes, defined "civilized" men as those who "cultivate the ground, live in houses, ride in Studebaker wagons, send children to school, drink whiskey (and) own property." By then, a federal agent assigned to oversee the reservation had already compelled families to leave Like-a-Fishhook, where they farmed communally, for individual plots of land. Those who refused were deprived of annuities. In 1884, the agent set fire to Like-a-Fishhook, and within a few years, the village was abandoned.

Old Man Yellow Bird was among those forced to move. He settled on the east bank of the Missouri, on a bluff overlooking a forest of willow and cottonwood, where the Arikara formed a village called Armstrong. In 1904, 380 Arikara remained. They hunted, raised livestock, and grew corn and beans, among other crops they had adapted over centuries to the northern plains. They dug wild turnips to boil with meat. They gathered water from creeks and timber from forests and berries from along the river, which they dried and mashed with corn. In 1924, they renamed the village Nishu, after a late tribal chief whose traditional name meant "arrow."

Slowly they remade themselves. Through subsistence farming and leasing their allotments to white ranchers, reservation families became self-sufficient, and in 1920, the local Indian agent reported he had not had to distribute rations for five years. Around that time, the three tribes filed a claim against the United States, and, in 1930, won a $2 million settlement for land the government had taken. Each citizen received $1,000, deposited into an account managed by the Bureau of Indian Affairs, and it was due, in part, to this money that they fared better during the Great Depression and the Second World War than their less self-sufficient white neighbors. Two-hundred-and-fifty tribal members served in the war, and each time a serviceman returned, his village honored him with a feast and a dance that often lasted all night.

In 1944, the U.S. Congress passed a flood control act, proposing a series of dams on the Missouri, which, as the longest river in the nation, had become central to its economy. A year earlier, the river had flooded millions of acres of farmland, and although the floods were later blamed on the Army Corps of Engineers—on levees constructed downriver, preventing the natural flow of water into the floodplains—the Corps was tasked with corralling the river into a series of reservoirs to regulate flow and ensure safe passage for grain barges. In 1945, the year the Second World War ended, the Army Corps, without official approval from Congress, began constructing the Garrison Dam at a site ten miles downriver from Nishu. The dams on the Upper Missouri, called the Pick-Sloan Plan, were located so as not to disturb white settlements. Instead, they would flood the bottomlands of eight reservations, land guaranteed to tribes by treaty and home to thousands of families. Pick-Sloan, the Lakota historian Vine Deloria, Jr., wrote, was "the single most destructive act ever perpetrated on any tribe by the United States."

In 1947, the year Congress officially approved the Garrison Dam, Madeleine Yellow Bird gave birth to her first of fourteen children, whom she named Irene. Five years later, Madeleine and Willard left Nishu and moved nineteen miles north to a flat, treeless plain, where Willard and a cousin gathered signatures on a petition to name their new community after an Arikara leader, White Shield.

Nishu disappeared into the reservoir. Later, in the stories reservation families told, the water would become as much a divider of time as it was of geography. *Before the flood* and *after.*

After the flood, the Bureau of Indian Affairs built a headquarters in New Town, on the northern border of Fort Berthold, and, as directed by an act of Congress, opened a "relocation" office where tribal members could apply for work in Phoenix, Albuquerque, Denver, Minneapolis, Atlanta, the Bay Area, and Los Angeles. In 1969, when Lissa was less than a year old, Irene took a job in a Los Angeles relocation office, and after that, it would seem that she and her daughter were set indefinitely adrift. Theirs was a shared fate: Among citizens of more than five hundred tribes recognized by the United States, a majority had become "urban Indians," and "Indian Country"—defined as Indian land, land not entirely stolen—had become, in reality, a patchwork of reservations and cities and the highways threading between them, on which Native people were always moving, always leaving and coming home.

THE WAY FROM FARGO TO White Shield is almost three hundred miles and has only two turns—north, toward Minot, then west, past a bridge over the Missouri River and the outflow of the Garrison Dam. In midsummer, humidity blots out the horizon, cleared now and then by drenching rain and lifted, again, with new gusts of heat. The prairie grows lush and green. It hums at night with frogs and cicadas, and sings in the morning with birds. All along the way are rapeseed fields, yellow in July; and corn and wheat; and grain silos that rise like tiny silver cities; and thick groves of trees that hide farmhouses from view. The first town past the river is Garrison, a gas station and some brick city blocks; and twenty miles on is the reservation, a green sign marking the border. There is no change in the landscape. Like the fields surrounding Fort Berthold, the land here is cultivated in large part by the descendants of Scandinavian and German homesteaders who bought reservation tracts from the U.S. government over a century ago. Soon after the border, White Shield appears: first a gas station, the only business in town; and then the community complex, a steep-roofed wooden building where funerals, fundraisers, and elders' birthday parties are held, among other celebrations. By the complex are the powwow grounds; past the grounds is the Catholic church; and past the church is the school and the housing clusters built after the flood, which include the apartments known as "the Jungle" and a row of large dwellings locals call "Knots Landing" after a 1980s soap opera about rich white people who live in big houses, drink too much, and kill one another.

On the morning she drove to White Shield to attend the Yellow Bird reunion, Lissa had washed her hair and brushed it, plucked her eyebrows, and painted her nails a light, iridescent pink. As she studied herself in the mirror, she had seen that her skin was still marked with the traces of her drug use, but in other ways her body had restored itself. Her lips were bright with natural color, and her hair, once short and fried to platinum, had grown past her shoulders, dark and thick. She was not as skinny as she once had been, but she was not yet fat, either. She had pulled on a pair of tight jeans and a black cotton shirt with a scooped neck, and slipped a ring onto her left thumb. "You're an attractive woman," a friend had told her recently, and that morning, Lissa had allowed herself to agree.

But on the road to White Shield, her confidence cracked. She imagined her relatives preparing for her return, stowing away their needles lest she raid the diabetics' closet. She knew they were ashamed of her. No one else in her family had gone to prison except for an uncle, a Korean War veteran who once had threatened a cop. Lissa's mother could not even bring herself to say the word "prison." That "other college," Irene called it, as if prison were a school she sent her daughter to, to do a little more growing up. It was Irene who had sent Lissa there, Lissa believed—Irene *and* Shauna who notified the police. Lissa had not seen her mother since the arrests. Nobody except for Shauna and Shauna's kids had visited her in prison.

It was even longer since Lissa had seen her grandmother, Madeleine. She remembered clearly the last night she had spent on the reservation, in the winter of 2001. She had left Minneapolis, where she lived for almost ten years, in hope that by coming home she could leave her addiction behind. As soon as she arrived, Madeleine had not wanted her. One night, after Lissa went to bed drunk, an uncle had shaken her awake and told her to get out. It had been almost midnight, thirty degrees below zero. Micah and Obie had been sleeping beside her. *Are you serious*, Lissa had said, and as she packed,

Madeleine had stood as still as a shadow in the bedroom doorway. *Fuck you and your fucking white man God,* Lissa had screamed. *You're a fucking sinner just like everybody else.*

Now it was summer, and the White Shield powwow grounds were full with color—feather roaches and beaded yokes, and tin cones on the jingle dresses. Beyond the church, Lissa turned onto the road to Madeleine's old farmhouse, a lane that tunneled through waist-high grass and curved along a row of poplars. There was a Quonset hut that Lissa's grandfather had used as a shop and a studio where he practiced saxophone until he died in 1997, and the farmhouse—gray, with a pale-yellow door and a red porch strung with icicle lights. The lawn was lush and groomed, and in the backyard, a cradle of trees had formed. There were gardens marked with railroad ties; flowerpots, stacked; petunias blooming by a birdbath. And in a chair in the yard sat Madeleine, wearing a blue headband, gray shirt, and khaki pants.

She looked older—that much Lissa could tell from the way her grandmother did not rise when they embraced. Madeleine's eyes were narrowed toward the sun, which felt hot on Lissa's back.

To the east, toward the border of the reservation, the surface of a slough glinted. Lissa scanned the property but did not see her mother. An uncle caught her eye and winked. "You got my money?" he said. A half joke. Lissa knew an Indian was sort of joking when he followed his line with a guttural, "Ayyyeee."

She glanced around once more for her mother but did not see her. "Say," Madeleine said, "get me a pop from the kitchen," and Lissa cut gratefully toward the farmhouse.

The inside was dark and sweltering, with shades pulled over the windows, fans propped on chairs. From the entry, Lissa could see into the living room where the glow of a television caught the bare, sweating skin of children sprawled on the floor—cousins, though they did not look up when she came in, and anyway, they were too young for her to recognize. The couch was new, the pictures rearranged. Everything else looked the same. Lissa followed a hallway into a kitchen, where food was laid out for dinner that night. She crossed to the refrigerator and stopped. On a shelf against the wall were three boxes of syringes. Lissa reached for a box. There were five syringes in all, alcohol swabs, and a finger poker to check blood sugar. She lifted a syringe and twirled it in the window light. A milliliter. This had been a good size, she thought, the right hit. She tried to remember the needle sinking into her, the cold and then the warmth. Once, in Minot, when she ran low on meth, she had gone to a liquor store, purchased a bottle of vodka, and shot that up instead. She had hardly noticed the difference. Sometimes, she had wondered if it was the needle she was addicted to. The rush had been the same.

She twirled the syringe again, noting the tiny orange cap, the tab wings. That was when she saw her aunt Donna standing in the door-way of the kitchen.

"Lissa, what are you doing?" Donna said.

Lissa glanced once more at the syringe and returned it to the box. "I was trying to remember what was so important about it," she said.

Donna paused. Then she crossed the kitchen and wrapped her arms around Lissa. "I'm glad you're back," she said.

As far as Lissa knew, Donna never told anyone about the incident in the kitchen. Her relatives' fear that she would relapse was palpable without them mentioning it. "Don't say that," an aunt had chided when an uncle made a prison joke, as if the mere reminder of her crimes might incline her to commit more of them. The reunion was the beginning of a strange new discomfort Lissa felt in the company of her family. In the visits she made afterward—to Madeleine's house in White Shield; to Minot, where her mother lived and taught social work at the university; to the shores of the lake where Lissa went with her cousins to fish and camp—she was able to create an illusion of closeness in which it seemed no time had passed. Illusions had always come naturally to her. Lissa knew how to make people who were distant appear close. She could enter their conversations at just the right time, make them laugh, soothe them with her bluntness. She could fill the too-quiet spaces—not with small talk, but with important things: losses they had suffered; things they still feared; stories they shared from their childhoods and adulthoods. Lissa could almost make her relatives believe she was the same girl they had known years ago—though if they thought too hard about it, inevitably they would remember. She saw the unease come into their eyes. She could not shake them from their watchfulness.

They had every reason to be afraid. Before her release, Lissa's confidence that she would not relapse had bordered on smugness. Once, a caseworker at the halfway house had suggested she open a savings account, and Lissa had joked, "Indians don't do that shit." When the caseworker asked what she would do if she got out and blew a paycheck on drugs and died, Lissa replied, "I'll be dead." The caseworker was a prim woman named Jan, and Lissa liked to give her a hard time. In the end, Lissa and Jan had made their peace. Lissa started a savings account, and after she was paroled, Jan invited her back to offer advice to inmates. Lissa still did not want to relapse, but now, a year into her parole, the fact of her sobriety had begun to seem less a matter of desire than of circumstance.

The first year was the easiest. It was in the second year that Lissa came perilously close to using again. In September 2010, a man hit her with a truck as she crossed the street near her apartment and dragged her body for ten yards before realizing what he had done. Lissa broke an ankle, her pelvis, and her left arm, and cracked five vertebrae in her neck. She spent weeks in a nursing home, where Irene and Madeleine visited, as did Bruce, her boss at the laundry. Micah rode his bike there after school or caught rides with men from the recovery group, until at last, against her doctors' wishes, Lissa went home to the apartment.

She could not work and filled her days with other things, like journaling. On October 26, 2010, she wrote:

I have come to the conclusion that everything happens for a reason. . . . Now that I am stuck in this wheelchair, I have one of two choices. I could whine . . . and get nothing done while feeling 100% miserable or shut up and use my time wisely to do all the things I always said I never had time to do. I think I will go with option #2. Get something done and try to figure out what exactly God wanted me to slow down for. . . . I figure now I need to develop a plan, ie structure my time, prioritize my goals and recovery. Organize! Something my OCD loves to do.

She healed from the accident faster than her doctors expected. Even her children wondered at the speed of her recovery. "My mom is like a cat with nine lives, except her nine lives never run out," Shauna said. Lissa did not deny it. How many times had she come this close to death? Accidents. Fights. The wrong cocktail of drugs. She supposed she was lucky, though at times this luck felt like a chain tethering her to life. Lissa had always believed she would die young and had lived with this in mind. Once, she had taken matters into her own hands and swallowed a bottle of pills, but a friend found her in a pool of her own vomit and delivered her to the hospital. Lissa called this attempt at suicide an "overdose" and described it in her journal like this:

The people that witnessed my overdose never really said anything to me about it except for Bart, one of my true friends. Not only was he the one who rescued me but he said I had better not ever do that again cause it traumatized him and then he died of an overdose a couple years later in Atlanta all by himself. Bart had left Minot because of warrants and to try to start anew elsewhere. It didn't take him long to get back in the dope game. His girl, Jess, and their two babies went with. The dope took over and Jess returned to Minot. . . . The story was that one day she got sick of Bart and his dope and got the kids ready, they went to the store and never returned. She took the bus back to North Dakota without telling him. One day Bart called me out of the blue. We were on the outs when he left Minot. He asked me if I would kill him if he returned. I stated that no matter what we would always be friends. He told me that he was coming back to be with the kids and Jess and could I pick him up on Monday 2 a.m. in Bismarck. I agreed. I received a call from his sister on Friday. Bart would not make the trip. . . . They had his funeral instead on that Monday morning. I didn't make it to the funeral.

When Lissa got bored of writing to herself, she wrote letters to friends she knew before she went to prison. In one, she admonished a man who had relapsed and gone back to treatment:

So you're back in!? Wow! Figures. I know what you're thinking. After October you're done. Done! . . . No more bullshit, right? Well good for you! All I can say is that if you didn't PLAN on fucking up anyway you wouldn't have had anything to worry about. But oh well. As you can probably tell I'm disappointed. Nice of you to think about your friends let alone your kids before your addictions! ASSHOLE!

On the next page, she listed his options:

1. Productive happy sober life.
2. Dysfunctional addictive life with jail, institutions, cycle, or . . .
3. DEATH

When she reread the letter, she would wonder if she had written it for herself as well as for her friend. One day, as she sorted through her old belongings from the storage unit, she came across a quarter ounce of meth in a container buried beneath some papers. She kept it for three days and then dropped it in the toilet, watched the crystal soften into gel. For a moment, she considered fishing it out, shooting it up with the toilet water, but then her body began to quake. She flushed.

. . . . .

IN THE DISTANCE LISSA FELT from her relatives—in the years after her release from prison, before she heard of Kristopher Clarke—she drew unexpectedly close to her oldest uncle, Charles Yellow Bird. Chuck, or "Chucky" as Lissa called him, was a year and eight months younger than her mother, Irene. He had spent much of his life in Denver and Albuquerque, where he worked for the Bureau of Indian Affairs. Although not as accomplished as his older sister or his brother Michael, who were university professors, Chucky was, according to his siblings, the smartest of them all. He read endlessly, especially about history and politics. Once he had been offered a scholarship to a program at Harvard, which he turned down. As Michael would put it, Chucky was "driven only so far"; he wasn't interested in "the old American Nightmare." For a while, he lived at home in White Shield and taught art at the school, where he pushed for an Indian-led school board and founded a club called Arikara for Survival. Chucky had noticed that few young people knew their language, let alone their culture. He gathered elders, recording the stories they told. He wrote grants, pooling money for the club, and hired staff—Michael, whenever he was home from college, and Irene, who kept the books.

This was the Chucky his brothers and sisters bragged about: Chucky who saved the Arikara language. Chucky who liked to call his mother on the phone and say, "How's my fat little Indian lady?" Chucky who loved books, Ford Mustangs, and playing pool. Chucky who loved music most of all and whenever he came home drove his Mazda 280Z right up to the house, blasting Rickie Lee Jones's "Chuck E's in Love."

The Chucky Lissa had known when she was a child was different. After he left the reservation, she saw him only when he came home, and Chucky came home when he was having a hard time. Lissa remembered one particular summer, in 1984, when she had been living on Fort Berthold with her uncle Michael. One day, she and a friend took off around the state, stopping at powwows and sleeping on strangers' floors. It had been late at night some weeks later when they came to White Shield. As they neared her grandparents' house, they saw headlights coming fast on the dirt lane. A car pulled up. It was Chucky. He had a gun. "I'm going to blow your head off," he said, and so they had skidded down the lane, dashed into the house, laid breathlessly on the cold enamel of the bathtub.

He could be violent when he drank, but with Lissa his tussles were more often abstract. He liked to tease younger kids to get their attention, calling out to them as they ran through the house. While Lissa's cousins shied away from Chucky, Lissa had always quipped back. He challenged her to riddles. Some were logic problems he culled from books; others, questions he dreamed up about the world. Lissa did not solve his riddles right away. Often, days elapsed before she presented him with an answer. She would try to surprise him, offer it in passing as if the riddle had been too easy. Later, they admitted to each other that there was nothing amicable in this exchange. Chucky described it as "a battle of the minds" and took pleasure in stumping her.

So it surprised both of them when, after Lissa's release from prison, they became close. In 2011, Chucky left Albuquerque and moved to his mother Madeleine's house, where Lissa found him one day in the living room.

"Why are you moving home?" she said.

"What's it to you?" Chucky replied.

"I think I have an idea."

"What is it, then?"

"I think you came home to die."

Chucky frowned, dark brows crowning his narrow eyes. He had been lost in the city for too long, Lissa thought, unmoored, alone to practice his addiction. He looked tired, like he had given up. Lissa told him so and crossed to a bay window where she had left her cigarettes.

They sat on the porch, looking south toward the lake. Chucky asked what she had meant. "You used to look impenetrable," Lissa said. "Like you could shoot an arrow and it would bounce off you, but now I think it would kill you."

Chucky said nothing.

"Well, you got cirrhosis now or what?" Lissa said.

"I've had cirrhosis. I'm in the later stage of cirrhosis."

"You don't think you can heal yourself?"

"Your mom and grandma are always trying to get me on medication, but I'd rather just go out like this."

"Gee, Uncle, that's kind of sad."

"You say it like it is," he said.

The next time Lissa visited White Shield, Chucky had slipped into a depression. He rarely came out of his room anymore. "What's going on?" Lissa asked Madeleine, but her grandmother didn't know. Lissa knocked on his door until he opened it. His bedroom was small, dim, cluttered with books and papers. She took a folding chair from a corner, set it between the bed and the wall, and reached for a book, flipping the pages mindlessly.

"I'm moving back to Denver," Chucky finally said.

"For what?"

"They just don't want me here."

"Are you drinking again?"

"I'm a grown-ass man. I can drink."

"Hey, I'm not the enemy here. Go ahead! I don't have a problem with it."

After that, whenever Lissa visited Madeleine's, she went straight to Chucky's bedroom. He did not go back to Denver. She often found him studying Article 25 of the Code of Federal Regulations, which defines the relationship between tribes and the U.S. government. From the look of it, the article would have taken a lifetime to decipher, with seven chapters, twenty-four subchapters, and hundreds of parts, not to mention an exponential number of subparts. It concerned, mainly, the management of Indian land from the enforcement of federal laws and regulations to the duties of federal officials in regard to reservation resources. The basis for the code was a series of treaties through which the U.S. had promised to act as "trustee," furnishing tribes and members with the necessities it had stripped

from them when it stole their land. These included food—no longer
annuities, but commodity programs—and education, housing, and
law enforcement. According to the code, the federal government held
Indian land "in trust," which meant that if a tribe or individual wished
to use their land—build a house, dig a well, run cattle, drill for oil—
they needed approval from the Bureau of Indian Affairs.

Chucky had spent his career working for the Bureau, and yet he
distrusted the arrangement. He knew how federal agencies lost titles,
sold land out of the tribe, paid leasing fees to the wrong landowner or
to no landowner at all. He had sued the government himself, but
although he knew the law better than most, he had been left near the
end of his life with some philosophical questions: Who, really, owned
Indian land? And what did "tribal sovereignty" mean if federal agencies determined the land's fate?

Lissa and Chucky parsed these questions and then turned to others. They discussed the U.S. debt to China, wars in the Middle East.
They indulged in conspiracy theories. Their riddles lost their hard
edges, and they took pleasure in each other's company. This was how
Lissa would remember her uncle after he was gone: Chucky at his
desk, she in the folding chair, sifting aloud through the strange logic of
the world. He was her proof of intellect, confidence that her mind
had not dulled in their years apart—and still, there was no denying
that Chucky was the brightest Yellow Bird.

He died on December 6, 2011, eleven weeks before Kristopher
Clarke disappeared.

2

Missing

After Lissa wrote to Clarke's mother on June 2, 2012, she heard nothing. June passed. Then, July. In early August, Lissa drove to the Spirit Lake Indian Reservation, 150 miles northwest of Fargo, where she danced in her first sun dance, an annual religious ceremony that originated among tribes in the Great Plains. Before prison, Lissa never had any interest in traditional ways; it was after she got out that she became curious. Though her family was Catholic, they had not abandoned their ways entirely, and if a relative fell ill, they often asked medicine people to pray at the bedside. One day, while visiting an aunt in the hospital, Lissa met a Lakota man whom her mother had summoned to hold a ceremony. The man invited Lissa to the Pine Ridge Indian Reservation in South Dakota, where he lived, and after that, Lissa made frequent trips. He taught her how to prepare for sun dance, how to pray, how to fashion a medicine pipe from red pipestone. One of Lissa's uncles, who worked as a Native American commissioner for the city of Fargo, helped secure a small plot of municipal land on the outskirts of the city to erect a sweat lodge. Soon Lissa was attending several nights a week, bringing her son Micah along and arranging for inmates at her old halfway house to attend as well. After the sweat, they gathered in lawn chairs around a firepit, drank water, and ate sloppy joes. Now, wherever Lissa went, she was ready for ceremony. In her car, she kept a suitcase packed with tobacco, eagle feathers, medicine wheels, inserts for her moccasins, bitterroot for her throat when it got sore from singing, a knife, dresses she sewed herself—applying a skill she had gained in prison—and scalpels and hemp thread, which she used to pierce her shoulders under the skin, stitching to her body the feathers and medicine wheels that were torn from her during the sun dance. The dance lasted four days, through which Lissa consumed no food or water. Suffering, she was learning, could be a gift, and flesh the only thing that belonged to her, that she could give of her own body.

On August 11, 2012, the day Lissa returned to Fargo from Spirit Lake, Clarke's mother, Jill Williams, replied. "I just need info," she wrote. Perhaps Lissa could "ask around" on the reservation. She should be careful though, Jill warned: "Someone around there is responsible for KC's disappearance and I don't want to put anyone in danger."

Lissa knew from Jill's original plea that the last her son had been seen was at the trucking company offices where he worked, in a segment of the reservation called Mandaree. Fort Berthold had six segments, drawn up after the flood. White Shield made up the east segment, Twin Buttes the south, and Mandaree the west, while Four Bears, New Town, and Parshall spread from west to east across the north. On the twenty-fourth of August, a Friday, Lissa drove with Micah and Obie to White Shield and spent the night at her grandmother's house. The next day, she continued to Mandaree. Across a bridge over the lake, the land scrunched like a dry blanket, where the flatness of the prairie gave way to badlands, to canyons cut by seasonal creeks. Red clouds hovered over the grass—dust devils, Lissa thought at first, but when she looked closer, she saw that they were the billowed wakes of trucks. There were roads where she had never seen roads before, curving through pasture like suburban culs-de-sac. Even the contours of the land had changed, cliffs cut, hills reshaped, as if giants had pressed their fingers into clay.

It was her first sight of the oil boom. She had heard about it from relatives—about a man who came by her grandmother's house promising bonuses if Madeleine signed. That had been in 2007, while Lissa was in prison. The man happened to be Madeleine's nephew, hired by an oil company called Dakota-3 to persuade his fellow tribal members to lease their mineral rights. By the time Lissa was paroled, every scrap of land on the reservation had been leased, and the first oil wells had been drilled.

The land Madeleine leased out was in Mandaree, across the lake from White Shield. It was a small share she had inherited from her father, Ben Young Bird, upon his death. Ben was Hidatsa. Before the flood, people crossed the Missouri freely by three bridges connecting towns on either side, but after the bridges were submerged, the distance became vast, irreconcilable. Arikara families moved to White Shield, Hidatsa families to Mandaree, and after that, Madeleine rarely saw many of her Young Bird relatives. Even when a bridge was rebuilt in 1955, connecting Four Bears to New Town, those living in the southernmost segments—White Shield, Twin Buttes, and Mandaree—crossed the reservation less often, the drive being one to three hours.

Madeleine had never seen her land before she leased it to the oil company. When she later heard that the leases were sold to a different company for a higher price than the one her nephew offered, she regretted having leased the land at all. Her check had been small. It had shouldered the weight of grocery and electricity bills, and then, as easily as it had come, it was gone. When Lissa heard her relatives brag, "We got oil on our rez," she struggled to believe them. The boom had hardly touched White Shield. Mandaree was different, she knew, and still, Lissa had found it difficult to believe the rumors circulating on the reservation. Some Mandaree families, people said, were collecting hundreds of thousands of dollars a month. "Are you serious about that?" she challenged her relatives. "When do Indians ever get their due?"

But now here it was: the boom. Lissa could not deny it. Roads, dust, trucks, rigs. And flares, too many to count, shooting from pits and tall metal pipes, the air shimmering with heat.

The road dipped into another canyon, the flares disappearing from sight. Here the land looked as it had before, broad and unmarked. She passed a pale-yellow house where an aunt and uncle lived and thought of stopping for a visit. Then, remembering why she had come, Lissa continued on.

Some miles past the canyon, the road forked west toward Watford City and south toward Mandaree Village. On a far corner were the trucking offices, larger than Lissa had expected. They were a metal building with few windows, a garage tacked to the side. Vehicles had lined up by what appeared to be a main entrance, and semitrucks were scattered in the yard. There were workers everywhere, most of them white, lying beneath trucks, climbing in and out of cabs. Lissa parked at the edge of the yard, hoping someone would notice her, but no one did. When a worker came near, she called out to him.

"Is this the place where KC Clarke used to work?" she said.

The worker stopped, looked. "Who?" he said.

"There was a kid that went missing out here. Is this the spot where he went missing?"

"I don't know nothing about that," the worker said.

He had an accent she couldn't place. He had left his home a few months earlier, he explained, when the bank took his car and nearly his house. He had never heard of Kristopher Clarke. He made good money, though the cost of living on the reservation was high. In the beginning, he had rented a cot in a Quonset hut for $300 a week, but the cots were closely spaced, and whenever he rolled over he had found himself face-to-face with an "ugly son of a bitch" beside him. Now he slept in the cab of his truck, in the yard by the trucking "shop."

As it happened, the shop was owned by the chairman of the MHA Nation, the worker said. The chairman's name was Tex Hall.

The day had cooled by the time Lissa said goodbye to the worker, the sun lower on a range of mountains past the west border of the reservation. She knew she should return to White Shield—her mother would be worried she was gone so long—but instead she drove toward Mandaree Village, beyond a cluster of houses and a blue water tower, to where the prairie opened toward the lake.

Lissa wondered if there had been a time when people called the lake a "reservoir." She never heard her relatives use this word. "When the waters came" was how they described the flood, as if to remind themselves they had no choice in the matter. But to Lissa the lake meant something different. She knew the history, and still she loved the lake. When she was twelve years old, she had often gone fishing from the shore in Mandaree with her stepfather, Wayne White Eagle. Wayne was Lakota from Eagle Butte, a tall man, big-featured. In the early eighties, he had worked in New Town for the Indian Health Service, where he met Lissa's mother, who was teaching at the tribal college. Wayne and Irene fell in love and, in 1983, they married.

It was through Wayne that Lissa had first heard of Tex Hall—the chairman of her tribe whom the worker had mentioned. Tex had been Wayne's best friend. They met in the nineties, when Wayne took a job at the school in Mandaree where Tex was principal. After that, Wayne and Tex sat together at basketball games and often stayed out until late at night. Wayne had a degree in Native American studies and knew quite a lot about Indian law and politics. When Tex ran for tribal chairman in 1998, Wayne campaigned on his behalf. As far as Lissa knew, her entire family had voted for Tex—a surprise, since although Tex was family, related to them through Madeleine, he identified as Hidatsa. Bloodlines had long blurred among the three tribes, but families still tossed insults across the lake. Some Arikara liked to point out that the Hidatsa were "mixed-blood"—part white—and thus untrustworthy, while some Hidatsa did not fail to mention that

the Arikara had aided General Custer in the U.S. government's bat-
tles with the Sioux. That a Lakota Sioux man had convinced an Arikara family in White Shield to vote for a Hidatsa from Mandaree
struck Irene as extraordinarily funny. After Wayne died, in November
2011, she told the story at his funeral, and when she came to the
punch line, Tex had laughed and laughed.

Lissa spoke at Wayne's funeral as well, though her memory had
been overtaken by a later funeral, for her uncle Chucky, who died
three weeks after Wayne. Lissa hardly knew Tex. After he won the
election for chairman in 1998, he had won again in 2002, and again
in 2010. He served more terms as chairman than anyone in the tribe's
history. Had Lissa not been hit by a truck and bound to a wheelchair
at the time of the past election, she would have voted for Tex. Irene
spoke highly of him, and Wayne had liked to brag he was "a powerful
man." Lissa never bothered to ask Wayne what he meant.

She had little interest in politics, but she was surprised to hear the
worker mention Tex's name. Lissa had not realized Tex owned an oil-
field company. She wondered if Tex even knew that a worker had
gone missing from his shop. She decided she would give Tex a call;
perhaps he could then pressure authorities to focus on the case.

The sun was setting, Lissa miles past Mandaree Village now. To
the north a church appeared, tucked into a wooded swale. Lissa had
come to this church many times as a child in the summertime, when
the Catholic families of Fort Berthold sent their kids to bible camp. All
the Yellow Birds had attended camp at Saint Anthony, including Lissa's mother, Irene, who once ran away and hitched a ride home with
the tribal judge. But Lissa had not minded camp. She had liked
Brother Bernard, a scruffy white man with a ten o'clock shadow that
left scratches on the cheeks of every Indian kid he hugged. Brother
Bernard had made pancakes, and on hot afternoons let the campers
ride in the bed of a truck out to the shore of the lake.

The camp looked as it had before, the dorms more crooked but
upright. A gas flare hissed in a nearby field. The road to the church
bent east, past a house where the priest lived, and dipped into a brushy

creek, emerging at the entrance to a cemetery. Lissa's father, Leroy Chase, was buried here. She found the graves difficult to make out, some marked with headstones or simple plaques and some with no markings at all. She searched until it became too dark to see. Her mother called: "Where are you?"

"Don't worry," Lissa replied.

As LISSA CROSSED THE LAKE back to the east side of the reservation that night, her phone rang again. It was Jill Williams, Clarke's mother. Jill had a sweet-sounding voice as she shared with Lissa everything she knew. On the morning KC disappeared, he had left his rental house in the village of Four Bears and driven south to the shop where he worked in Mandaree. Indeed, Jill said, the shop belonged to the tribal chairman, Tex Hall, who owned a company called Maheshu Energy that was partnered with another company called Blackstone. Blackstone was owned by a husband and wife, James Henrikson and Sarah Creveling, who, like KC, were white and from Washington State. James and KC had met years earlier racing motorcycles and become friends. Then, in 2008, KC moved to Brownwood, Texas, to live with a girlfriend. He had been working at a car dealership when James found him one day in 2011. James had moved to Texas, as well, and had a masonry business there, but work was slow, and he had decided to leave for North Dakota to start a trucking service in the oil fields. He offered KC a job. KC was at first reluctant to leave Texas, but when he and his girlfriend broke up, he moved north. For several months, he lived in a trailer with James and Sarah in Van Hook, a town on the north shore of Lake Sakakawea, until he moved into the rental house that December. James had several trucks, which he sub-contracted under a company owned by a tribal member named Steve Kelly. The arrangement had not lasted long. By Christmas, James, Sarah, and KC moved their trucks to Tex Hall's shop in Mandaree. The work had been good—so good, Jill learned, that her son hardly slept. In February, James suggested KC take a vacation. On the morning of his first day off, KC drove to the shop, arriving around ten, and turned in his company credit card to Sarah, whom he told of his plan to visit his grandfather in Oregon. Then he disappeared.

KC was close to his grandfather, Robert Clarke, who helped raise him. They spoke regularly, so when weeks passed without word from KC, Robert called the Mountrail County sheriff, stationed north of the reservation. "It's not a crime to go missing," the sheriff said. Men fled the oil fields all the time, and KC would probably show up. But on March 23, 2012, the sheriff received a different call from the mother of KC's ex-girlfriend, who had reported him missing to the Brownwood Police Department. KC still leased a house in Texas and that month had failed to pay rent. A Mountrail County deputy filed an incident report. The next month, KC missed another rent payment.

His case languished. Jill, from whom KC had been estranged for years, did not learn her son was missing until months after he disappeared. Then, in June 2012, a detective in Brownwood received a call from a man who had discovered KC's truck, a white Chevrolet Silverado, parked on a street in Williston, roughly an hour west of Fort Berthold. The man lived on the street and had seen the truck parked there for months. One day, he had approached out of curiosity and found a door unlocked. He located the registration, noted the owner's name. He entered "Kristopher Clarke" in a records database and learned that KC had a DUI in Minot. A court date was scheduled; KC had not appeared. The man also came across a notice that KC had been reported missing. The notice listed a license plate matching the one on the truck and a phone number for the detective in Brownwood. The man called the detective. The detective called the Williston Police Department.

When officers searched the truck, they found latex gloves, an atlas, a water bottle half-drunk, a box of ammunition for a handgun, a Bible stuck with receipts and business cards, a pill bottle—empty, unmarked—invoices, employee lists, a set of needles and syringes, and a bottle of liquid labeled TESTOSTERONE. Jill had suspected her son used steroids, but the thing she considered most strange about the truck was not what was in it but what was not. Officers had found no wallet, no phone, and no handgun.

A few things confused Lissa about the story Jill told. First, for whom was KC working when he disappeared? If Tex Hall owned the shop as well as the company called Maheshu Energy, then what was Blackstone, the company supposedly owned by James and Sarah? That a company owned by white people had a base on Indian land was in itself unusual. There were laws discouraging this. In 1983, the tribe had passed an ordinance establishing a Tribal Employment Rights Office, known as TERO. The office, sanctioned by an exemption to federal civil rights law, made incentives for companies to give hiring preference to tribal members; and on tribal business owners, it conferred "tier one" status, granting them the right of first refusal of any contracts on the reservation. How, Lissa wondered, was Blackstone operating on Fort Berthold?

On the Monday after she visited the Maheshu shop, Lissa drove north again from White Shield, this time to the TERO office, a small building on the main drag in New Town. The office kept paperwork on every company doing business on the reservation. Lissa requested two files—Blackstone's and Maheshu's. The arrangement became immediately obvious to her. Maheshu was a shell, Blackstone its subcontractor. Blackstone paid 20 percent of its profits to Maheshu. By partnering with Tex Hall, James and Sarah had tier-one status and could bid on contracts normally reserved for companies owned by tribal members.

This brought Lissa to the second thing that confused her: If a worker had gone missing from Tex's property, why had Tex not said something? One would think, as leader of the tribe, that he would at least show concern and try to get to the bottom of it.

"Have you talked to Tex himself about this?" Lissa messaged Jill one night after she returned to Fargo. In two years, Tex would be up for reelection, she explained. "This could have a big impact on his turnout if this were to be blown up in his face."

Over the following weeks, Lissa and Jill attempted to reach the chairman several times. Neither woman was successful. Once, Lissa spoke to a secretary in the tribal office who asked what a missing man had to do with Tex Hall. "He worked on our chairman's property," Lissa explained, adding, "I'm a relative—a tribal member." The secretary said she would give Tex the message, but days passed, and Tex did not return the call.

One evening in late September 2012, Jill received a Facebook message from the wife of a Blackstone truck driver: "I seen that you are trying to reach Tex Hall. Good luck. When my husband was having problems with James he tried to reach Tex and never was able to reach him and then when he did get the chance to speak with him about James Tex didn't want to hear it. James is his golden boy."

Jill often received messages like this. Months earlier, she had created a Facebook page to solicit tips, amassing more than two thousand followers, and although most people who wrote had never met her son, many were familiar with Blackstone. In the time KC worked for the company, it had expanded into a successful operation, acquiring contracts with all the major drillers on the reservation and hiring dozens of full-time staff and drivers. In spite of this success, some employees disliked working for Blackstone. Many truck drivers complained to Jill about not being paid what they were owed, and some who knew KC had suggested that he, too, was dissatisfied. In fact, Jill had learned, KC was preparing to leave Blackstone. Jill wondered if this might explain his disappearance. Perhaps, she wrote to Lissa, KC knew "what really goes on" at the company. According to one rumor, Blackstone was a front for selling drugs.

"Now we are getting somewhere," Lissa replied. "So there is dope involved? What kind? I know you don't know me, but I have a history also. I'm not perfect. I'm clean now. About this dope. I know everyone in the dope game. Pretty much everyone."

Jill did not know what kind. She had heard only that dealers hung around the Maheshu shop. She was fearful, she told Lissa—"I don't know who to trust"—and had begun to lose confidence in even law enforcement. After police searched KC's truck, a detective in Williston had made calls and collected statements, and the case had been assigned to an agent in the North Dakota Bureau of Criminal Investigations, who acquired KC's phone and bank records. Neither showed any activity after February 22, 2012, the day KC disappeared. The agent had made no progress beyond this. He was hindered, he told Jill, by having no body, no evidence that a crime had been committed. It was as the sheriff had told KC's grandfather: *It's not a crime to go missing.* And even if it was a crime—even if police were to open a criminal investigation—Jill suspected the case was complicated by the fact of having occurred on a reservation. "There is a division between the tribal (Indian) police department and the county (white) police department, and a total lack of them being able to work together on any incident," one woman wrote to Jill in a message that Jill forwarded to Lissa. "My mom has a flower shop there," the woman continued. "She is white. She witnessed some Native Americans vandalizing her building so called the native police. They said 'We can't help you if you're not an enrolled member of the tribe.' So she called the county police, they said 'We can't help you because those kids are native.' . . . The natives stick together like gangs. Many crimes on this Indian Reservation never get reported to the police, especially if the crime is against a white person."

Lissa knew that what the woman said was partly true. In 1978, a Supreme Court case, *Oliphant v. Suquamish,* had stripped tribes nationwide of their criminal jurisdiction over nonmembers. Now any crime committed on Fort Berthold by a nonmember against another nonmember was the province of the state, and crimes involving both members and nonmembers belonged to federal authorities. The Department of Justice had a poor record of pursuing even major crimes in which only tribal members were involved. In other words, the problem the woman described to Jill struck both ways. A white person could commit a crime on a reservation and get away with it as easily, if not more easily, than a Native person. And when both victim and perpetrator belonged to the tribe, the victim rarely saw justice.

It bothered Lissa that Tex would not respond to her messages.

Still, she did not believe him capable of murder, and she worried the
tips Jill received through Facebook had stoked an irrational fear of the
reservation. It did not help that the oil fields already had a reputation
for being lawless. "We had reporters saying it was the 'Wild West,'"
Lissa would say. "We had the cowboy and Indian thing going on. It
wouldn't have surprised me if she was thinking, *There's an arrow sticking
out of my son's back, and the Indians are responsible.*"

IN THE EARLIEST MESSAGES SHE traded with Jill, Lissa was brash, boastful: "I can show you everything," she wrote when she first invited Jill to
the reservation, adding, "Before I was an addict full time, I was a tribal
attorney for some years." It was true Lissa had worked as a licensed
advocate in tribal court, where she represented defendants, often relatives, in hearings before a judge. She was particularly emphatic about
her familial bond to Fort Berthold. Once, when Jill mentioned that
she had heard James was "in good" with Tex, Lissa replied, "Nobody
is in good with Tex Hall. Not even me, and I'm related."

Still, her claim to the reservation was more delicate than she made
it seem. While it was likely, as Lissa had first written to Jill, that she
was related to most members of her tribe, and while blood conferred
on her a right of access to the reservation that Jill lacked, it did not
make Lissa any privier to the sort of information they sought. In truth,
her home had changed radically in her absence, in ways that even her
relatives who had remained there did not fully understand. Although
the boom brought more jobs to Fort Berthold than there had been
before, few tribal members worked in the oil fields, and fewer owned
businesses. Lissa could think of only one relative who had taken a job
on the rigs. That was her brother Percy Chase.

Percy and Lissa shared a father, but as far as Lissa was concerned,
calling him her "half brother" was a "white thing." A brother was just
a brother, no halves about it.

She had met Percy when he was a toddler. He had been too young to remember her, and it was not until their father died in the winter of 2007, and Lissa's name appeared in the obituary, that Percy realized he had an older sister. Lissa had been in prison, unable to attend the funeral, but she heard her brother was looking for her and found him on Facebook when she got out. They met in New Town. After that, they called each other on the phone, and whenever Lissa came to the reservation, she visited Percy. He was skinny, shy, twitchy with nervous energy. He had grown up between the reservation, often in the care of an aunt in Mandaree, and Yakima, Washington, where his mother lived. His upbringing had been "isolated," as Percy put it. He had preferred to be alone, drawing in his bedroom or playing in the coulees near his aunt's house. Not until he finished high school had he found a group of friends. They were Native and Latino men from cities in Washington State who often came to the reservation with drugs. They liked Percy. His shyness made him good at keeping secrets, and among them, Percy felt that he belonged.

By the time Lissa connected with her brother, he had distanced himself from that life. Percy was going to sun dance, and he earned good money on oil rigs. Then, not long after Lissa found him, he quit.

He had been working on a rig in Mandaree, not far from his family land, and although the badlands were familiar to him, the site had looked the same as all the others where he had worked—the same motor house and pump house, the same rig and pits and stacks—and in this sameness Percy had felt that he was nowhere and anywhere at once. He never told the other men on his crew where he was from. He did not think it mattered, since none of them stayed long. For two years, Percy had been a floor hand, assembling and disassembling rigs. He worked sixteen hours a day, all night if necessary, earning twenty-six dollars an hour, which, in the beginning, had seemed like a lot, but over time diminished in value. His back ached. Once, he fell carrying heavy material, and his supervisor asked him not to report his injury. This angered Percy: "I seen other young guys get hurt, and they try to make it the kids' fault, when really he just didn't know where to put his hands." He had never been trained properly. "It's almost like they were counting on us to get hurt," Percy said.

It had not taken him long to realize how risky the work was, or how little he was paid given this risk. While mixing chemicals into a slurry called "mud" one day, Percy wondered what the chemicals were made of. That night, in a trailer where he often slept on-site, he skimmed the Material Safety Data Sheets. They were bound in a book thicker than anyone would ever read, he thought, and in it he learned that some of the chemicals he frequently handled were carcinogenic. He had never worn a mask or gloves.

There were many reasons why Percy quit the job, but one incident rattled him in particular. They had been "tripping pipe," feeding one steel tube after another into the wellbore as the drill bit ground into the earth, when the bit broke. His crew's response was routine: They removed the pipes and set them on a rack in sets of three, each one called a "stand." It was the derrickman's job to secure the stand, but now and then, he dropped one. "If a guy messes up," Percy recalled, "the other guys call him a worm"—an amateur. One day, the derrick-man dropped a stand, and Percy called him a worm: "He didn't like that, and so he comes down and blames me. I'm like, 'So what? You lost a stand. It happens all the time.' We get into a squabble, and the driller comes in and breaks it up and then just leaves me to clean up the mess. My driller, who's supposed to have my back. You know what I mean? What if I got my head cut off? Would they just leave me there, put me in a ditch and say hush hush? You start hearing these stories where they obviously don't care about you. 'Don't rush, take your time,' they say, but when it comes down to it, they're screaming at you to get it done."

Lissa was the first person to whom Percy admitted how disposable he had felt, how easily he could have disappeared. "It used to eat away at me, Sis," he said, "but money is power, right? Sometimes I think nobody on the rez would have cared. As long as they're getting lease checks and driving nice cars, nobody would have believed me."

Lissa believed Percy. The news was plastered with oil workers' deaths: On May 10, 2011, a fifty-two-year-old man named Joseph Kronberg had been electrocuted at his work site. Four months later, a well west of the reservation exploded, killing two men and injuring others. In 2012, North Dakota became the most dangerous state to labor in, its workers dying at a rate four times the national average. The first worker to die on Fort Berthold had been Dustin Bergsing, a twenty-one-year-old father from Montana who was monitoring a Marathon Oil well in Mandaree when, in January 2012, he was found slumped on a catwalk, asphyxiated. An inspector who worked for Marathon told investigators he had been concerned by gas emissions at the site and had notified the company multiple times. Marathon had done nothing. That May, when another worker was similarly poisoned but survived, Marathon fired the inspector.

It seemed to Lissa that the oil fields contained endless ways for a person to disappear. Had KC died in an accident at work, a hasty cover-up, his body stuffed in a borehole? Or had he been murdered, his killer guided by a vague motive of the sort that had been suggested to Jill? Drugs seemed possible to Lissa, if only because she was familiar with them, though among the tips Jill received on Facebook, another motive had emerged as more likely than the rest.

The tip had come from a man named Rick Arey, a roughneck from Wyoming who knew KC at Blackstone. Rick, thirty-four years old, had worked in the oil fields since he was twenty-one and arrived in North Dakota in 2008, not long after the boom began. In 2010, he moved to the same campground in Van Hook where, the following year, KC lived with James and Sarah, the owners of Blackstone. James recruited Rick to Blackstone, where Rick hustled contracts to deliver water to drilling sites and haul away toxic fluid after the wells had been fracked. Rick and KC worked side by side. Often, they hung out at the casino bar or at the house KC moved to in December, where, one night, KC made them pasta with Alfredo sauce for dinner. When KC mentioned he was planning to leave Blackstone, taking with him to a new trucking company many of the contracts he had personally arranged, Rick decided to go along.

By the end of September, Lissa and Jill spoke so often that their conversations lost their beginnings and ends. Jill could talk for hours, straying from her missing son to other dark corners of her life. Lissa did not stop Jill. Sometimes, she put the phone down, fixed dinner, and let Jill go on alone. The only thing Lissa felt certain of was that KC was dead. One day, she told Jill that she would soon make another trip to the reservation. "You think you would be interested in accompanying me?" she wrote. "You as his mother would 'know' once you traced some of his footsteps. I could help you with that." Jill agreed on the condition that she bring guns for protection. "That's fine," Lissa said. "Just keep them to yourself. I'm a felon. I'm not going back to the clink because of you."

ON THE MORNING OF OCTOBER 6, 2012, Lissa met Jill, Rick, and Percy in a parking lot on the main street of New Town. The day was bright and cold. Jill had driven from Washington the day before and spent the night in a hotel near Williston, as far from the reservation as she could manage. She was short, with pale, translucent skin and the air of someone younger than her age. She had arrived with Rick, who drove up from Wyoming, where he had been living since he shattered his femur in a drunk driving accident months earlier. Rick was blue-eyed, chubby, leaning on a cane. Lissa liked him immediately.

They did not linger for long on the street. They boarded Lissa's olive minivan, which she had purchased when the little blue car died, and headed west—past a Jack & Jill grocery, a post office and a liquor store, past towering grain bins and the Bureau of Indian Affairs, past the oil-company offices erected on the city outskirts, past billboards advertising RAPID HOT FLOW, LLC: WE'LL MAKE YOUR FRAC'N WATER HOTTER!, past the river and casino and tribal headquarters, past flames licking from pits and pipes and pump jacks nodding their steely heads—to where they turned south, drove through coulees and wider canyons, and came to Bear Den, where Percy had lived years ago with his aunt.

It was a likelier place than most to hide a body, being not far from the Maheshu shop and the only area within miles that wasn't trampled or dug up by industry.

By the road was the yellow house Lissa had passed on her recent drive and, higher on the hill, an old clapboard where her father had grown up, carried from the bottomlands and since abandoned. There was a bridge near the lower house and a creek flowing under it, widening toward the east and emptying into a narrow bay, and a faint two-track along the creek that passed through a gate by a cottonwood tree. Where a slope rose to form the north bank of the canyon, the two-track faded into a trail along a fence, through bluestem and cactus and coneflowers shriveled on their stalks. The grass was thicker by the creek. Trucks echoed in the canyon. Then the trail departed from the water, ascending a bank through sagebrush and the hardened stacks of cow dung, to a cliff overlooking the marshy tendril of the lake. Blackbirds perched on the bones of flooded trees, and ducks drifted along the edges of the bay. The sound of the road vanished, and there was only the rattle of insects, the croak of frogs, the fat shadows of catfish drifting in the amber stillness of the creek.

Rick had not made it far from the car, while Percy, turtled in a hoodie, had wandered out of view.

As Lissa and Jill walked, the sun rose higher and the sagebrush glistened in the autumn light. Later, Lissa would say that it was as if the reservation had expanded around them. The lake widened. The coulees deepened. The grass thickened to fill disturbances in the land. And as the space in which her son had been lost grew, Jill seemed to shrink inside it. In a photograph Lissa took that day, Jill would appear blurry and overexposed, staring into the camera. The nylon jacket was tied around her waist, and the wind was blowing her long, red hair, and her lips were parted, and her hands were clasped in loose fists. "If KC ever shows up, I'll give him a piece of my mind," Lissa would remember Jill saying.

"I don't think he's going to show up, Jill," Lissa replied, and Jill began to cry.

·····

THAT OCTOBER MARKED TWO YEARS since Lissa had been hit by the truck, a year since she had returned to work. She had not gone back to the laundry. Rather, through a vocational rehabilitation program, she enrolled in welding school, where the owner of the school hired her to his company. The company merged with another, TrueNorth Steel, and Lissa was sent to a shop not far from her apartment. It was tall and airy, cold on autumn mornings. She wore thick gray coveralls, a hard hat, safety glasses, and her hair pulled into a ponytail. The building was divided into four separate bays, and Lissa was assigned to the fourth. The projects were smaller there—ducts, handrails, simple frames—though it was not long before she transferred to the first bay, where she made structural pieces for bridges and a hospital in Fargo. She liked the work—the measuring and cutting, the punching of holes and blasting off of rust. She liked the firework smell that filled the bay and the way the whole building rocked with sound, with clanking metal and whining saws and the rumble of carts on the floor.

As the work became routine, and then familiar, Lissa retreated into her daydreams. She could not stop thinking about KC. While the vastness of the reservation had seemed to empty his mother out, Lissa had felt charged up as they searched. She had taken Jill everywhere KC might have been—the casino, the Maheshu shop, the street in Williston where his truck had been found. In Bear Den, they had traced the contours above the creek, and everything they noticed Lissa documented with her camera: a patch of grass marked with pink paint; the track of an excavator cutting through sagebrush; a wide ravine cluttered with oak; a juniper; a scrap of tarp; a meandering creek, the banks silted and green; the clavicle of a cow; and among signs more difficult to discern, a mark in the mud by an animal or a boot, a beaver stick that from a distance resembled bone, and a wheel rim stuck in a tree, hung there by either a person or a flood.

There was no clue in this ensemble of obscurities, as inscrutable in form as in their relation to one another, but this was not the point of the photographs. What Jill had appeared to lose in hope, Lissa gained in purpose. Each detail seemed to her a piece of a larger riddle to which she had been fatefully drawn and now was determined to solve.

In the evenings, after Lissa returned from the welding shop, she opened Google Earth on her computer and panned across the bad-lands. The landscape was indeed vast and relentlessly featured, but it did not seem impossible that a body hidden there might be found. Lissa often called Rick, KC's friend, on these evenings, and it was through their conversations that she gained a clearer sense of KC's movements in the days preceding his disappearance.

According to Rick, KC had been plotting to leave Blackstone for weeks before he disappeared. Rick believed KC's frustration began in December 2011, after the company cut ties with Steve Kelly, the tribal member who owned Trustland Oilfield Services, and relocated to the Maheshu shop. James's decision to move was as Lissa suspected: He hated losing 80 percent of the money his trucks earned on each job to Kelly. By partnering with Maheshu, the fraction inverted: Blackstone earned 80 percent, while Tex Hall earned 20. Rick rarely saw the chairman. In the beginning, Tex was scarce around the shop, and then entirely absent. Rick heard he had fallen ill but never inquired further. Anyway, the arrangement proved lucrative. That they could name-drop the chairman did not hurt, nor did their willingness to work, as Rick liked to joke, "twenty-five hours a day." James, who worked harder than anyone, expected KC and Rick to keep up, but he never paid them more for it.

One night in January 2012, KC and Rick were drinking at the casino when they spotted a tan, blond woman with eyeliner arcing toward her temples. As Rick put it, "KC's head went sideways." The woman, Tesha Fredericks, was a manager at the casino and a member of the MHA Nation. KC began hanging out with Tesha and often invited Rick along. She was building her own trucking company—Running Horse—and offered them jobs. KC and Rick decided not to tell James or Sarah until the move was final.

In February, they slept even less. They were working for Blackstone, still, while quietly arranging contracts for Tesha, hoping some
of their clients at Blackstone would follow them to Running Horse.
KC had begun to look unwell. He was not tall, but he was muscular
and trim, with short brown hair and a shadow of a beard. He had an
easy sense about him, a gaping smile that made him appear far from
serious, so it struck Rick as odd when, one day, KC gave him a number for his grandfather, Robert Clarke, instructing Rick to call Robert
if anything should happen to him.

James and Sarah noticed a change in KC, too. At a Blackstone
meeting one day in the middle of February, they suggested he take a
two-week vacation. The day his vacation was to begin, the twenty-
second of February, was the last day Rick spoke to KC. They talked
for thirty-eight minutes as KC drove to the Maheshu shop to turn in
his company credit card and made tentative plans to meet Tesha in
the evening at the casino. That afternoon, Tesha called Rick. "She
goes, 'KC won't answer his phone,'" Rick recalled. "I call. Nothing.
She says, 'Rick, run out to Mandaree to see if KC's truck is there.'"

The truck was gone. As Rick wandered the Maheshu lot, he
noticed it was full of workers. Inside the offices, he found Sarah, who
told him KC had been there just that morning, and James, who said
KC had left for Oregon. This sounded possible to Rick, but something
else James said bothered him: "James looks right at me and says, 'Are
you quitting, too?' It threw me back. I said, 'What do you mean?' He
says, 'I heard you're quitting.' I said, 'I can't get ahold of KC.' He
says, 'Yeah, that son of a bitch. I've been trying to get ahold of him all
day, too.'"

When Rick returned to New Town that afternoon, he called
Tesha. She didn't believe KC would leave without telling them, so the
next morning, at Tesha's request, Rick dropped by the house in Four
Bears where KC lived with Judd Parker. Judd was in his forties, a
"goofy guy," as Rick put it, "cool, but real monotone." They had met
when they both worked for Steve Kelly at Trustland, and a few times
they had hung out. Judd liked to talk, especially about the Grateful

Dead, but on the morning Rick knocked on his door, Judd took Rick straight to KC's bedroom. The door was open, the bed made. A pair of jeans and a T-shirt were laid out on the bedcover. Rick had never been inside the room, and its neatness surprised him. "Me, I stuff my clothes in a drawer and call it a day," he said, "but all of his clothes were hanging in his closet. Even his jeans were on hangers. He had these Puma racer shoes. He loved them so much, he had two pairs. They were sitting next to these high-dollar vitamins—he was always eating healthy—and a couple Snap-on tool sets. I said, 'Judd, do you know if KC's toothbrush is here?' Because wherever he was, he had a toothbrush. And his toothbrush was still there."

Lissa listened carefully to Rick, fitting together each piece of the story as he handed it to her. Rick did not return to Blackstone, he said, but he called James once, who told him KC had a habit of running off. As KC requested, Rick also called his grandfather, Robert Clarke. The first time Rick called, Robert had no idea where KC had gone, but a few weeks later, Rick called again. This time, Robert had received a message from someone who said he knew KC was alive, at work on a remote location in Montana. KC did not want to be contacted, the caller said. Rick asked Robert who the caller was, but Robert told him that the caller had not identified himself.

Lissa assembled a list of names—James, Sarah, Tesha Fredericks, Robert Clarke, Judd Parker. She had tried to reach Judd several times, and when at last he answered his phone one evening, he told Lissa he was glad she had called.

One day in February, Judd said, he had come home from work and found a beer can propped in a tree at the end of the driveway. KC had been target practicing. Judd thought this odd, but not as odd as what happened early the next morning, when a woman knocked on his door. "I'd say it was nine o'clock," Judd recalled, "and this girl is like, 'Is KC here?' I said, 'No.' She's like, 'He's missing.' She was adamant. 'I know he's missing.'" Judd recognized the woman as Tesha, the owner of Running Horse, but before he could ask what the matter was, he said, "she turned around and booked. So I called James. Not instantly. I sat there thinking of that beer can in the tree. So I called James. I said, 'Is KC around?' He said, 'No, he went to his grandfather's, I think.'"

Judd did not speak to James for a while after that. He did not see Tesha again, either. Rick dropped by; they looked in KC's room. When weeks passed and KC still had not appeared, Judd tried to file a missing person report. According to Judd, the sheriff told him—incorrectly—that only a relative could file a report, so Judd called his roommate's ex-girlfriend in Brownwood, whose mother was allowed to file. In May, when Jill called Judd, he was rude to her: "I said, 'Your son's been missing for three months, and you haven't bothered to call me. No one's bothered to call. Do you know how frustrating that is? I have a roommate that disappears, and it's like no one cares. The only people that care are an old girlfriend in Texas and a grandfather who thinks he's somewhere else.'" Judd felt bad for saying it and was kinder to Jill after that.

But something about James had bothered Judd, and one night Judd called him again: "I said, 'Hey, KC's nowhere around. Do you have any idea where he's at? I mean, aren't you his best friend?' He's like, 'You know, I'm not really his best friend. I don't really know KC that good.' I said, 'Really? I thought you guys had known each other for a long time.' I thought it was interesting to hear him say that, knowing how they were. At least a few times I'd talked to KC about motorcycles and racing and James and stuff. James had known him a long time. So it wasn't too much longer after that, I called James again. I just struck up a conversation. 'Things are going all right?' He said, 'Yeah, we've got some work.' And I said, 'Man, I heard that KC was going to damn take some of your business and go to Running Horse.' And he said, 'I know, can you believe my best friend would do that to me?' *My best friend.* He probably remembered, too. He probably wished he would have caught himself. I thought, *Really, your best friend?* That was the last time I talked to him."

3

Oil Kings

WHEN I THINK NOW OF THE DAY I FIRST ARRIVED ON THE RESERVATION IN April 2011, ten months before Kristopher Clarke went missing, I think of how muted the place looked, how a late winter storm had flattened the deadened grass, how the snow had withered into dusty patches and the sloughs were still hardened with ice, how the only forests to speak of were the gray brushes of cottonwoods filling the canyons and junipers dotting the clay cliffs, and how all of it blended and washed out, faded into a low, gray sky. I drove from the south on a two-lane road through a border town called Killdeer, dropping into the valley of the Little Missouri River fifteen miles west of the confluence with the Missouri. There, on the far bank of the tributary, a sign marked an entrance to the reservation. Then the road cut through cliffs and emerged on a prairie where houses appeared—lone bunkers battered by the wind—and Mandaree Village, its homes of all the same size and shape, and a water tower standing garishly at odds with the flatness of the landscape. The road straightened. To the west rose Thunder Butte and the Killdeer Mountains, and then I turned east and glimpsed the Missouri, feeding from the north through a narrow passage and widening toward the south.

The 4 Bears Casino & Lodge is on a spit of land that forms the west bank of this passage. I arrived after dark and parked between two pickup trucks. A sign blinked the dates of a wrestling match already past, and lit the insides of cars with its fluorescence. The lodge was full, I soon found out, so I continued over the bridge into New Town, where I knocked on the door of a motel. The proprietor didn't answer. I returned to the casino and waited in the lobby in a leather chair until the receptionist took pity on me, called an oilman who had booked a room but not shown, and learned he would not be coming for another week.

I had been sent to Fort Berthold by *High Country News*, a small magazine where I had just begun to work, my first job out of college. Five years earlier, in May 2006, a company from Texas had drilled an exploratory oil well in the northeast corner of the reservation, near the town of Parshall. The oilmen used a new technique called horizontal drilling: Rather than bore straight into the ground, they maneuvered their drill bit downward and then across, needling through a deep layer of shale. Into the well, they pumped a mixture of chemicals, sand, and water, the pressure of which fractured, or "fracked," the shale. The well gushed oil, outdoing the company's expectations, and it was not long afterward that men and women began appearing at the doors of reservation homes with offers of bonuses and royalties.

The formation the company had tapped was called the Bakken, a miles-deep shale layer extending from western North Dakota into eastern Montana and southern Saskatchewan. It contained, by conservative estimates, four billion barrels of recoverable oil, enough to supply the nation for six and a half months. Geologists had known about the Bakken for years, but it was the advent of new techniques—hydraulic fracturing and horizontal drilling—that made the formation accessible. In the summer of 2010, after the boom had already overtaken western North Dakota, it arrived on Fort Berthold, as well:

the tearing up of sod and blasting of rock, the setting of culverts, the molding of embankments, the piling, compacting, and surfacing of roads, the laying of track, of rails and ballasts, the filling of water depots like giant backyard swimming pools, the digging of trenches and fitting of pipe, the drilling—switchboards, generators, tanks, mud pumps, masts lifted and set erect, wells bored and cased—the hauling of fresh water, of used water, the injecting of sludge into old wells, the assembling of pump jacks and lighting of flares, the building of man camps where workers slept—engineers, operators, surveyors, scaffolders, welders, mechanics, riggers, supervisors, dispatchers, janitors, electricians, pipe fitters, carpenters, journeymen, tool pushers, drillers, mud men, floor hands, derrickmen, motormen, and roustabouts.

On the heels of the Great Recession and the highest national unemployment rate in three decades, North Dakota's population grew faster than any other state's. Fort Berthold—located in the center of the Bakken—was no exception. By the time I arrived to write about the oil boom, the reservation population had doubled with non-Native workers. In the course of a month the summer prior to my arrival, the Mandan, Hidatsa, and Arikara Nation had earned more than $1.5 million in taxes and royalties, while its members who owned land earned, collectively, $2,781,670. It was estimated the reservation contained a third of the oil in North Dakota, more than most nations in the world. In a matter of five years, one billion dollars would land in tribal coffers, placing it among the wealthiest tribes in the United States.

During my first days on Fort Berthold, I spent a lot of time at the casino. It had been built in the early nineties not long after the U.S. Congress passed a law allowing gaming on reservations nationwide in a rare effort to foster economic development among tribes whose poverty seemed intractable. You could visit almost any reservation in the country and find a casino of the same vintage and similar design. The 4 Bears had two entrances—one that led to the game room, a dim, smoky parlor crammed with slot machines, poker tables, a dance floor, and a small bar; and the second into the lobby, a round room with a vaulted ceiling, sparsely furnished with pinball machines and the leather chair where I had waited that first night. When I had nowhere else to be, I often sat in the leather chair and observed the goings-on of the lobby. It did not take me long to realize the casino was at the center of a constellation of transactions. I saw fishermen come to fish the lake; a woman looking for a job; elders cracking crab legs at the casino buffet—one of two restaurants on the reservation that served breakfast, lunch, and dinner; and a steady flow of men in suits. One morning, I watched a tour bus disgorge a hundred elderly passengers and learned they had come from a senior center in Bismarck. They were among the few patrons I saw come solely for the slots. The other gamblers were oil workers and tribal members, many of whom lived in the lodge. I would learn that around four hundred tribal families had inadequate or no housing—a number that had risen as workers competed for shelter—and for all its capitalist ambition, the casino was in certain ways an equalizer of wealth. A portion of its revenue went back to the tribe, helping to pay for salaries and houses and medical bills, among other reservation services.

It was at the casino that I began to note signs of the oil boom: "No vacancies for 5 weeks," I wrote, and, "Oil worker surprised at $400/mo camping fee, says it was 300 only last month." Beyond the casino, the most obvious sign was the number of trucks. All day and night, semis groaned on the bridge over the lake, hauling fresh water to drilling sites, used water to evaporation pits, oil to storage facilities, and modular homes, tanks, pipe, and concrete among all the other materials that assembled into a boom. One day, in the course of twenty-four hours, deputies stationed at an intersection north of New Town counted twenty-nine thousand vehicles headed for the reservation, 60 percent of them large trucks. Roads had been crushed under the weight of these trucks, pounded back to dirt, and new gravel tracks had sprouted all over, sending up plumes of red scoria dust in the wakes of speeding semis. There were frequent accidents. Months earlier, an oil hauler had strayed into oncoming traffic and killed a family of four. On the way from Mandaree to New Town, roadside ditches were littered with deer carcasses and plastic flowers memorializing the dead. One morning, I dropped by the health clinic, where I was told that ambulances were in short supply and, due to the traffic, trauma victims had died before paramedics could reach them. I continued on to the fitness center, in a building in New Town called Northern Lights, where I spoke to a receptionist who said she often caught oilmen walking on treadmills in their mud-caked work boots.

I began to feel like a doctor recording the early symptoms of an illness—the oil boom, like an illness, was all anyone wanted to talk about. Yet I also detected in my conversations with tribal members a sense of awe that their fortune had so suddenly reversed. The boom had just begun. Fewer than a hundred wells had been drilled on Fort Berthold; companies were waiting on permits to drill hundreds more. While I waited in a lobby to meet with a tribal official one day, I came across a brochure titled MANDAN HIDATSA ARIKARA: KEEPERS OF THE BAKKEN, and in smaller lettering, SOVEREIGNTY BY THE BARREL. It opened to a letter from the chairman, Tex Hall:

> *We are a sovereign nation, recognized by treaty with the government of the United States. Our sovereignty can be maximized by the number of barrels of oil taken from our Mother Earth. We call it sovereignty by the barrel. The potential is here to obtain financial independence for our nation, education for our youth, sustenance for our elders, maintenance of our culture, and above all to set the people of the Mandan, Hidatsa and Arikara Nation on the road to independence.*

OVER THE LAST TWO CENTURIES, the sovereignty of tribes—that is, tribes' inherent authority to govern their own territories and affairs—has been upheld by treaties, courts, and the U.S. Constitution amid avid efforts to dismantle it. So it seemed a reversal of policy when, in 1934, Congress passed the Indian Reorganization Act, halting the division of Indian land into allotments and the sale of land to white homesteaders. In the fifty years prior, tribes nationwide had lost two-thirds of their land base. The IRA allowed tribes to form governments to replace the traditional institutions colonization had suppressed, and in 1936, the Mandan, Hidatsa, and Arikara elected a council and adopted a constitution. Prior to the IRA, the three tribes had relied on a ten-member body to consult traditional leaders and lobby federal agencies, but the IRA restored more of the tribes' authority. The new council set about acquiring land it had lost and regulating use of its pastures, which the Bureau of Indian Affairs had long allowed ranchers to overgraze. Later acts of Congress permitted tribes to charter companies and manage schools, courts, police departments, and social services, and while federal agencies retained some major responsibilities, such as criminal jurisdiction and management of the Indian Health Service, the tribe largely became the entity on which its citizens depended, around which most aspects of reservation life revolved.

On the morning I was to interview the chairman, Tex Hall, I arrived at the tribal headquarters, a single-story brick building next to the 4 Bears Casino & Lodge, and found it empty. Nearly everyone, including the chairman, had gone to a funeral.

I waited in a lobby beside a glass case containing portraits of Hall. In all of them, he was wearing either a warbonnet or a cowboy hat. He had shiny cheeks, a long, firm nose, and thick, dark eyebrows shaped like upside-down birds. "Isn't he handsome?" his press secretary plied when she saw me studying the photographs. The last journalist to write about Hall had described him as possessing "a John Wayne swagger" and "a Clint Eastwood squint," she said.

Our appointment had been for eleven o'clock. At noon, the secretary led me into an office where I was greeted by a tall man with a ponytail and a crushing handshake. He offered me a seat beside his desk and then leaned back in his own chair as if we were about to watch a football game.

I had known before I met Hall that he was among the most influential politicians in Indian Country. He was fifty-four years old, born to cattle ranchers in Mandaree. When his segment elected him to the council in 1996, he had been a superintendent of the Mandaree schools. Hall quickly ascended political ranks, becoming chairman in 1998 and, three years later, president of the National Congress of American Indians, an assembly of tribes that lobbies federal agencies. Hall was a fixture at congressional hearings. He befriended the Clintons and members of Congress and often appeared at White House parties in his warbonnet or cowboy hat. It was rumored he would run for governor, but in November 2010, he was elected to his third term as chairman. In the five months since, it had become clear this term would be unlike any other he had served. Presiding over a cache of minerals worth billions of dollars, Hall's influence in Washington, D.C., had grown. Recently, he had testified before a Senate committee, requesting that it force the Interior Department to speed the approval of drilling permits. "This boom should create a once-in-a-lifetime opportunity for our tribe," Hall told me. "The curse of it is that we have a very aggressive industry that wants the oil, and the price is right now, and they don't like the bureaucratic red tape."

The "red tape" Hall spoke of was the process through which companies gained access to Indian land. The allotment era had made a mess of this land—divided it into a checkerboard of plots, each with its own kind of ownership. There was "allotted land" that belonged to individual Indian landowners but that the federal government managed in trust; "tribal land," which the tribe had reacquired after losing it to allotment, but which the government also managed in trust; and "fee land," held privately and taxed by the state, which had been sold a century earlier to white homesteaders. To drill on fee land, companies approached landowners directly, offering an up-front payment—the "bonus"—and a percentage of their profits to be paid later in royalties. But on "trust land" the process was more complicated. Companies could approach Indian landowners directly with offers, but they had to deal with four federal agencies, including the Bureau of Indian Affairs, which approved leases, and the Bureau of Land Management, which issued drilling permits. The process, Hall said, was too cumbersome. The BLM had a backlog of applications to drill, and some companies had been waiting on permits for months. The price of oil was the highest it had been in decades. Hall worried that if the permits were not granted soon, the boom would pass the tribe over.

I glanced around his office. It was bright, lit by a window and decorated with old photographs. In one of the photographs, fourteen men in suits gathered around a desk where a white man was signing a document. Beside him stood a Native American man who had taken off his glasses and was weeping into his hand.

I would learn that the photograph had been taken on May 20, 1948; that the white man was J. A. Krug, the secretary of the interior at the time; that the weeping man was George Gillette, chairman of the Three Affiliated Tribes; and that the document was the contract with which the tribe relinquished the bottomlands of the Missouri after the United States had claimed them by eminent domain for the construction of the Garrison Dam. This was after the tribe had fought the proposal for years. In 1945, four councilmen had met with the Senate Committee on Indian Affairs to present a resolution:

> *Whereas construction of the proposed Garrison Dam . . . would inundate 200,000 acres of the best irrigable land of our reservation; and Whereas this will force approximately 200 families to move from their permanent homes . . . ; Whereas it will flood or cause them to be useless, all Government buildings and improvements at Elbowoods, Nishu, Shell Creek, Independence, Beaver Creek, Lucky Mound, Charging Eagle, and Red Butte, including the hospital, school buildings, total value over $1,000,000 . . . ; and Whereas cause to be either cut and removed all timber now growing along the bottoms, thus destroying natural shelter for the cattle and taking away the continual fuel supply of our people, and source of income from sale of timber, fence post, lumber, and firewood . . . ; Whereas the cemeteries of our forefathers will be destroyed, and with it all our memories and kind remembrances of these burial places that have been held sacred for all; and Whereas this large body of water will separate the reservation . . . ; and Whereas the various treaties and Executive orders have given the people of this reservation*

promise of a perpetual use of this land . . . ; Whereas we have permanently
located on these lands, and our forefathers also have lived on these grounds,
and it is the hopes and plans to have our children and their children to occupy
this land continuously forever; and money or exchange for other land will not
compensate us for the land, landmarks, and sentimental attachments . . . :
Now, therefore, be it Resolved by the tribal business council . . . That we
oppose the present plan of constructing a dam at Garrison, or any other plan
which will destroy the flood areas of the Missouri Valley.

It was this event, more than any other in the tribe's history, that had cast on the boom a certain karmic power. "The white man thought they were going to put us on the badlands where nothing would grow," Hall told me. "Do you think they would have put us here if they had known?" I shook my head. Hall smiled. "Before the dam we were self-sufficient. Then they flooded us and destroyed our economy. If we've been blessed with this fuel, here, there's no reason why we shouldn't try to bring it back, what we lost. If managed right, this development could make our tribe self-sufficient again."

THE DAY BEFORE I GAVE up my hotel room to the oilman, I met a tribal historian, a woman, who invited me to stay in a house that had belonged to her late sister. The house was in Parshall, east of New Town, and over the following years, I would stay there whenever I came to the reservation. One day, while perusing a bookshelf, of which the house had many, I found a collection of old newsletters issued by the Bureau of Indian Affairs. The first, dated May 18, 1953, announced the visit of a government "Oil and Gas Supervisor" who met with the tribal council regarding the leasing of land. The Bureau would hold eighteen auctions, through which companies acquired the mineral rights to a third of the reservation. At an auction in December 1953, bonus offers ranged from $5 to $190 an acre, and landowners earned $3.5 million collectively. By the following September, tribal members had earned $6 million, but the figure came with a caveat:

"Not all of the Fort Berthold Indians share in this income," a Bureau agent warned in a newsletter that month. "The truth of the matter is that only 710 individuals have shared in this oil income out of a total enrollment of 2,751, and 105 of these are Indians who reside off the reservation permanently." Even among those who earned bonuses, the money was unevenly dispersed. Twelve people received more than a million dollars between them, while a majority earned less than five thousand apiece. For a few, the gift was well timed: The Garrison Dam was nearly finished, and tribal members were preparing to move. According to the newsletters, most of the oil income went toward new houses, while "35 individuals purchased 628 head of cattle; 12 individuals repaid their loans in full to the Tribe," and "approximately 4,196.45 acres" were bought for home sites. Thousands had been spent on "furnishings and equipment, wiring of homes, four barns, sheds, corrals and fencing, and for food and clothing"—all "worthwhile expenditures," noted the agent, "but the fact remains that for over 2,000 Fort Berthold Indian people, a major job of rehabilitation is still a serious immediate need."

No one would ever mention this money to me, perhaps because no one on the reservation remembered it. The oil boom that began in 1951, later eulogized in books and plaques and North Dakota school curriculums, hardly arrived on Fort Berthold, where only a few dozen wells were drilled. The first of these wells was on land belonging to an Arikara woman named Helen Gough, who willed her royalties upon her death to build and maintain a museum. The Three Affiliated Tribes Museum, a modest A-frame in the casino parking lot, was the sole relic of the first boom I found on the reservation, as if the memory of the dam had eclipsed the memory of this boom, and what was lost to the dam had lasted while what was gained from the boom had not.

Booms by definition are temporary, strung along by the whims of international markets. In the sixties, the price of oil fell; then, in the seventies, it rose, and the industry flourished again in North Dakota. Even fewer wells were drilled on the reservation this time due to the problem of heirship: Allotments had fractionated among landowners' progeny, and it was not uncommon for hundreds of owners to share in an allotment. By federal law, to drill on an allotment, a company needed consent from every landowner—nearly an impossible task, since so many had scattered after the flood. Unable to secure enough leases, oil companies considered it hardly worthwhile to drill on the reservation. By the end of the second boom, forty-two oil wells had been drilled on tribal or allotted land, and by 1996, only ten of these wells were still producing.

For decades, the tribe's entire annual budget came from congressional appropriations. This changed in 1992, when the tribe won a $142.9 million settlement for land it had lost to the flood. The next year, the tribe opened the casino. The settlement and casino gave the tribe leverage it never had before, and as the tribe sought loans, it also sought new sources of income. In 1995, the council drafted a report on their oil and gas potential and sent it to hundreds of companies. Few responded, but those who did were unanimous in their concern that the fractionated heirship of Indian land made leasing prohibitively difficult. Only one company made an offer: For exclusive rights to drill on the reservation, it would pay the tribe 18.25 percent of its profits and a $2 million bonus, on the condition that three-quarters of allottees also agreed to lease their land for 12.5 percent royalties and twenty to thirty-five dollars an acre.

The company, Alenco, based in Alberta, had been connected to the tribe through two white brothers in Williston, North Dakota, who owned Powers Energy Corporation. Alenco agreed to pay Powers 4 percent royalties on all the oil it extracted from the reservation. In 1997, one Powers brother accompanied the tribal chairman to Washington, D.C., where they testified before Congress on a bill that would alter the heirship laws on Fort Berthold, requiring only a simple majority of landowners to agree to lease before their allotment could be drilled. The bill passed.

The first day most tribal members heard of Alenco was March 14, 1997, when the *Minot Daily News* reported that the tribal council, in a

closed session, voted to accept the deal. Only two councilmen had dis-
sented. One of them was Tex Hall.

The reservation erupted in outrage. Tribal landowners demanded
a meeting with the Bureau, which they blamed for not informing
them of the deal. When the council held a private meeting with
Alenco, landowners protested until they were let in. "Will the Council
place their interests above that of the private landowners?" one
woman wrote in a letter to the Bureau. "Oil development of a vast
area of land lends itself to political maneuvering. The request by the
oil company to waive a number of Federal regulations was of grave
concern to us, and we wondered if allotted lands would be adequately
protected." Letters elicited no response. After months of silence, the
Bureau released a report in which it found that the deal was "not in
the tribe's best interest" and suggested Alenco amend it. A year later,
the company presented a new deal not all that different from the first.
Hall walked out of the vote, followed by two other councilmen. The
deal never passed. A year later, Hall was elected chairman.

Nearly every tribal member I interviewed about Alenco shud-
dered to think what might have happened. The royalties and bonuses
Alenco offered were far below federal standards, let alone market
value, but perhaps the most terrible aspect of the deal was one that
glimmered out in retrospect: The company would have had exclusive
access to the reservation for a period of fifteen years. Hall opposed the
deal because it was "not a fair price" but also because it would have
broken one of the last levers of sovereignty the tribe possessed. He
was not opposed to drilling, but he believed that the tribe, rather than
give up control of its land to an outside company, should develop the
resources itself.

Hall never had this chance. During his first two terms as chairman, the tribe slipped perilously into debt, and in 2005, when a company called Black Rock Resources, with no prior record of oil
development, offered to lease twelve thousand acres of tribal land for
thirty-five dollars apiece, the council voted, excluding Hall, to accept.

Hall was furious. Among his most vocal detractors was Steve

Kelly, the chief counsel for the tribe. Kelly, a pale, portly tribal member who had been raised off the reservation in the oil fields of eastern Montana, believed the tribe was incapable of drilling its own oil and thus better off leaving the job to outside companies. It was Kelly who facilitated the leases with Black Rock and a majority of the tribal leases that followed.

Kelly was not the only one with whom Hall began to spar. In 2006, the manager of the casino, Spencer Wilkinson, Jr., made an offer to the council, proposing that a company he owned called Dakota-3 operate an old oil well that belonged to the tribe. In exchange, Dakota-3 would earn 75 percent of the well's profits.

Spencer was from White Shield but grew up in Oklahoma and moved to the reservation in 1993, when his uncle, Wilbur Wilkinson, was elected chairman. The casino opened, and Spencer got a job. His uncle's tenure ended in scandal when Wilbur, with Spencer's help, embezzled $20,000 from the tribe. Spencer testified against his uncle and kept his job at the casino, while Wilbur was sentenced to twenty-one months in federal prison. In the mid-2000s, Spencer came to own Dakota-3 with several partners. The council accepted his offer to operate the tribal oil well, but before the Bureau of Indian Affairs could approve the deal, Dakota-3 began drawing payments from the tribe. On August 28, 2006, two months prior to the next election for chairman, Hall sent Spencer a letter, reminding him that the Bureau had yet to sign off on the deal. Hall also noted that he had heard Spencer was attempting to lease minerals from the tribe. "I will not process or sign any assignment of the Tribe's mineral leases," Hall warned. That fall, he lost the chairmanship after Spencer campaigned for his opponent.

The following year, the tribal council leased 42,842 of its acres to Dakota-3 for fifty dollars each and 18 percent royalties. In March 2008, Spencer posed with the new tribal chairman, holding a giant check addressed to the tribe for $2.1 million. Meanwhile, Spencer went door-to-door, leasing around as many acres at the same rate from Indian landowners. Then, in 2010, an Oklahoma-based company,

Williams Oil, purchased Dakota-3 for $925 million, earning Dakota-3 a profit roughly two-hundred times what it originally paid for the leases. Not since Alenco had a deal generated so much outrage on the reservation. Tribal members wondered why the federal government, its trustee, had not held an auction or warned the tribe and landowners that their minerals were worth more than Dakota-3 offered. In November, Hall won reelection on the promise that he would fire Spencer.

Spencer kept his job, and by the time I arrived on Fort Berthold, his clutch on the tribal government had become legend. I often heard members speculate as to how he had enticed the council to lease the tribe's minerals for such a low price. But what Spencer had done was common practice in the oil industry: Companies often purchased leases for little money before landowners knew what their land was really worth and sold them for enormous profits. Every company that acquired the first leases on the reservation, including Black Rock, "flipped" them to other companies. Spencer's deal drew more ire because he was related to many of the landowners he fooled. "I felt really ashamed that I had been taken like that," a cousin of his told me. In a culture where family mattered more than anything, she explained, she had trusted him. Spencer had exploited the tribe's strength at the same time he exploited its poverty and vulnerability to federal mismanagement. "None of us knew there were billions of dollars under Fort Berthold," another woman told me. "How do you believe that if you've been poor all your life?"

One morning in April 2011, I met with the tribe's tax director, an energetic man with short, dark hair and an affinity for brash metaphors. "It's a David and Goliath situation," he told me. "When you're worried about how you're going to pay your electric bill, or you can't buy your kids school clothes, or you're an elder on fixed income, and you're way below poverty level, and somebody throws $30,000 at you, and you don't understand that it's worth $300,000, you've just made a huge error. That's what happened to our people. The oil companies have dictated this process. It's not their first rodeo."

The director, Mark Fox, was in his late forties and had spent most of his adult life working in tribal government. The tribe was unprepared for the boom, he believed. After centuries of colonization—of federal entities weakening and displacing tribal institutions—it did not have the resources, let alone the expertise or regulatory power, to control the oil industry. It had no environmental agency to monitor leaks or spills; no transportation department to track trucks; and what was more troubling, it had no criminal jurisdiction over the thousands of non-Native men and women who had come to work, since the U.S. Supreme Court had stripped tribes nationwide of the right to criminally prosecute nonmembers.

"It's like the lottery winners you see on TV," Fox said. "Their lives get worse, because they're not ready for it. We're the same way. My biggest fear is that we end up like other reservations I know—industry comes in, money's thrown around, everyone celebrates for a while, and when industry leaves, the reservation is in worse shape than before."

After I left Mark's office, I thought about what he said. Not everyone had been blindsided. In interviews with landowners, I had begun to recognize the names of individuals who seemed to have gotten ahead of the boom. I heard these names over and over, saw them in court documents. These were the men and women whom oil companies had hired to appear at their relatives' doors with lease forms in hand. How had they known? the landowners I spoke to wondered. Had they been smarter, wiser? Had they had the gift of foresight? In fact, it appeared they had been chosen to know, plucked up from the casino, from tribal government, from influential families. These "consultants" earned both direct payments for their services and a small percentage of royalties from oil produced on the land they helped lease. Oil companies had found their proselytizers, and after these men and women acquired all the reservation land there was to lease, many had started their own companies servicing the oil fields. For this, they had earned a moniker I would hear often on the reservation: "oil kings."

Spencer Wilkinson was an oil king, but he was not the only one.

There was also Steve Kelly, the lawyer for the tribe who had sparred with Tex Hall over the oil deals. In 2008, Kelly left his tribal position and founded the company Trustland, through which he acquired leases for many of the same companies whose deals he negotiated on the tribe's behalf. When there were no more leases to acquire, Kelly had expanded his services, and Trustland grew into the largest truck operator on the reservation. That was before the company called Maheshu encroached on Kelly's business. Maheshu was owned by another oil king—the tribal chairman, Tex Hall.

ONE EVENING THAT APRIL DURING my first visit to the reservation, rain fell so hard that trucks idled on roadsides and potholes roiled with mud. I drove east from New Town on Route 23, paused at a crossing of asphalt and dirt where a horse had slung its head over a barbed-wire fence and a pump jack nodded relentlessly. When the rain let up, I went on to the Scenic, a restaurant perched on a rise with a view of Lake Sakakawea. Three roughnecks smoked beneath the eaves, their dirty boots propped against the siding, knees protruding into the storm. A waitress seated me near an elderly man who caught my eye when I came in. He wore glasses and a nylon jacket, his hair thin and wispy. He invited me to eat with him. "The thing you must know," he said once I had joined him, "is that this was our big chance, and we missed it."

The man's name was Ed Hall. The chairman was his nephew. Ed had been born in Elbowoods, a town in the Missouri bottomlands, and, in 1953, a year before the flood, left the reservation to join the Marine Corps. Over the next forty-eight years, Ed had lived all over the country: on the Turtle Mountain, Cheyenne River, and Standing Rock reservations, where he designed and built tribal roads; in Crow Agency, where he served as Bureau of Indian Affairs superintendent; in Washington, D.C., where he advised the assistant secretary of the Bureau; in Albuquerque, where he worked in a Bureau transportation department; until he came home in 2001 to assist with a redesign of the bridge over Lake Sakakawea. All those years in the bowels of the federal-Indian bureaucracy had kindled in Ed a fondness for reports. I would see him often on later visits to the reservation, and whenever I asked how he was doing, he would reply, "I'm working on a new report."

The evening I met Ed at the Scenic, he told me about a report Tex asked him to write. After regaining the chairmanship in 2010, Tex had assembled a team, including Ed, to investigate corruption in tribal government. Tex meant for the report to remain private, but someone had acquired a copy and posted it online. The findings were troubling—money wildly mismanaged over the four years prior; $1.4 million spent on councilmen's travel, almost half of that for the former chairman alone; a tribal debt exceeding $100 million; dubious leasing of tribal minerals, such as the sale to Spencer Wilkinson, Jr.; and a system of spoils that made it far too easy for councilmen to buy their constituents' votes. There was widespread "fear of retaliation if one speaks up to address injustice, fraud or corruption," according to the report. "This fear of retaliation is not only for the individual, but for one's entire family. Tribal goods and services, once open freely to all, have been restricted and made available only to those who are politically connected." Perhaps most troubling was that the oil boom had fueled this corruption. An ethics ordinance held that elected tribal officials could not "own interests in or conduct business with" oil and gas companies, and yet multiple councilmen already had been recruited as partners in oil-field ventures or owned companies themselves. The report did not offer names, but it occurred to me that among the councilmen violating the ordinance was the chairman himself. After Tex lost the election in 2006, he had made the curious transformation of founding Maheshu, through which he acquired leases for outside oil companies, and then entered the trucking business.

After I said goodbye to Ed, I drove to the casino. There, in the parking lot, I came across two white men cooking chicken on a charcoal grill. They were in their forties—mechanics, they said. They wondered if I wanted to sit and offered me the metal steps that folded from the doorway of a camper. The shorter man lived in the camper. He had come from Washington State, where he lost his house to fore-closure and where his wife now lived in a rented apartment. The taller one also lived on Fort Berthold, in a backyard shed with no windows or heat. He paid $300 a month—a good deal, he said—and when I asked how he liked the reservation, he grinned: "It's crazy. You run a truck for fifty-four hours straight, and no one here will stop you."

The shorter man nodded. "I got taillights out. I seen guys with no seatbelt, no mud flaps, just rolling through stop signs."

"Keep your eyes open with toothpicks, and you're making money."

"A cup of coffee, you're making money."

The taller one laughed, paused. He looked at me, and his eyes widened. "You can do anything you want short of killing somebody," he said.

I remember thinking that they were nice men and that they needed something to laugh about and so they did.

Eventually I left them and went inside the casino and ordered a drink. The bar was thick with smoke and the singsong of slot machines. Women with their hair pulled in tight, dark buns dealt cards to sun-burnt men. A Leonardo DiCaprio movie was playing on the televi-sion, and a white woman in a feather boa was flirting with some oil workers. I took my drink and sat beside a man who introduced him-self as "Pancho the Bull Rider." Pancho was from Texas but lived in a man camp twenty-five miles to the north, where "all there is to do is drink," he said. We talked until the music got too loud. A man and a woman rose to the dance floor, laughing so hard their eyes shut. Then, clasped in each other's arms, they spun around, and around, and around.

4

The Great Mystery

THE DETECTIVES ASSIGNED TO THE KRISTOPHER CLARKE CASE WORKED in a three-story brick building on the edge of downtown Williston, seventy miles west of the reservation. On the bottom floor was the Williston Police Department; on the top, the McKenzie County Sheriff and the state Bureau of Criminal Investigations; and in the basement was a coffee room where officials from all departments met at eight-thirty each morning. They gathered at a table and passed around a stack of pawn tickets—computers, guns, watches, gold. If a ticket matched a theft, they had a case, and then they moved on to what had happened overnight. A man shot a urinal in a strip club. A woman had been raped. The calls came at all times of day. In 2012, the police department would field almost triple the calls it had received three years earlier, while detectives' caseloads would double. Among these cases were some that languished for months: front-end loaders missing, the thieves long gone across state lines; city parks overtaken by roughnecks who, like wasps, constructed shelters under the bridges; sex workers insisting they were there on their own, though they seemed to have misplaced their IDs and the rooms they rented were in men's names; and the case that had gone unsolved longest of them all: the disappearance of Clarke.

After the truck had been found in Williston in June, the case was assigned to a city detective, Ryan Zimmerman. He was the same age as Clarke, twenty-nine, bald, earnest, and relatively new to his job. From a storage closet repurposed as an office, Zimmerman phoned Clarke's acquaintances. "KC is always out to have fun, but not the type of person to walk away from everything," he noted in an interview with a childhood friend of KC's. The detective paraphrased:

- *KC is a very private, very outgoing person.*
- *KC break up with his ex-girlfriend was not the best, but it was not the worst.*
- *KC never got in trouble unless it was racing his bike on the street.*
- *KC Grandfather was his best friend.*
- *KC walking away from his pickup would not happen, let alone leaving it unlocked. That kid does not leave anything unlocked.*
- *He does know James HENDRICKSON and James is not good news.*

By the middle of June, it became clear to Zimmerman that the city did not have jurisdiction in the case, so he passed it on to Steve Gutknecht, a Bureau of Criminal Investigations special agent. Gutknecht was older than Zimmerman by more than a decade—a serious man reputed among his colleagues for being a dogged investigator. Gutknecht had served long enough in the position to know how the oil boom was changing North Dakota. Prior to the boom, he had investigated five murder cases over his lifetime; since the boom arrived, in 2008, he had worked an average of one homicide every year.

Gutknecht approached the Clarke case as he had each one before it, sorting every shred of rumor, following every lead. The report he released in July contained thirty-nine points. "On June 15, 2012, S/A Gutknecht interviewed a confidential informant from the Fort Berthold Indian Reservation who had some theories as to what may have happened to CLARKE," one point read. The informant told Gutknecht "it was possible that Blackstone Trucking, because of its political affiliation with Maheshu Trucking, which is run by the Tribal Chairman Tex Hall who has strong political power on the Fort Berthold Indian reservation, may have ordered the killing of CLARKE because of his attempt to take business away." This same informant theorized, alternatively, that Tesha Fredericks, who owned Running Horse, had an ex-boyfriend who murdered KC out of jealousy. Gutknecht ruled this out quickly; querying the boyfriend's name, he learned the man had been in jail at the time KC disappeared, having beaten another man nearly to death.

Among the tips Gutknecht collected in the report, a majority pointed at James Henrikson. This did not make James a "suspect"—as Gutknecht explained to Jill, they lacked evidence to prove a crime had been committed—but it did make James a "person of interest." So, that July, Gutknecht called James, and on the first of August, James appeared at the police department for a voluntary interview.

Zimmerman watched a live recording of the interview from an office down the hall. Gutknecht and James entered a small, carpeted room furnished with a wastebasket, a table, and two chairs. "I'm just closing the door for privacy," Gutknecht said. "You can leave anytime you want."

James sat down on the front of a chair, his legs splayed as if ready to spring out of it. His eyes were shaded under the bill of a hat, his skin tan, his hair neatly cut. He wore new jeans and a T-shirt fitted tightly across his bulging chest. His voice was high and nasal, incongruous with his body, and he had a giddy, confident manner that seemed especially odd given the occasion.

"He was fun," James said when Gutknecht asked about KC. "Always happy. He worked pretty hard. We had him go on vacation, because he was pretty tired. We were like, 'Hey, you've got to go on vacation, catch up on some rest, because you look like shit.' But he did awesome with our company guys. Everyone loved him." It wasn't until after KC disappeared, James explained, that James heard KC had been planning to leave Blackstone. He heard it from a "company man"—a foreman who lived on drilling sites and oversaw the operations—who told him that Rick Arey had been approaching other company men to steal contracts from Blackstone for Running Horse. "I guess Rick and maybe KC had been trying to work for Running Horse for like four weeks," James told Gutknecht. "We've been friends forever. I don't see him doing that to me. I've given that kid probably fifty grand, easily. Meals and stuff like that."

Gutknecht asked James about the day KC disappeared. The agent had heard that on the morning of February 22, KC had dropped by the Maheshu shop to turn in a company credit card. Had KC given this card to James?

"No, not to me," James said.

"Sarah?"

"I don't know." James was talking faster now. "He didn't tell me, not once, that he was leaving. I was always asking him if he was all right, and he was, like, so tired. He didn't look good. I don't know if he was drinking hard, partying." Recently, James told Gutknecht, he had been talking to a guy named Johnny about it. Johnny thought maybe KC had gotten into drugs.

Had James any idea where KC's gun had gone? Gutknecht asked.

James folded his arms, thought for a moment. "He always had it with him," he said. "I don't know what that was about."

"So you don't have anything to do with his disappearance?"

"No," James said, laughing as if the question were preposterous.

"You guys never had a physical altercation?"

"No, never."

"Because I think something bad happened to him," Gutknecht said.

"What if he shacked up with some girl?" James said. He had been talking to Johnny about this possibility, as well.

"Who is this Johnny you've been talking to?" Gutknecht asked.

"He's out in Washington," James replied. He couldn't remember Johnny's last name. "Johnny Donkey," James always called him.

Gutknecht changed the subject. "When I talked to Rick, he said he had concocted a plan with KC to 'bring Blackstone to its knees.'"

"What?" James said. "I don't believe that for a second. KC would never do that to me. I love KC to death. There's no way KC would do that to me. I'm probably one of his best friends, so I don't see that happening."

GUTKNECHT TOLD JILL WILLIAMS VERY little about his interview with James. He did not tell her, for example, that although James looked nothing like criminals Gutknecht typically encountered, James had bragged like a criminal, extolling his past crimes while denying the one now in question. Once, James told the agent, he had lost millions of dollars in a marijuana bust. "I felt like he was making stuff up as he went along," Gutknecht later would recall. One thing remained clear to the agent: "Henrikson was the only one with a motive. In my career, as soon as you see a guy with a motive, that's usually who it turns out to be. It's not like storybooks or movies where there's some type of surprise."

Among the few things the agent shared with Jill was the fact that both James and his wife, Sarah Creveling, refused to take a polygraph test. Their refusal confounded Jill. Sarah had been eager to help in the beginning, and her distress at KC's disappearance had seemed genuine, but since then, Sarah's attention had waned. She wrote less often to Jill, and in this silence, Jill had grown suspicious.

The tips Jill received on Facebook hardened her suspicion, as did her and Lissa's conversations with Rick Arey. Rick said that when he first met James, he was "fucking charmed by the guy." James did not look like any man Rick had known in the oil fields before. His hair was carefully combed, and instead of canvas pants and old sweatshirts, which most men wore on the job, James worked in T-shirts and a puffy vest no matter the weather. "I'm not gay," Rick said, "but this guy is a pretty good-looking dude. He makes you feel good when you're around him. He's somebody you want to like you."

Rick's impression changed on the day James interviewed him for a job with Blackstone in the late fall of 2011. They met at Better B's, a busy café on the main street of New Town, where James chose a table in the center of the room. "He was loud, like he wanted everyone to see him," Rick recalled. "The waitress comes up, and he says, 'Rick, get whatever you want,' and he orders steak and eggs, three pancakes, a glass of water, and a cup of coffee. I'm watching him eat, and he's cutting big chunks up and piling them into his mouth, and he's chewing with his mouth open. He was a fucking slob. He had that vest on, and he was flexing his muscles. He didn't eat half of his meal. He had four bites out of three pancakes. He might have finished the coffee. I'll never forget it. Them pancakes were as big as dinner plates."

The job James had offered Rick paid $1,500 a week, a bit more than roughnecking on oil rigs, which paid $28 an hour. For never having to climb a rig again, Rick thought the deal sounded good. In January 2012, not long after they moved into the Maheshu shop, Blackstone received a contract from the tribe to spray water on a road to suppress dust. Rick dispatched trucks for weeks, until a worker for another company spun out on the road and died. "Nobody got in trouble for it," Rick said, "but we looked like jackasses, because every swinging dick knew who was watering the road. We were the ones making an ice rink." Rick ordered the trucks off the job, but James ordered Rick to send the trucks back. "He wanted the image that Blackstone was successful, that we put people to work," Rick said.

James was ruthless with money. Drillers paid truckers by the load, so the faster truckers hauled, the more money Blackstone made. It was not uncommon for truckers carrying contaminated water to open the valves of their tanks as they drove, letting fluid pour out, or to dump in remote corners of Fort Berthold to avoid having to drive to waste disposal sites located beyond the borders of the reservation. James encouraged this, and it bothered Rick, who had started his career as a roughneck in Wamsutter, Wyoming. BP, the company he worked for, had trained him not to spill. "I know they fucked up the Gulf of Mexico," he said, "but in Wamsutter, a fucking drop of antifreeze was a spill. On the reservation, people don't understand that. *Hey, this is dirty Indian land. Fuck it.* That's the mentality. That's James's mentality."

By the time Rick left Blackstone, he had been glad to never see James again. But was James capable of physical violence? Rick was not sure. He was even less sure about Sarah. Rick believed James relied on Sarah more than James let on. Sarah kept the books, made payments, and rode to drilling sites with James, who rarely went anywhere without her. If James seemed out of place in the oil fields, the impression they made together was even more startling. Sarah was tall, lithe, blond, with bleach-white teeth. It was her teeth that had made Rick distrust her: Sarah drank coffee through a straw.

Jill also had trouble believing that James or Sarah had killed KC, but their silence suggested to her that there was something they were not saying. One day in October 2012, Jill posted a public message naming James and Sarah on her Facebook page: Why wouldn't they take a polygraph test? Why didn't they write to her anymore or donate to her fund to find KC? Why didn't they spread the word about his disappearance?

Neither James nor Sarah responded. A few days later, Jill asked her followers to send letters to the tribal council requesting a public hearing about Blackstone and their "refusal to cooperate" with investigators. She had heard the next year was an election year, she noted. "I'm sure that Tex, being a tribal bigwig, would certainly want to use his power to do good and wouldn't want to dirty his good name covering for a piece of crap like James." Tex did not respond, either. When Jill made a poster for her supporters to hang around North Dakota, at the bottom, she wrote, "As if the horror of my son being missing is not enough, I have had to deal with the fear of there being a possible danger to my own life from the people who are involved with the disappearance of my son."

On October 19, Jill was served with a lawsuit. She had just left her house in a suburb south of Seattle when the papers landed in her yard. The complaint was brief, six pages in all. Jill photographed the

pages and sent them to Lissa, who called Jill and read them aloud:
"The defendant . . . regularly posts defaming statements. . . . Defendant has accused the plaintiffs for causing or contributing to the disappearance of Kristopher D. Clarke. . . . The Plaintiffs have cooperated
with the police. . . . [James Henrikson and Sarah Creveling] are not
connected with the disappearance of Kristopher D. Clarke and have
no knowledge of his whereabouts."

LISSA ENCOURAGED THE COMMENTS JILL posted and, in some cases,
drafted them herself. After they met on the reservation, Jill had made
Lissa an administrator of the Facebook page, and Lissa often spent
nights culling the messages, which had become too numerous for Jill
to respond to on her own. Among them was an assortment of condo-
lences and tips, many hopeful if far-fetched. A hotel clerk writing from
Brownwood, Texas, said she had checked in a man who bore a resemblance to KC and later noticed he had registered under the name
Christopher Clark. "Please note that I don't know if it was for sure
him," she wrote. "I felt very odd telling you this because I don't want
to bring your hopes up. Also I am not supposed to release any guest
info because I can get in trouble & lose my job. So please keep me
anonymous!" Others speculated that KC was alive. An oil worker who
had known him wrote, "It makes me sick to think something might
have happened, and [I] pray he just needed to get away from it all, as
he was very stressed and burnt out from the work the last time I saw
him. I wish you and your family the best."

Among the messages from people familiar with Blackstone, Lissa
noticed a common thread. The worker who knew KC claimed to have
stopped using the company's services "due to various issues that made
me question their integrity." Others noted more specifically that
Blackstone had underpaid them or that workers in the company had
a history of making threats. One man had been working for a shop
that serviced Blackstone trucks when a mechanic in the shop overheard a Blackstone employee brag "they were going to get someone to

beat a guy up." Another man writing under the name "John Doe" offered, "There is a lot of hearsay on the reservation and rumors are created out of thin air. So for what it's worth . . . I heard that when KC went out to Blackstone that he was wanting to get paid for some work. The situation had gotten out of control and KC got beat up pretty bad."

It occurred to Lissa, KC's disappearance aside, that among workers at Blackstone there was an undercurrent of violence. She sensed it not only in the theories they shared but also in the fear their messages expressed. Everyone who wrote to the page asked to remain anonymous—afraid, it seemed, of some vague retribution.

One night, Lissa reread the defamation suit James and Sarah had filed against Jill. A final point most interested Lissa: "Plaintiffs have experienced a loss of business due to the Defendant's action." It appeared that comments Jill posted on Facebook had reached some of the companies that hired Blackstone. James and Sarah were seeking monetary damages. This worried Jill, who could not afford to pay for the company's lost profits, let alone for a lawyer, but it gave Lissa an idea: If they could convince drillers to sever ties with Blackstone, then perhaps Tex would end his partnership, too. Blackstone would lose its tier-one status in bidding on contracts. It would have to leave the reservation.

"We need a strategy," Lissa told Jill. "You know what I think? I think these guys built an empire around Tex, and the only way we'll get inside is if we take it down, brick by fucking brick."

LISSA CHOSE A PSEUDONYM—NADIA REINARDY. She had made up the name in the nineties when she worked as a stripper during her first years out of college. She had liked how "Nadia" sounded—exotic, the way it rolled off the tongue—and "Reinardy" she had stolen from an old boyfriend, Tom Reinardy. A white guy. He had roomed with CJ's father at the University of North Dakota in Grand Forks, and after they all graduated, Lissa had decided she got along better with Tom and followed him to Minneapolis. The relationship had not lasted. In Lissa's telling, she wasn't good enough for his family, and Tom tried to control her. After they broke up, Lissa worked as a security guard at Mystic Lake Casino, south of the Twin Cities, where she met the only man she would marry and, within fifteen months, divorce. It was around that time, 1993, that she met another man, OJ Pipeboy.

He was a friend of her stepbrother, Wayne White Eagle, Jr. When OJ's brother threw a party in Minneapolis, Wayne invited Lissa along. Lissa was twenty-five, OJ eighteen. He had a ponytail, a baby face, a faint mustache like the stroke of a paintbrush. He had a thick neck and thick shoulders and thick arms and thick wrists. He had gold chains dripping down his chest, gold rings lacing his fingers, but it was his voice—a smoky radio voice—that attracted Lissa to OJ. It was his voice that made her fall in love.

His mother was Sisseton Wahpeton Sioux from the Lake Traverse Reservation in South Dakota, his father Lakota Sioux from Pine Ridge, but OJ grew up in the center of Minneapolis, in the only urban public housing project in the country that gave preference to Native families. Although federal programs to relocate Native Americans to cities had ended in 1972, the fraction of Native Americans who lived in urban areas had kept growing. By the nineties, roughly half lived in cities, and Minneapolis had more urban Indians than any city in the nation. Lissa had aunts and uncles who moved there, cousins who were born there. The American Indian Movement, or AIM, began in Minneapolis in the sixties when Clyde Bellecourt and other Movement founders organized neighborhood patrols to protect residents from police brutality. Due, in part, to the efforts of AIM, Minneapolis had Indian health clinics and community centers, as well as Little Earth, the housing complex where OJ's grandmother was among the first tenants. None of these resources made up for the fact that OJ grew up poor. His father, a medicine man, was always on the road and had girlfriends all over the country. His mother drank. OJ mostly took care of himself, waiting in line each morning at the Little Earth gym for cereal and a carton of milk. There were two things he remembered clearly from childhood: how often he fought with other kids and how hungry he had felt.

By the time Lissa met OJ, he had more money than most Indians she knew. At the age of thirteen, he had fled Little Earth and gone to live with a woman named Linda who worked as an aide in his middle school. Linda was a member of the Shakopee Mdewakanton Sioux Community, the wealthiest tribe in the nation thanks to its casino, Mystic Lake, and earned tens of thousands of dollars in payments from her tribe each month. The years OJ lived with Linda were the happiest of his life. They went on walks, gardened, hunted, fished, and tapped and boiled maple syrup. Then, when OJ was fifteen, he got in trouble, and Linda kicked him out. She gave him an option to come back, but by then OJ was supporting himself, earning, he claimed, $2,200 a day.

He had met a Vice Lord, a member of a black Chicago gang that had territory in South Minneapolis. The city had Native gangs, as well—raggedy kids who roamed Little Earth, scrapping it out with rivals—but it was the black gangs OJ admired, with their gold chains and expensive cars. The Vice Lord was a cousin of his sister's boyfriend and took OJ under his wing. When OJ met Lissa, he had begun dealing on his own, copping his drugs from Vice Lords and selling them at Mystic Lake.

He had heard about Lissa from her brother Wayne—how smart she was, how she was trained in law enforcement and had a college degree—but Lissa was not what OJ had expected. She could talk smarter than anyone he knew and still sound like she came from the streets. She was pretty, too, with perfect skin and long, curly hair. OJ wanted Lissa because "everybody wanted her," he would say. He wasn't sure if he was attracted to her himself, but he knew that other men thought she was beautiful, and when she paid him attention, it made OJ feel good.

In 1995, Lissa moved with Shauna and CJ into a house in St. Paul, where she found a job assisting homeless families. That year, OJ called her, looking for a place to stay. One day, in lieu of rent, he gave her a baggie of cocaine.

It was around that time that Lissa asked OJ to call her Nadia Reinardy. After that, everyone they hung out with in the Twin Cities knew her by this name. *Nad,* OJ called her. *Nadicus.*

She would assume other names throughout her life, each one an escape from the shadows that trailed her, but Nadia was a different sort of name. Nadia *was* the shadow that trailed her, more ruthless and clever than Lissa had ever been. Where Lissa was loving and compassionate, Nadia was vindictive and petty. Where Lissa played by the rules, Nadia went behind everybody's back. It was as Nadia that Lissa became an addict. Now when she remembered that time of her life, she marveled at how easily she had moved between her halves, like an actress in a one-woman play, inhabiting a role and then another. She supposed this should not have surprised her. She had long walked a line that separated cop from criminal. She believed in this line, in its thinness. She believed everyone had inside themselves the capacity for evil and for good.

ONE DAY IN EARLY NOVEMBER, Lissa made herself a Facebook account under the name Nadia Reinardy. That she should become Nadia again made sense to her. She believed the skills she acquired as a criminal might help her in solving a crime. She knew what fit within state juris-diction and what constituted a federal case, and she could inhabit the psyche of a criminal: Already, she recognized in James's behavior some tactics she had used herself. When she searched for him on the Inter-net, she found him associated with multiple spellings of his last name—Henrikson, Henderson, Henricksen, and Hennikson. Lissa believed James had caused this confusion intentionally, since more names made a person harder to trace. Rick had mentioned that James had a crimi-nal record, and indeed, one evening, when Lissa typed "James Henrik-son" into a records database, she came up with twenty-two pages of results. James had been arrested and charged with crimes ranging from sexual assault of an ex-wife—he had been married twice before Sarah—to theft and manufacturing drugs. Once, he had been arrested for growing marijuana and spent a year in prison. James was still on probation.

That night, Lissa logged in to her Nadia Reinardy Facebook account and posted James's criminal record to Jill's page. "Had to do it," Lissa captioned her post. "I blew some cash just to prove a point but didn't realize it would be this fruitful."

A few days later, as Lissa was driving home from the welding shop, a song came on the radio by a band she liked, Evanescence. Lissa had never listened closely to the lyrics, but now they caught her—*Isn't something missing? Isn't someone missing me?*—and gave her an idea. Once, she had made a video for her uncle Chucky after his death by assembling a slideshow of images and setting it to a song. She decided to do the same for KC.

At home in the apartment that night, Lissa printed a few dozen photographs that Jill had sent her, trimmed them with scissors, and arranged them on the living room floor as she played the Evanescence song on repeat. *Please, please forgive me,* the singer crooned, and Lissa lifted an image of Jill in a hospital bed holding her newborn son. She chose another image of KC in a bathtub and a third of Jill holding his tiny body, pressing her lips to his forehead. Lissa surveyed the other photographs. There were more of KC as a baby and one when he was an older child, his hair darkened. Then he was an adult, posing with a motorcycle, and in the next photograph, he was in a hospital bed, the tube of a respirator curling from his mouth. It was a miracle, Jill had said, that KC survived the motorcycle accident. After he could walk again, he left Washington for Texas. Here, Lissa's options thinned: KC in a bowling alley with his ex-girlfriend; signs reading NEBRASKA THE GOOD LIFE and WELCOME TO NORTH DAKOTA; sunsets over Lake Sakakawea; and, finally, James and Sarah.

Lissa worked through the night, left for the welding shop in the morning, and began again the following afternoon. It was a Saturday, the third of November, when she finished. She uploaded the video to YouTube under the name Nadia and sent Jill the link.

"I hope you like it. Was hard to pick and choose," Lissa wrote.

It was "perfect," Jill replied, thanking her.

"It's Nadia! Not me. Lol."

Lissa could not sleep. She wrote Jill at eleven that night, when the first comments appeared below the video, and again at eleven-thirty, when it had been viewed five hundred times. By one-thirty in the morning, Jill was asleep, but Lissa remained awake. She toggled between the video and Jill's Facebook page, which seemed to blink every minute with new messages. Lissa read each one carefully, making note of those she would mention to Jill the next day.

When Lissa woke in the late afternoon, on Sunday, she was still at her desk. The apartment was quiet, her children gone out. She had received a text from a friend that there would be a ceremony at the sweat lodge in Fargo that evening.

She went into the bedroom and, from a mess of clothes strewn about the floor, chose a T-shirt and a long, cotton skirt. On the dresser, she found her pipe and a drum, which she wrapped in a beach towel and carried to the car. She drove west on Ninth Avenue and south on Forty-fifth Street, past the grocery store where she shopped, past soybean and sugar beet fields and the hard, square growth of new apartments, to where the city faded into storage lots. There, behind a low berm of earth, was the sweat lodge, and in a trough beside it, a set of mudstones smoldering on a bed of coals. A man tended the fire, raked the coals with a pitchfork. Other men and women had gathered. Lissa greeted them one by one. She lowered to her knees, unwrapped the pipe. Pressing a plug of sage into the bowl, she sang a quiet song. The others rose and formed a line, and Lissa rose, too. At the door to the lodge, she spun once around. Then she went inside.

......

BY THE MIDDLE OF NOVEMBER, Lissa was spending so much time on the case that her apartment had fallen into neglect. If Shauna stopped by to visit her mother, she found the laundry unfolded, the shower unscrubbed. The kitchen floors were tacky with spilled sugar, and bowls sat dirty in the sink, where the hard remnants of meals had blossomed into mold. Paper accumulated like fallen leaves, forming loose piles on the desk and on the floor of the hallway into the bedrooms. Lissa had not lain in her bed in weeks. If the boys saw her asleep, it was at her desk, mouth agape. This was not exactly unusual. Lissa claimed to prefer chairs to beds, and the apartment had long ricocheted between states of chaos and order. But now it seemed there was no order, and the boys, sensing their mother had little time to worry as to their whereabouts, came and went as they pleased.

It had been months since Lissa attended her addiction recovery meetings, having relinquished her leadership role to another woman in the group. Even to the sweat lodge, she was going less and less. Instead, she spent so much time on the phone that the boys took to imitating her. Obie, now fourteen, would coolly enter the apartment, while Micah, thirteen, pretending to be on the phone, would wave wildly for his brother to be quiet and then storm into a bedroom and slam the door. Shauna, now twenty-five, was less amused. "Our mom cares more about a stranger than her own kids," she complained. She had moved to Fargo to see her mother—recently, she had relocated to an apartment next door—and now it seemed that on the rare occasion she discovered her mother at home, Lissa had no time to talk. Lindsay, twenty-two, sympathized with Shauna, while their brothers swung between their sisters and mother, defending Lissa one day and harping on her the next.

The tension between Shauna and Lissa had risen not long after Shauna came to Fargo. While working full-time, Shauna had enrolled in classes to finish her undergraduate degree. Lissa encouraged this and offered to watch her kids—an arrangement that suited them both in the beginning but over time strained their relationship. Shauna could be sullen and critical of Lissa, who reacted by refusing to watch her grandchildren, deepening Shauna's resentment.

"My older kids are very judgmental, accusatory, disrespectful," Lissa wrote one day in her journal:

> *CJ called me a "pill head" and told me to go back and lay in my room and pop some more pills. I believe "addict" and "junkie" were thrown in there a few times. But it doesn't matter. All in all, basic old argument. I always owe him. Owe him for the awful life I gave him. I owe, I owe, and I owe. It seems no matter what I do I will never make up for the past. I fucked up here and there but the past is the past. . . . No matter what I will never be good enough for my older kids. The damage is done. They can continue to hate and ridicule me all they want. They can do it AWAY FROM ME.*

Now even Lissa's younger kids were seeming bothered by her work on the case. One evening in November, Micah told Lissa he believed a spirit had taken up residence in the apartment. He had been napping on the couch after school when he felt the blanket he was lying under lift and fold across his chest. He thought for a moment that his mother adjusted the blanket, but when he realized Lissa was nowhere around, Micah leapt up and ran to his bedroom. After that, strange things kept happening. Obie noticed them, too. They would be alone in the apartment when a cupboard would open or a shampoo bottle would drop to the bathroom floor. It was not a coincidence, they insisted, and their stories confirmed something Lissa already suspected—that KC had been visiting her, as well.

She had been raised to believe in spirits, whose existence few in her family questioned, but Lissa's sense of how spirits behaved was shaped less by her culture than by her own inquiry.

Her first real encounter had come while she was in prison. Dakota Women's was located in an old Catholic boarding school, which several of Lissa's uncles had attended decades earlier. Lissa noticed the spirits as soon as she arrived, clinging to other inmates like masks, possessing them, making them say strange things. The spirits scared

Lissa, and one day, she told a priest about them. Though she had been raised Catholic, she had not yet been confirmed. The night before her confirmation, she had stolen a bottle of her grandfather's liquor and drank most of it herself. The reservation priest had rescheduled, but Lissa missed that date as well. She never had much use for religion, believing it a ploy of white men to control the behavior of Indians, but what the priest at the prison said surprised her. While the Catechism acknowledged the presence of spirits, it warned against delving into the spiritual realm, since although God created spirits, like people spirits had free will and like people they could turn away from God. The spirits Lissa had seen among her fellow inmates were real, the priest said. He believed Lissa had a gift for seeing, but he told her to be careful.

After that, Lissa developed her own theories about the way spirits occupied the living world. She wondered if they did not drift in the air as she once thought but instead took shelter in everyday objects—in doorknobs, hot dogs, cigarettes touched to lips. In needles sunken in the crooks of arms.

She believed spirits were around all the time, and it was at night, when things got quiet, that it became easier to register their presence. The first time spirits entered her dreams had been in the summer of 2010, on a camping trip in White Shield with her relatives. They had erected a canopy by the lakeshore and gone fishing. One evening, Lissa climbed a bluff above the beach and found several large stones arranged so deliberately she was certain they were an effigy. That night, as she fell asleep, a man and three women came to her in a dream. Lissa was on a bluff picking sage when she noticed them standing on a far hill. Each time she glanced up at them, they moved impossibly closer. She picked frantically, arranging the sage in a circle around herself, and when she looked up again, the man and women were standing beside her, their eyes cloudy and white.

Later, she sent a photograph of the stones to an anthropologist, who told her they were shaped like the constellation Auriga. She also told the story to the Lakota holy man she knew, and after that, she paid more attention to her dreams. None would be so vivid as the one that came to her that night by the lake, but when a spirit began visiting her dreams in the fall of 2012, Lissa had no doubt it was KC. "I don't know why but he likes it here," she wrote Jill one night. "I'm sending him to pester u cause I'm wiped out. I just offered my pipe up and I talked to him."

If Jill was bothered that a woman who had never known her son was claiming to have spoken to his spirit, she did not let on. Once, when Lissa wrote, "It's him keeping me up but I'm going to ignore him tonight," Jill replied without a hint of sarcasm that her son could be "persistent." Jill, as Lissa put it, was "more open-minded than your average white girl." She often visited a psychic, whom she believed had communicated with her son. Lissa distrusted psychics. They preyed on desperate people, she thought, whom they gutted of all ability to reason. Jill received frequent messages from psychics offering services for a fee, and Rick had even spoken to one who propositioned him to engage in something called "astral sex." Rick was creeped out, but even he was more open-minded than most white people Lissa knew. "You know," he mused one night, "before this KC thing happened, I was fine going through life drinking beer and hanging out with my buddies." Now, he said, "It's like God smacked the shit out of me. He's like, *Listen, you've got to wake up to what's going on.*"

Rick meant "God" not in a religious sense but in a spiritual one. "Everyone says, 'the Bible, the Bible, the Bible,'" he said, "but everyone interprets the Bible different. I choose to have my own relationship with the Great Mystery. I've been ostracized by my family for that. Once, I was like, 'Hey Uncle Bobby, if you don't take Jesus as your lord and savior, are you going to hell?' And Uncle Bobby said, 'Yes.' He's fucking sixty years on the planet and he believes that bullshit? I've kind of gone anti-religion, even as far as, like, pagan ritual, the old yin-yang version, where they chop heads off lambs and put them on the altar. It's all ridiculous when you get down to it." Rick was done with God, he told Lissa—at least with the one he had known as a child—but into the space made vacant by his doubt had come a new way of seeing that was, he thought, more holy than the way he had abandoned. Rick believed in spirits. He believed people saw only what they allowed themselves to see: "God ain't going to show you nothing that you can't fucking comprehend yourself. I'm sorry to cuss, but I'm passionate about it. We're talking about what's wrong with the world, here. We're talking about why people suffer. Because God can't give them a fucking answer."

IN THE DAYS AFTER LISSA posted the video, she monitored the number of views obsessively. In less than a week, the video had been seen 120,000 times. Eighty-five percent of those who shared it were women, a majority based in North Dakota, Idaho, Washington, and Wyoming—states many oil-field workers hailed from. Lissa even sent the video to James's parole officer, noting in an email, "This man is on probation under your watch."

About a week later, the video vanished from the Internet. On Jill's Facebook page, a black box occupied the space where the video had been, and the YouTube link opened to an error message. Lissa wondered if someone had contacted law enforcement to have it taken down. She posted the video again.

James had never been active on social media, and Sarah had deleted her Facebook account, but now others appeared on Jill's page in their defense. "I do not know where KC is, but I know for a fact this mother has twisted SO MUCH of the info on this site," one man wrote. The man, whose name was Brian Baker, wished to correct Jill's story: "KC said he would be back in 2 weeks. I don't think James or Sarah knew anymore than that. James and KC were good friends, they never had a fall out or argument of any kind! . . . Blackstone did end up finding out that KC and Rick were working for the other company. But there was nothing 'shady' going on. Rick told Blackstone he just wanted to be paid more, so all that stuff he says does not make since to me."

Lissa had not heard of Brian Baker before. Oddly, neither had

Rick. Brian had no information on his Facebook page, and his name was too ordinary to summon with a Google search. Then, one morning in early November, Brian wrote to Jill directly:

> *You can't be trusted! . . . You don't want help, you only want money. James and Sarah would gladly help you. You've never reached out besides for money, why don't you publicly apologize and see where that gets you?*

Jill forwarded the message to Lissa, asking if "Nadia" could post a reply. Lissa logged in to Nadia's account and wrote to Brian, who replied immediately. She responded in a private message: "How could you be so mean to a mother that is missing her son?"

"I was never being mean," Brian wrote. "I'm sorry you thought that. . . . I want answers just like you do and everyone does, I want to help!"

Lissa considered her opening. "Who are those people to you anyway?" she asked. "You sound as though you take everything personal like they are siblings of yours or something."

"They are very dear friends I've known for years. What is Jill to you?"

Better to stay as close to the truth as possible, Lissa decided: "I met her through the page, and I flew to North Dakota to meet her when she went there with a lady from the reservation to look around."

If Brian believed "Nadia," he did not say. He was concerned, he wrote, that Jill had targeted James and Sarah when neither were yet "suspects." He had no idea where KC had gone, he repeated, and he mentioned the anonymous caller who told KC's grandfather that KC was working in Montana.

Lissa baited Brian: "I pulled James's criminal history and . . . he is a drug dealer, a thief."

"Why would you think he's a drug dealer?!"

"You obviously have never seen his rap sheet."

"Yes I have, and better yet I know him."

"Well why won't they take a polygraph to shut everyone up?"

Brian did not respond right away. After eleven minutes, Lissa assumed he had abandoned the conversation, but then a new message appeared: "They were given legal advice to never take one. And a lot of the time the results are not admissible. And the police said they were very helpful. . . . Doesn't that make since to you?"

Since instead of *sense*. It was the second time Brian had made this mistake.

"I mean NO disrespect for Jill what so ever!!!!" he continued. "But she doesn't even know KC was missing for 4 months. KC told many people he didn't like his mom. I'm not trying to be rude. I can imagine her hurt, but he told people that."

"And you're real tight with your mom?" Lissa replied. "Don't a lot of people have resentments towards their parents? I don't talk to my mom very often. Resentments. You know. You haveta know. That's why you're way far away from your home."

"I'm close with my mom, maybe a week or two could go by. But never 4 months."

"Good for you. I can't say the same. I have nothing against Sarah. She seems like a nice person, young, a lot going for her, but she needs to lose that loser! That girl would be better off without him. You watch! The minute she tries to gain some independence from him, she will be missing, too, or beat up. People like him are predictable. It's just a matter of time."

"I know them both, and James is not a loser. He does not look good on paper but he is a good person, he's helped anyone who's asked! And Sarah is very very sweet and kind, always putting others before her."

"What do you think happened to KC?" Lissa asked.

Brian didn't know. "It's driving me nuts!" he wrote. "I feel like there has to be some sort of clue. . . . What do you think?"

Lissa took several minutes to compose her reply. "I think James killed him or had him killed cause KC knew things about James and about that business. Also I think Sarah knows something about it after the fact. But I also think that money is a terrible demon. I think KC will be found soon and everything will come to light. James is a socio-path and he has most people fooled, including his wife, and including you."

"Wow, you're very opinionated ha ha," Brian wrote. "I don't believe at all James killed or had KC killed. There's nothing to know about the company. . . . James and Sarah are very open with books and checks and there's nothing weird going on."

Lissa printed the conversation with Brian and reread it several times. Then she printed all the incriminating information she had gathered on James and called an investigator she knew in Minot, a North Dakota Bureau of Criminal Investigations agent named Mike Marchus.

They met one day in early December on a street near the Minot police station. Mike remained in his car as Lissa handed him the crim-inal record. He was pudgier than she remembered, with arched eye-brows and military hair. "A friend," she called him, though he had helped send her to prison. For years he had monitored her when she lived in Minot, kept track of her drug deals, until one day, in 2005, officers had acquired a warrant and raided her house. Still, Lissa trusted Mike more than any other cop. Even while he surveilled her, they had spoken often on the phone, and once, when a little girl disap-peared from a house next to Lissa's, and Mike was assigned the case, Lissa had tried to help him. The girl was never found.

"It's a classic RICO case," Lissa now explained to Mike—a con-spiracy eligible for federal prosecution through the Racketeer Influ-enced and Corrupt Organizations Act. If James was guilty of theft or fraud or trafficking drugs on the reservation, as his record suggested he might be, then the case "could go federal," to the FBI and U.S. attorney.

"I'm not federal," Mike told Lissa.

"I know," she replied. But perhaps he could share the case with a detective who was. She suspected there was more to James's crimes than the record she had found online contained, and she planned to find out. Jill had invited her to Washington for Christmas, and since the courthouse in Bend, Oregon, where James's arrest records were kept was five hours south of the town where Jill lived, they intended to make a trip. Lissa promised to bring Mike these documents, as well.

IT WAS BELOW ZERO, THE highway dusted in a powder of snow, when Lissa departed Fargo with Obie and Micah on the evening of December 21, 2012. The boys had been reluctant to miss Christmas with their relatives, but Lissa had offered to take them to see the ocean and had added that perhaps they might lure west whatever spirit was haunting the apartment. So, they had packed the van with changes of clothes and driven to Bismarck, where they spent a night with a cousin, before continuing on to Washington.

Jill's house was no larger than a double-wide trailer, on a cul-de-sac at the edge of a forest. It was modest, loosely cared for, with latticework around the front and gardens gone to seed. After Lissa and the boys had settled in, Jill served beef and barley soup for dinner and fretted over what they would do the next day. Obie and Micah were eager to see Seattle, but the idea upset Jill, who said things wouldn't be right the day being so close to Christmas. So Lissa waited for Christmas to pass before she took the boys out.

She could recall seeing the ocean three times herself, first with her mother in 1971, when she was three years old. They had been living in Los Angeles, Irene one of forty students selected to attend a new Indian Studies program at UCLA. One day, Irene and Lissa took the bus to San Francisco and a ferry to Alcatraz Island, which, when they arrived, had been occupied for more than a year by Native American activists. AIM would later lead similar occupations—of Mount Rushmore; of the Bureau of Indian Affairs headquarters in Washington, D.C.; of Wounded Knee, South Dakota, where, in 1890, a cavalry massacred around three hundred Lakota men, women, and children—but Alcatraz was the first.

By then, Irene had met a Yakama Indian from Wellpinit, Washington, named Willy Phillips, who had been hired as an undercover spy to sleuth out drug users among students in the Indian Studies program. Irene learned this only after they started dating, though it had not mattered anymore, since Willy, a decorated Vietnam veteran with PTSD, was fired for drinking too much. They married and moved to San Jose, and then Willy took up with another girl, and Irene did not see him much anymore. One night, in an Oakland bar, Willy was stabbed to death. This Lissa remembered—how suddenly Willy was gone for good; how Irene, after three years in California, phoned the reservation and said she was ready to come home; how Lissa's grandparents, Madeleine and Willard, appeared in San Jose with a station wagon and, while their daughter packed, took Lissa to the beach.

That was the second time Lissa had seen the ocean. The third time she remembered had been in the winter of 1997, when she was twenty-eight years old. She had been two years into her addiction by then. Her house had been raided, and her children, Shauna and CJ, taken and placed in foster care. Lissa had been desperate to get clean, so she and OJ had fled Minneapolis in a hurry, rented a car and pointed it west until they came to the edge of the continent and could not drive any farther. The beach had been flat, cold, vast—somewhere south of Seattle. Lissa had taken off her shoes and socks and waded into the frigid water. Then they had driven to Portland and rented a motel room on Division Street, which OJ had wanted to leave as soon as they arrived. One day, Lissa returned to the motel and found him high, laid out on the bedcover. He screamed at her, acted crazy. She took him to the emergency room. That evening, when they returned to the motel, OJ beat her brutally and then left on a bus for Minneapolis.

Lissa remembered wandering a wide boulevard on the east side of Portland. She entered the first strip club she came to. It was a lingerie modeling shop, under renovation. The proprietor took one glance at her bruised face and said she could not dance looking like she did. He found her a room in a hotel nicer than the one she and OJ had been living in. When she said she would not sleep with him, he had told her this was okay, and when he left, she lay on the bed and cried. The proprietor was kind to her. While Lissa waited for her bruises to heal, he tasked her with monitoring cameras in the club, keeping an eye on the dancers as they greeted clients. He paid her forty dollars at the end of each day, and when he realized she had a knack for business, he invited her to partner with him. He even gave her a car for her birthday and hired an attorney to get her kids back, but Lissa told him she could not stay. At the end of that summer, she went home.

That was the last time she had seen the ocean. Obie and Micah were not yet born. Now they drove as far west as they could go, to the edge of the city, and parked beneath an overpass, a highway roaring overhead. Obie was acting sullen and refused to leave the car. It was afternoon, the shadows of homeless men shifting in the almost-dark, and when one approached for a cigarette, Lissa gave him a whole pack. "Keep an eye on my son," she said. The man brought over a chair and sat, looking dutiful as he smoked.

They rode the Ferris wheel, lights spinning over a boardwalk, and then stood on a pier that jutted into the sound. The day was damp, the water the color of clay.

Lissa's phone blinked with a message from Jill: Were they sure they wanted to go to Oregon the next morning? Jill was broke and hated for Lissa to cover the cost of gas and court records. She hoped they were having a good time. She had saved them leftovers.

"We are going tomorrow," Lissa replied. "Regardless end of story."

LISSA HAD BEGUN TO LOSE patience with Jill. The intimacy they had found over the phone had waned upon her arrival in Washington. Still, they acted close, and this posturing made Lissa feel claustrophobic. At the house, Jill hardly took her eyes off Lissa, asking where she was going if ever Lissa stepped outside. After days of this, Lissa was glad to leave for Oregon and would have preferred to make the trip alone had she not planned another stop after the courthouse requiring Jill's presence—Sweet Home, the town where KC's grandfather, Robert Clarke, lived.

Jill had not seen Robert in years. He was the father of KC's father, who had long been absent. It was no secret KC favored Robert over Jill, and it was for this reason, Lissa suspected, that KC had been missing for months before Jill even emailed Robert. Jill and Robert had spoken intermittently after that, trading what information they had. Robert told Jill about the anonymous caller who had claimed KC was in Montana, and he sent her the last emails he exchanged with KC a day after Christmas in 2011:

> *You are my thoughts, you are the fireplace on a cold morning, you are the constant reminder that I still have a life. So much for sentiment, all is true. Wishing you the best, Love Gramps*

KC's response had been no less sweet:

> *I feel the same about you. You have done more for me and cared more than anyone else on the planet. Still lots of work here. I got a sinus infection and been sicker than shit the last few days. I've been taking antibiotics and getting better though. Love you with all my heart.*

Reading those emails had to hurt, Lissa thought, but in reply, Jill had sounded strong. She suggested the anonymous caller was, in fact, James, and she worried Robert was in danger.

Now as Lissa and Jill drove to Oregon, Jill did not seem as strong. When they arrived at the courthouse in Bend, they found it under renovation and were forced to sit cross-legged on the floor as they read the pages Lissa had requested, sorting them into piles for the clerk to copy. They would have more time to read later, but Lissa could not help herself. When she came to a document that excited her, she handed it to Jill, who showed little interest.

The next day, they left Bend and continued west toward Sweet

Home. When they came to Sisters, a piney enclave on the east side of a range of mountains, Jill's phone blinked with a message from Robert. He was "sicker than hell"—they better not come. Jill wanted to turn around, but Lissa refused.

The boys had fallen asleep. Snow fell. Their wheels spun on a slick of white. The banks on either side of the road were taller than the van and the trees so laden with snow that they formed a tunnel through which Lissa drove. The snow seemed to calm Jill, and when they reached the top of a pass, they stopped and got out together to photograph the trees. Then they descended through a mossy valley, so green that they might have entered another world.

They found Robert's trailer some distance out of town, on a thin lawn beside a creek. It was getting dark, but there were no lights on inside. Lissa knocked gently at first, then harder. Jill looked like she might cry. "We came all this way," she said, forgetting her earlier reluctance.

"Is he hard of hearing?" Lissa asked.

"Yes, very. Yes. I forgot that."

Lissa knocked again and waited. A minute passed. Then she heard footsteps, and the door opened revealing a man with stooped shoulders, long ears, and white wisps of hair retreating from his forehead. His jeans hung on a pair of suspenders. He did not look pleased to see them. "Huh," Robert said. "You're here anyway."

His trailer was crowded, boxes stacked on the surfaces as if he was preparing to move. "Find someplace to sit," Robert said. "Can't believe what it's like living in one of these when there's nowhere to put anything."

"At least you got somewhere to put something, right?" Lissa said.

"Some people got, yeah . . ." Jill said, trailing off. She was breathy, talking to herself.

Lissa pushed aside a box and sat at the table. She noticed a set of photographs and reached for them, listening quietly as Jill and Robert spoke. In one photograph, KC was no more than five, smiling largely on a leather sofa in the crook of his grandfather's arm. In another, taken some years later, the two of them stood in a parking lot against a backdrop of forest, a camera slung around Robert's neck.

"That Mountrail County sheriff—boy, he was a real ass," Robert told Jill. "I don't know what his name was. I don't remember. He says, 'Even if I find him, I don't have to tell you anything. He's twenty-nine.'"

"I got the same story," said Jill. "I got, 'Well, maybe he wanted to disappear.'"

"After I found out that was a phony call, it must have been two, three weeks, and I still hadn't heard from KC. That caller told me the only reason KC hadn't called was there was nowhere to get service in eastern Montana up around the oil fields."

"Somebody's trying to throw you off," Jill said.

Lissa looked up. "Did you ever get the phone records?" she asked Robert.

"No, see, I wasn't smart enough to save the records. I thought everything was all right. I didn't—" Robert sounded tired, like he was ready for them to go. "What a mess," he said. "How'd you find this place?"

Jill nodded to Lissa. "She can find anyone," she said.

Robert didn't seem to hear. "I have to take Tom"—a neighbor—"to the doctor once in a while. He's had hip replacements, knees. Albany—you go down a one-way street, turn, go a block, and think you can go back the other way, but hell, you don't know where to go."

"How often was KC calling you then?" asked Jill.

"Oh, I don't know, probably average once a week, maybe go two weeks without a call. When he was in Texas"—working at the car dealership—"he'd get upset 'cause he couldn't sell anything and then he wasn't very friendly. Then he'd have a good week, and he'd call. In [North Dakota] he called me on the road. Sometimes we'd talk for twenty, thirty, forty minutes, but all of it was about the job, and how the job was going, and the hours he was working. A couple times he mentioned that he was saving money."

"Did he ever tell you he had any problems with James?" Lissa said.

"No," Robert said. "It was all a big surprise that there were any problems. I found that out from Rick Arey. I was trying to figure out where that house was that Judd and KC lived in. I finally called Judd on the job where he was working, and he talked a little bit, but he had to get back to work. [Then] I called Sarah, and she went into hysterics. I didn't get anything out of her. She just said, 'I don't know, I don't know,' and hung up. The bawling hysterics, I mean, not laughing."

"Do you have any other pictures of KC?" Lissa said.

"That box right there is full of them."

"Can I look?"

"Help yourself. Turn the lights on overhead there."

Lissa rose, lifted the box, carried it to the table. Once, Robert continued, he visited his grandson in Washington and "took a whole pile of pictures," which he later gave to KC. "I don't know if he ever went through them or not," Robert said. "The people he was renting from, they sent the box to me." His voice cracked and quieted. "They're not organized. You can keep any of those you want."

Jill began to cry. "It's okay, Jill," Lissa said. "It's part of what we got to go through." Lissa lifted a photograph from the box and handed it to Jill. "Is this you?"

"I don't know," Jill said. She had left her glasses in the car.

Lissa lifted another, this time of Robert's late wife—KC's grandmother. She had planned to make an album, Robert explained, but then she had surgery and never woke up. That had been a few years ago.

Now night was falling across the windows of the trailer. "I don't have anything to give you guys," Robert said. "I've got coffee if you want it."

"We should probably hit the road," said Jill.

"Would you mind if I did a video of you?" Lissa said. "If you had something to say to KC—"

"Oh, I don't know. I'm not very good at that sort of thing," said Robert.

"If he was alive?"

"There's no way that he's alive, as far as I'm concerned. I don't think there's any use wondering anymore."

A WEEK AFTER LISSA AND Jill visited Robert Clarke, they heard that he had died. This did not surprise Lissa. In Fargo, she loaded onto her computer an audio recording she had made of their visit and listened to it over and over. Even in the distant scratch, Robert's grief was deep and unmistakable. As Lissa and Jill left the trailer that night, Robert had put on his shoes and followed them outside. "Got to bring the cat food in," he said. "We trapped a coon the other day and it chewed the cage up so bad trying to get out that it bloodied itself, must have broke teeth." Lissa had barely heard Robert over the crickets singing in the fields beyond the property, above the wind scattering leaves across the lawn, but in that moment, she recognized in his voice something she had heard in her uncle's on the day, now more than two years ago, that Chucky told her he had come home to die.

It was not, as people sometimes said, that they had nothing left to live for. It was that the living became too much. It was the living, not the wanting to die, that weakened a person, Lissa thought, and it was this weakness that invited bad spirits. So it had been for Chucky: A bad spirit had taken hold, and he could not let it go.

5

What Good Is Money
if You End Up in Hell

In the winter of 2013, the oil boom slowed in North Dakota. Although the price of oil remained high, at ninety dollars a barrel, companies would drill only the wells they had begun or those where their leases would soon expire. Many workers fled south to oil fields in Oklahoma and Texas, while those who remained braced themselves for the cold. They skirted campers with plywood, stuffed scraps of insulation into makeshift walls, lined the insides of huts with emergency blankets, and reinforced windows with duct tape and sheet plastic. They installed propane heaters, praying they would not leak. They lived as many tribal members lived, burning what fuel they could find.

Snow came. The roads iced over like plates of glass, causing semis to jackknife across the highways.

Lissa visited the reservation almost every weekend, though the snow made it difficult to search for KC on foot. Instead, she drove, stopping here and there to take photographs. She took particular interest in the tribal dwellings she passed that winter: in one image, a pale-yellow shed; in another, a concrete bunker with plastic sealing the windows; then an old blue clapboard, the paint peeling; and a trailer set crookedly in its lot. Later, when asked why she had taken the photographs, Lissa would say she was documenting "our oil-rich reservation." The irony of the season had not been lost on her—that while many reservation families struggled to heat their homes, the oil that once had lain beneath their feet had gone to keep others warm.

She often stopped in White Shield to visit her grandmother Madeleine. Since Lissa's first summer out of prison, the tribe had built Madeleine a new house—a single-story white house at the end of the same dirt lane, with a window looking east over fields and sloughs past the border of the reservation. The farmhouse Madeleine lived in previously had been coming apart for years, crawling with freeloaders that rambled in from the prairie—mice that scurried through cracks in the walls and snakes that crept through the plumbing. The snakes in particular were a problem. They bobbed in the toilet bowl and climbed the curtains in the living room. Once, when Irene asked Lissa to fetch beets from the cellar, Lissa had gone down barefoot, and when she pulled the chain that dangled from a light at the bottom, the snakes had writhed and scattered. Lissa had screamed. An uncle laughed from the top of the stairs. "Better put some shoes on," he warned. Lissa suspected it was because of the snakes, and the mold, that the tribe had granted Madeleine a new house. She suspected also that the tribe had taken pity on her grandmother for having lost her oldest son.

Chucky's death had shocked the family. Even Lissa, whom he told of his intent to die, experienced a strange lack of feeling whenever she visited White Shield after he was gone. It was as if, in dying, her uncle had clipped the thread that bound her memory to the reservation, and now the two existed separately for her, parallel but never touching. Her grandmother's new house felt too sterile, and the old farmhouse, though it remained standing, and though an uncle had moved in and filled the rooms with his belongings, seemed emptier than it had ever been, a museum of forgotten objects.

The first family reunion after Chucky's death, in the summer of

2012, had been a smaller gathering than usual. Lissa's children in particular seemed less eager to accompany her on trips to Fort Berthold. "I like the reservation," Micah said once, "but it's kind of like a restaurant you don't have in town. It's like Big Boy. It's great every once in a while, you look forward to it, but you don't want it in your city, because it kills the fun."

If asked where they were from, all of Lissa's children replied, "White Shield," but Lissa could not deny that they were city kids— and now, with Chucky gone, and the family overcome with grief, the reservation did not seem as fun to them anymore. Even Obie, always eager to see his grandpa Dennis, who had left Fargo and moved back to the reservation, appeared to have lost interest in visiting. On a recent visit, Obie had been shamed for taking bacon from the breakfast table before his elders had been served.

Lissa did not mind going alone. In winter, the cottonwoods faded in the bottoms of the coulees, and the grass was cut to its stiff, sharp stems, and the prairie turned gray and brittle. The weather shifted wildly. Some days were warm, the next mornings cold, the snow so dry it blew away in a light wind. Madeleine's house thronged with relatives. Lissa's aunt Cheryl had moved in, and there were more cousins than Lissa could count, who trailed babies through all the rooms. Lissa rarely went to the old farmhouse anymore. Once, when she passed by, she had peeked in Chucky's bedroom and noticed his furniture had not been moved.

"There's too many spirits in there," Dennis told Lissa. Dennis wanted to burn the house down, and Lissa agreed. If the house was gone, her memories might return to her, she thought, but as it was, Lissa felt nothing for the house, and this nothing reminded her of her family's loss.

"At least when it's gone you can romanticize it," she said. "I'd rather it be 'the house that used to be there' than have to look at it and feel nothing."

......

THE NEW HOUSE WAS THE fourth Madeleine had occupied since moving to White Shield in 1953. Her first house had been an old clapboard, dragged up from the bottomlands and propped on cinder blocks just in time for the flood. Then she had moved across the street, to a cluster of homes the government built for relocated families. In 1981, when Madeleine and Willard bought their third home, the old farmhouse, they turned the second house into a store. YB's, they called it. They sold candy, pop, and sandwiches, which you could not get from the government commodity truck that delivered rations monthly to White Shield, and eggs and meat they raised on the land they had purchased, where they resurrected the old farm. In addition to chickens and hogs, they kept horses and planted gardens from which they harvested and preserved much of their own food. Lissa's generation of Yellow Birds helped on the farm but more often roamed the property. They tied belts around the hogs, loose enough to slip a hand underneath, and took bets on who would hold on longest. In the summertime, they swam in sloughs and rode horses to the lake, where they played along the banks. Sometimes their elders joined them there and told stories from the years before the flood. It was not far from shore where Nishu and the other villages had been—where the schools and churches and forests had been—so one could imagine, looking out on the lake, another world beneath the water.

It was this world Madeleine had tried to replicate when she and Willard bought the old farmhouse. She had been raised some miles north of Nishu, on the road to Garrison, where her family grew carrots, corn, potatoes, peas, and rutabagas, and raised hogs for bacon and cows for cream, which they delivered to Nishu. Madeleine spent much of her childhood in Nishu with her grandfather, Clair Everett, and grandmother, Fannie Bear, who lived in a frame house on a bluff overlooking a slough. Below the house were thickets of chokecherries, Juneberries, plums, and gooseberries, which her grandparents harvested and preserved, and forests so lush and tall that nothing grew beneath them. Here, in the springtime, Clair came to hunt, departing the house before dawn, and often when Madeleine woke, a duck would be roasting in the oven.

Clair Everett's original name had been Elk Tongue, but in 1901, when he was nine years old, a government agent rounded up children from Fort Berthold and placed them in boarding schools. Elk Tongue had been sent to the Carlisle Indian Industrial School in Pennsylvania, where the superintendent was a U.S. Army captain, Richard Pratt, famous for his punitive pedagogy: "Kill the Indian and save the man." If students spoke a native language, teachers beat them or washed their mouths with lye soap. Elk Tongue, who spoke only Arikara when he arrived, was severely punished. One day, he went with some younger boys to a pigpen on the school property, where older boys had been riding a sow and, by accident, killed her. The older boys told the younger ones to say yes when asked if they had done it, tricking them into believing that "yes," in English, meant no. And so the younger boys admitted falsely to killing the sow and were whipped and deprived of food. They quickly learned English. After five years at Carlisle, Elk Tongue returned to the reservation as Clair Everett, and in 1936, he would be among the first men elected to serve on the new tribal council.

He still spoke Arikara, though rarely around Madeleine, who learned words but never became fluent. She did not blame her grandfather for this. As Madeleine later understood it, her elders were protecting her from the shame and punishment they and their own elders endured. For decades, Indian agents had kept tribes from practicing their traditional ceremonies, and in 1887, Congress codified the ban, allowing agents to arrest holy men. What ceremonies the Arikara carried on they practiced in the privacy of their homes. Many of these ceremonies made use of bundles, assemblies of sacred objects wrapped in wool blankets, each containing at least a pipe, tobacco, and an ear of Mother Corn. There were many of these bundles—for childbirth, for women, for men, for each of the twelve Arikara clans—but those containing the most power were the medicine bundles, capable of healing physical and spiritual wounds. Clair kept several medicine bundles, having inherited their stewardship from his parents, and their use was documented by Melvin Gilmore, a white anthropologist who visited Fort Berthold in the 1920s. One bundle contained bear medicine, which treated fractures and injuries to the abdomen. Another comforted mourners after a death in the tribe—"to wipe away their tears," Gilmore wrote. In one of these ceremonies, a holy man retold the Arikara origin story, and when he came to a part at which death entered the world, the women began to wail. Then, all at once, the women stopped. Together, the mourners smoked a pipe contained in the bundle, and one by one they stepped forward, wrapping their lips around the ear of Mother Corn and drinking from a mussel shell dipped in tea. They spit the tea into their hands and washed their faces in its medicine.

Madeleine was born a few years after Gilmore recorded the ceremony but would never witness anything like it. When she was six years old, her parents enrolled her in a missionary school in Elbowoods, the reservation town fifteen miles west of Nishu, where she hardly noticed that students were forbidden from speaking their native language, since most had never learned their language anyway. Madeleine was a devout Catholic. She recited the rosary every morning and rarely missed Mass. For high school, she returned to Nishu, where she met Willard Yellow Bird, who served in the military for two years following the Second World War. When he returned, he and Madeleine married and had their first child, Irene.

In 1948, the year that the Three Affiliated Tribes signed a contract with the U.S. government approving the Garrison Dam, Madeleine gave birth to Chucky. With young children, she had no time to attend meetings about the dam, so what little she knew she heard from her father, Ben Young Bird, who had been elected to the tribal council. By then, the dam was inevitable, the council grasping at any rights it could salvage from the designs of U.S. congressmen. In 1952, Ben made several trips to Washington, D.C., to lobby for a bill ensuring that the mineral rights beneath the lake would be returned to the tribe and that landowners would be able to go on grazing their horses and cattle along the banks. The bill succeeded.

By 1954, 586 graves had been dug from the bottomlands and reburied. That March, pools formed in the Nishu lowlands, and a newsletter issued by the Bureau of Indian Affairs warned of the coming flood: "When the spring runoff starts coming down the Missouri River, the waters will rise rapidly." The first village to flood would be Beaver Creek, and then Red Butte, and then Nishu: "The Nishu School will be flooded in June. The road from Albert White Calf's old place, east three miles, and the old Fort Berthold Public School, will be flooded sometime during July. The old Rapp Store and the Lucky Mound Corner will be under water about the first of June. . . . By August, the bridge at Lucky Mound, the bridge at Shell Creek and Sully's Lake will be flooded. . . . By December, the site of Elbowoods will be under some 55 feet of water."

Madeleine and Willard moved to White Shield. There were no trees or coulees to block the wind, and whenever they went outside, the cold cut through their clothing. Many people would cry for their loss, but not Madeleine, who in those years did not cry much at all. "I felt really sad about it," she would say, "but, you know, when the government wants something, they take it."

NOT LONG AFTER MADELEINE MOVED into the newest house, the basement flooded, destroying boxes of old photographs. Among the few that had been saved was a portrait of Madeleine and Willard taken a year before Irene was born. They stood by a fence in Elbowoods on a blustery day, Madeleine in heels and a dark, slim dress, Willard in a button-down and an undershirt. They were close but not touching, laughing but in different ways. Willard cast his eyes to the ground, while Madeleine looked straight into the camera.

A relative made copies of the photograph and distributed them at the reunion one summer. Lissa hung hers above the desk in her apartment, where she saw it whenever she walked in. "Grandpa's got that shy, puppy love," she observed, "and she's just like, *What's up?* And look at them shoes! Grandma was stylin'."

The circumstances of the photograph added to its nostalgia. Lissa felt proud of having come from such handsome people, but her pride was muddied by the bitterness of knowing how soon her grandparents' lives changed. After the flood, the unemployment rate on the reservation rose to 70 percent. The only jobs available were with the Bureau or the tribe, and the tribe's only income came from federal appropriations, the leasing of its pastures, and several small settlements it had lobbied for and won to account for the loss of the bottomlands. Never had the Mandan, Hidatsa, and Arikara been so dependent on the U.S. government. Since the land to which they had been moved was dry and infertile, families no longer grew their own food, relying on surplus "commodities" such as flour, oil, canned vegetables, and processed cheese and meat. Some families tried to live on the land allotted to them, but without water or electricity or neighbors around, the living was almost impossible. In 1967, 81 percent of people living on the reservation had to haul water to their homes from a half mile or more away. Most families moved to housing clusters such as those in White Shield, erected in each reservation segment, or to already established towns, like New Town and Parshall. Willard drove buses for the White Shield school and worked for the tribe, and although YB's drew some income, Madeleine was generous with credit, particularly toward relatives who could not afford food. The store lost money, and in 2000, two years after Willard died, Madeleine shut the store down.

It was due to this poverty that Lissa's grandmother believed the drinking set in. Lissa had heard various theories about the drinking. Some said it had been a problem since fur traders brought liquor to the plains, while others thought it began with World War II. No one denied the war had made it worse. Among various men who returned from the war, drinking was a common pastime. Madeleine had three uncles who fought in France and in Okinawa, and the one her age— sixteen when he left—came home an alcoholic. He had developed a taste for liquor in battle, he told her, thinking it would make him braver. Madeleine believed him, though she did not believe the war was wholly or even largely to blame. Her husband had never gone to war, nor had her father, and both drank. Madeleine blamed the drinking on the flood.

When Lissa was born in 1968, White Shield had existed for sixteen years. Her memory of the reservation began four years later, after her stepfather, Willy Phillips, was murdered in Oakland, and she returned to North Dakota with her mother.

In Bismarck, Irene worked as a secretary at a tribal college while Lissa attended school. Lissa spent many weekends in White Shield, the reservation largely foreign to her. She was two years younger than her mother's other child, Cory, whom Madeleine had taken to raise as her own son, and roughly the same age as her uncles Loren and Rodney. The four of them went everywhere together. To wander so freely across the reservation was a novelty to Lissa, and she moved with righteous curiosity. In Bismarck, she had few relatives apart from an aunt and cousin who lived in an adjacent apartment, so she spent much of her time in the company of her mother's friends, most of them white lawyers and professors. Lissa was good at making conversation with these friends, at offering coffee when they visited and answering their questions, but she never felt the city belonged to her in the way the reservation did.

The longer Lissa lived between the city and the reservation, the more complicated her perception of both places became. Lissa was the only Native American in her first-grade class, so each return to Bismarck felt like a return to hostile territory. The students called her "yellow turd," "yellow piss," "blackie," "blanket ass," and "squaw." Often boys followed her home, yelling "Indians are dirty" and "Indians are drunks."

The more Lissa heard these things, the more she believed they were true, and each time she returned to the reservation, it revealed itself to her in sharper relief. She saw that some of her relatives were indeed dirty; that their hair was long and uncombed; that their houses were crowded and in disarray. She noticed empty liquor bottles, the relatives off-kilter, heard whisperings that so-and-so drank himself to sleep.

The reservation became her paradox, a source of her shame but also the place where she felt most free. In a sense, the reservation saved her. One day in Bismarck, when she was six years old, the boys who followed her from school caught up. They punched her, pulled her hair, tore apart her shoes. As soon as Irene took one look at Lissa, she had gone searching for the boys, and when she did not find them, she called a friend, a lawyer, who threatened to sue the school on her behalf. Irene also called her dad, Willard, and when Lissa returned to White Shield the next weekend, her uncles had been ready. They padded her fists with socks and cinched tape around her wrists. They showed her how to kick and punch and how to slip from choke holds. All that weekend they had fought, in the fields and in the house, and the next week, when the boys followed Lissa home again, she hurt them, and they ran away.

Her mother would say Lissa had been a precocious child before she could even speak. At seven months old—when Irene regained custody—Lissa learned to propel herself out of her crib. At eight months, she learned to walk, and then it had not seemed long before Lissa spoke in whole sentences. She plied Irene with questions, her curiosity unflagging, and she was clever, always discovering ways to thwart her mother's rules. After Bismarck, they had moved to Minot, where Irene enrolled again in college. She would often try to study at night after she put Lissa to bed, but instead of sleeping, Lissa would lie awake with a handheld mirror, cocked at an angle to watch her mother work. Lissa had so much energy as a child that she often got in trouble in school. Her mother took her to psychologists, one of whom recommended testing and, upon seeing the results, concluded that Lissa was bored, her intelligence unusually high.

When Lissa was young, these qualities endeared people to her, but as she grew older, her precociousness hardened into defiance, and her defiance broke into a reckless rage that scared even her own mother. Lissa was thirteen when they moved to Milwaukee with Irene's

husband, Wayne White Eagle, where she developed a habit of pulling
fire alarms and stealing her mother's things. Among the items she
stole were photographs Irene had saved to make an album to give to
Lissa when she was older, but Lissa had resolved to not grow old, to
kill herself or disappear, and it was not long after they arrived in Milwaukee that Lissa ran away. She was found living with a Laotian family in another part of the city. When Lissa refused to come home,
Irene called her brother Chucky for advice, who told her to report
the family to Lutheran Social Services. It worked; the family kicked
Lissa out. She was sent to South Dakota, to the Flandreau Indian
School, and then to Fort Berthold to live with her uncle Michael.
When her mother got a job in behavioral science at the medical school
in Grand Forks, Lissa joined her there. One day, Lissa and Irene got
in a fight. Irene fell, and Wayne called the police. Lissa was committed
to a psychiatric ward, where she remained for weeks until Michael
came and got her. She was sixteen years old.

If the reservation had been her paradox when she was younger, as
she grew older, it became her only constant. In all her flitting from one
city to another, the reservation always took her back.

After the fight with her mother, Lissa took a break from school,
and it was decided among her relatives that she would care for her
great-grandmother, Nellie Red Fox. Nellie was bone-thin, hard as a
statue, with a prominent nose and a wide, square jaw and eyes that
blinked like a deer's. She wore cataract glasses on account of her diabetes, the lenses shaped like marbles sliced in half. As a child, Lissa
made fun of the glasses that so many elders on the reservation wore,
which made them all look like bugs. When the glasses had fallen out
of fashion, Lissa had wondered, *Did the aliens claim their people?* But Lissa
knew where the glasses came from: They came from the flood, which
had brought diabetes by replacing farms with convenience stores and
commodity trucks and by destroying the hospital, which the U.S. government had promised, but had yet, to replace.

The year Lissa moved in with her great-grandmother, Nellie's diabetes worsened. Her toe became infected and then was amputated,

and Nellie was bound to a wheelchair. Each morning, as Lissa later wrote in her journal, "Grandma would wheel herself into my room."

"Say! You can't sleep all day," all whipping some kind of towel or material at me because her chair couldn't get close enough for her to wiggle me to get my attention. She would get me on task. "So and so is going to be here today, so straighten up. Make some coffee. Boil some meat." She would get on the phone and start to check in with people. "Say, are you coming?" She would dial up someone else on her rotary phone. "Say! This is Nellie. Are you going to stop over?" "Say" was her favorite word to get your attention.

Nellie's husband, Charles Yellow Bird, had died years before the flood attempting to save two boys who fell in the river. But Nellie never seemed lonely. She recruited her grandchildren to chauffeur her across the reservation to visit relatives or to attend prayer meetings. Sometimes these meetings were Arikara ceremonies, but more often they were Christian revivals, where devotees laid hands on one another's backs and sang and spoke in tongues. Nellie was not particularly religious—no one heard her say anything about Jesus—but her family understood the Holy Rollers gave her back something she had lost: if not spiritualism, then the company of other Indians all wailing and singing at once.

She was a social woman, the life of the party. She liked to laugh at the white rock stars who twisted their hips and shook their butts and sang in funny voices on TV. She spoiled her grandchildren, most of all Irene, but with Lissa, whom Nellie resented for causing her favorite grandchild so much trouble, she was stern. "Leetza," she called Lissa. Arikara was Nellie's first language. She could not pronounce the soft *i* in Lissa's name, and since the Yellow Birds deferred to Nellie, their matriarch, even Irene started calling her own daughter "Lisa."

One June day, Nellie commanded Lissa to bring her a scrap of paper, on which she sketched the leaves of a wild turnip plant and sent Lissa out to dig. Lissa did not want to, but her great-grandmother scared her, so she did what she was told. She had never dug turnips before and at first struggled with a shovel to pierce the clay earth; then a neighbor gave her a pitchfork, which made the digging easier. Lissa filled two coffee cans with turnips. That night, Nellie showed her how to trim the stems and peel the skin, revealing the bright, white flesh, and how to braid the long roots into a rope, which they hung on the kitchen wall.

After that, Nellie was kinder toward Lissa. As her diabetes worsened, infection spread to her foot and then her leg. One day, after another amputation, a man visited the house. Lissa remembered this man clearly: He was short and wore a jacket and carried a rolled wool blanket. When he handed the blanket to Nellie, she cradled it like a baby and then pressed it to her face and cried.

Lissa never saw inside the blanket, but her grandfather, Willard, explained it to her afterward. He told her the visitor was Bobby Bear, the hereditary chief of the Arikara people and keeper of a medicine bundle. Then he told her that Nellie would die soon and that Lissa should return to school. He gave her a loan of $2,000. In the fall, Lissa moved to Bismarck where she lived with an uncle and then on her own. In June 1987, before her nineteenth birthday, she earned a GED. She gave birth to Shauna that August and started college in Grand Forks. A year later, her great-grandmother died.

NOW IT WAS JANUARY 2013, and the oil boom still had not come to White Shield despite rumors that it would. An oil company had leased land on the west edge of the segment, though by the time the company gathered the resources to bid, most of the reservation had been leased. According to seismic reports, White Shield had little oil. The leases there were table scraps—land no other company wanted.

Irene preferred it this way. She saw how the boom was changing the north and west segments of the reservation, and she was grateful—or, at the very least, hopeful—that White Shield would be spared. Altogether, Irene had lived on Fort Berthold only a few years since she left at age eighteen, but she planned on moving back when she retired from her job as a professor of social work at Minot State University. There, every semester for twenty-two years, she had lectured a new class of students on the less heroic foundations of their country—on Indian boarding schools and genocide—and every year, some of her students could not believe that either ever happened.

It relieved Irene to go home to the reservation where few people questioned these things. Of course, not everyone agreed with her on everything. For instance, while she hoped the boom would never come to White Shield, many tribal members regarded the drilling rigs across the lake with jealousy. "Jeez, we were born in the wrong stars," Irene heard them say. "Jeez, those Hidatsas got money over there."

In fact, some tribal members who lived in White Shield received royalties for land they owned in Mandaree. Their checks varied in size—some large, $10,000 or more, and some very small—which swelled and shrank with the price of oil and were inversely proportional to the size of one's family. The larger the family, the greater the fractionation, the less a person earned in royalties. Most Arikara families were like the Yellow Birds in that they received little to no royalties, but there were a few exceptions. There was the man and his aunt who one day appeared at Madeleine's door with a crate of meat and said, "This is for you." And there was Candace, Irene's cousin, who had always been less fortunate, since so many of her relatives had died or gone to prison. To put herself through college, Candace made and sold crafts, but with the boom, her luck had turned. "Irene, did you hear?" she said one day when they saw each other at a wake. Candace was now earning $85,000 a month and already had spent a large portion of the money on cars for her kids.

Jeez, that would be nice, Irene thought, but to Candace, she said, "Let me tell you this: If anybody deserves that money, you do, because you had to put up with so much over the years, and nobody was there to help you."

Candace was also charitable toward her elders, and whenever she saw Madeleine in town, she reached into her wallet for a hundred-dollar bill. "Grandma, is there anything you need?" she would say. Madeleine always assured Candace she did not need anything, but once, when Candace insisted, Madeleine mentioned her grandson was in the hospital and could use a laptop. Candace gave Madeleine a thousand dollars.

These tales of generosity spread across White Shield: A man shuttled people to AA meetings. An elder gave her money to Saint Anthony Catholic Church. Another woman, before she died, donated to the American Legion, while a man bought a vehicle for the addiction treatment center in Parshall, and his sister hired a bus to carry elders to casinos in South Dakota. Irene's best friend, Evangeline, bought Pendletons and star quilts to give to those who could not afford gifts for the pallbearers at their funerals.

As Irene put it, it was the "way of our people" to help those in need. These were also the ways, she sometimes complained, of people who had more money than they knew what to do with. When her friends posted photographs on Facebook of vacations in Mexico and Hawaii, Irene wondered when their fortunes would run out. Most tribal members appeared to spend their money on harmless things, but some, she knew, spent it on drugs. With all the new money around, drugs were proliferating on the reservation. Irene knew of a man in Minneapolis, an addict who earned $30,000 a month and blew each check in a matter of weeks. Sometimes, he asked her sister Cheryl for a loan. "Can you give me forty dollars until my check comes?" he would say, and Cheryl would wire him the money. He never paid her back.

The story disturbed Madeleine. "Gee, he could be helping people instead of killing himself or the people he's with," she griped to her daughters. "You know it says in the Bible, What good is money if you end up in Hell?"

Madeleine was not fond of the boom, but her distance from it by living in White Shield had seemed to foster, more than anything, indifference. She was glad some families were getting a break after suffering for so long, and she appreciated her friends' generosity. Irene, on the other hand, believed her mother was blind to the darker ways the boom was changing their community—to the ways it had changed even their own family.

It was Irene who noticed when her mother's spoons went missing, who said one day in her blunt manner, "Mom, your son is using. He's taking your spoons and using them for drugs."

"Oh my," Madeleine replied.

No one could blame Madeleine for failing to notice something unfamiliar to her. Lissa liked to joke that her grandmother could not tell the difference between sage and marijuana: "She smells weed, and she's like, *Gee, that's good. My kids are praying.*" But to Irene, at least, the change was obvious: Alcohol was becoming a side note to more devastating addictions.

If the flood had tethered the people to the same past, money was dividing them by their futures.

And it was not only tribal members suffering the impacts of the boom. "You know a white boy went missing from Mandaree," Lissa announced one day. "He went missing from Tex's place."

Now even Irene did not know how to respond. Madeleine simply replied, "Oh my," and no one said anything after that.

WHENEVER LISSA VISITED THE NEW house in White Shield, she sat in the living room or at the kitchen table and talked over the din of the television, or if the day was warm, she went out on the porch, drank coffee and smoked cigarettes, and watched pelicans lift up from the sloughs. Her visits had become easier since the first reunion after her release from prison, but they were not exactly comfortable. For one thing, her mother, who wore her hair in a tight perm, still regarded Lissa distantly, as if at any moment she might pull a childhood stunt. The rest of her discomfort Lissa owed to how hot her relatives kept the house during the winter. The heat made Lissa want to shout,

"Mitákuye oyás'in!" like one did in the sweat lodge before the holy man threw open the door.

Lissa rarely mentioned KC to her mother. The first time she did, it seemed that Irene did not hear. The second time, Irene replied, "You better be careful. These people are not good people. They could come after you or somebody in our family." Madeleine had agreed.

Lissa recognized in their warnings a fear so familiar to her that she regarded it as its own species of fear, endemic to the reservation. "When you leave back to Fargo, we still have to be here," her relatives said, as if Lissa's distance shielded her from the political reality of reservation life. In a certain sense it did: The tribe provided almost everything on Fort Berthold—work, shelter, lunch for elders, grants to pay medical bills or attend the Indian National Finals Rodeo. People said it paid to be a friend of a councilman or, better yet, family, and if friend became foe, the consequences could be grave. "You remember Evangeline," Irene said—Irene's best friend who once spent a winter in a tipi outside her tribally owned house after someone in tribal government locked her out on a grudge.

Still, Lissa knew it was not just out of fear that her relatives warned her—they also respected Tex Hall. His reputation had grown in the year since Wayne, Irene's husband, died. Recently, a photo had circulated of Tex shaking President Obama's hand at a White House Christmas party, and it seemed, anyway, that he spent more days traveling to Washington, D.C., and other cities than at the tribal headquarters. The boom had given him this power, in part, with Fort Berthold already producing a fifth of the oil coming from North Dakota. Tex wielded this fact like a club, threatening to pull out of a state tax agreement if the legislature did not amend it in the tribe's favor. He had come to be seen by many as a gatekeeper to the reservation. To do business on Fort Berthold, it was rumored, one had to win his favor. This was of little consequence to the Yellow Birds, none of whom worked in the industry, but it mattered to them that Tex was powerful and, more important, that he was family.

"Tex, I admire him!" Irene told Lissa one day. "He is a leader in a lot of different ways. But when people start going up the ladder, you know, sometimes they start losing their mind as far as greed is concerned. You be careful. There's different layers to people, and sometimes we don't know all the layers. These people he's working with, they could go after you."

HER RELATIVES' DEFENSE OF TEX disturbed Lissa. Even if their chairman was not responsible for the disappearance of a man from his property, should they not hold him accountable to find out who was? And if James was responsible, then why did they not worry that a murderer was at large on their reservation, enabled and enriched by their chairman?

Lissa wondered if her relatives even believed her. No doubt it was hard for them to imagine that Tex could be involved in something so sinister, but the way they averted their eyes when she shared the story with them made Lissa suspect they were even more loath to believe it for the fact that it had come from her. She hated to feel disbelieved. She brimmed with an old anger as her memory ushered forward old complaints: *Everyone was suppressing their pain with something,* Lissa thought. Madeleine buried hers in the church, prayed it away with beads and rosaries, while Irene hardly seemed to do anything but work. Even Michael, who had taken Lissa in so many times, and whom she called her "dad," had his own methods of escape, she believed. He had been a professor at universities all over the country, and by the time he returned to direct the Tribal and Indigenous Peoples Studies program at North Dakota State University in Fargo, he had taken up traditional methods of meditation. The way Michael put it, he was "decolonizing" his mind. He wrote books on the subject, delivered lectures around the world. He believed that by returning to spiritual ceremonies and contemplative practices, Indigenous people could rewire their brains to heal from the trauma of colonialism. "Neurodecolonization" he called it, as if you could will the settlers to leave your body, exorcise their whiteness right out of you.

What her dad said made sense to Lissa, and she had been influenced by his thinking. She admitted that, at times in her life, she had felt proud of her relatives' successes, their piety.

But now, suddenly, she resented it all. The rosary beads. The university titles. The fancy words used to describe the Indian Condition. These seemed to her like props in a performance meant to trick an audience into believing everything was okay. But everything was not okay. What was wrong with plain suffering, with showing the world how much you hurt? This, Lissa decided, was why she had drawn so close to her uncle Chucky. While others hid their shame under glossy exteriors, Chucky had not tried to hide his anymore. Chucky had suffered in the open.

In the final year of his life, his slip toward death had become a march, louder and more determined. He had begun to pass out standing up. Lissa saw him in this state only a few times, but her relatives told her it happened often. Some no longer seemed to notice when Chucky fell, numbed by the regularity of his drinking.

One day, while Lissa was visiting White Shield, Chucky passed out in a ditch by her grandmother's house. Lissa went to look. His pants were wet, so she returned inside and laid towels on Chucky's bed. A cousin helped her carry their uncle to his room, where, with the gentle precision of a hospice nurse, Lissa stripped his clothes, bundled them, and stuck them in a bag. In the kitchen she found a pair of latex gloves, which she wore as she scrubbed the mess from his skin. She rolled him onto his back and washed him again, pulling the towels from beneath him and lifting his torso to straighten the bedsheet. Over his groin she laid a hand towel. Then she went outside and scoured the dirty towels with a hose.

The next time Chucky fell in a ditch, Lissa had been in Fargo. Her relatives told her their versions of the story—how Chucky had been drinking when an acquaintance pushed him out of a car not far from his mother's house. Madeleine and Irene had gone out for an errand, and when they returned to the house, they found Chucky inside, still drunk. He lunged at his sister, pulling on her perm, as Madeleine yelled for him to stop. He spent that night in a mental health clinic in Minot, where Lissa reached him by phone.

"I pulled your mom's wig out," he said.

"I heard," Lissa said. "That's fucked up, Uncle, but kind of funny."

Chucky did not remember the fight. He knew only what he had been told—that he had yanked on his sister's curls, and then his mother had leapt up and they all fell to the floor, and he had kicked someone in the face.

"Come down here to Fargo," Lissa said.

"No, you're sober. I don't want to do that to you."

"I tell you what, they opened a wet house here," where he could drink but still have shelter. "Let's get you a room. That way we know you're safe. It's too cold for you to be just running around anyway."

"All right."

"Seriously, Uncle. If you want to die, go ahead. You're grown. You said that before, and that's your decision, but I just want to be there with you."

Chucky did not call Lissa when he arrived in Fargo. She heard he was there from an aunt, whom he had visited in Bismarck.

"Shit, nobody even told me," Lissa said when her aunt called. After her aunt hung up, Lissa tried to call Chucky, but he had lent his cell phone to a cousin. Finally, Chucky called her from a hotel bar. He would not tell her which hotel.

"I'm drinking," he said. "I don't want you to come over here."

"I'll come sit with you," said Lissa.

"You're on probation."

"Fuck probation. I want to know where you're at," she said, but still Chucky refused.

After he left the bar, he called Lissa again from his hotel room. She pleaded with him to tell her where he was, but he would not. He told her he would die that night, so Lissa borrowed Micah's phone and kept her uncle on one line while she dialed relatives on the other. It was late; no one answered. Now and then, Chucky fell quiet, and in these pauses, Lissa dialed every hotel in the Fargo phone book. None had a Charles Yellow Bird.

At five A.M., her phone shut off. She was still in her clothes from the day before. She brewed a pot of coffee and took Obie and Micah to school.

She had made Chucky promise to call her again, to meet her for breakfast, but he did not. Just after eleven o'clock, Lissa received a call from a relative she had tried to contact the previous night. Chucky had been found in his hotel room, the relative said.

Two days after her uncle's body had been returned to the reservation, Lissa went by the hotel where her relative said he died. It was one she had dialed while she spoke to Chucky, a grim building with a hallway like a basement corridor. "You're sure he's not there," she had pleaded with the clerk, but now she knew why the clerk had said he was not: He had checked in as "Charles Bird."

Lissa passed the clerk without stopping and walked straight to the door of the room where she was told he had been. "Can I help you?" a janitor asked. Lissa explained; the janitor nodded and said he was sorry. Did she want him to open the room?

"No," she said.

She stood at the door, thinking of her uncle's body. She had been told the belt left no marks. The ceiling was low, so he had landed on a knee, kneeling as if before a woman, or God, his arms lifted slightly and stiffened by his sides. It was an odd pose, but it made sense to her, as if Chucky had at last confronted the spirit that possessed him. She hoped he had. She hoped he had broken free of it. On the phone, she had tried to coax this spirit away. "You can take his physical body," she had warned, "but you're never going to take his spirit, because I love him, because my power is stronger than yours."

As she stood at the door, a wan woman came into the hallway, and then the clerk appeared around the corner and began hollering for someone to get out, and Lissa thought the clerk was hollering at the woman but then realized the clerk was hollering at her.

Lissa looked at the janitor, at the woman, at the clerk.

And then she saw that Chucky's spirit was gone, and the thing that had taken his body but not his spirit was still there—she could see it—in their skin and in their eyes.

She had to go. "I'm glad my uncle got out of here," she said to them. "May God save you."

Now two years had passed since Chucky died, and still Lissa recalled the night before his death so clearly that it was as if she had lived it not just once.

She often thought of what her uncle had said to her that night. He had said a lot of things, but one thing he kept coming back to. He had been reading about human DNA, about the way our family histories are imprinted on our nucleotides. He said that our bodies remember. Some scientists believed that our genes could be turned on or off by the things our ancestors had seen or done or the things we ourselves had seen or done, so it was possible that our fates were decided by former lives and that our lives, in turn, decided the fates of our grandchildren.

Imagine that, Chucky had said. No such thing as innocence at birth. Violence, like milk, passed from grandmother to mother to son.

Imagine that. Imagine how impossible it is to stop something like that.

6

The Flyer

THE STATE INVESTIGATION INTO THE DISAPPEARANCE OF KRISTOPHER
Clarke had stalled. In January 2013, after Lissa returned from Washington, Jill received an email from Steve Gutknecht, the agent based in
Williston. "Not much new," he wrote. "I still work on this case daily. . . .
I get calls from people claiming to have seen KC all over the world
but none ever pan out." Meanwhile, Lissa was trying to reach Mike
Marchus, the agent she knew in Minot. He seemed to be ignoring
her calls, and when she texted him to arrange a meeting—to give him
the documents she had collected from the courthouse in Oregon—
he replied that it was not his case.

In February, Lissa gained company in Fargo—her brother Percy,
who had sailed through the window of a pickup truck as it slid on a
patch of ice. Percy had lost a kidney, his spleen, and a significant
amount of blood. He spent a week in the Minot hospital before Lissa
took him home and set him up in her bedroom. Percy could hardly
walk, nor could he sleep, so he spent nights studying algebra from a
textbook one of the boys had tossed on the floor, and picking tunes on

an electric keyboard that stood beside the couch. Three times a day, Lissa came home from the shop to change his bandages. In the evenings, she made simple dinners—tuna sandwiches and avocados sliced in half—before going to work on the case.

She was beginning to assemble a list of workers who had come and gone from Blackstone, among them drivers who wrote to Jill with tips, as well as some whose names Rick Arey had mentioned to Lissa. In the months since Rick left Blackstone, there had been turnover, he said. James had hired a pusher to replace KC, and two investors had left the company. The first investor, Ryan Olness, was from Arizona; the second, Jed McClure, lived in Chicago. Both men were in their thirties and had met when Ryan ran a company that manufactured synthetic cannabinoids called "spice." Ryan would claim he delivered "chemical" to Jed; Jed would deny ordering the drug. In any case, authorities had determined that spice was illegal, and Ryan was being criminally charged. When Jed met James through a mutual friend, he and Ryan decided to give the oil fields a try. As Jed explained in an email to Jill, James returned their initial investments but not their agreed-upon share of Blackstone's profits. Jed planned on confronting James but was fearful of doing so in person. Ryan had spent several months working in the Blackstone office, and in the spring of 2012, he had fled North Dakota. Ryan was afraid James would "send someone after him," Jed explained, and had asked that his contact information be removed from Blackstone records.

There was also an odd story involving two truck drivers who left Blackstone and then came back. George Dennis and Justin Beeson were their names. According to Rick, Justin was a "whiner," a "spoiled brat," and George "smoked too much pot." Rick doubted either was capable of murder, but Lissa did not want to rule them out. It intrigued her that both George and Justin had left Blackstone around the same time as the investor from Arizona, Ryan Olness. She wondered why they left and why, later, they returned to work again for the company. George interested Lissa in particular, since his cousin was in touch with Jill. Three months before KC went missing, this cousin had traveled with George to Fort Berthold and observed that George was "really close to James." George asked James to give the cousin a job, but "the day I talked to James to inform him of my abilities as a mechanic he asked me a question that gives me chills," the cousin explained. "I am in the military and told him I have small arms experience. He asked me, 'So that means you can kill people for me?' He said it with a smirk which I took as a joke because I have never been asked that before."

The strangest story of an employee quitting Blackstone involved a driver named Paul, who was friends with Rick. Paul had been a reliable driver, and unlike other men, he claimed James never cheated him. Still, after KC disappeared, something had not seemed right at Blackstone, Paul told Rick. Paul moved into a trailer behind the Maheshu shop with a new worker James had recruited named Robert Delao. Paul had no idea where Delao had come from, and he had a bad feeling about him. One day in the trailer, Paul was scrolling through Jill's Facebook page when Delao entered and asked what Paul was doing. "Paul kind of got freaked out," Rick said. "He closed his laptop and went to make a sandwich or something, and when he came back, his laptop was open. Delao had been looking at what Paul was looking at." That night, Paul got drinks with James and Delao. "They were trying to feed him shots, and Paul was like, 'No, I better not.' He went home the next day. He called me. He was like, 'I swear to God, I'm next.' A week later, Delao calls. He says, 'We've got all kinds of work. We need you to get back here.'" Paul did not go back.

One evening in February, Lissa called Paul. They did not speak for long. When Lissa asked about Robert Delao, Paul insisted he knew nothing more about the man.

The next day, after work, Lissa opened an Internet browser and entered "Robert Delao" in the search bar. Delao had no address, no phone number. It was as if he didn't exist. She went to a public records site and entered his name again. Now she realized why Delao had so little information online. He had spent his life "in the system."

His criminal record began in 1995 with a shooting in Spokane,

Washington. He had been riding in the backseat of a car when a fellow passenger fired shots, injuring a member of an opposing gang. Delao had been twenty and belonged to the Sureños, a Latino prison gang that originated in Southern California. Three years later, he murdered a man and went to state prison for eight years. Shortly after his release in 2007, he and three other men held an elderly woman at gunpoint while attempting to burglarize her home. He faced twenty-four more years in state prison but served only three in a federal facility. Lissa found it interesting that Delao's case was prosecuted by a U.S. attorney, while an accomplice's case remained with the state. Delao testified against his accomplice, who in court stated that "Delao was a 'good friend, old gang member, we go way back.'" The filing noted Delao had "cooperated" with the government, and for this "Mr. Delao received a safe harbor from all state prosecution." In other words, he was a snitch.

Lissa forwarded a news article about the armed robbery to Jill. Then she sent it to Paul, the former Blackstone driver.

"Wow!" he replied.

"Oh and there's more," Lissa wrote. "Murders, theft. Guy spent most of his life locked up. What does he do at Blackstone?"

"He is basically running the damn company for James."

"Like a manager?"

"He is in control. He only answers to James."

Minutes passed before a new message appeared on Lissa's phone: "Never mention his name on Facebook," Paul wrote. "I don't want this news to be linked to me. No one else on that KC page even knows of his existence." He added, "When was his last offense date?"

Delao had been arrested in 2009 for dealing heroin, around the same time he was cooperating with federal prosecutors.

"Wow," Paul wrote again. "Please understand that I am worried only for my family. I just don't want this fool trying anything stupid."

"I understand," Lissa replied. "I really do. I won't reveal anything." That night, she wrote to Jill, "DO NOT MENTION TO ANYONE WHAT I JUST SHOWED OR TOLD YOU."

On other evenings, as Percy lay bandaged on the couch and the boys drifted in and out of the apartment, Lissa studied the documents she had collected at the courthouse in Oregon. James's criminal record was thinner than Delao's. It began in 1999 when James was twenty years old. His first wife, with whom he lived in Bend, reported a domestic assault, and not long afterward, she filed for divorce. Several months later, she alleged that James entered her house and raped her. Both charges were dismissed, and that was the last time he was accused of violent crime. In 2000, he stole steroids from a veterinary clinic and a trailer from a construction site. Eight years later, he was arrested for growing 542 marijuana plants in a barn behind his house.

Lissa was less interested in the crimes James committed than in the way he went about committing them. He was brazen, stealing in broad daylight and lying about it to police. The barn where he grew marijuana was on the corner of two main roads. He had been discovered when he threatened a worker's dog; the worker had complained to his own mother, who told a friend, who called the police. It was as if James thought, *The more obvious the crime, the better*. The fact that KC had disappeared in the middle of the day no longer struck Lissa as odd, nor did the stories James told to explain KC's disappearance. James, she now realized, often told stories that drew on truth but were altogether bizarre. When caught stealing the steroids, he had claimed to be looking for a vaccine for his sister's horse, when neither he nor his sisters had horses, police learned. The story he told about the trailer he stole was similarly unconvincing: He claimed to have purchased it with cash in a grocery store parking lot, not realizing that his dealer had stolen it.

The documents contained other odd details. In 2010, an ex-girlfriend reported to police that James wrote "obsessive" letters to her from jail. He "bought her roses on a daily basis" while they were dating and was "obsessed with money," she said. Another document noted that James had a habit of mentioning people whom his friends suspected did not exist. When questioned by police about his marijuana farm, James mentioned that a man named "Aaron" was in charge, but when police questioned Nathaniel Lancaster, a friend who had, in fact, helped James on the farm, Lancaster said Aaron was "just a made-up person that Henrikson tells people about to take some of the pressure off of him."

According to police reports, Lancaster had met James through a mutual friend with whom they raced motorcycles. Lissa suspected Lancaster knew KC, and one night she dialed his number, which she found in a report. Lancaster answered by text message. Lissa asked if he still spoke to James. "No," he wrote. "I steer very clear of him."

"Good! That's probably why you're still alive!" Lissa replied. "I wanna talk to you about James. I'm a tribal member where KC came up missing. Just want anything I can get my hands on to find KC's body."

"Well I value my life as well," Lancaster wrote.

"Do you know KC?"

"Yes I raced with him and James."

"Who was Aaron?"

"Aaron was fake."

"I see. Do you know Robert Delao?"

"Sounds familiar."

"Gang banger. Snitch. Murderer."

"Nope . . . Never heard of that guy but that's kinda scary."

Lissa asked if she could call him the next night. Lancaster agreed, but when Lissa tried to reach him, he did not answer, and when she tried him again some weeks later, she found that his number had been changed.

With each dead end she encountered, Lissa was growing more frustrated. Then, one day, Mike Marchus, the Bureau of Criminal Investigations agent in Minot, called her back.

He told her there was an agent in the Department of Homeland Security who worked with him in the Minot office. The agent was young, looking for new cases, and noticed on Mike's desk the criminal record Lissa had given him in December. James's drug charges intrigued the young agent, who had called Steve Gutknecht in

Williston, offering to use his federal authority to acquire James's phone records. The agent's name was Darrik Trudell. Mike gave Lissa his number.

The night Lissa first spoke to Trudell, she relayed their conversation to Rick: "The DHS guy sounded pretty aggressive and excited. Told me to call or text anytime with updates." She had shared with Trudell everything she knew without giving away names of her sources. She told him about the truckers whose wages James allegedly skimmed and the investors whose assets he never returned. She told him about the men who left Blackstone fearing for their lives and the rumors that James was selling drugs. Trudell was mainly interested in the drugs, since in the documents Lissa had given Marchus, there was a suggestion that James had once tried to purchase a chemical used in copying prescription opiates. If investigators could arrest James for a drug violation, Trudell reasoned, then they had a better chance of gathering the evidence necessary to charge him with murder.

The week after Lissa called Trudell, federal agents subpoenaed phone records for James and several of his associates. Trudell called Lissa with the news. "My job is done," she later wrote to Rick. It would take investigators twelve weeks to interpret the records. Then, "It's a wrap. Just a matter of time now so hopefully they find KC!"

LISSA AND JILL WERE SPEAKING less and less. Before Christmas, they had often exchanged dozens of messages in a night; now, days passed without either reaching out. Even the messages they had exchanged before said altogether very little, containing few insights into Jill's daily life and fewer into her past. Instead, Jill's messages to Lissa grasped at friendship: "I don't know what I'd do without u," she texted. "U know how people have soul mates? To me u r my soul sister." Lissa did not reply. A few days later, Jill wrote, "I love u more than words can say." This time, Lissa wrote, "Love you guys!" and Jill replied, "Love you more!"

The kinship Lissa had felt with Jill was fading. "I would call, but I don't feel like it," Lissa wrote to Jill one night. Her son CJ had gotten in a fight and been arrested, and Lissa had visited him in jail:

During and after my visit I believe I have felt some of what you have felt. Pardon my directness. (You know how I roll.) This whole situation is NOT YOUR FAULT! Don't you EVER take on guilt for "not doing enough," or the shoulda, coulda, woulda's! Now, regardless if KC is alive or dead forgive HIM! forgive YOURSELF for teaching him to behave that way and forgive him for coming up missing. Forgive him for not giving you the answers you seek. And mostly, forgive him for not displaying the same kind of love you showed him. And then . . . let him know you still love him no matter what happens. . . . I love you Jill. . . . and I know KC does too . . . Things were supposed to happen this way and just because we don't understand why, doesn't mean there wasn't a justified larger plan of Gods.

At the beginning of their search, Lissa had reasoned that once KC was found, Jill would allow herself to grieve. But the longer KC was missing, the more Lissa doubted this. She had begun to wonder if Jill cared less about finding her son than about the company she had drawn in the wake of his disappearance. Seven thousand people now followed the Facebook page, and although Jill had never met most of them, some, like Lissa, had become friends. Lissa could imagine losing a child was lonely, and if all Jill needed was for people to listen, Lissa was glad to. But over time it had become harder for her to listen, their phone calls a litany of the suffering Jill endured—marriage problems, poor health, the defamation suit, bank accounts drained by legal fees, the silence of investigators, and above all, the smugness of James and Sarah, whom Jill believed could get away with murder. These injustices were not insignificant, but they struck Lissa as cries for pity, not help. This was what irked Lissa most: When Jill appealed to her Facebook followers, it seemed that she, not KC, was the victim of a crime.

"I'm sorry," Rick told Lissa one day, "but you've got to take it easy on her. She lost her son. What would you do?" Rick thought he knew what Lissa would do. He figured she would kill James and go back to prison.

Lissa mostly kept her frustrations to herself until one morning in February, when Rick wrote her asking if KC was found. Lissa opened Facebook and saw that Jill had posted a plea for KC to call her, having received a tip that her son was spotted vacationing abroad with a girlfriend.

Rick thought this was absurd. "Great," he told Lissa. "They're in fucking Bora Bora drinking mai tais, and we're all freaking out, and he's not going to call because he's had one too many mai tais? There's no fucking way." But Lissa was too angry to laugh. She posted a public comment on the Facebook page:

This is not a daytime drama! The footwork has been done. It has been turned over to the authorities. Believe me it is just a waiting period. The page is starting to look ridiculous and uncredible. This isn't about us or how many "likes" . . . its about kc . . . lets keep a FOCUS here!

That night, Lissa received a private message from Jill: Why had she not written directly rather than embarrass Jill in front of her followers? The message fanned Lissa's anger. "Please do not play the 'victim' card with me," Lissa wrote. "I have seen why KC left and never looked back. . . . In order to make any of this right you're going to have to come clean with yourself."

"Take a look in the mirror," Jill replied. Lissa was in no place to criticize her, given what Jill knew about Lissa's own past. "Once an addict, always addict behavior."

"I don't claim to be mother of the year," Lissa wrote.

Jill blocked Lissa from the Facebook page. The day after their fight, Lissa tried not to think about the case. That night, she wrote to Rick, "Tell you what she will never find someone from that rez to put their neck on the line for her like I did." Some mornings later, Lissa woke with an idea.

It involved Jed McClure, the Blackstone investor from Chicago who had written to Jill in the fall. Earlier that winter, Lissa had spoken to Jed. He had a formal manner, confident if a bit stilted. Lissa was not sure she could trust him, but she believed they shared a common goal—to force Blackstone off the reservation.

Their reasons were different. It bothered Lissa that a company owned by white people could profit so easily from Indian land. It bothered her more that, if the allegations were true, the company stole from its workers, dumped toxic frack water, and trafficked drugs. It bothered her especially that her own chairman was partnered with this company and profiting from it. Jed's reason was simpler: money. He was prepared, he said, to "take over Blackstone." He had been talking to a tribal member, a friend of Tex Hall's, who wanted to enter the oil business. If the friend could convince Tex to partner with him instead of with James, Jed would invest. First, he needed the money James owed him—he had sued for it—and then he needed James out of the way. The deal sounded crooked to Lissa, who did not want Jed profiting off her land, either, but it seemed to her that if he had money to spend, she might convince him to put it to good use.

One night in late February, Lissa shared her idea with Jed: Perhaps they could make a flyer warning against James and Sarah and fax it to the companies that worked with Blackstone. Jed liked the idea and suggested they take it a step further: What if they printed copies of the flyer and sent a mass mailing? Jed would cover the expense if Lissa mailed them herself. Given that he was suing Blackstone, he did not want to risk having the flyers traced to him.

That week, Lissa sent Jed copies of the documents she had gathered in Oregon, noting James's arrests in chronological order, which Jed listed on the flyer. At noon the following Monday, Jed sent Lissa a draft. BEWARE: CON-ARTISTS AND THIEVES, the flyer read at the top. In the center were headshots of Sarah and James, their teeth strikingly white, and then a list of their identifying characteristics. At the bottom of the page, Jed had composed a cautionary note: "James is very charismatic and charming. He may claim to have money in order to build confidence with vendors or companies to steal from them. James and Sarah may also have been involved in the disappearance of former Blackstone employee Kristopher D. Clarke (K.C.), but have refused to cooperate with the BCI. Consider them dangerous!"

"AWESOME!" Lissa texted from the welding shop. That evening, after she returned to the apartment, she studied the flyer again and noticed an error—Jed had spelled Sarah's name wrong. "Sorry I'm such a critic. Just want it to b PERFECT," she texted.

Lissa hardly slept as she waited for the flyers to arrive. Each night as her brother and kids slept in their bedrooms, Lissa sat awake, the apartment lit by the kitchen light and the cold, blue radiance of her computer screen. She glanced at Facebook—Jill had posted vaguely about their fight—and closed it. She reread Jed's messages. His suit was not going well. Sarah claimed Blackstone had not yet made a profit. Jed suspected that this was a lie, that Sarah and James had hidden their profits elsewhere. They offered to settle for $50,000, far less than what Jed believed he was owed. James suggested they meet in Chicago to talk about it in person, but Lissa told Jed this was a bad idea. "That's what KC did," she warned.

Instead, Jed's lawyers met with Tex Hall. Afterward, Jed told Lissa that Tex "denied all responsibility" for James's failure to pay Jed. Her chairman's rebuffs no longer surprised Lissa. In January, after she returned home from Washington, she had mailed a copy of James's criminal records—all 450 pages—to the tribal office. She had not expected a reply, nor had she received one, but, curiously, a new affidavit had appeared in the defamation suit against Jill. It had been filed by Tex's girlfriend, a tribal member named Tiffany Johnson, who was apparently fed up with the calls and letters she and Tex had received regarding Blackstone. "I have had businesses and friends and family approach me too many times in regards to the allegations being made to James and Sarah," she wrote. "I am afraid for James and Sarah's safety as well as my own since we Tex/Maheshu Energy are being brought up. We are now being attacked by this Jill Williams via telephone. I am now not only fearful for James and Sarah but now fearful for my family and self as well. I really feel that this Facebook page is violating our rights and privacy."

The affidavit was proof that Jill's calls had, at least, reached Tex, and it was evidence that James and Sarah were as close to Tex as Lissa suspected. But while Lissa felt certain of this closeness, Tex denied it. On the last day of February, as Lissa was still waiting on the flyers to arrive, Jed asked a friend to fax the flyer to every oil-field company operating on the reservation. The fax to Maheshu included a summary of Robert Delao's criminal record, which Lissa compiled for Jed, and a cover letter with a phone number for Delao's probation officer. Several days later, Jed confronted Tex in a hallway of the tribal building. According to Jed, Tex tossed the flyer in the trash right in front of him. Tex claimed that he had met James only a few times, that his partnership was with Sarah—she owned Blackstone, not James—and that he hadn't realized James and Sarah were connected because they did not share a last name.

On March 8, 2013, Lissa drove Percy to a doctor's appointment in Minot and then dropped by the police station for a scheduled meeting with the young Homeland Security agent, Darrik Trudell. She arrived at the station fifteen minutes early. "These fuckers always think we're running on Indian time," she later complained. "Hurry! Lol," she texted Trudell as she paced the station lobby. It had changed little in the years since her arrests—scuffed linoleum floors, wooden pews snagged from either an old courtroom or a church, a drinking fountain set crookedly in the wall. A fixture by the door dispensed hand sanitizer, and when Mike Marchus, the Bureau of Criminal Investigations agent, appeared in the lobby, Lissa had taken a glob and rubbed it into her hands.

Mike sniffed, as Lissa would recall. "Been drinking much?" he said.

"No," she replied dryly. "It's hand sanitizer."

She followed Mike through the station offices and into a small spare room where Trudell joined them. Trudell was in his early thirties. His face, soft and clean-shaven, looked to her like the face of a Boy Scout. She had googled Trudell weeks prior to their meeting and learned he had been a student of her mother's at Minot State University. He was "a good student," Irene had said when Lissa asked about him, "always respectful." Irene had been surprised to hear Trudell was now "a cop." After college, he had worked as a parole officer and then as an investigator for the U.S. Secret Service based in Philadelphia. When Lissa called him, Trudell had been in the Department of Homeland Security little more than a year.

She passed him the stack of courthouse documents and watched as he leafed through them. Finally, Trudell looked up. "We could've gotten these," he said.

"I know," Lissa replied. "But you didn't."

She blustered past his comment with other things on her mind. She was thinking again of the anonymous caller who told KC's grandfather that KC was in Montana. If Trudell requested Robert Clarke's phone records, she thought he might identify the caller, whom she suspected was James. She promised to send Trudell Robert's phone number and the recording of their visit, and she had a new lead on "the drug angle" from the investor, Jed McClure. Recently Jed had told Lissa that the friend who introduced him to James had first-hand knowledge of James's efforts to copy prescription opiates. Unfortunately, the friend was unwilling to speak to Trudell, and Lissa was beginning to wonder if drugs, alone, made a weak case. She believed Trudell would have better luck pursing a RICO case, as she had explained to Mike Marchus already, by classifying Blackstone as a "corrupt organization" for its swindling of investors and employees. If Jed was correct in his suspicion that James and Sarah were concealing Blackstone assets, both might be guilty of fraud.

Trudell did not sound convinced. The suit Jed had filed was civil. Trudell needed evidence of a crime, but he promised to call Jed anyway.

Four days after Lissa's meeting with Trudell, she arrived home from work to find two cardboard boxes taking up the kitchen. Percy was on the couch, looking stronger.

"What's this?" he said. "You getting bodies sent here, Sis?"

"No," Lissa said. "But I'm putting you to work."

WHEN PERCY WOKE THE NEXT morning, he staggered to the kitchen table, donned a pair of blue latex gloves, and lifted a handful of flyers from a box. There were five thousand in all, stamped and pre-addressed to the governor, every legislator in the state, and most homes and businesses in the oil-field region, including the reservation. Percy recognized many of the addressees. He imagined his friends and relatives opening the envelopes and studying the flyers, but in his daydreams, the recipients tossed the mailings without much thought. The flyers were a waste of time—too "old school," Percy believed. Still, he felt he owed his sister, and although it hurt him to move, he liked having something to do.

According to Lissa's instructions, he was to mark the front of every mailing with a stamp she had specially ordered—a website address—which would direct recipients to an online database where they could read more about the case and peruse original documents; and he was to wear gloves whenever handling the flyers so that no one could trace his fingerprints. Lissa had decided that they would mail the flyers from Dickinson, a town south of the reservation. Blackstone was the return address, so any failed deliveries would end up in the company PO box.

For three days, Percy rose after Lissa left for the welding shop. He worked at the kitchen table, which was cluttered with papers and dirty plates and baggies of loose-leaf tea, as the boys wandered in and out. Sometimes CJ or Micah sat and helped, but more often Percy was left alone, the apartment silent except for the heavy steps of a woman upstairs and the jingling of keys in the hallway.

Percy finished on a Friday. That afternoon, Lissa loaded the envelopes into totes, and together they set off for Dickinson. The day was overcast and dry. Lissa was in a good mood. Later, they both would laugh as they told the story: How Percy assumed they would carry the flyers inside and deposit them with the postmaster. How Lissa had said this was a terrible idea, and, instead, they had donned fresh pairs of latex gloves and stuffed all twenty thousand through the drive-through slot. How long this had taken. How cars had lined up behind them. How, when the slot filled, Lissa had reached in with her arm to pack the flyers down. How a man started honking—they let him through—and when at last he fit his own letter into the slot, he yelled in their direction, "What the fuck are you guys doing?"

Percy was embarrassed. "Oh man," he said. "We probably look like a bunch of meth cases. Or terrorists. 'Hey, look at those terrorists putting anthrax in envelopes.'"

When he and Lissa finished, their hands damp with sweat, they peeled off their gloves and threw them in the trash and then drove north to the reservation.

What struck Percy as paranoid at first—the gloves, the return address, the driving hundreds of miles to deposit the mail to fool the recipient with a postmark—in fact made some sense. Only a week earlier, when they had driven to Minot for his doctor's appointment, they had hardly made it an hour out of Fargo when Lissa's van swerved and bucked and came to rest on the highway shoulder. Lissa had gotten out to inspect the wheels. The bolts on one were loosened, the wheel nearly fallen off. They spent the night in Valley City and, the next morning, had the van towed to Fargo where they rented a car, continuing on to Minot. It was during their ride in the tow truck that Lindsay, Lissa's daughter, called. She had been driving her own car, she explained, when a wheel had fallen off. Lindsay did not know what to make of the incident, but it did not seem a coincidence to her that her car lost a wheel only a day after her mother's almost did. She suspected her mother was being targeted, perhaps due to her work on the case. "I'll never fucking live with you again," Lindsay told Lissa. She was moving out.

When Lissa and Percy returned to Fargo from mailing the flyers,

Lissa walked the perimeter of her apartment building, the rows of parked cars. She felt unsettled, like she was being watched.

"Mom, I have a serious question for you," Obie said when Lissa returned inside. "With the shit you're doing, are we safe?"

"No," Lissa replied, "so you should be alert."

She had been cautious in the beginning—now she became more so. She installed blinds on the patio so that people could not see her when she went outside to smoke, and she was rarely spotted with her children on the streets and sidewalks that ran past the apartment; they staggered their departures and rode in separate cars. Lissa instructed the boys never to speak of her. If a stranger asked, "Is Lissa your mom?" they were to reply, "I don't know what you're talking about."

Micah accepted these measures stoically. It was harder to tell what Obie thought. He had become withdrawn in the months since Christmas. It seemed he wanted nothing to do with the case. "Hungry as hell bring something home to eat!" he wrote on his mother's Facebook wall one weekend while she was gone. His anger was unpredictable. One Sunday, Lissa returned to Fargo and found the kitchen spotless, the dining chairs stacked artfully like a cairn in the center of the floor.

Then, one night, Obie lost his phone and asked Lissa to call it. She discovered it on her desk under a heap of papers. The caller, she noticed, was "Nadia."

"Why does it say 'Nadia'?" she asked.

"So that if anybody ever took me, they couldn't find you," Obie said. "I'd never want them to ruin what you've got going on."

If Obie meant this as a reproach, Lissa did not notice. Later, she would recall the comment without a hint of guilt as the moment at which she knew her sons' lives "had totally changed to accommodate the case." Obie's anger deepened her resolve. "I never want what happened between Jill and KC to happen between you and me," she told him. But it seemed that her work on the case had only generated more tension—first with Shauna, now with Obie and Lindsay, and finally with Percy.

In April 2013, Percy returned to Fort Berthold and found work in

New Town at the Northern Lights building, mopping floors and set-ting up tables for events. He did not go on another search with his sis-ter. After he moved out, he and Lissa rarely spoke. Lissa would assume that her brother was scared—that the numbness he inhabited in the wake of his accident had lifted, revealing the true stakes of their involve-ment. But Percy denied this. It was true he was cautious and did not tell anyone about the flyers, but this had little to do with fear, he said. He figured, rather, that no one would believe him. When friends and relatives mentioned seeing the flyers, he found it easiest to say, "What do you think about that?" or, "Jeez, that's too much," as if he knew nothing about them. To Percy's surprise, after he returned to the reser-vation, he saw the flyers everywhere he went, in the windows of main-street businesses and on the walls in tribal offices. One day, while getting gas at a station in Parshall, he discovered a flyer taped to the pump, and when he went inside, another was resting on the countertop.

"What do you think about that?" he said to the cashier.

"I see them in here all the time," she replied, as Percy would recall. "You'd never know they'd killed a guy."

Percy would later say that people had tried to kill him before—"over money, or something bad happens to someone's relative, and someone says you did it. They don't ask no questions. They don't get to the bottom of it. They just come after you." It wasn't fear, he insisted, but drugs that made him draw away from his sister. "I was getting high again. So I quit hanging around her, out of respect."

7

The Church

THE TRIBAL POLICE WERE AMONG THE FIRST WHO NOTICED THE CHANGE on Fort Berthold—track marks creeping up handcuffed arms, paraphernalia tossed in the backseats of cars. In 2012, for the first time, officers arrested a tribal member for heroin possession, and after that, a majority of crimes they responded to had something to do with drugs. The boom expanded the market for meth, while pills, more common among oil workers, became common among tribal members, as well. Local drug dealers yielded territory to men and women from out of state who, in an effort to increase demand, hawked drugs for free. It was money, more than the demand for drugs, that drew these dealers to the reservation—money that deepened the addictions of those already addicted and made families without money more vulnerable. This was another of the many ironies that had come to define the boom: The generosity Madeleine and Irene observed among rich families did not end with blankets or meat. Addicts with royalties were similarly generous: They got poorer people high.

In the summer of 2012, the U.S. Department of Justice reported that over the three years prior, federal case filings on reservations in North Dakota had risen 70 percent. I was curious if this had to do with the oil boom, so I called Timothy Purdon, the U.S. attorney of North Dakota. He resisted my theory. In 2010, the same year that the Department of Justice declined to prosecute 62 percent of criminal cases referred to them from reservations in North Dakota, Congress had passed the Tribal Law and Order Act, which established an Indian Law and Order Commission to examine how the federal justice system systematically failed tribal communities. As part of the reform effort, the federal government gave more money to prosecuting crimes in Indian Country, enabling attorneys to pursue more cases, and in 2011, Purdon appointed an assistant U.S. attorney to work specifically with the MHA Nation. There was a growing sense among Native American victims that the crimes they reported would be prosecuted, he explained, and this had encouraged more victims to come forward. Still, Purdon said, the boom was having an impact. Just that summer, he had noticed that more cases than usual coming from Fort Berthold involved non-Indian perpetrators. "We had five or six in a month," he told me. "We realized it's non-enrolled folks moving to the oil patch."

I returned to the reservation that summer to report on the rise in crime. It was a July evening when I arrived at the tribal police station in New Town, a brick building with an aquarium-blue lobby that had not been renovated in some years. I had arranged to ride along with an officer named Dwight Sage, a tribal member in his thirties with short-cropped hair and a shy smile. When he appeared in the lobby, I followed him outside, and we drove west out of New Town, emerging through a pass on the edge of a butte, where we could see flares flickering on the horizon and trailers clustered in pockets of the prairie. We ascended a bluff toward Sanish and turned onto a dirt road. The sun was setting, clouds gathering to the west, birds dipping in and out of the grass. A trailer appeared, and then a dozen campers parked down a hill where some oil workers had gathered, chatting. A tribal member emerged from the trailer. He had called in "a domestic,"

Sage said—a fight over oil royalties, the man and his sister in a pushing match—but the sister had fled. I remained in the car while Sage
spoke to the man, the workers eyeing us warily. Then Sage and the
man waved goodbye, and we headed back north.

"He's a bad alcoholic," Sage told me. "He started getting his oil
money last summer, and that's when things got really bad. His wife
was getting him drunk, taking his pills. The whole family has been
fighting over money since they leased their lots to a company to house
oil workers. They're pain pill users. Hydrocodone. Valium."

It had begun to rain. We turned west and crossed the bridge. Sage
pointed to his landmarks: a café where he detained two undocu-
mented workers and had them deported; a street where he found a
white sex offender with shotguns stashed in his trunk; the ditch where
a truck hauling contaminated water tipped, spilling 1,200 gallons; the
yard where Sage chased two white roughnecks after they assaulted a
Native woman; the house where he kicked in a door too late, where a
tribal member died of an overdose.

On the main road, Sage stopped an SUV with Wyoming plates
for going sixty-five in a forty-miles-per-hour zone. Although tribal
police have no criminal jurisdiction over non-Indians, they can ticket
reckless drivers. It was the only legal power the tribe had over non-
Indians, and the records did not carry off the reservation. "Forty dollars, no points," Sage announced when he returned. "When I tell
them that, they're pretty happy. This guy asked, 'Will I get in trouble
if I don't pay?' I said, 'You won't really get in trouble, but we'll have
you on record if you get stopped again.'"

I thought of the mechanics I met in the casino parking lot more
than a year ago. *You can do anything short of killing somebody*. What they
had said was not technically true—cases that fell outside tribal and
federal jurisdiction belonged to the state—but several tribal officers
had told me that crimes committed by non-Indians on Fort Berthold
were a low priority for deputies and sheriffs, who were already over-
worked by the oil boom outside reservation borders. Each county
overlapping Fort Berthold had only one or two deputies stationed

there. If an incident required a deputy, he could take hours to arrive due to the volume of calls he received and the reservation's enormity. The sheriff of one county admitted to me that his deputies often escorted non-Indian drunk drivers home instead of arresting and delivering them to county jails, which were far away and often full. If jurisdiction was ever in question, getting the right officers on the scene could take a while. "Time is sensitive," a tribal criminal investigator told me. Sometimes it was the difference between finding a perpetrator of a crime or having no evidence at all.

Fort Berthold, like many reservations, already had a long history of crimes slipping through jurisdictional cracks. According to a report issued by the Indian Law and Order Commission, "When Congress and the Administration ask why the crime rate is so high in Indian country, they need look no further than the archaic system in place, in which Federal and State authority displaces Tribal authority and often makes Tribal law enforcement meaningless." Now tribal officers told me that the boom had exacerbated the problem and that the tribe's lack of jurisdiction over non-Indians had created a culture of lawlessness. Most could recount being told by an oil worker, "You can't do anything to me." According to Sadie Young Bird, director of the tribe's domestic violence unit, rates of violence against women were rising. Recently, three oil workers had offered a tribal member a ride home from the bar in New Town, driven her to a remote area, raped her, and left her on the road. They returned several times and, each time, raped her again. The woman survived, but finding these men would be difficult. Once, when Young Bird visited a man camp to check on a domestic violence victim, the manager told her women were not allowed there. "Perpetrators think they can't be touched," she told me. "They're invincible."

Regardless of the effort to prosecute more crimes on Fort Berthold, no one I spoke to could deny that the crime rate had risen with the boom or that the violence had turned inward. In 2012, the tribal police reported more fatal accidents, sexual assaults, domestic disputes, gun threats, and human trafficking incidents among tribal

members than in any year prior. According to the police chief, since
the reservation population had, by some estimates, tripled with the
boom, the tribe needed forty officers, and yet the department struggled to retain them and rarely employed more than thirteen at one
time. Affordable housing was hard to come by, and some officers lived
in their cars. Sage told me that most did not stay long in the job,
forced so often into taking double shifts. Several had quit; one committed suicide. The longest-serving officer had been in the department
for five years. His name was Nathan Sanchez, and he was twenty-five
years old.

I rode along with Sanchez a few times in the weeks I spent with
the department. He was Latino, from Indiana, engaged to a tribal
member with whom he had two kids. He had tattooed forearms and
hair cut so short I could see the damp of his scalp. He seemed tired,
nervous, the first night I rode with him, flicking a cigarette between
his thumb and forefinger as I stared quietly out the window. The
ditches alongside the road were littered with plastic bags that tossed
in the wind and caught on pasture fences, and with bloated carcasses
of unlucky deer. "Do you swim in the lake?" I asked Sanchez as we
neared the bridge.

He shook his head. "This lake still has tombs down there," he
said. "You know they didn't have time to relocate their dead? Swimming in a liquid tomb, no thanks."

The reservation felt sleepy that evening, like we were waiting for
something to begin. We crossed the lake and turned at the casino. By
the shore was a tackle shop, some pavilions, and a campground—
a few hundred tents and trailers tucked into the trees. I had been here
only a few times since my encounter with the mechanics. The trailers
were gone from the casino lot, but along the grassy banks of the lake
were more shelters than there had been before. Men cooked dinner
on outdoor grills, nodding as we passed. Most of the shelters looked
empty, their inhabitants, I assumed, at work.

As the sun set, we left the campground and drove to New Town.
Streetlights cast the buildings in dull yellow. We wound through a

neighborhood where the houses all looked the same; and around the Northern Lights building, which was quiet except for a man turning doughnuts in the parking lot. We had heard the squeal of his tires from a distance, but when we arrived, his car was still, and the man— eyes bloodshot, alert—was smoking a cigarette in the passenger seat.

Sanchez received only one call that night, a domestic dispute at Prairie Winds, a trailer park in New Town located behind the railroad tracks. The tribal police often responded to calls in the park, since some residents there struggled with addiction, but lately there had been more calls than usual. The residents were stressed, Sanchez explained; all of them would soon be evicted. The owner of the park had sold it to a man who planned to build houses for oil workers and employees of a local energy company. Tribal members had protested, marching in the streets with signs that read RELOCATION ENDED IN THE '70s. In response, the council had invested $2 million in a park east of town. The new site had no water or electricity yet, and residents had only a month before they would have to move.

We circled New Town until midnight and then lingered outside a bar on the main street. A woman in a silver skirt waited by the door. Sanchez had pointed her out earlier, spotting her by her house. He believed she was a sex worker, and when I asked why he thought this, he explained, "I work eighty-some hours a week, and I sit in front of these bars every night. I know that this night she left with that guy, and last night she left with this guy, and then the night before—" Sanchez hedged. "I know that doesn't prove anything," he said, but sometimes, in his patrol car, women admitted they were sex workers. Sanchez had noticed other signs as well: a man who hurried women into a car when police drove near; women captured on the casino security cameras moving in and out of hotel rooms; meth addicts whom investigators suspected of trading sex for drugs in the man camps; girls who arrived at school with new iPods and jewelry. On a reservation where everyone once knew everyone, noticing was easy. "I know these girls," Sanchez told me. "I know their parents, and I know for a fact that their parents cannot afford to buy them these things."

The tragedies these officers tended to often involved their own relatives. "I ask them, 'Are you using clean needles? Did you get tested for hep C?'" one officer, Dawn White, told me as I rode along with her one evening. "There are quite a few who cry in the backseat and tell me all about their addictions. It's hard. How I rationalize it: If I have to put them in jail to save their life, I'll do it." Sometimes, parents begged her to arrest their children. "They'll say, 'Arrest them, Dawn, because I don't want to bury them.'"

It was the middle of July, and we were driving to the powwow in White Shield. White was in her early thirties with radiant skin and slick black hair drawn into a bun. She had been talkative when I met her at the station, but as we drove along the edge of the lake, she quieted. The radio filled our silences. A man was having a stroke; a couple was fighting in a parking lot. The dispatcher had a drowsy voice. The calls were meant for another officer, and I sensed White wasn't listening.

"When I come to White Shield, I just feel so happy and calm," she said. "You look out there, and there's no blowtorches, no rigs, no trucks." The road curved west and south again and climbed a hill that sloped toward the lake. At the top of the hill, a church appeared—first a steeple and then a roof, and windows and steps, and a grove of pines sheltering a cemetery. White stopped the car, and for a moment we sat looking at the church. It had been carried up from the bottomlands, she said. Her elders remembered attending services before the flood. Now it was weathered, sky showing through. I considered suggesting we go inside, but White got a call—a reckless driver on the road near the powwow—and we continued south.

The fields were blooming yellow. Buildings appeared amid some trees, and then came the sound of drums, low and tinny in the distance.

We did not stay long at the powwow but rode slowly around the outer circle. It was a flash of color, men whirling across a green, glowing turf. White chatted with a cousin, asked a boy to pick up his candy wrapper. Then we left the grounds and turned north.

We made one more stop that night in White Shield, at a house set nakedly in a field. The family living in the house had a twenty-eight-year-old son who overdosed and died a week earlier while riding around with his cousins. I waited in the car as White approached the house. A woman came onto the porch and embraced White. The sun cast the porch in shadow so that I could not see the woman's eyes, though I knew that she was crying. Then another woman emerged, nodded to White, and took off in the direction of the sun, on a path cut through high grass. A dog trotted after her. There were many dogs around, and birds on the power lines, and old cars with grass grown up between the wheels, circles mowed around them.

The door opened once more. This time it was a girl, nineteen, I guessed. She wore a U.S. Navy T-shirt, her shorts baggy, her hair in a ponytail. She had seen me from inside the house and approached with her eyes pointed toward the powwow grounds. "Are these your cousins?" I said, nodding to the parked cars.

"A bunch of killers," she said. "He was dying, and they didn't do nothing. Just kept driving, then took him to the house when he was already blue."

The girl cursed quietly, resting her forearms on the window frame, and together we surveyed the porch. The woman was no longer crying but talking in whispers to White, who had a hand on a hip and, with the other, wiped sweat from her brow.

THE ATLANTIC PUBLISHED MY ARTICLE in February 2013 under the title "On Indian Land, Criminals Can Get Away with Almost Anything." It began with an anecdote about a white teenage girl who followed her father from Texas to the Bakken. He refused to let her stay with him, so she wound up in Prairie Winds, the trailer park, living with a friend. One night at a bar in New Town, she met an oil worker who bought her drinks and took her to his camper. She would remember some men and a woman were having sex, and they raped her. Officer Sanchez found the girl that night, scrambling out of a ditch near a man camp. He wrapped her in a blanket and took her to the tribal police station, where an investigator, Angela Cummings, interviewed her. The girl could not remember the races of her rapists. First she said yes when Cummings asked if they were Native; then she corrected herself, believing they were white and Latino. If the latter was true, neither tribal nor federal officials had jurisdiction in the case. Cummings called a county deputy, who took the girl off the reservation.

Days after the story ran, I got a call from Steve Kelly, the former tribal lawyer and the owner of Trustland Oilfield Services. We had never spoken before, but he had found my number because he was troubled by a paragraph in the *Atlantic* piece in which I noted that the man camp where the teenager had been raped was located behind the Trustland offices. He had no connection to the man camp, he said, and hoped I would clarify this in the online story. He worried my mention of Trustland had been "something political." I assured him it was nothing political, though I was curious what politics he was referring to. "I can't compete with the chairman," he said, explaining that Tex Hall's outfit, Maheshu Energy, was "fronting" for a white-owned company. Kelly knew quite a bit about the politics of the reservation and was glad to help with my next story, he said. I thanked him, promised to make the clarification, and then hung up the phone.

In the months after I reported for the article, crime on the reservation escalated. A man who had come to Fort Berthold for the boom stabbed a tribal member to death; the victim was Officer Sage's younger brother. Then Kalcie Eagle, the son of a councilman, broke into a house in New Town and shot a white woman and her three grandchildren. Mike Marchus, the Bureau of Criminal Investigations agent in Minot, photographed the crime scene and later would tell me it was the most difficult case he ever worked. Eagle killed the grandmother first; and then two boys, thirteen and six; and a girl, ten, who was in the bathtub. Sanchez and another officer tracked Eagle to Parshall, where Eagle brandished a knife and slit his own throat.

When I heard the news, I remembered Eagle from the summer. I had been with Officer Sage at a Marathon Oil facility—an alarm gone haywire—when a call came and we sped through open pasture, yellow with rapeseed, to New Town. Sage had walked slowly toward the house. The councilman answered the door. It was the councilman who had called the police; he had been calling often, lately. Eagle was addicted to meth and could be violent when he was high, but that evening he was docile and let Sage escort him outside. This was all I saw of Eagle, pale and sweating as he passed through our headlights. I remember he squeezed his eyes shut before vanishing into the dark of another police car.

In the months following the murders, the tribal community struggled to make sense of them. Tex Hall, in the *Washington Post*, called Eagle's crime the "worst tragedy" on the reservation in his memory. The horror was made larger by how well people had known both Eagle and the victims. A woman I contacted when I heard the news had seen the grandmother just days before she died. People were more reluctant to speak of Eagle, perhaps out of respect for his parents. His father drowned in the lake soon afterward, and fewer spoke about that. Those who did speak seemed to fall on one of two sides: Either Eagle had always been troubled, enabled by his own family, perhaps even destined for violence; or drugs had changed him in awful, unnatural ways. In this second telling, the boom was a coconspirator, having made meth, as Sanchez put it, "as easy to find as a gallon of milk."

In November 2012, the same month Eagle murdered the family, the tribe earned almost $10 million in oil royalties and production taxes. By the end of the next year, this figure would double as the tribe's total earnings since the beginning of the boom approached a billion dollars. The tribe did not make its expenditures public, but some of my sources grumbled that little of this money had yet been spent on social services or public safety. Millions of dollars would go toward expanding the casino, while the domestic violence unit would continue to be housed in a single-wide trailer across the street.

Still, the murders had an effect. In December 2012, the tribe asked federal authorities to determine where Eagle's meth had come from, which led them to Michael Smith, a white man from Colorado living on the reservation. One morning that winter, the New Town police attempted to arrest Smith, who barricaded himself inside a house and for twenty-four hours would not come out. The house belonged to a tribal member trapped inside. She was addicted to heroin—Smith, her dealer. When night passed and neither emerged, police hired a front-end loader to tear a wall off the house. The woman and Smith were arrested, and it was decided that day by the tribal council that the drug situation had gotten out of hand. Hall called an emergency meeting and recruited tribal members to serve on a drug task force.

On March 27, 2013, Timothy Purdon, the North Dakota U.S. attorney, charged Smith and twenty-one others, including twelve members of the tribe, with conspiracy to distribute meth and heroin. Investigators had traced the drugs sold on Fort Berthold to Chicago, Minneapolis, and Southern California, where two brothers were the conduits between Mexico and North Dakota. The next year, Purdon would indict sixty others for trafficking drugs on the reservation.

Tribal officers and social workers told me they were grateful for the federal help, but if the arrests made a difference, it hardly showed. At the end of 2013, the task force would assemble data from tribal departments into a report: Three years earlier, 30 percent of the crimes committed on the reservation had been drug-related; now, the number was 60 percent. Three years earlier, 69 percent of domestic violence cases had been drug-related; now, the number was 100 percent. Since 2010, all cases filed with the tribe's Children and Family Services had been drug-related, and the number of cases had tripled over three years. Ninety percent of the health center budget was being spent on drug-related cases. Hepatitis C had spread among tribal members, with 10 percent of health center clients testing positive, a quarter of them pregnant. Children as young as eight years old had been admitted to the juvenile justice center showing signs of heroin and meth use. Meanwhile, rates of domestic and sexual assault were rising, according to Sadie Young Bird, the director of the domestic violence unit. The unit would counsel more victims in 2013 than in any year prior. Ninety-six percent of these cases would involve alcohol and drugs.

"When the boom's over, what's it going to be like here?" Young Bird had asked me. She guessed: "They're not going to take their trailers with them. It'll just be deserted, with a lot of broken people."

8

What She Broke

Among the tribal members Tex Hall appointed to the drug task force was Irene Yellow Bird, on account of her expertise in addiction treatment. Irene did not mention this to Lissa, who found out one day in March 2013, when she visited her mother in Minot. Irene lived in a small, carpeted house with a bedroom, a living room, and an eat-in kitchen. She had lived alone for some time now. In the years before Wayne's death, they had divorced, and then he had moved back in, and then they had split up again. He was "running around with a Puerto Rican girl," as Irene put it, and living with the woman when he died. Irene had received the news of his death while at a doctor's appointment for an oncological exam, and when her doctor tried to leave the room, the door had stuck. "Your dad was visiting," she later texted her stepson. "He wouldn't let me and the doctor out of that room. I suppose he's being jealous again."

Her living room was furnished with a love seat, a television, a recliner where she often slept, and an expansive library containing books on all aspects of social work—chemical dependency, diabetes, family violence, child welfare—as well as on grant writing, Indigenous spirituality, and pedagogical theory. Beside two volumes of the *Diagnostic and Statistical Manual of Mental Disorders* were books by Vine Deloria, Jr., a Lakota writer and historian, and Wilma Mankiller, the first woman elected principal chief of the Cherokee Nation. There were cookbooks, self-help manuals, and a biography of Mother Teresa, and memoirs by famous American Indian Movement activists like Dennis Banks, Leonard Peltier, Mary Brave Bird, and Russell Means. Irene knew Russell when she lived in Bismarck. She admired his stern demeanor, his gift for oration. That was in 1973, as the occupation of Wounded Knee was ending. Irene attended some protests, including a Bismarck event hosted by the John Birch Society, at which Doug Durham, an FBI informant who infiltrated the occupation by posing as an activist, was invited to speak. Lots of Indians attended his talk, including Russell's cousin, Dennis, who sat right up front and glared at Durham. When it came time for questions, Irene asked Durham what impact his work had on his family, and she swore she saw regret flicker across his face.

The books of which she was most proud were her collections of Arikara stories, recorded and translated by Douglas Parks, a white anthropological linguist. In 1974, Irene attended a workshop hosted by the Inner Peace movement, where she met the director of the language program at Mary College in Bismarck, whom Irene told about her brother Chucky and his efforts to preserve the Arikara language. The director offered to reach out to Parks, who was studying Pawnee, a language in the same family as Arikara. Not long after that, Parks visited Fort Berthold, where Irene introduced him to Chucky and various elders, among them Nellie Yellow Bird. Over the following years, Parks became the preeminent scholar of the Arikara language, and Irene's brother Loren studied under him. Now Loren was a cultural expert for the National Park Service and had been hired by a Hollywood director, Alejandro González Iñárritu, to teach Arikara to Leonardo DiCaprio for his role in *The Revenant*.

On the walls not taken up by books were portraits of Irene's grandchildren and great-grandchildren, as well as a photograph of Lissa in her final year of high school. It was remarkable that Irene still had the photograph—that Lissa hadn't stolen it with the rest. Her shoulders were draped in black, her left hand rested on her right arm. Her skin was smooth, her eyebrows arched, her cheeks dimpled in the corners of her mouth. Her eyes laughed out of the dark.

On the day in March that Lissa visited her mother, she stood in the doorway to the kitchen, Irene watching from a recliner, as she sifted through papers stacked on the table. It bothered Irene, Lissa's habit of nosing through her things, and now Lissa made a show of it. When she came to some papers labeled DRUG TASK FORCE, she paused and then ran to the bedroom.

Her mother's closet was neat, her clothes evenly spaced, and Lissa took theatrical pleasure in pushing them back and forth. Irene had risen from her recliner and watched from the bedroom door. "Lisa, what are you doing?" she said.

"It's in here somewhere." Lissa dropped to her knees, peered beneath the bed.

"What are you looking for?"

"For your SWAT team outfit."

Irene looked confused.

"What's this task force, Mom?"

Her mother straightened. "Tex asked me," Irene said. This was not out of the ordinary. He had asked her to serve on committees and give presentations to the tribe before.

"Mom, you can't tell me that this guy isn't trying to buy you out. Who else is on it?"

"Cheryl." Also, Madeleine's younger sister.

"You're fucking kidding me. Don't tell me Grandma's on it, too?"—Madeleine, who could not tell marijuana from sage. Lissa wanted to laugh and then scream. She saw that her mother was becoming angry, too: Her lips had tightened. Her chin lifted. Her eyes cast on Lissa a familiar disappointment. "This is to silence me, Mom,"

Lissa said. "This is a fucking psychological game. If this is how it's going to be—"

"You be careful now," her mother said.

THAT WAS HOW LISSA RECOUNTED the incident. Irene would not recall specifically how her daughter learned about the task force but, when presented with Lissa's version of the story, offered that while she did not remember the "SWAT team outfit," Lissa rummaging through her things sounded "about right." Apart from worrying for Lissa's safety, Irene wondered why Lissa cared so much for the child of a stranger. Did she not have her own children to care about—children she had hardly seen in the past decade of her life? Still, Irene knew better than to expect her daughter to heed her advice. She thought that if she could give Lissa an "Indian name" she would call her "Tells It Like It Is." Then she thought of a better name: "No Ears Don't Listen Woman."

Irene's grievances echoed her granddaughter's. "Our mom loves dead people more than her own kids," Shauna still complained—so often now that her brothers Obie and CJ had taken to repeating what she said. Lindsay, who had rented her own apartment after the wheel fell off her car, encouraged this, leaving only Micah to defend Lissa consistently. "We should just be happy that we still have a mom," Micah said.

Lissa told her children that they were lucky to be alive; that there was a murderer at large in their home, the reservation; that a dead person could not defend himself; that if any of them ever disappeared, she would search for them as she did for KC; that KC was now "family," in a sense; that she could have lost a child as easily as Jill had lost her son. It was not true Lissa cared more for KC than her kids; she cared about KC *because* of her kids. As for Irene's warnings to be careful, Lissa replied with variations on a point she once made to Jill: "James can do nothing to me that my addiction hasn't already."

None of this comforted Shauna, who had no desire to revisit the sort of life she had occupied before her mother went to prison. That was a life of absences and separations, of feeling more like an orphan than a daughter. And now, with her mother gone so often, her memories of those separations returned.

Shauna remembered each one clearly—her age, the length of time, the names of strangers and relatives in whose care she had been placed. The first separation came in 1993, when Shauna was six years old. Her mother left Grand Forks for Minneapolis to join her boyfriend, Tom Reinardy, and while Lissa searched for a house and a job, Shauna and CJ had lived with their grandmother in Minot. Not long after that, they moved to Prior Lake, south of the Twin Cities, where Lissa met the casino security guard whom she swiftly married. The man was abusive, which led to the next separation, when Lindsay went to live with her father and Lissa placed CJ and Shauna in foster care while she found her own place. For reasons Shauna never understood, they remained in foster care for a year until the fall of 1995, when she and CJ rejoined their mother in the house in St. Paul, with OJ. Less than a year passed before police raided their house, and they packed their bags and fled. Shauna never saw that house again. She and CJ were taken into custody. CJ went to live with Irene in Minot and Shauna with Madeleine in White Shield.

It was the only time Shauna lived on the reservation. She had been nine years old then and still remembered how lonely she had felt—how she made few friends at the White Shield school in spite of being related to many of her classmates. White Shield was quieter than anywhere she had lived, as foreign to her as places she had seen on TV on other continents or in earlier times. There was something freeing about this, Shauna thought—the way the reservation felt like another world that few others paid any mind. Dennis taught her how to drive, and no one cared when she took Madeleine around. It was the elders, Shauna learned, who kept the order in White Shield. "Call his grandma. She'll get him in line," she heard people say. No one had to get her in line. Madeleine often remarked how different Shauna was from her mother. She was diligent with her schoolwork. She attended Mass, counted beads and said the rosary, and took her first communion. She accompanied her grandmother on visits to relatives' homes, where she listened, keeping her opinions to herself—how the houses all smelled the same, like water left to sit, and dust from roads and pastures, and commodity dinners of hamburger and pilot bread, and the rank sting of propane. A "poor smell," as she would put it, "the smell of barely getting by."

The Yellow Bird house was not much different, but Shauna clung pridefully to the idea that her family was more successful because they owned a store. She often worked in the store, which had two rooms, a bathroom, and a closet furnished with a cot for visitors. The place was stocked with basic groceries, candy, and instant meals. A bench had been placed in a corner by a microwave, where customers warmed their sandwiches and sat to eat. The cigarettes were kept behind the counter, and on a wall near the entrance hung a list of customers late on credit payments and thus prohibited from charging more items. Some tried anyway, but Shauna had been firm. She came to know the drunks who lived beside the store in the complex called the Jungle, and the elders who asked the first time they saw her, "Who's your grandma?" When she told them, they nodded and said, "You look just like Lisa."

Whenever the store was empty, and Shauna had been left alone, she sometimes looked around and tried to imagine her grandparents living there with all their children. In reality, they never lived there all at once, due to their different ages and the fact that many attended boarding school, but in her daydreams, her relatives occupied the house together. It comforted Shauna, this thought of them all in one room. Later, when she tried to explain the feeling, she would say, "I've always felt in between. I've never felt like I totally belonged on the reservation, and I've never really been part of the white people's society either." In the store, among the illusory bodies of her relatives, she had felt, for a rare moment, at home.

Shauna had no idea what her mother did during that time. She had heard Lissa was in Oregon. Then, one day in the summer of 1997, her mother reappeared.

After that it had seemed they were always on the run. Shauna's memory of those years was as fragmented as their movements: The neat piles of weed. The men wandering in and out. Her mother gone and back again. The *pop-pop* of handguns. The warnings not to answer a knocked-on door or a ringing phone.

It had not always been clear to Shauna whom they were running from—police? social workers? her mother's boyfriends?—but the longer they ran, the more these threats coalesced in her mind into a single, indiscernible force. No matter where Shauna slept, she had been ready to escape. The oddest thing about this childhood, she now believed, was how normal it seemed at the time. Shauna could not remember feeling scared. In certain ways, Lissa hid her addiction from Shauna, who had never seen her mother stick a needle in her arm or wrap her lips around a pipe. Years later, after they moved to Minot, Shauna had known when her mother was using meth by her strange, hostile energy, by the smell of the drug on her skin, but with crack it had been harder to tell. Perhaps the best childhoods lacked frames of reference so that even depravity felt like innocence. Either Lissa concealed the highs or it had all been too routine for Shauna to notice.

This was not to say Shauna never rebelled. After a boy who lived in a neighboring apartment learned Lissa had been a stripper and teased Shauna for it, she had taken to snipping the strings of her mother's thongs whenever she did laundry. But she remained loyal to Lissa to a degree that baffled her other relatives. *You always go back to her,* Irene complained, and it was true, Shauna always did. Even in the care of her grandmother and great-grandmother—in the stability they had fashioned from their own loosened foundations—Shauna, admittedly, grew bored. She missed not just her mother but the entropy of her mother's life, the daily flowering of new crises.

As Shauna grew older, her loyalty toward her mother had waned, but it was only in the course of their longest separation, after Lissa went to prison, that it had occurred to Shauna that their life, as a family, could be different.

Later, when asked what she envisioned, Shauna would describe two photographs, both taken while her mother was in college, before the addictions set in. In the first, Lissa posed with Shauna in lipstick and a blazer. In the second, Lissa held Lindsay in a garden, wearing a pink blouse and matching bow, her head tilted to kiss her daughter's neck. *This* was what Shauna had wanted—a version of her mother she believed existed but which she knew only from photographs—but instead, her mother reminded her of a past Shauna wished to forget. When Lissa left on weekends, Shauna remembered nights she and her siblings spent wondering when their mother would return. When Lissa warned them not to speak about the case, Shauna remembered how she had been forbidden as a child from answering strangers' questions. When Lissa hung blinds on the patio, Shauna recalled the paper they had taped over the windows of the apartments where her mother sold drugs. And if ever Lissa mentioned KC, Shauna remembered the time she disappeared herself.

Her mother had not looked for her.

SHAUNA SPENT SEVERAL MONTHS DECIDING what she would say. Then, one night in the spring of 2013, she went by her mother's apartment. She sat at the computer desk, Lissa at the dining table. "When you came back from prison, I thought you were going to be different," Shauna began. "I thought sobriety would make you this perfect mother, but the only thing different about you is that you're sober. You've substituted what you do now for things you used to do."

Shauna cried. "I like to hold it together, make it look all pretty on the outside," she would recall. "I learned that from my grandma. But I couldn't anymore. There was just so much I wanted to ask her about my childhood. I wanted to tell her how I felt. I wanted her to have some remorse, some sort of accountability. I envisioned it playing out differently. I thought I would cry to her about all these things, and she'd feel bad, and it'd be a huge awakening for her, and she'd be like, 'Oh my God, I had no idea. Let me change.' But it didn't work out like that. She just sat there, no emotion on her face. She stared at me the whole time I broke down. And when I was done, she said, 'You sound like you got some really serious emotions that you need to deal with.'"

Shauna left her apartment on Ninth Avenue Circle for a temporary lease across town. She told the landlord not to bother painting the walls. She asked her employer for a transfer, and on July 1, 2013, she would move with her children to Minneapolis.

THERE HAD BEEN NO "AWAKENING" for Lissa, because everything her daughter said, Lissa already knew. She heard each word Shauna spoke, and in the days after Shauna cried to her in the kitchen, Lissa could think of nothing else. *What did her daughter want from her,* she wondered? Did she want her to relapse just so she could see how much her mother hurt? What would it take for her children to understand that it was the moving on that made her well again?

Remorse was not the only thing Shauna wanted, Lissa knew. "How about you search for my missing dad," Shauna had said, a fair criticism. Lissa had never told Shauna who her father was. Lissa did not know, she claimed—or did not care to know. There were some things she still never spoke about. The circumstances of her first pregnancy was one of those things. So was the time, at age four, she was molested by a man who watched after her while her mother was at work. So was the time she was trafficked for sex—in the eighties, during the second oil boom. These were the things, sexual things, that Lissa believed would bring the most shame to her family. OJ was one of few people she ever told who Shauna's father might be. To everyone else, Lissa explained it like this: She had found herself in a dangerous situation, and when she got out, she had not looked back.

Now Lissa retraced her path to other origins of her daughter's resentment. There was the decision she made to place her children in foster care in 1994. She had made this decision hastily: Her husband started beating her; Lissa worried her kids would see it. She had intended for them to live with a family in the area for only a few months, where she could visit often while she worked and saved money to rent her own place. The plan had gone wrong immediately. Lindsay's father had claimed custody of her, and whenever Lissa visited Shauna and CJ, they begged Lissa to take them back. There was *something going on,* they said, but would not tell her what it was. Lissa requested that they be placed with another family, and it was after that, she believed, that Child Protection began giving her a hard time. First, they denied anything was wrong; then, they required that her visits be supervised. Lissa had assumed that by placing her kids voluntarily, she could take them back any time, but suddenly she was confronted by a variety of reasons why she could no longer have them: She missed some visits. (She worked two jobs.) She was "too transitional." (She was homeless, living with friends.) Her work was not suitable for children. (She bartended, the most lucrative job she could find.) In surrendering her children, it seemed she had given up her right to be a mother, but what defined a mother in the eyes of the state was unclear to Lissa, and in the end, the reason she got her children back had seemed as arbitrary and unknowable as the reason she lost them. One day, after Shauna and CJ had been in foster care for a year, a social worker called and said Lissa could come and get them, offering no explanation. Nor did the social worker explain how CJ ended up with a traumatic brain injury. It was Shauna who later admitted that he had been abused by a foster care mother.

The next time Lissa lost her children, the reason was clearer to her: She lost them because she was an addict. In 1996, after police raided her house, Cheryl, Lissa's aunt who lived in Minneapolis, told Irene that Shauna and CJ were in danger and called Child Protection. Lissa did not remember losing them—that was how strung-out she had been. She and OJ were together still, or maybe at that time they were apart. Later, when asked how he started beating her, each would tell a different story. OJ would say Lissa made a joke about sleeping

with another guy, and he hit her, and it had seemed to him she liked
it. Lissa would say OJ came home drunk one night and, without warning, broke a VCR over her head.

They started selling crack together not long after Lissa started
smoking it. There was a dope house they sold at most often, where a
dealer named Cuba hung out. "Yayo," Cuba called cocaine, so that's
what they called it. Yayo. Selling drugs was the easiest thing Lissa ever
did, because the drugs sold themselves. She drove a hard bargain—
harder than OJ, who often gave away his drugs for free.

He was soft like that. In certain ways, OJ was helpless without
Lissa. He had no driver's license, no credit. He had never paid taxes
or applied for a job. It was Lissa who drove him around in her sports
cars, who taught him how to pump gas and change the oil. She taught
him to cook. All OJ had ever wanted, he sometimes said, was to have
a family to sit down with for dinner. He was good with Lissa's kids. He
loved them. He fed them when she was absent. But it was her absences
that bothered OJ, that filled him with rage and made him act like a
different person. She believed her sex work made him jealous. By
then, she had a full-fledged business, with many women and returning
clients. The women paid Lissa seventy-five dollars each session for
making their arrangements and ensuring their safety. Lissa often
brought OJ to her own calls, who waited outside in the car. Her clients
were doctors, foreigners, businessmen. If ever she worried one was a
cop, she encouraged him to pleasure himself, and when he had suffi-
ciently jacked off, she offered help. It was not just sex these men
wanted. They wanted comfort, purpose. One paid her to dress him in
only an apron and order him to sweep the floor. Another liked to call
at all hours of the night and ask if there was anything she needed.

She became an expert in the sadness of men. When OJ hit her,
she hit him back, and then he hit her harder. She called the cops on
him but never showed up for her court dates. Charges were dropped;
she took him back. She inured herself to violence. Once, she was selling crack to a man when another addict sank a screwdriver into her

buyer's head. The attacker dragged her buyer onto the street, and Lissa never bothered to figure out what happened to the victim. She was ruthless. Sometimes she flung a pea-size crystal against the wall and watched the addicts scatter like starved animals to sweep the pieces up. She laughed at them. *Go ahead,* she would say. *That's a fucking devil's drug.*

When Lissa became an addict, everything she loved turned to water in her hands, and everything she lost—that slipped through her grasp—she believed she deserved to lose.

After she fled Minneapolis and ended up in Portland, she got sober, and after she returned to Minneapolis, she reclaimed her children, but not in the way she had planned. Willard Yellow Bird died that September, in 1997. The day before his funeral, Irene insisted Lissa take Shauna and CJ for the day so Irene could focus on her father's arrangements. Lissa took her kids but did not bring them back. When weeks passed and Lissa still did not return, Irene reported her for taking them.

Lissa had enrolled them in school in St. Paul. One afternoon, she went to pick them up, and they did not emerge from the building. She was still waiting when a social worker called to inform her that Shauna and CJ had been detained by Child Protection. Police arrested Lissa on the sidewalk, threw her on the concrete, and pulled so hard on her hair that her neck cracked, she would recall. They let her out of jail that night, after her kids were gone. She wandered downtown, where a man drove up beside her and offered a ride in exchange for sex. Lissa agreed on the condition that he take her to a dope house first. When they came to the house, Lissa ran inside and never saw the man again.

She was pregnant. She and OJ were back together, and the next July, she gave birth to their child, Obie. OJ came and went. Lissa became pregnant again, but this time the father was not OJ.

When she relapsed in 1999, she would not remember when or how it happened. It was OJ who would later say how he had shown her his stash in the hopes that she would relapse. When Lissa was sober, she intimidated OJ. He found he loved her even more, but he could not control her.

On the evening of December 22, 1999, Lissa stopped at a friend's house, bought some crack, and got high. Obie was seventeen months old. Micah had been born just that summer. OJ was home with the kids that night, and Lissa had left her phone in the car because, as she would later explain, she "didn't want to hear him calling all the time."

The story Lissa would tell of that night would match the police reports and court records. She had returned to the car in the early morning and listened to her messages: If she didn't come home soon, OJ said, he would murder the kids. "I was hysterical," Lissa would recall. "I drove up to the building. When I went in the first door, there were people in the hallway. They were like, 'Don't go up there, something's happening.' I pushed past them. I opened the door. I said, 'Where are my babies?' OJ was standing there. He hit me with a bat."

By the time the ambulance arrived, Lissa's body was cut and bruised, her wrist broken, the bone showing through, her left eye swollen shut. She was unconscious, so what else she knew of that night came from interviews police conducted with Shauna. Her daughter would say that it was the sight of her mother after the attack that shook her more than anything—her face so disfigured, Shauna could not bear to look at her—but during the beating Shauna had remained calm. Later, in court, a prosecutor would note how serenely Shauna described the scene to police. At 3:45 A.M., she had risen from bed, walked to the kitchen, and found OJ with a fistful of her mother's hair, striking her limp face with his knee. For a moment, Shauna watched as CJ threw his body between OJ and their mother. Then she called to CJ, whom she told to dial 911. He handed her the phone.

And this was the remarkable thing, the prosecutor said: how coolly Shauna told the dispatcher, "My stepdad is trying to kill my mother," and when the dispatcher had not understood, how Shauna said it again.

My stepdad is trying to kill my mother.

The words were the clearest memory Lissa had of that night, though they were not her memory; she could not have heard them; and it was after the court hearing that she claimed them as memory, as vivid as if she had heard them herself.

OJ pled guilty and was sentenced to thirty-three months in prison. Lissa spent two days in the hospital and rejoined her kids at the apartment. Later, she would say that the winter and spring were when things really fell apart. She stopped paying rent. She was evicted. She went on smoking crack. She had loved OJ. She had let herself be hurt by him, again and again, and in the end, he had stolen from her the choice to take him back. "Kill me. You don't have the balls!" she had screamed at him in the minutes before she lost consciousness. She had been ready to die, and when she survived, she had wondered why she was still alive.

It was Shauna who changed the most after that—who drifted from her mother—so it had not surprised Lissa when, one morning, Shauna disappeared. Lissa did not hear the hotel room door when it opened or closed, but when Lissa woke, she knew her daughter was gone.

ON THE NIGHT OF JUNE 14, 2013, Lissa sat in the kitchen, her sons gone out, and composed a message to Shauna:

> *You know I was thinking about what you said regarding the time I spend looking for all these "Missing People." I didn't know what to say that day and I didn't want to say anything I didn't mean. But now that the words have revealed themselves to me here is what I have to say. When you were a teenager and that day you left the hotel, I knew already in my heart why you left. I knew it was a result of my addiction. I knew that I was unable to help myself let alone try and track you down and bring you back to the misery and despair I created for you. I have apologized and I also knew that the words "sorry" would never be enough to compensate for the wrongs I have done to you as a result of my addictions. You ask why I didn't look for you? I'll tell*

you at first I couldn't bring myself to believe that I had lost my daughter because I fully chose drugs over you. Even though I couldn't help it. I was gone inside. I pretty much knew you were with friends. I felt you were safe in my heart. Call it intuition if you will. Insight. Whatever. Even though I was emotionally and spiritually bankrupt at the time I always felt you were ok. I hoped and prayed you were. I didn't see the point of coming after you and bringing you back into my world of chaos, immorality, and despair. The shame I harbored, the sick emptiness in my gut knowing that I had lost you emotionally and at that time physically. Our relationship has never been the same since that day. Until that day you were MINE. My treasure my baby my everything. I had realized that I had pushed you so far away that you would never come back the same person and I hated myself for that. I have known you never trusted me since that day and you have always looked at me with a sense of hate in the background of your mind. I tried to change my life and SHOW you my love and it seems it hasn't helped the hostility within you every time you think of my name. The way I look for KC . . . IS the way I would have looked for you if I was sane and drug free. I'm sorry I was not that person for you back then. I am now. I am drug/alcohol free and I try to live right. These things I do, I do for you. This is how I would have done for you. I keep doing them to show you my persistence and my love and that I will never give up again. I will never make myself vulnerable enough to not wanna fight back. This is my explanation. I hope this helps you to move forward. I am proud of all you do to help others. I would hope that it is a little reflection of me. Maybe not, but someday. Remember Shauna . . . I love you! Every time I am out there looking for others helping others I'm thinking of you too. You were the real inspiration. Love MOM

Shauna did not reply, and Lissa did not write her again. After that, Lissa tried not to think of her daughter too often, as doing so filled her body with emptiness.

For Shauna, the feeling was different. Shortly after she moved to Minneapolis, she bought her first home, a condominium in a quiet, wooded suburb south of the city. She felt relieved. She decided she would no longer expect anything from her mother. She would not speak to her, and in this silence, there would be less to remind her of their past.

She had read the letter once, and quickly. She had been too angry to give it much thought, and, anyway, it made little sense to her. "I more or less was like, *Not only did you not care when I ran away then, but you're completely ignoring me now,*" Shauna said. That she had inspired her mother sounded too convenient, and it angered Shauna that Lissa rationalized her obsession in this way: "It's easier to accept guilt for what you've done than admit to it. By accepting that guilt internally and trying to change your life around so that others on the outside can see a change, you're still not making those amends where that hurt was done. You know, you murder somebody, you feel bad about it, and next thing you know you become an advocate out in the real world, but what about that family you took from? It's two different things, to accept the guilt and to admit it. She wasn't able to admit to the guilt. She wasn't willing to repair what she broke. She was just trying to fix it in other places, through other people, but she failed to fix the one thing that she broke. I didn't care how many other people's lives she was trying to fix. It's still broken here."

Sarah

In the months leading up to Shauna's departure for Minneapolis, Lissa settled more deeply into her investigation. She had achieved a significant breakthrough: In March 2013, a week after Lissa and Percy mailed the flyers, Tex had canceled his partnership with James.

The flyers were indeed, as Percy described, everywhere: taped to the windows of reservation stores, tacked to telephone poles and to the bulletin boards that hung in post offices and schools. Lissa could not say with certainty what effect the flyers had, but the timing of Maheshu's and Blackstone's separation struck her as more than a coincidence. A week after Tex ended the partnership, Lissa received an email from Brian Baker, the man who had defended James and Sarah on Facebook, with whom she previously engaged as "Nadia Reinardy." Brian had visited the website Percy stamped on all the flyers and wanted to know who was behind it. He had asked Jill, who said honestly that she didn't know. She wasn't "bold" enough to make a website like that, but Lissa was. It was Lissa, Jill told Brian, who composed many of the comments posted on the Facebook page. Brian forwarded his exchange with Jill to Lissa.

In fact, Lissa had been in touch with Brian since mid-February, not long after she and Jill stopped talking. "An acquaintance of mine"—Nadia Reinardy—"said you knew some things about the KC ordeal and that your ok to talk to . . . is this true?" she had written him. Her overture was strategic. It occurred to Lissa that her distance from Jill presented an opportunity to align herself with someone else, and so she had expressed to Brian sympathies for James and Sarah. When Brian forwarded her Jill's emails accusing Lissa of publishing the website, Lissa denied responsibility. She explained to Brian that Jill had blocked her from the page due to their disagreement. On March 15, the day after Brian forwarded the emails, Lissa composed one to Sarah Creveling:

> *I know I'm probably the last person you would ever want to hear from, but this is Lissa and I would like to firstly say, that I'm sorry for jumping on the band-wagon with the others on the KC page and made some harsh comments about you when I didn't even know both sides of the story. I sincerely would like to apologize to you and in making amends I truly would like to hear your side of the story so that I can set the record straight. My goal is to find KC. If you are interested, I believe I can help you also get the TRUTH out there instead of all this drama. I can't even imagine how you are feeling. I think we can help each other out. I understand if you don't feel too much trust in answering but I thought I would give it a try. Keep your chin up, cause this too, shall pass! ;)*

Two mornings later, Sarah replied:

> *Hi Lissa,*
>
> *I can't say how much I really appreciate you contacting me and apologizing for some of the things you've said. . . . First off I know many people have quite the opinion about my husband and I and I know his past record sure*

doesn't help. But the hardest thing for me is that I DON'T have a record! I have a speeding ticket, and people are just dragging us through the mud. It is hard to wake up every morning and check the page to see what terrible things have been said about me today. . . . I tried reaching out to Jill many times, she never gave us the time a day and then turned around and hurt us. We have feelings to, we care about KC! I think about him everyday, and just think if only he would come back and set everyone straight.

I understand its human nature to want to put blame on something or someone. But . . . Some days I barely hold it together. I worry a lot that someone is going to show up at the house and hurt me. There are a lot of crazy's out there. I just wish people would ask me questions or come to me before they jump to conclusions.

Sorry if I am writing a lot. Your just one of the few to actually ask me questions. I'm more than happy to talk to anyone about this, just no one seems to care. North Dakota is my home now, I have very few friends and family here, and now I hardly feel welcome.

Thanks again for taking the time to listen Lissa.

Thanks

Sarah

Lissa knew little about Sarah. In the photographs Jed had chosen for the flyer, she had blond hair, straight and dyed; small, shiny eyes; and bright white teeth. She was thin, athletic, dressed in sports tops and jeans. The Blackstone drivers Lissa spoke to had all mentioned how pretty she was, but beyond this, none seemed very fond of Sarah.

It was true she had no criminal record. The most incriminating thing Lissa could summon about her was the story KC's grandfather told—how Sarah had cried to him on the phone and then hung up. *The bawling hysterics, I mean, not laughing.* A week after Robert Clarke died, Lissa had opened KC's Blackstone email account by guessing his password and written to Sarah from his old address. "Surprise!" she had titled the email:

Doesn't it bother you that my family is suffering over what you and James have done? have you no conscience? you and james run around acting like nothing has happened. . . . you can pacify yourself with money for now but eventually you will lose everything. you think james is going down alone?. . . . if he doesn't kill you first . . . you'll see. and you'll be chased off the rez. . . . my grandpa took his own life last week because of what you and james have done. there is one more soul lying on your shoulders but he is with me and you can't touch us here . . . that phone call you got from rob when you went into hysterics and started crying and going crazy tells me you had somewhat of a conscience back then. hopefully you are able to clear it before its too late.

Lissa spoke on the phone to Sarah for the first time at the end of March. Sarah was polite, to the point. She shared her side of the story—that she cared about KC, that she tried to help Jill until Jill attacked her and James—and Lissa told Sarah about her falling out with Jill, though she did not offer details. It soon became clear to Lissa that Sarah was distressed and that the reason for her distress was the flyer. Sarah first heard about the flyer from acquaintances who received it via fax, before receiving her own fax at the Maheshu office. Sarah asked if Lissa knew who was behind the flyer. Lissa told Sarah she did not know but offered to help find out.

Lissa suggested Sarah begin by looking up the fax number she received the flyer from and tracing it to its origin. The number, it turned out, belonged to a veterinary clinic in New Town. This confused Sarah more. She had never been to that vet, she told Lissa, nor did she know anyone who worked there.

"I'm scared for you!" Lissa texted in reply. "Did you call the vet? Want me to?"

If Lissa didn't mind, Sarah said. "I think thousands of faxes and letters have been sent now. People are calling and texting me from everywhere." Sarah had been studying one of the flyers that she had received in the mail. It was "nice glossy thick paper, expensive," she wrote. It looked professionally done. She wondered if she called around to print shops in the region, she might identify the one that processed the order.

"And what if it was done online?" Lissa replied. She suggested Sarah check the postmark on the flyers.

The flyers appeared to have been sent from Bismarck. Mailing them from Dickinson, Lissa now privately realized, had made no difference. She advised Sarah to mail herself a letter from Watford City to the Blackstone PO box in Minot. That way, Sarah would be able to confirm that all letters distributed to that part of the state were routed through the capital. Sarah did as Lissa advised.

A week later, Sarah drove to Minot and checked the Blackstone mailbox. The letter she had sent herself was there—postmarked in Bismarck, she told Lissa, which meant it would be difficult to trace the flyers to their origins. What was worse, Sarah had opened her mailbox to find it stuffed with hundreds of undeliverable flyers, many addressed to towns she had never heard of. "Makes me nervous now that everyone knows what I look like," she texted Lissa. "That's like literally half the state that has received them. This is a ton of money spent."

Sarah was becoming more distraught. The morning after she went to Minot, Lissa texted, "Wake up! Because today is a great day and its gonna be better than yesterday!" It was late March, Easter weekend. Sarah was in Washington visiting family. She was close with her parents, she told Lissa, and thankful to leave the oil fields for a while. But some nights later, she called Lissa, upset again. Jill was attacking Sarah on Facebook.

Lissa had recommended that Sarah stop reading the page. "I know it must be hard," she wrote one day, "but try to keep your own sanity. What does your husband think of Jill's rants?"

"He's learned to ignore them," Sarah replied. "Says if she really wanted our help she would reach out to us, since she put us in the bad light. He tells me not to look on that page."

"You should listen to him."

"I know. It's just so hard Lissa. I wish I could talk to every person who's read that page, received or seen the letter. I just wish I could sit down with all of them and explain."

Lissa had been waiting for an opening like this and now composed her message carefully. She wondered if Sarah would be willing to answer questions about the day KC disappeared. Did she remember what time he arrived at the office? How long did he stay? Did he speak to James? Did he mention that he "needed to tie up loose ends"?

Sarah answered eagerly. She could not remember what time KC arrived, exactly, but she believed it was in the late morning or early afternoon. She had seen him for only five minutes, when they talked about his plans to go to Oregon. "I honestly don't know what he did after he left the office we were in," she wrote to Lissa. "James said he said hi to him, talked about his grandpa's health and drinking too much." She couldn't remember KC saying anything about "loose ends."

"Did he have his truck with him when he arrived or when he left?" Lissa asked.

"Oh, that I don't know," Sarah replied. "I was never outside while he was there. I would assume he was in his truck."

"And no calls after he left?"

"No calls that I know of!"

It was almost eleven o'clock. "Well I'm going to head to bed," Sarah wrote. "Thanks for talk as always. I hope I didn't keep you up too late. Have a good night:-)"

Over the following months, Lissa asked Sarah many questions about KC. Often, Lissa repeated these questions—whom did he talk to, what did he say—as if sorting a complex array of details, though what Sarah had witnessed was rather simple, and it became clear that Lissa was searching for inconsistencies in her account.

The story Sarah told did not vary, however: KC had come into the office, handed her his company credit card, and chatted for five minutes about his vacation plans. He had not wanted to take a vacation, but he had seemed tired and depressed, and at a company meeting prior to his disappearance, everyone decided he should take a break. When Sarah saw KC, he had been more upbeat, she said, looking forward to visiting his grandfather. Then he went outside, and Sarah never saw him again. James told her he had spoken to KC, but not for long, since "whenever James is at the office people swarm him asking questions." She had tried calling KC in the weeks after that, as did James, but KC did not answer. When it seemed he was gone, Sarah canceled his paychecks.

Sarah knew KC had been miserable in Texas, heartbroken by his breakup with his girlfriend. "I actually never met her," she wrote Lissa. "KC made her seem like she was so sweet and so nice. He always said he expected they would get back together." About other employees, though, Sarah knew comparatively little. She knew Ryan Olness—the investor from Arizona who eventually fled the reservation—perhaps the best, since he had lived with her and James. "It was sort of strange," Sarah wrote to Lissa. "He had all these big plans for ND like restaurants and roustabout and a million other things and nothing ever happened." She knew the least about Robert Delao, the worker who arrived after KC disappeared—whom Lissa knew to be a snitch. When Blackstone left the reservation, Delao stayed behind to work for Tex at Maheshu. Delao still lived in Mandaree, while Sarah and James lived in Watford City, the town off the reservation where they relocated Blackstone. They rarely saw Delao anymore, Sarah said.

"If [Delao's] such a bad person why are they not focusing on him too?" Lissa texted one day.

Sarah didn't know: "I've wondered that too."

"I mean cause he's a convicted murderer."

"He claims that info isn't true, but I don't know."

"Between you and me I know it's a fact. He did time for it. Lots of time."

"What!?! Really, lots of time?"

"I never told ANYONE but you! I don't see putting him out there like that cause he did his time and I heard he regretted it."

"Wow, I won't say anything. It's not my place to. But still crazy."

Lissa felt Sarah was being mostly honest with her—more honest, perhaps, than Lissa was being with Sarah—but she did not believe Sarah was above a lie. In late April, Jill claimed on Facebook that Sarah and James had been "kicked off the rez." Lissa asked Sarah if this was true, but Sarah denied it. "We're not working on the Rez by choice," she wrote. "We had to shut down our business on the Rez because people were being so rude. Why is Jill so focused on us:-(. . . It's crazy, it's like she gets bored and just wants to get people going again." Three weeks later, Lissa tried once more, this time mentioning she had heard a rumor that Sarah and James "got into it with Tex." Sarah denied this, as well: "We are completely on good terms we just don't have a company working with him anymore. People just think since Blackstone water doesn't exist then something bad must have happened and it didn't."

The nature of Blackstone's separation from Maheshu was one thing Lissa suspected Sarah was lying about. Another thing was Brian Baker, whom Lissa now believed was a pseudonym, just like Nadia Reinardy. Once, Sarah had lamented to Lissa about the posters, "It just doesn't make since," and Lissa thought, *Sense, not since*. Brian had made the same mistake. "Hey how's Brian?" Lissa texted Sarah. "Now that I talk to you I never talk to him." Sarah replied that he was busy but well and "happy that he got us two talking." A few weeks later, Brian was back in touch.

Still, Lissa believed Sarah was beginning to trust her. One day in May, Lissa asked why James and KC used steroids. Sarah said she didn't know, and Lissa replied, "White folks are funny! Ya'll never really talk about the IMPORTANT things! Lol." Her bluntness seemed to put Sarah at ease, and Sarah began to share more about herself: James was always working, she said—more than she was willing to work—and they had been spending more time apart. Sarah often left North Dakota to see friends in Arizona and California, or to visit her parents in Washington. Her father was a doctor; her mother, a wildlife biologist. "She's obsessed with birds and animals," Sarah wrote. "Every time we went on vacation as kids, the first thing my mom would do was buy a bird book so she could identify everything while we were there. Even with plants and trees, like which ones you could eat. And which ones you could use if you touched stinging nettles to make it stop hurting." Sarah was twenty-six, a year older than Shauna. In college, she had studied hotel management.

Lissa was beginning to think Sarah was innocent in that she truly did not know what happened to KC, but other things perplexed Lissa. Could Sarah be guilty of the fraud Jed McClure, the investor, accused her of? And how could Sarah not wonder about James, with everything in his past?

Lissa often asked after James. "Same as always with him," Sarah once replied. "Nothing stresses him out I swear and I'm always stressed over everything."

"What does James say about all this?"

"I always ask him stuff after we talk, and he always says people will make whatever stories they can cause he says for some reason people always want to tear him down. Then he apologizes to me for having a record because he knows how sad this all makes me. It kills me that people claim to hate me or think I'm a bad person. I always tell him as long as he's honest to me I'll stay by his side, but I NEED honesty."

"I understand his point," Lissa replied, but had Sarah never at least wondered? "I mean for real you can't tell me it hasn't crossed your mind."

"Yes I'll be honest, I do ask what if . . . But I made him promise me NOTHING bad after all his past . . . and he promised . . ."

"What if it was just some accident that he can't admit?! Like a fight that got outta hand? I mean, those two"—KC and James—"were messing with steroids!!!!"

"Honestly I never saw either of them really upset. They're surprisingly both really happy people."

Lissa tried one more angle: "Well between you and I," she wrote, "I have heard stories about how demeaning and controlling he is towards you."

"Really?" Sarah wrote. "I won't say anything to him." They fought over business, she said, over truck repair bills and employee troubles, "but nothing crazy."

"Just don't let anyone cut you down and make you feel like you're not worthy cause you are. If you ever feel like he's all you got don't feel that way. Sounds like you have a lot of people who care! I'm one."

"Thanks Lissa:-)!!! I'll tell you one thing, I honestly hate business ha ha. James loves it and it's what he does. But it's hard for me cause everyone has problems or is mad all the time, and I just want things to be smooth."

"I feel for you."

"Talking with you has BEEN SO NICE!!! I definitely consider you a friend."

"I worry bout you ya know? I know YOU didn't do anything to KC! If I thought that I wouldn't be talking to you. I just hope he's found and all this bs goes away! Hope you keep in close contact with your folks so they don't worry so much!"

"Oh I hope he's found!!! And hopefully he's just hiding from all of us. You know what someone told me the other day? They thought maybe KC was behind all these posters, met up with someone with a bunch of money who knew James from years ago."

"Really?" Lissa replied. "Who has that much money to blow?"

IT WAS IMPOSSIBLE TO DISCERN Lissa's true feelings toward Sarah from their messages, or, for that matter, Sarah's feelings toward Lissa. Both seemed to be masterful liars—cheerily aware of being lied to, if unable to identify the lies the other told. "Do you ever speak with Nadia anymore?" Sarah wrote not long after Lissa asked about Brian. Lissa replied that she did not and changed the subject.

But between lies, their dialogue was strangely genuine. When Sarah spoke of her closeness with her parents, her frustration with James, or her sense of displacement in the oil fields, Lissa believed her; and Lissa's concern for Sarah's well-being was not all fakery, either. By the end of the spring, Lissa realized she cared for Sarah, as if all her pretending had made it so. They called or texted nearly every day. Lissa looked forward to their conversations and stayed on the phone as long as Sarah was willing. She believed Sarah had no one else to confide in. Once, Sarah described her parents as "really nice" people who think "everyone is good and the sky is blue and life is perfect." Sarah had told them about the defamation suit she filed against Jill, she said, but she withheld almost everything else, doubting they would understand.

Lissa's feelings toward Sarah were hardly an exoneration. Sarah still believed in James's innocence, a state of denial that Lissa found maddeningly irresponsible. Later, Lissa would reflect, "It wasn't so much that I thought Sarah was guilty but that maybe she knew more than she's ever led anyone to believe." Lissa often thought about Sarah's call to Robert Clarke, when she cried into the phone: "It made Sarah sound like less of a sociopath than James. I mean, why would she start crying, other than the fact that she was probably adding things up on her own already, wondering how she could have gotten herself so involved in something? But she turned around and carried on. What did she think? This was all going to go away on its own? My guess is she thought there would be a reasonable explanation someday, and it just kept getting worse."

Lissa could think of one more reason why Sarah would remain loyal to James: Lissa recognized in the way Sarah spoke of him the mentality of an abused woman—not physically abused, necessarily, but manipulated and controlled. The more Sarah came to trust Lissa, the more Lissa wondered if she could break Sarah's trust in James. Friends of Sarah's would later say how strange it was to them that someone so independent and smart ended up with a man like James. Lissa did not find it strange at all. People had said the same thing about her. "Put me in a room with twenty men, and you can be sure I'll pick the abusive alcoholic," she said.

Lissa knew how it was to be controlled, as acutely as she knew how to control. Once, when asked if she felt guilty for exploiting a mentality she knew so well—a mentality that, at one time in her life, had led her back to a man who tried to kill her—she said she did not. Lissa believed that although Sarah was controlled by James, Sarah was his "backbone." James needed her clean record to register their companies, establish credit, and purchase equipment. Beyond that, Sarah was, in Lissa's terms, "a perfect lieutenant." None of James's ventures had ever worked so well until he married Sarah: "I saw that James would be nothing without her, and I wanted to break him down any way I could," Lissa said. "I wanted him to lose his business. I wanted him to lose all the power he had. I didn't want to destroy Sarah, but in one sense I kind of had to, to get what I wanted. I kind of had to help her, in a tough love kind of way, to evolve. She was clueless. She couldn't smell the danger that was right under her nose."

10

The Search

BY THE END OF MAY 2013, WINTER LOOSENED ITS GRIP ON THE RESERVA-
tion, and people emerged from the dark warmth of their homes, and
weekends filled with picnics and softball games, and the lake echoed
with pop songs thrumming from the radios of drifting boats. The
powwows began in June, first in Twin Buttes, the southernmost segment; and then in Lucky Mound, White Shield, Mandaree, and Four
Bears. For many years, the final powwow, in early August, on the bank
of the lake, had attracted the best dancers and singers, but on the first
weekend of July that year, Mandaree drew a lively crowd as well. Oil
companies donated $20,000 to the celebration, which, with private
contributions from Mandaree families, amounted to the largest pot of
powwow cash in the segment's history. Dancers and singers came from
all over the continent—Arizona, Montana, Wisconsin, Saskatoon—
to compete for the generous prizes, and the Mandaree councilman,
in a nod to industry, named the powwow "The Heart Beat of the Bakken." In addition to the dancing and singing contests, there were
horse races, bingo games, a rodeo, fireworks, an egg toss, tug-of-war,

a basketball tournament, a chili cook-off, a battle of the bands, and a parade of rez cars. There were contests to determine who had grown the biggest turnip or beaded the prettiest earrings, who could rattle her tongue the fastest or war whoop the loudest, who could devour the largest watermelon or fry the most delicious fry bread.

Lissa attended many of the powwows that summer to hand out missing person posters and spread word about KC. Some men and women in her sun dance circle avoided powwows, lamenting the capitalization of spiritual tradition, the conspicuousness of tribal wealth; and indeed, the dancers' regalia appeared more expensive every year. Still, Lissa liked to go. Her aunt Cheryl had been a champion traditional dancer, and when Lissa was a child, Cheryl taught her how to dance. Lissa came to prefer traditional dancers, who wore simpler clothing and moved more subtly, to fancy dancers, who wore neon ribbons and feathers. "If you watch closely," Lissa would say, "you'll see the ones that really have the spirit, the teachings, because they're the ones with the footwork."

She enjoyed perusing the stalls that formed a ring around the grounds. She bought gifts for relatives, fabric for a sun dance dress. She tried on turquoise necklaces and ran her hands over leather. The quality of goods had improved since the boom. The vendors, like the dancers, had come from farther afield, since tribal members had more money to spend. Lissa liked to take it all in—bison hides and deer antlers, medicine wheels and packets of herbs, and all the trappings one needed to sew a dress: porcupine quills, feathers, fringe, Venetian glass beads, tin cones for the jingle dresses, cowry shells, bone pipes, abalone disks, fabric, ribbons, needles and thread.

In summer, clouds descended on the prairie like flocks of birds, constantly landing and lifting. The sky weathered to dark gray. The mustard bloomed bright yellow.

Lissa rarely stopped in White Shield anymore but went straight on to Mandaree, where she drove the back roads and sometimes wandered on foot through the draws and wider canyons. Before the boom, it had been easier to wander the reservation, and many tribal members

did. They fished, camped, hunted, and gathered medicine. Although
fences divided cattle pastures, it had been easy to slip between strands
of barbed wire or to lay down a gate. Now hundreds of oil wells dotted
Mandaree, and on new roads bisecting allotments, companies posted
signs reading OILFIELD TRAFFIC ONLY BEYOND THIS POINT. The companies had little legal ground to keep people off the land, since they did
not own it, but the signs, if not the traffic, discouraged tribal members
from wandering.

Lissa considered it an act of resistance to wander, and that summer she covered more ground than in any year before. Marks of the
boom were everywhere. Even land that remained intact was on its
surface changed: creeks and sloughs sucked dry, the water purchased
or stolen; the prairie littered with food wrappers, plastic bottles, scraps
of carpet, aluminum flashing, jerricans, busted work boots, bullet casings, oily rags, electronics, cigarette cartons, and empty tins of chewing tobacco; and a dense smog overlaying it all. Recently, the
Environmental Protection Agency had sued a company for failing to
properly limit pollution at their well sites on the reservation. One day,
Lissa wandered behind the Maheshu shop and came across what
looked like a heap of giant condoms. They were filter socks for strain-
ing contaminated water after it had fracked a well, before the water
was injected, again, into an old well for disposal. Each gram of a used
sock contained up to seventy picocuries of radiation, fourteen times
the amount allowed in North Dakota landfills. Since the Bakken generated seventy-five tons of filter socks a day, and since the only landfills that accepted the socks were located out of state, the socks were
often found stashed in abandoned buildings or dumped in fields.

Among the places Lissa searched most often was a canyon near
Mandaree, where the border of Fort Berthold skirted the Little Missouri River. An allotment there belonged to an uncle on her grandmother's side and, being so close to the river, reminded Lissa of the
bottomlands before the flood. Cattle roads threaded between tall clay
bluffs and groves of cottonwood thickening toward the bank. Lissa
had chosen the area because it seemed a likely spot for a body to be

buried. It was not far from the Maheshu shop, nor from the main road, and yet it felt remote, the topography too varied and too close to the river for it ever to be drilled. A gate guarded the entrance to the allotment, but apart from an earthmover rusting on a hillside, there were few signs anyone went there. The roads cut through sagebrush and canyons formed by sudden rain, one road so impassable that Lissa had to park and cross on foot over fallen logs onto a grassy rise on the other side. There, poking from a vast, green slope, were prairie dog mounds. The rodents stood on their back legs to greet her, sounding an alarm, and if she stayed long enough, they forgot her as they grazed and dug new portals to their underground city.

She was not systematic about the way she searched. She plotted no transects, no GPS points. She considered the distance of a site from a road, the density of the soil. She looked for disturbances in the land—mounds of hardened dirt, concavities in the grass, cigarette butts tossed carelessly behind. Beyond this, she relied on intuition. If she had a feeling about a place, she went, and if the feeling lingered, she went again.

Lissa documented her findings meticulously, like an archaeologist on an endless dig, unearthing the scraps of former lives as the boom chafed at the reservation around her. She often thought of what was being lost to the boom. She remembered the stones on the bank of the lake where she had gone camping with her family years earlier—stones arranged like the constellation Auriga—and wondered what other effigies or burial grounds had been paved over by roads and drilling pads. Once, an oil worker brought her a plastic bag containing bones he found near a well site. He had heard Lissa was searching for someone. "Shit, I ain't taking them," she joked with the worker. "That might be some mean old Hidatsa." She advised him to give the bones to law enforcement.

She found many bones herself, most of cows, horses, and deer. Once, she found a human sacrum in White Shield not far from the lake. It was so old, so soft and porous, that she felt it could have turned to powder between her fingers. Lissa gave it to a police officer, who sent it to a museum in Bismarck, where an archaeologist carbon-dated the bone and learned that the person to whom it belonged had been dead seventy-five years. Lissa wondered if the bone had risen up in the lake after the flood, from a grave that was never moved.

She rarely searched alone that summer. Dozens of people from the reservation and neighboring towns saw her posts on Facebook and offered help. They arrived with sandwiches, water, shovels, and metal detectors, following Lissa wherever she went. Her most reliable companion was Micah, who now rarely missed a trip with his mother. He was fourteen, taller and leaner, not quite skinny, with ears that stuck out like tiny wings. He no longer seemed haunted by KC but rather excited by the prospect of finding him. Micah wondered if one day he might become a detective or a forensic anthropologist. He was, in Lissa's words, "down for the cause," and when volunteer searchers complained about ticks or sore feet, Micah shook his head. "I know, man," he liked to say. "The struggle is real."

Among her other regular companions were two members of the tribe, Tiny Crows Heart and Waylon Fox. Tiny lived half the time in Sanish, in a trailer not far from the apartment where Lissa lived as a child, and the other half in Twin Buttes, where he was developing a Hidatsa language program. Both men were tall, gaunt, and wore their hair long. Waylon was Lissa's cousin on her great-grandmother Nellie's side but had grown up nowhere in particular. This nomadism had crept into his adulthood. Waylon slept under bridges and on the couches of patient relatives. He was a good singer and for years had followed the powwow circuit, hitching rides from reservation to reservation, winning enough money to pay his way in between. Eventually, he had decided powwows were fanning his bad habits and turned to traditional ceremony. This was how Lissa met Waylon, in the sweat lodge on the south side of Fargo. When Waylon was sober, he made good company. He brought his drum and practiced prayer songs as they drove. Often, he thought up his own songs, and the lyrics made Lissa laugh.

It was on these searches of the reservation and of the towns just beyond the border that Lissa frequently encountered oil workers. She would tell several stories from her encounters that summer: In one, she had been driving on a street in Williston, an hour west of the reservation, when she came across a man grilling cheese sandwiches in the bed of a pickup truck. She had noticed him because of a line of workers extending along the street. They were standing in the bright sun, fanning themselves with dollar bills. Lissa had not seen what they were waiting for, at first, so she parked and approached a man in the line. "What are you waiting for?" she asked. When he told her, she walked to the front of the line and called out to the man making sandwiches. "How much are they?"

"Five bucks."

"What if I wanted another piece of cheese?"

"I'll give you one more for a dollar."

Lissa did the math—sixteen slices of cheese cost three dollars; a loaf of bread, one—and suddenly was struck by the absurdity of the boom, by the gross fact of men waiting in the sun to pay five dollars for a grilled cheese sandwich.

Her second encounter occurred on the reservation, in New Town, on a day even hotter than the one in Williston. Lissa spotted a man on the road on the east edge of town, swinging a bag of candy. He was young, an immigrant from an African country he would name but she would forget. The man wore jeans and a long-sleeved denim shirt. When she yelled to him, "Where are you going?" he smiled.

"To the man camp," he said.

The camp was seventeen miles away, in a northeast corner of the reservation. The man seemed grateful as they drove, and spoke cheerily in English. He had recently immigrated to the United States, he said, and had come to the oil fields to pay off debts. He had no car, but he was accustomed to walking. "In my country" was the phrase he used. Lissa hated this phrase. The refugees who lived in her building used the phrase, and she wanted to shake them, say, "Like it or not, this is your country now," but to the man she was polite.

They turned south toward the lake. A cluster of trailers appeared, and the man got out. Lissa never saw him again. Later, she would wonder what became of him: "I said, 'It's cool to meet you,' and he said, 'No, no, the cool all mine.' He was probably eighteen, nineteen— barely legal to be working. You hear of people blowing up on rigs, dying in car accidents, and here this kid was walking on this dusty, congested road, and he was just happy. Maybe he was one of the ones making twelve grand a month. Even if he was, you could see the sac- rifice people were giving for this."

Her relatives regarded the oil workers who had overtaken their reservation warily, but Lissa found herself feeling more sympathy than suspicion. It seemed to her these workers had been caught up in some- thing beyond even their control. "I hated oil," Judd Parker, KC's for- mer housemate, said once. "I never thought in my life I'd do oil. I ended up in the oil fields because I had nowhere else to go."

One day that summer, Lissa dropped by the house where Judd still lived, tucked into a knoll above Four Bears Village, not far from the casino. It was a nicer house than most on the reservation, with a wrap- around deck and large windows and a curtain of trees that hid the houses below from view. Judd came to the door wearing pajama pants. He was in his forties but seemed younger, with blond hair brushing his shoulders and a blond shadow of a beard. He looked a bit like Gen- eral Custer, if Custer had smoked a lot of pot.

Judd led Lissa into the kitchen and through a corridor into KC's bedroom. The room was empty. Jill had reclaimed her son's belong- ings except for a bottle of vitamins KC had left in a cupboard and a pair of boots, which Judd handed to Lissa. "What was that day he disappeared—the twenty-second?" Judd said. They returned to the kitchen. Judd was meandering and apologetic, rarely finishing sen- tences, blending one into the next. He was from North Carolina, where his father owned a successful record company that had pro- duced hundreds of albums of Southern gospel music. Judd grew up loving gospel more than anything, until he heard the Grateful Dead. In the nineties, he had followed the Dead "until Jerry died" and then returned to North Carolina, where he worked for his father and sold albums at flea markets on weekends. By then, Judd had a wife and two sons. They needed money, so he took a job in Aspen, Colorado, building a Ritz-Carlton hotel. The recession hit; the work ran out. Judd called a drill foreman he knew in North Dakota whose company had contracts with Steve Kelly, the former tribal lawyer who owned Trustland Oilfield Services. Kelly gave Judd a job, and that was how Judd met KC.

"Did you see him much?" Lissa interrupted. It was a Sunday evening, and the sun was setting. She had to work in the morning.

"KC? Not much," Judd replied. He had seen him only when they came home to sleep. "I mean, you think you know someone, but you can live with someone your whole life and not know them."

Judd began another story, and when Lissa glanced over at him, she realized that he was crying. *Jeez, these guys are so sensitive,* she thought.

"I was following this dump truck back from Williston," Judd said, "and, well, a car went in front of the dump truck, hit him head-on. I watch him, closer than I am to you. I watch him die. For four minutes, I watch him die." That evening, Judd called a fellow oilfield worker— "and he's like, 'Did you steal his wallet?' I'm like, 'Fuck you. I watched this guy die.' It was emotional for me. It kind of affected me."

Judd went on: "I swear, with all this money, people turn against each other. My landlord and his sister—they don't talk. It's all about mineral rights, this property, that property. I know an Indian lady. She's got a single-wide trailer that's trash, but she's got sixteen oil wells. People say, 'I don't see why she wouldn't build a real house.' How do you not understand that? Money doesn't change anything."

Lissa supposed Judd was an exception to the workers she met in the oil field. Yet every worker she met seemed to have wound up there for a different reason. Or was it the same reason? Even Rick Arey, who had spent his adult life on oil rigs, and whom Lissa now knew better than any oil worker given how often they spoke on the phone, had misgivings about the industry. "This is the only place I've seen this kind of carnage go on," he told her. The longer he lived in North Dakota, the more his pride in the industry had faded.

Rick was a decade younger than Lissa, born in Denver, Colorado, the middle of three children. His father had been a truck driver while his mother raised the kids. As a child, Rick had been fond of pyrotechnics. Once, he lit his mother's can of hair spray on fire and burned a hole in the carpet. On another occasion, while his family was asleep, he set off a firecracker in his bedroom. His mother bought him books on safety and took him to the fire department, but none of this had worked. When an uncle found Rick in a closet with his cousins, lighting matches beneath racks of clothes, the uncle beat him until his bottom was bruised and, for days, forbade Rick from entering the house. Rick and his uncle camped in the backyard, where Rick was to imagine he burned the house down and killed all of his relatives. He never played with fire again.

His mother said that of all her children Rick had the biggest heart, but he did not stop getting into trouble. When he was nine years old, his family moved to Wyoming and then back to Colorado after his mother and father divorced. His mother married six times. Rick attended five high schools before he turned eighteen and dropped out. He was often left alone at home and used a lot of drugs. He got addicted to meth. He stopped eating. A friend rescued him and took him to live with his own mother in Fort Collins. Rick found work as a groundman on a rotomill, walking behind a machine as it chewed up asphalt. He worked that job for two years and then enrolled in the Spartan College of Aeronautics and Technology in Tulsa, Oklahoma.

It was his mother who made clear to Rick how important money was. She had been raised poor and, at age thirteen, taken out of school and forced to work. All the money Rick's father earned had never been enough. Rick wanted to make money but did not know how. People told him to use his brain, but Rick had more confidence in his brawn. "I can read like the wind blows," he said, "but I never had the patience to sit behind a desk." After less than a year of college, he realized how much debt he already owed and quit. He worked three years for a moving company and then, on his father's recommendation, got a job on an oil rig in Wyoming. BP operated the well; Nabors Industries, based in Texas, did the drilling. Rick began as a floor hand, "tripping pipe" into the drill hole and keeping the area clean, and worked his way up to derrick hand, one step below the "driller." When BP shut down the rig—a worker was almost killed—Rick took a job on a Nabors practice rig, training roughnecks how to operate it safely.

By then, Rick was twenty-five years old. He felt proud of his work. Roughnecks, he said, had a reputation for being "the toughest motherfuckers around," and the money was not bad either. Rick earned $5,855 every two weeks, which he spent haphazardly. In 2004, he got a DUI and, not long after that, at a gas station met a woman whose car had broken down and later got her pregnant. He learned he had a daughter when he received a subpoena for his DNA. After that, between car insurance and child support, drilling was the only work Rick knew that paid enough to cover his bills.

In North Dakota, something changed. Maybe it was KC going missing, or maybe it was the chaos of the boom on a scale Rick never witnessed before. Men were pushed to work so fast that inevitably they made mistakes. Amid so much negligence, Rick felt helpless. "I got to thinking," he said. "The middle class, we don't run shit, we're just herded around like a bunch of cattle, and the powers that be, the people running this country, they're not doing anything to stop it. They're not doing anything to find alternative energy. They're not doing anything to save the environment, but they bitch at all the Americans using plastic, that are going to McDonalds. It's like, Alright motherfucker, we didn't really choose this. This is what you've given us to survive. You're the one that built the roads, put up the stoplights, invented the car. Don't tell me you did it to make my life easier. You did it because you wanted to be a multibillionaire, and you're power hungry, and this was the fastest, easiest way to do it. Nobody sat down and said, *If we go forward with this, what's America going to look like two hundred years from now?* They didn't fucking care about that. And they don't care about it now. They tell us to stop using plastic, but that doesn't

mean shit in the grand scheme of things, you know? The only alterna-
tives to save the environment have got to come from the people that
made the trillions of dollars. They've got to think of a new way,
because a guy like me—I know, 'Don't limit yourself, Rick'—but I
can't reinvent the fucking wheel. It's just that I'm not that guy. I'm not
that smart. Even for the Einsteins, it's not that fucking easy."

In the middle of an oil boom, there was no such thing as choice,
Rick believed. Booms obliterated choice. "We're born into this money
machine, and it's all we know. We go through the motions. We work
hard. We retire at sixty. We go golfing or run around a nude colony.
That's the American dream. Quick money. Dodge diesels and women
and drinking beers with your buddies. And there's camaraderie in that.
We all felt like we were really doing something. We were contributing to
the economy. But that's what sucks about money. When it's gone, you
figure out it's not even real. It's just a dopamine rush. We know what an
oil field does. We know what drugs do. We know these things wreck
everything about the human spirit, but we keep doing them."

THE SUMMER OF 2013 SETTLED on the prairie, turning everything a lan-
guid green. Lissa and Jill were speaking again—Jill had written an apol-
ogy, Lissa gave her a call—although they spoke less often and less
intimately than before. Jill called Lissa whenever she had news or heard
from Steve Gutknecht, the Bureau of Criminal Investigations agent in
Williston. Investigators had completed an analysis of James's and KC's
phone data, finding that on the morning KC disappeared, his phone
had been active until it entered the vicinity of James's phone, at which
point KC received messages and calls but no longer answered or made
them. That same afternoon, the phones moved in tandem toward Watford City, where they remained until that night, when both traveled to
Williston. There, KC's phone had been deactivated.

The analysis made investigators more certain of James's culpabil-
ity but did little to build their case. It was not a crime for a phone to

follow another. To indict James for murder, they needed much more than the analysis—a body or, at the very least, a witness.

Lissa was beginning to think their only hope was finding KC, but as the summer wore on, this was seeming even more difficult. She wanted to organize a search of the reservation with support from the tribal council. One councilwoman, Judy Brugh, replied to her inquiry, suggesting that Jill draft a letter requesting assistance from tribal police and a speaking slot at a council meeting. Jill drafted two letters—one to the council and another to Tex asking permission to search his property. Neither the council nor Tex responded.

Lissa urged Jill to come on a search anyway, but Jill considered the trip a waste of time. She had asked Gutknecht for a copy of the phone data, hoping it would suggest a specific location, but he would not give it to her. "I just can't break the law and get myself in trouble," he wrote. "Rest assured if there . . . was a good place to search and not just blind searching it would have been done long ago. Sorry I can't be of more help with a place to search but if I had that I'd be searching it."

Lissa disagreed with his suggestion that searching was futile. She knew the chances of stumbling upon KC were low—"Finding a body in the badlands is harder than finding a needle in a haystack," she often said—but this was beside the point. If they had one good reason to go on searching, Lissa thought, it was to show James that the case had not languished. There was still the possibility that a witness would come forward—that by a tip or a fluke, KC would be found.

Lissa arranged for a professional search team to meet Jill in North Dakota in late June. Jill said she could not come. She believed they should be more "realistic" about their prospects of finding KC, she said, and she was tired, still fighting the defamation suit. Sarah had updated the complaint:

> 25. I believe the defendant also started to post "Beware" of my hus-
> band and I all around town and on the internet. My bank received this
> poster and Tex Hall received this poster as well. It states that we are

con-artists and thieves. These allegations on the poster are untrue. Tex Hall gave me the envelope address to him with this flyer. . . .

26. People in town are constantly asking us if we are involved with Mr. Clarke's disappearance. Many businesses have stated that they don't want to do business with us because of these rumors. We are the center of the town's gossip and live under a constant cloud.

27. As a result of these posters and false allegations, our contract between Maheshu Energy was terminated on March 16, 2013, which was also around the same time the flyer was sent to Tex Hall. . . . We were forced to dissolve the LLC.

Lissa argued with Jill: "It breaks my heart to know that I have invested nearly a year of my time, effort, resources, etc. to make this happen FOR YOU and you are not willing to do what is necessary to find KC. Pushing it off is only giving the person or persons involved with KC's disappearance more time to tamper with whatever scraps of evidence have been left." They compromised, and in July, Jill drove to North Dakota.

The search did not go well. They met in New Town—Rick, Lissa, Jill, and Jill's husband—as they had before, but this time Jill appeared to have little interest in searching. Lissa was impatient; Jill, withdrawn. They rode in separate cars to Mandaree and north along the lake edge, where the shoreline meandered along bays and coves and peninsulas jutting into the water. The day was hot; a haze descended; the prairie crawled with wood ticks. Jill did not want to leave the car. She wandered a short distance through the grass, through coneflower and thistle, and retreated again to the pavement.

When they went by the Maheshu shop that afternoon, Tex was not there. Jill and her husband began to bicker in the parking lot. Lissa lost her patience. "Everyone shut the fuck up," she said. There was something strange about the lot, she thought. Then she saw what it was: A white man, parked in a red sedan, was watching them. Lissa took a photograph of the man. He looked away. "Let's get out of here," she said.

KC WAS NOT THE ONLY one for whom Lissa searched that summer. In the months before and after he disappeared, at least three other men had gone missing from the oil fields. Mike Marchus, the Bureau of Criminal Investigations agent in Minot, sent Lissa a list of names, which included Ron Johnson—"74 year old male, 5'11", 220 lbs, gray/blonde hair, beard and mustache, wears glasses and has diabetes"—who had last been seen on the morning of October 16, 2011, at the 4 Bears Casino & Lodge. There was also Eric Haider, thirty years old, who had a "full beard" and "multiple tattoos." He disappeared about three months after KC, on a construction site south of the reservation. Lissa took particular interest in his case, since the circumstances of his disappearance were similar to KC's, but she found no overlap among the people each man had known. She spoke to Haider's mother, whom she helped by posting on social media and distributing missing posters on her drives around the oil fields. That was how Johnson's family heard of Lissa and asked for her help. Lissa created a Facebook page to which she invited many of the same people who followed Jill's page and, in June, with assistance from law enforcement, planned a search for Johnson. She did not believe he had been murdered. Johnson had intended to stay with his sister in a town east of the reservation the night he disappeared but never arrived at her house. His family said he had a history of depression. Lissa thought it was more likely that he had driven off the road. She planned to walk the edges of the lake and various sloughs and invited Sarah Creveling to join her.

The search was on a Saturday, the prairie blanketed with a still, heavy heat. Lissa met two deputies and some volunteers at the gas station in Parshall. When Sarah arrived, Lissa laughed at how the deputies looked at her, fumbling with recognition. Sarah was more composed than her photographs on the flyer had let on. She was taller than Lissa by several inches, and slender, her hair pulled in a ponytail and eyes darkened with mascara. Her thin lips opened into a confident smile. She wore diamond earrings, a baseball cap, and a blue zippered shirt.

Lissa and Micah rode in Sarah's truck to the lake, the volunteers and deputies following behind. "She had a really nice truck," Micah later recalled, "like a Ford F-150, with the big-ass thousand-dollar-apiece tires. Everything she owned was so nice." Micah was smitten with Sarah and made no secret of it, proposing that if she dumped her husband he would be available. This made Sarah and Lissa laugh. They joked about what James would think. The lake appeared to the west and was lost again behind the bluffs, behind fields of corn and purple flax that formed a loose seam with the horizon. They passed the old Congregational church, the sky showing through the steeple, and a cemetery where Arikara soldiers were buried, its thin white stones stuck like cigarettes in the earth. They turned east toward White Shield, toward the border of the reservation, and south, again, toward the lake's edge, where roads dropped right into the water. They followed faint tracks, skirting washouts until they came to a ravine. Sarah paused and stared down into it. It was steep on both sides—they could easily get stuck—but Lissa assured her she would make it. All Sarah had to do was give the truck a little gas. Sarah did not seem sure, and for a moment, Lissa wondered if she would go a different way, but then Sarah shifted into a lower gear and, as Lissa instructed, gathered speed. The truck rocked as it plunged, and when they came up the other side, Sarah was smiling, pleased with herself.

"Awesome spending time with you crazy girl! It was a blast!" Lissa wrote her the next day.

"Yesterday was a lot of fun!" Sarah replied. "I had 3 more ticks when I got home OMG I about died ha ha. I threw them on the ground and James was looking for them!"

They would try to meet again that summer but miss each other. Their messages grew friendlier still. One day, Sarah sent a video of her and James cuddling a puppy. She rarely mentioned the flyers anymore, chatting instead about work and weekend plans. She had enrolled in an exercise class called Insanity, which relieved her stress, she said.

"That would be FATALITY for me," Lissa wrote to Sarah. She had little use for deliberate exercise. It was August, and she was preparing to go to sun dance: "No food or water. Just dance ceremony and prayer."

"No food or water?!" Sarah asked. "Can you last that long without?"

"Yeah," Lissa replied. "Once a year."

Lissa had begun to share more about herself. Though she did not name her kids aside from Micah, they were ever present in her messages, which contained the relentless detail of a family in flux. Obie and Lissa were fighting more and more. One day, he had tried to run away. As soon as he disappeared, Lissa went to the computer in Obie's bedroom and looked at his Facebook messages, where she learned he had gone to meet up with his father, OJ, who had been out of prison ten years. Lissa called the police, who located and returned her son.

Even as a child, Obie had held OJ against her. The first time he said, "You kept me from my dad," he had been six years old. "I didn't keep you from your dad," Lissa had replied. "Your dad kept himself from you." They had been living in Minot before Lissa went to prison. Eventually, she had gotten sick of hearing it, loaded Obie and Micah into a car, and driven through the night to Little Earth, the housing complex in Minneapolis, where she pounded on OJ's sister's door. "Fuck, Nadia's here," she had heard his relatives yell, and when she pushed her way into the apartment, they had begged her not to kill OJ. She found him facedown on the carpet, nudged his face with her foot. "Hey, Dad, get yourself up and talk to these boys," she had said, and when OJ lifted his head, she saw that his cheeks were bruised, his eyes swollen, his lips broken and bloody. He had been in a fight. "That ain't my dad," Obie said. "The hell it ain't," Lissa replied. "Damn, Nad," OJ had said. "Why you got to be so mean?"

Now Obie was fifteen, and his bitterness had sharpened. Once at the top of his class, he was doing poorly in school. He passed tests easily and was popular among his classmates, elected to student council, and recruited to the football team. But he rarely put in effort, and as soon as he joined something, he quit. When Lissa asked Obie what he wanted to be when he grew up, he replied, "An alcoholic. You and Dad are alcoholics, so I guess that's what I'm going to be."

For every mistake her children made, Lissa felt a twinge of guilt, driven deeper by the fact that they, too, blamed her for their problems. She worried most of all for CJ. He was whip-smart and acted tough, but Lissa believed he was her most sensitive child. He was often depressed, which she attributed to the traumatic brain injury he suffered while in foster care. A few years earlier, CJ had tried to take his own life. They had been driving together across Fargo when Lissa lost her patience with him, stopped the car, and told him to get out. A few days later, he had called, asking if he could come over. When he arrived at her apartment, he went into the bathroom, and when he emerged, he had tripped, dropping an empty pill bottle. Later, in a hospital room, as CJ's pulse loosened, a doctor had grabbed Lissa by the chin. If she had anything to say to her son, she should say it, the doctor had said. Lissa did not remember what it was she said. She remembered the way the doctor held her face, looked her in the eyes, and in that moment, Lissa knew the doctor was a mother, too. As machines sang out the rhythm of her son's dying, Lissa had lost her breath. Shauna and Lindsay stood near, and when a chaplain walked in, he had looked from Lissa to her daughters. "He did this because of her," Lissa heard them say, and the chaplain, taking her daughters' hands, commanded them to pray.

Lissa believed her daughters. She believed them even after CJ explained that he had swallowed the pills because his girlfriend broke up with him. "It's not your fault," he tried to assure his mother, but the guilt she felt preceded the incident, and there wasn't much he could say.

It was Micah who consoled her then and every other time Lissa fought with her kids. "I try my hardest," she told him once.

"I realize that, Mom," he replied. "Why do you think I stick by your side?"

Micah's older brothers called him their "bigger little brother" because they thought he had grown up faster than them. Lissa just figured she had been a better mother to Micah than to her other children. Already, Micah was two years past the age at which his doctors believed his lungs would give out, damaged so severely by anhydrous ammonia when the train derailed in Minot a decade earlier. Lissa refused to believe his doctors—refused to allow Micah to believe them, too. In prison, she had come across the book *The Power of Intention* by Wayne Dyer; and later, at a garage sale in Fargo, she found a collection of his books on tape. After that, whenever Lissa drove Micah to appointments at the nearest Indian health clinic in White Earth, Minnesota, she had made him listen to the tapes. According to Dyer, a person had the power to change his own DNA. *Do you hear that, Micah?* she had said. *Do you know what that means? It means that what these doctors are telling us is wrong. If you believe them that you're going to die, you will die. I don't want you to listen to these people. I want you to live.*

Lissa thought of those tapes whenever Micah accompanied her on trips to the reservation. He was not wholly uncritical of his mother. He often teased Lissa for applying an excessive level of intensity to even the most mundane tasks. Later, they both would laugh when they told a story from one day that summer in 2013, when Lissa dropped by the tribal headquarters to find a map of her land in Mandaree. She had inherited the land from her father. She never would have known about this land had an oil company's request for a right-of-way not appeared in her mail. She had gone first to the Bureau of Indian Affairs to find a map, since she had no idea where the allotments were located, but an administrator had claimed the information was proprietary and refused to give one to her. Lissa figured she would have better luck at the tribal land office.

She had been inside tribal headquarters a long time when she burst through the doors at a run, clutching a roll of paper. Two men she met in the land office had been reluctant to give her a map. "They wanted eighty dollars," Lissa later complained. "I'm a landowner. How am I supposed to know where my land is if they won't give me a map? I had to go half-ass traditional. I'm like, 'What's your name? Okay, we're related.' I start bringing up names, and this guy's like, 'Oh, shit. Here, you can borrow this map,' and the other guy's like, 'Hey, wait a minute.' I said, 'No, man, he already borrowed it to me.' He gets on the phone, starts texting his boss. Then he's calling security, so I grabbed that map and got the hell out of there."

Micah sighed when he saw his mother dashing out of tribal headquarters: "I said, 'Mom, how come every time I'm here with you they've got to call in the militia?' It felt like that movie *National Treasure*, where they get the Declaration of Independence, and they're taking off. She was breathing heavier than ever. She just put the car in reverse, and we were gone."

That same summer, Lissa bought an aluminum dinghy with an outboard motor in which she searched for Ron Johnson and took Micah fishing on the lake. They would head out on one of the dirt roads in White Shield that dropped into the water, lower the dinghy down the bank, and motor toward the depths. Micah could fish all day if Lissa let him. Sometimes Tony, her cousin, and other relatives joined. Lissa liked to fish, as well, though she liked as much to talk and look around. The bluffs looked smaller from out on the water, the prairie almost flat, and if the boat floated into the shallows, it would have been easy to entangle a line on a cottonwood tree. There and along the shore, silver snags protruded at odd angles from the water, the last stubborn residents of the bottomlands.

ONE DAY AT THE END of the summer, while driving in Mandaree, Lissa dropped by the cemetery at Saint Anthony Catholic Church. This time, she found her father's grave.

She had met her father, Leroy, only a few times, and they had spoken infrequently on the phone. The last time he called, he had told her, "You sound just like your mother." He had not intended it as a compliment.

Lissa had long resented her mother for not staying with Leroy.

Lissa knew that her resentment was unfair—that it had not been just her mother's choice to leave. She suspected her grandmother had pressured Irene to give Lissa up, and she knew it was because of Catholicism—a "white way" of thinking inflicted on her family—that her grandmother believed this necessary. But what, exactly, had changed her mother's mind? This had never been clear to Lissa, who still wondered about those first seven months of her life in the custody of other relatives. Delphine and Ed had been their names. Had they loved her as much as her mother did? Had they missed her when her mother took her back? After that, they adopted another girl to take Lissa's place, and years later, when Lissa was in college, this girl had appeared at the door of her apartment. She just wanted to see what Lissa looked like, she had said.

As Lissa grew older and had children of her own, she resented her mother less for leaving her father, but the feeling had not gone away entirely. By then, there were other reasons for her resentment: all the times her mother decided Lissa was unfit to raise her own children, and times before that, when her mother expected her to be something she was not. Clean. Well-dressed. Sober. Was this *really* what her mother wanted of her, Lissa had wondered, or had she just been worried what white people thought?

For years these questions had trailed Lissa, and then, one day, they simply had not mattered anymore. The change came a few springs after her release from prison, on a road trip with her brother Percy. His own mother lived in a nursing home in Idaho, and Percy had wanted to visit her; so Lissa applied for permission from her parole officer to join him. She remembered most vividly, when they arrived at the nursing home, how small and shriveled Percy's mother looked. In that moment, Lissa thought of her own mother's impossible strength. She could summon no more anger toward her mother and decided that day to forgive her.

Forgiveness did not erase all resentment, but Lissa found it easier to let go of her anger now. Irene was approaching seventy years of age and soon would retire and move home. Now and then, Lissa considered moving home to the reservation, as well. In August, her probation had come to an end, and for the first time in seven years, she had no one to report to. The thought of moving unsettled her. She had rarely been so stable as in her years in Fargo, and yet every time she returned home, she felt a pull stronger than before. "The rez is the rez," she once would say. "Everybody wants to be on an adventure somewhere, but when you run out of resources, you run out of time, you run out of whatever, it's where everybody goes. It's the end of the road in a lot of ways. A lot of people from here don't even live here most of their lives, but they'll get buried here. It's home. It's an unconditional place. You walk in, and it's exactly where you left off."

On the few occasions Lissa visited White Shield that summer, she went to the cemetery in the south of the segment where her Yellow Bird relatives, among them Chucky, were buried. She missed Chucky. Once, she had sent a message to his number, and someone replied. Lissa apologized. It had not occurred to her that his number had been reassigned, but the new recipient told her not to worry: "He must have been an awesome guy because a lot of people text and call him still."

She wondered what Chucky would have said about the boom. He probably would have sued the government over something, because that was what he liked to do. It was as if Chucky had hoped the government would make things right. Or maybe it never had anything to do with hope. Maybe it had been his way of proving that history repeats itself. That was more likely. Chucky had been a cynic. In all the riddles they had tried on each other, Lissa could recall stumping him only once. They had been in his bedroom, her uncle seated at his desk, Lissa in the folding chair. "Chucky, what's the ultimate ruler of everything?" she had said.

"Money?" he ventured.

"No. Love—unconditional love."

11

The Gunman

THE OIL BOOM REACHED ITS PEAK ON FORT BERTHOLD IN THE SUMMER OF 2013. That September, after the tribe had been earning a steady average of $12 million in oil and gas production taxes each month, suddenly, it earned almost $20 million. A year before the next primary election for chairman, tribal councilmen found themselves in an unfamiliar position: No longer beggars for investors and grants, they became the bestowers of wealth. They funded building projects such as schools, powwow grounds, tribal offices, and housing developments, and created summer programs for youth. Under Tex Hall's direction, they established a People's Fund, from which they issued an annual five-hundred-dollar payment to each member of the tribe. It had long been true that members who could not afford to pay their bills petitioned the council for help. This reliance on the tribe for basic needs had hardly diminished with the boom, but now members were not the only ones for whom the tribe opened its coffers. At council meetings, white men dressed in company shirts populated the chamber, peddling their services with phrases like "Your Honor," "your people," and "Mother Earth."

I attended several of these council meetings on my trips to the reservation. I wondered if councilmen thought it funny, all these white people stumbling over words, but they seemed to enjoy the attention and had no problem making people wait. Once, while interviewing a tribal administrator in his office, I saw two white men dressed in matching shirts pass the door a half dozen times, and when I went into the lobby an hour later, I saw the men again, on another lap around the building. "Just making the rounds," one said, and smiled as if I understood.

Most of the visitors were industry lobbyists waiting on drilling permits or rights-of-way across tribal land, but a surprising number had little to do with oil. They were real-estate investors and salesmen pushing boom-time goods such as software, water filters, and GPS systems that traced the whereabouts of trucks. It was remarkable all the things the tribe was told it needed when suddenly it had money. The council seemed wary of the offers and took few of them, though it did accept several that drew its constituents' ire—among them, a $1.2 million yacht named *Island Girl* that would take casino guests on the lake, and a helicopter that the tribe leased to fly patients to hospitals and diabetics to dialysis. Both were Tex Hall's idea. While his fans considered the helicopter a good investment, his detractors felt he had acted in self-interest and claimed he used the helicopter more than anyone else. As for the yacht, it was kept onshore, since the tribe had yet to secure permission from the Army Corps and Coast Guard to put it on the water. Anyone who crossed the bridge saw the yacht perched on the beach like a trophy, and the longer it remained—amid an addiction crisis and heightening violence—the more it smacked of carelessness and poor judgment.

It was no secret that some councilmen were profiting from the boom. Most tribal members I interviewed had heard of Maheshu and knew Tex earned significant royalties from oil wells on his allotments. Judy Brugh, who represented the Four Bears segment, told me she earned $50,000 a month from wells drilled on her land; meanwhile, she had relatives who owned oil-field service companies. Mervin

Packineau, who represented Parshall, was a partner in U.S. Sand, a Texas-based corporation that shipped silica and ceramic proppant, used to frack wells, from Tianjin, China, to North Dakota.

Most tribal members knew only the gist of their councilmen's arrangements. The *New Town News* rarely reported on tribal politics, and the tribal newspaper, the *MHA Times*, was funded by the tribe and thus could not report critically on the council. (The editor I knew would be fired when she did.) It was not for lack of trying that members had so little information about their own tribe's affairs. I knew many who had launched citizen investigations, interrogating councilmen at meetings and requesting documents from state and federal agencies. These tribal members attended public hearings in Bismarck, and when bureaucrats failed to answer their questions, they found the answers themselves. Often, I would visit their homes, and they would present me with boxes of photos and paperwork. Everything that could be witnessed was documented—spills, oil-field waste tossed in fields, traffic, well explosions, men wandering where they should not be, car accidents, and potholes.

Among these tribal members was Ed Hall, the elderly man I shared a meal with on my first visit to the reservation. Ed would hear I was in town or see me at a meeting, and later he would call and say he had something to tell me. The secrets he shared were never revelatory, and I wondered if he just enjoyed the company. One day, when I saw him at the grocery store, he dropped all pretense and said, "Call me, and we can gossip." I picked him up at his house in Parshall that evening, and we drove west toward the lake. He had heard a councilman had built a mansion by the water. Ed wanted to see the place, but we drove and drove and could not find it.

THE INVESTIGATION INTO KC'S DISAPPEARANCE had languished once more. While Blackstone no longer operated on the reservation, it appeared to be doing fine from its new base in Watford City. Meanwhile, it was dispatching a fleet of oil trucks from Williston, Lissa learned. As for Tex, his separation from James and Sarah seemed to have had no effect on his willingness to return Lissa's calls, and if what Sarah said was true, then Maheshu, with help from James's acquaintance Robert Delao, was also still turning a profit.

Then, in the fall of 2013, a new rumor circulated on the reservation: The chairman's stepdaughter, a nineteen-year-old woman named Peyton Martin, was pregnant with James's son.

Lissa had reason to believe the rumor. In the summer, Jill had forwarded her a tip that came via the Facebook page. It was from a waitress at a diner in Keene, a town near the west border of the reservation, who claimed that the winter KC went missing, she often saw him come in to eat. Sometimes, she saw him with another man—"a built, buff, tall guy"—who made her feel uneasy. "He dresses very nice and is very charming in a puke kind of way," the waitress wrote. Lately, this man had been appearing at the diner with a young woman the waitress knew: "She happens to be the chief of the Fort Berthold Indian Reservation's stepdaughter."

Lissa knew little about Peyton Martin. Peyton's mother, Tiffiany Johnson, had worked on Tex's staff during his previous term as chairman and was described by many as an "attractive" woman—dark hair, sharp features. The compliment, however, came with a caveat. Tiffiany wore her oil wealth shamelessly. Her hair was strange, people said, cut short and dyed red at the tips, and her eyelids, painted green and purple, were dabbed with glitter. She wore beaded jackets, Pendleton purses, jeans and leather belts crusted in rhinestones, and jewelry so heavy with silver that it hung like chains around her neck. Tiffiany owned a retail business called The Sparkling Spur. On Facebook, Lissa had found photographs of Tiffiany, Tex, and Peyton at a gala, dressed in Tiffiany's adornments.

Sarah had never mentioned Tiffiany or Peyton to Lissa, but the rumor of James's affair gave Lissa another idea. "We need to talk," she texted Sarah one day on her way home from the reservation. "Where's James right this second?!? He is not with you is he?!"

"He's at the house with me, why?"

"Honestly?"

"Yes, what's wrong?"

"Tell James to call me right now!!!"

"Really?! Is everything ok?"

"Call me!! But would like to talk to James."

Lissa did not record the conversation, nor would she remember all of it, though she committed to memory a few important details with help from Micah, who listened to the call. Her first impression, she later would say, was that James sounded confident, and when she asked if he cheated on Sarah, he denied it without hesitation. Lissa asked again; James spoke over her. He was a smooth talker. She let him talk, and when he seemed to have talked himself out, she asked another question: "Aren't you worried Robert's going to snitch on you?"

James paused. "No," he said.

"Well you need to be," Lissa replied. "Once a snitch, always a snitch."

After they had spoken a few minutes, as Lissa would recall, James handed the phone back to Sarah. It seemed to Lissa that Sarah had been listening to the conversation, but if Sarah heard Lissa ask about Delao, she did not mention it. Rather, Sarah wanted to know why Lissa believed her husband was having an affair. Lissa did not bring up Peyton but invented a story about a woman from Arizona who called with tips regarding KC. Lissa told Sarah that the way the woman spoke about James made her suspect they were romantically involved.

"Do you think he's a cheat?" Lissa texted Sarah.

"I don't think so," Sarah replied. "But there are so many rumors out there now, I can't help but wonder. . . . I wonder why she's curious about KC but . . . she really just wanted to talk shit about James."

"She said she believed James had KC taken out."

"Seriously?! Agh that makes me sick to my stomach, I just can't imagine that. Or why he would even do that or have a reason. Did she have any guess as to what a motive would have even been? That's what I always think about."

"What did he say about it?"

"He said no way has he cheated. Has no idea who she is."

A month later, Lissa tried again. She told Sarah the truth this time—that she had received a new tip from a relative who said James and Peyton were seen on a well site in James's truck. According to the relative, Peyton's uncle had spotted them while at work on the site. "He's a dirty fuckin dog and you should ditch his ugly ass!" Lissa texted.

"I need to know details," Sarah replied. "I have to present it to him, date, well site, anything else."

"Call me."

"I'm trying to call James."

"Keep me out of it."

That night, Lissa and Sarah spoke briefly. Sarah admitted she had been hearing rumors that Peyton was sleeping with James. Tiffany had said she didn't like the way Peyton looked at James, and drivers had also mentioned the rumors to Sarah, but Sarah dismissed them. Jill had begun attacking her on Facebook around the same time, and Sarah suspected the rumors were part of Jill's effort to discredit her. But in November 2012, when she and James joined Tex, Tiffany, and Peyton for a football game in Dallas, Texas, and James and Peyton disappeared together, Sarah began to wonder if the rumors were true.

Lissa instructed Sarah to delete their messages. "Ok, I'll be ok," Sarah wrote. "He knows I'm just sad, he's not an angry person."

The next night, Sarah wrote to Lissa, "Sometimes I look back at the past year and can't believe I've kept my sanity. I see my friends all moving to Cali and relaxing and I'm like wow our lives are so different. And mine nothing like I had ever expected."

"Just make sure you have a backup plan," Lissa replied.

"I know. Another thing I never thought I'd have to worry about."

"You don't talk to anyone about that shit do you?"

"No not at all."

"Gonna shower and hit the hay. You're a good person with a good heart."

"Thanks Lissa."

. . . . .

In November 2013, Peyton Martin gave birth to a boy. Sarah still denied the rumor that James was the father, while Lissa spent evenings on the phone trying to convince Sarah otherwise. The tip that James and Peyton had been spotted together on a well pad came, originally, from Peyton's uncle, but after Sarah asked the uncle about the sighting, she received a message from Peyton herself. "She told me to stop being insecure cause she would never want to be with someone who had a record like James," Sarah texted Lissa. Sarah had said something similar about Peyton: "James has a type, and she for sure is not it." Even if James had taken an interest in Peyton, Sarah could not see how Peyton would have gotten pregnant, since by that time Sarah had put James "on lockdown."

Lissa suspected Sarah was not confident in this belief. At the same time that she denied James's infidelity, Sarah privately insulted Peyton and Tiffany. Lissa responded gamely to these insults, both in the hope that it would lead Sarah to acknowledge the truth and to indulge her own disdain. According to Sarah, from the start of the Blackstone and Maheshu partnership, Peyton and Tiffany had taken a watchful interest in her and James: "I honestly think Tiffany wanted to be my friend cause she wanted to be white. She always talked shit about being native. Wanted to know what I wear, where I've traveled, and like everything about my life." Peyton, meanwhile, had a non-Indian father but "thinks she's the 'chairman's' daughter. I've heard her drop Tex's name all the time. She always says do you know who my dad is?! I'm like wtf Tex isn't your real dad. . . . She always calls the reservation 'rezy' she said it's her way of saying 'white trash.'"

"Rezzy means like ghetto. Not white trash," Lissa replied. "She of all people should know white trash when she sees it."

One day, Lissa asked Sarah to send her a portrait of James as a baby and, to make it as obvious as possible, placed the photo side by side with an image Peyton had posted on Facebook of her son. Sarah saw no resemblance—James was blonder with bluer eyes, she said—and, in reply, sent a photograph of Peyton's most recent boyfriend. He bore a striking resemblance to James, Lissa thought. "You know what Indians say," she wrote to Sarah. "All white guys look alike! Lol."

WITH THE FALL HAD COME a damp wind, and with the beginning of November, light snow. One weekend, Lissa took the dinghy to the sloughs east of White Shield to search for Ron Johnson, but she found them drained to their muddy bottoms. Instead, she drove to Watford City and south into the national grasslands. There, in a draw above the Little Missouri River, police had recently located the body of a worker who committed suicide. Lissa wondered what spirits the man had left behind. For hours, she wandered among the meadows and wooded coulees, but she felt nothing. For a moment, she wondered if KC was buried there. She decided he was not.

There was something bothering Lissa about Sarah. She felt that Sarah was withholding information from her, and at the end of November, Lissa learned what it was: Blackstone was working on the reservation again.

The tip came from Paul, the former Blackstone trucker who first told Rick and Lissa about Robert Delao. Paul had recently returned to the reservation to drive trucks for a different company, and one day, on a drilling site, he spotted a man who had worked with him at Blackstone—George Dennis, the driver Rick once mentioned to Lissa who was particularly close to James. Paul called Rick, who called Lissa. According to Rick, Paul said, "I saw George on a Petro-Hunt location, and he's in one of James's trucks, but it's called Bridgewater now."

As soon as Rick shared the news, Lissa googled Bridgewater. The company was licensed to a man based in Spokane, Washington. James's name was absent from the records, which did not surprise Lissa. She suspected the man was James's new front man, a face no one in the oil fields recognized. To confirm her suspicion, she called the Tribal Employment Rights Office. Indeed, Bridgewater was licensed to operate on the reservation. Listed with the company was a phone number. Lissa left a message, but no one returned her call.

The man who owned Bridgewater was named Doug Carlile. Sarah had never mentioned Carlile to Lissa. In fact, Sarah rarely spoke about work anymore. Several times she had insisted to Lissa that Blackstone stopped hauling water, but she had never spoken of other companies. Had James instructed Sarah not to mention Bridgewater, Lissa wondered, or had Sarah made this choice herself?

Lissa decided to reach out to Tex one more time, and in early December, she sent a text message to his cell phone: "You have to be concerned for your safety as am I but I think we could help each other out."

To Lissa's surprise, Tex replied, asking who she was. He didn't have her number.

"I'm a relative," Lissa wrote.

They spoke on the phone shortly after that. Lissa told Tex about Carlile and Bridgewater and gave him the date and time that George Dennis had been spotted at the well site. Tex told Lissa he would investigate.

She also called Carlile many times that week. When finally she reached him, "He didn't want to hear what I had to say," Lissa would recall. "I said, 'Hey, Doug, do you know you're a front person? Do you want to know what happened to the last front people?' He said, 'Lissa, everyone has a past.' I said, 'Yeah, I know everyone has a past. I have a past. I'm a felon. But I don't keep reliving my past. There's some people who rehabilitate to change their lives, and there are others who rehabilitate on paper to get to the next move, and that's the guy you're dealing with.' He kind of threw it in my face. 'Look, you have a past. How would you like it if people did that to you?' I said, 'It happens all the time. But there's a distinct line between who I am today and who I was. You're working with a guy that hasn't made any changes. You're going to become a target.' It didn't last long. I did most of the talking. He just interjected with one-liners: 'Everybody's got a past, Lissa.'"

·····

As WINTER APPROACHED, LISSA WENT less often to the reservation. Something was wrong with her body. Her ankles began to ache, and then the aching crept into her pelvis and spine and up her neck and into her fingers. Her hands and feet swelled to twice their size. One day, Lissa could walk only on the outer edges of her soles; the next, she could only crawl. She called in sick to the welding shop and, for days, remained in bed. The boys peered worriedly through a crack in her door until, one night, CJ entered, passed her a joint, and ordered her to smoke it. Her pain subsided. The next morning, Lissa drove northeast to the clinic on the White Earth Indian Reservation, where a doctor diagnosed her with rheumatoid arthritis, an autoimmune disease that inflames the joints, and prescribed medication. The swelling went down, but the pain lingered.

Her diagnosis was in one way a relief to Lissa. Her body rarely failed her, and yet she lived with a persistent dread that it would. All it took was a common cold for her to wonder if the consequences of her drug use were, at last, revealing themselves. Once, not long after she arrived at prison, she had tested positive for hepatitis C, but when she was tested again years later at White Earth, doctors found an antibody in her blood—proof she had been infected—but no active infection. It was odd, because Lissa had never been treated for hep C. In prison, a few women had been chosen for treatment, and Lissa was not one of them.* Among those chosen had been Jayta Schmidt, a white inmate five years older than Lissa who had been in prison for fifteen years before Lissa arrived. Jayta was serving a life sentence for shooting a woman in the stomach three times. "You think you're hot shit because you killed a bitch?" Lissa asked her once. "I didn't kill a bitch. I killed a

---

* Prisons have a constitutional obligation to provide medical care to inmates. North Dakota corrections officials were unclear as to why Lissa had not been offered treatment but suggested that some inmates diagnosed with hep C do not receive medication if their prison term is shorter than the length of time it would take to complete treatment. Lissa's term, however, was long enough.

snitch," Jayta replied. One day in the sewing room, Jayta taunted Lissa, claiming she had been chosen for the treatment because she was "worthy." "You're not worthy," Lissa replied. "They're just giving you a chance at life, and you're going to fuck it up anyway, because you've been here so fucking long you don't know anything outside these walls." Jayta had brandished her scissors. Lissa told her to "sit the fuck down." On the day Lissa left prison, Jayta had cried. Years later, Lissa read in the paper that Jayta killed herself after she was denied parole a third time. Lissa called the prison and learned no one had yet claimed Jayta's ashes. "Can I come get them?" she asked. "I'm probably her only friend on the outs." But the prison did not allow it.

As soon as Lissa could walk normally again, she returned to work. She still spent evenings on the phone, exchanging messages with the men and women in whose lives she had planted herself. She was not sure what inspired Tex to reply after ignoring her for more than a year. She had heard from Sarah that Robert Delao quit Maheshu after Tex blamed him for conspiring with James to steal more than $500,000 from the company. Did that have something to do with it? Was Tex, like Jed McClure, the investor from Chicago, hoping she could help him get his money back?

Lissa had not spoken to Jed in some time, but she had spoken to Darrik Trudell, the Homeland Security agent, who, with help from a U.S. postal inspector and an IRS agent, was making progress toward indicting James and Sarah for fraud. He could not share details with Lissa, but the case was seeming solid. The story he and his fellow investigators pieced together went like this: In June 2011, James introduced himself to Jed as the owner of Blackstone LLC, his last name spelled H-E-N-R-I-C-K-S-E-N. Jed ran a search on the name, checking for bankruptcies and other signs of financial irresponsibility and, when he found none, wired his initial investment. Jed then prepared a résumé for James to solicit other investors, spelling his name H-E-N-D-E-R-S-O-N as he had seen James also do. (Sarah changed it to H-E-N-R-I-K-S-E-N.) That September, Jed and Ryan Olness, the investor from Arizona, signed a joint venture with Blackstone LLC, entitling them each to a percentage of monthly gross profits. In the first few months, they received returns on their investments, but then the money stopped coming. Jed confronted James, who told him Blackstone was losing money. Meanwhile, Jed heard another story: According to company employees, James and Sarah had founded a new oil hauling company called Blackstone Crude. Jed suspected they used Blackstone LLC money to purchase trucks for the other venture. He began to search for associated companies and found at least five more registered to James and Sarah or their aliases. Even Sarah had used multiple names—"Sarah Hendrickson" and "Amy Peterson."

On December 12, 2013, Trudell and his fellow investigators interviewed an employee who had begun working for Blackstone on or about the day KC disappeared. The employee confirmed what Jed suspected: James and Sarah were running companies on the side, depositing profits into these companies' accounts while paying expenses with Blackstone LLC's. One side company, Blackwell LLC, employed James's best drivers as subcontractors; 20 percent of the profits these drivers earned benefited Blackstone, while the other 80 percent went into another account.

The next day, Trudell interviewed Ryan Olness in Arizona. By the time the agent returned to North Dakota, he believed he had evidence to charge James and Sarah with fraud.

Two days later, on the fifteenth of December, Doug Carlile was murdered.

A DENSE COLD SANK INTO the prairie. Lissa's body gripped with a pain so strong she could not sleep, so, in the early hours of December 16, she noticed a message from Tex Hall as soon as it appeared on her phone. Lissa wondered why the chairman was awake. Then she read his message: Carlile had been shot in his Spokane home by an unidentified gunman.

Lissa texted the news to Trudell, who called the Spokane Police Department. Lissa wanted to text Sarah, too, but told herself to wait.

Instead, she monitored the news. An article in *The Spokesman-Review* noted that Carlile and James had leased an allotment in Mandaree and hoped to drill for oil. James wanted to buy Carlile out, but Carlile had refused. Before he died, Carlile told one of his sons, "If I disappear or wake up with bullets in my back, promise me you will let everyone know that James Henrikson did it."

A day passed. Sarah still had not mentioned the murder. In lieu of asking about it, Lissa texted Sarah a photograph of a milkshake.

"Dairy Queen!" Sarah replied. "I love blizzards ha ha." Given the circumstances, Lissa thought Sarah sounded oddly unperturbed. She had been at the gym, she told Lissa, and she griped about Jill, who had filed for bankruptcy with her husband, which did not bode well for the defamation suit.

The next morning, when Sarah still had not mentioned the Carlile murder, Lissa texted Sarah a link to the *Spokesman-Review* article. "I'm worried about you," she wrote. "Did he tell you about this?"

"Yes," Sarah replied. "I can't believe it. It's so sad, and I just hurt for that wife." Doug's wife, Elberta, had been inside the house when the gunman killed her husband. Sarah knew Elberta and Doug. They were working on some deals together, Sarah said, and Sarah had once visited them in Spokane. The night of the murder, Sarah and James were at home in Watford City eating dinner with friends. The police called James to ask where he was, because Elberta had said she believed James killed her husband. "But it wouldn't make since," Sarah wrote to Lissa. "That guy owes us and a lot of other people a lot of money. Why would James do that if money is owed? Right?"

Lissa suddenly felt tired of playing games with Sarah. She urged Sarah to go home to her parents and to believe the news reports, which were sounding more certain of James's involvement in Carlile's murder. But as they combed together through articles posted on the *Spokesman-Review* website, the news drove Sarah only deeper into denial. "Wife says shooter was a stranger," one subhead read: "Carlile's wife told police that the couple had just returned home when an intruder confronted Doug Carlile in the kitchen. Already at the top of the stairs, the wife returned to the kitchen, where she saw a white man she didn't recognize, clad in all black and wearing gloves, pointing a gun at her husband."

That the shooter was white ruled out Robert Delao, who was Latino, but when Lissa pressed Sarah for other ideas, she had none. Sarah fixated on money. Doug, she claimed, owed her and James almost $2 million.

"What did the project consist of?" Lissa asked.

"Oil lease, buying and reselling. Flipping." Now that Doug was dead, Sarah did not know what would become of the lease. "Doug was telling everyone they were getting paid soon. Now . . . someone else will have to take over."

"Sarah," Lissa wrote the next day. "You know this is basically the same story as KC. . . . Do you question or second guess any of this?"

"There's no reason for James to do this," Sarah replied. "And Doug and his whole family knew about everything we went through with KC. James made a point to let them know, hey this is what people say about me. . . . Of course I stop and think about things. . . . But it just doesn't make since."

"I'm worried about YOU in this whole matter."

"I don't know what to think. I do worry for my safety."

"If James is putting hits out on people . . . what happens to you if someone retaliates? Everyone knows James is totally dependent on you! . . . That makes you a target!"

"I don't understand why James would put hits on these people. Unless he has a whole life I don't know about."

"Answer me this. Honestly. Do you think James has the ways and means to carry something like this out? Fuck whatever the motive could be!"

"Honestly, I've thought about it. If it's possible I sure don't know how, and he would have done a good job at hiding it from me."

"Your parents must be hysterical!!!!"

"My mom called me this morning, she's freaking out. Wants me to leave everything and leave ND."

"I'm in total agreement with your mom! If you were my kid, you'd be hog tied in the backseat going home!"

Sarah did not go to Washington—she could not "abandon" her husband, she told Lissa—and Lissa gave up on telling her to. Instead, Lissa told Sarah not to speak to the press, nor to police, before consulting a lawyer. News outlets had called with interview requests; Sarah blocked their numbers. On January 5, 2014, when two police detectives from Spokane dropped by her house in Watford City, Sarah did not speak to them, either.

On the fourteenth of January, police raided Sarah's house. Sarah texted Lissa on her way home from Denver, where she had been with James on a business trip: "Oh man Lissa, I'm scared. People are really trying to hurt James and or me."

Lissa was asleep. When she woke the next morning—the fifteenth, a Wednesday—she was on the couch in her welding boots, her phone in the limp palm of her hand. She was late to work and did not text Sarah until her break. Sarah had arrived home to find a door kicked in, clothes scattered across the bedroom floor, the lining of her jewelry case ripped out, and her cash, computers, documents, and guns gone.

"Guns? Wtf you guys doing with guns?" Lissa wrote.

Sarah explained that she had a concealed weapons permit and owned "a couple hand guns" and "then like a hunting rifle"—"nothing crazy." They chatted briefly about Robert Delao, who was at the house gathering his things, before Lissa had to go. "I'm so confused and sad with what's going on," Sarah wrote.

Lissa replied that she would text Sarah after work. She wrote Sarah that evening four times. The next day Lissa texted, "If you don't wanna talk just tell me. But don't let me worry about you."

Sarah did not reply.

Confessions

THE HOUSE AT 2505 SOUTH GARFIELD ROAD, IN SPOKANE, WASHINGTON, was often mistaken for elegant, though anyone who had been inside knew it was cheerless and tacked-together, having had too many owners who had tried to renovate and given up. It was three stories, white, with vaulted arches over the entry and a sunroom lit with Christmas lights. There were two sets of double doors that opened from a sunroom into the main house, so that when a city detective, Brian Cestnik, arrived at 7:46 on the evening of December 15, 2013, he could see, from the street, a television on in the living room and a fluorescent glow emanating from the kitchen. He saw no one inside the house. The paramedics were gone, Doug Carlile pronounced dead. An upper floor where the wife had hidden in a closet was dark. Officers lingered in the street as Cestnik spoke with them. The first had visited a neighbor, a woman, who saw a white van pass her house three times in the hour before she heard the gun. A second officer had been the first to enter the house. A third had followed a canine into the backyard and noted some curious signs: footprints; water marks splashed across a wooden fence; and a welding glove, dry, which the officer found strange, since the ground on which it lay was damp.

Cestnik took notes and then delivered a warrant to the home of a judge, who signed it before midnight. By the time he returned to Garfield Road, a forensic team was waiting. They videotaped the residence, first from the street, leafy and meandering, and then up the driveway past a white Mercedes SUV and a blue Ford truck. The night was still, and the video would appear even more silent and granular. Beyond the driveway, in the darkness of the yard, the frame blackened and brightened again to reveal the fence, the metal gate, and the welding glove, palm-up on the ground. Then through a door came a bleach of light: A man laid out on the kitchen floor.

Carlile wore only boxers and shoes, his clothes tossed off by the paramedics, and in the hours that passed, death had flattened his raw, puffed nakedness to the hardwood. When the detective bent to inspect the body, he noted blood marbling the pale of Carlile's back and caked around his mouth, crusted in the folds of his neck and the hair around his scalp. There were four entrance wounds on his torso and an exit above his belly button, while a fifth bullet had entered by a nostril and lodged inside his head.

Cestnik would say that except for a tooth flung across the room, Carlile's body was relatively intact. It was the house that disturbed him—the promise of its exterior, the shabbiness once inside—and stranger, still, its adornments: colored lights blinking on a plastic tree, Bible verses scribbled on sticky notes throughout the rooms. Christmas was the detective's favorite holiday. "Here we are at the happiest time of year, and this guy brutally murdered," he would say. The radio was tuned to carols and soft rock. No one had bothered to turn it off. At times, Cestnik caught himself humming, and then the music would stop, the horror pushing above the innocence.

THE LEAD DETECTIVE ASSIGNED THE case was a tall, gray-haired man in his early fifties, Mark Burbridge, whose manners once inspired a colleague to liken him to a pit bull. In the fifteen years he had worked in the homicide unit, and in his years before that as a cop, Burbridge had become famous among Spokane prosecutors for his bluntness and disregard for politics. One would describe a courtroom incident in which he "was practically in fisticuffs with an attorney." What made him "a very good detective," the prosecutor noted, was that he seemed utterly lacking in self-consciousness. Cestnik was comparatively shorter and more polite. He had been in the homicide unit only a year, but the two detectives had become close. They went on family vacations together.

Burbridge believed that the relatives of murder victims fit into two categories: those who could not contain their grief, who had "this deep, soul-wrenching, guttural cry," and those who remained silent out of shock. But when he arrived at his office the night of the murder and found Doug's wife, Elberta, waiting, he noted she fit neither category. "She was detached," as the detective put it. She insisted he take her to her husband so that she could pray over his body.

Burbridge added Elberta to his suspect list, which would include a dozen names by morning. At the top were the Carliles' four sons, each involved to varying degrees in their father's business, as well as Doug's partners and investors. Doug was a contractor and, in 2013, he had taken an interest in the oil fields. He founded two companies: the trucking service, Bridgewater, with James Henrikson, whom Doug knew from a prior job; and Kingdom Dynamics Enterprises, with James and two other partners in Spokane. That July, KDE bid on an oil lease on the Fort Berthold Indian Reservation. The lease was 640 acres, located in Mandaree. Another company had leased the land in 2008 and decided not to drill, since the surrounding land was already leased, and the cost of bringing a rig to a remote location would have reduced their profits. But Doug had not been deterred. He solicited partners, among them James and others whom he promised a full return on their investments within ninety days. Even Burbridge, who knew little about the oil fields, sensed Doug's promise had been unrealistic, and indeed, as Elberta now explained, Doug had struggled to

lure investors. James had grown frustrated. One day, during an argument, he held Doug by his shirt collar as if to strangle him.

After Elberta left Burbridge's office, the detective phoned Doug's
partners in Spokane, both of whom were out of town—"Homicide
detectives hate coincidences," he said. Then he called Tex Hall, whom
Elberta had mentioned. Tex struck Burbridge as eager to talk. He told
the detective that he had never met Carlile but knew of him, and that
James had stolen $500,000 from his company with the help of another
"crook" named Robert Delao.

At eleven o'clock that night, Burbridge dialed James. Their conversation began cordially. James confirmed he had an oil lease with
Carlile but denied having any trouble on the reservation. His tone
shifted when the detective asked if James had assaulted Doug. James
replied that Doug was a liar who owed him almost $2 million. He
insisted he had nothing to do with the murder. Burbridge added James
to the suspect list.

Over the following days, twenty detectives in the Spokane Police
Department were assigned to investigate the case. Burbridge appointed
one detective to work solely on identifying the van spotted by the
neighbor, which was also caught on a security camera installed on
the grounds of a neighboring school, and another to sort through a
mounting pile of tips. *The Spokesman-Review* had published a police tip
line, and although most of the tips investigators received were unhelp-
ful, some had promise. One caller knew Carlile from a previous business deal. In the weeks prior to the murder, the caller said, Carlile had
asked him to encourage a common acquaintance to invest in the oil
lease on Fort Berthold. The acquaintance had not been interested, but
Doug lied to his business partners claiming that the acquaintance was.
James had suspected Doug was lying and had his wife contact the
caller, who told Sarah the truth.

Burbridge was wary to name James a primary suspect just yet.
Elberta's behavior still bothered him, and there was the coincidence
with the business partners, though both men had good alibis. There
was also the man Tex had named—Robert Delao—whom Burbridge

had heard of before. Among Spokane investigators, Delao was known as "a hardcore gangster" who could talk his way out of trouble. In 2010, he had cooperated with federal prosecutors to put seventeen gang members in prison.

Burbridge did not have to call Delao, because to the detective's surprise, three days after Carlile's murder, the suspect appeared at the homicide unit and requested an interview.

Delao was short and stocky, in his midthirties, confident and "personable," Burbridge noted. He explained he had seen the tip line in the paper a day earlier and driven all night to Washington. Despite his journey, Delao looked perky, in a bright blue shirt and matching baseball cap.

They spoke in a small, yellow room, where Burbridge recorded the encounter on videotape. "Robert, I want to talk to you about Doug Carlile," Burbridge began.

"Correct," Delao said.

"James Henrikson."

"Correct."

"And everything that's been goin' on back there in North Dakota. You need to be honest with me today."

"That's what I'm here for," Delao said.

Delao explained that he had known Doug and had been shocked to hear of his death. He worried that given his criminal history in Spokane, investigators might suspect he was involved, and he hoped to preempt a misunderstanding. Delao had met Doug in 2013 while working for Tex. That summer, Tex received a contract to haul gravel, and Delao went looking for drivers. "First person to call me back was James," Delao told Burbridge. "He says, 'Hey, I've got some friends, and I'm helping them build their company up.'" Delao met James and Carlile for breakfast in Spokane. Carlile wanted "to do business with Tex," and Delao promised to arrange it. The job fell through— Carlile did not get his license to operate on the reservation in time— but Delao hired him later to haul water for Maheshu. The job paid $38,000. Afterward, Tex told Delao he did not want to hire Carlile anymore. Many Indian-owned companies hired subcontractors like Carlile, but some owners considered this cheating. Tex told Delao to hire truck drivers directly instead.

"Do you still work for [Tex]?" Burbridge interjected.

"I don't work for him now, no," Delao replied.

"How come you don't work for him?"

Delao laughed, blinked, moved a hand up and down on his thigh. "Well," he said, "when I first met him and his wife Tiffany, he showed me he had pictures of President Obama, Bill Clinton, Hillary Clinton. I was actually like, *Wow, this guy's doing something right.* I felt honored. I was happy. I felt like I was in the right place in my life. Once I got to know him, I—my opinion changed. There's a fine line between ambition and greed, and greed—he radiates it. I didn't want anything to do with it. I was tired of people calling with lawsuits. I was tired of people calling me, threatening my life because they weren't getting paid, and I was tired of his wife interfering with everything, including telling me what to tell law enforcement if I deal with them. It was just too much drama. James and Sarah and Tex and Tiff, they're like the Hatfields and McCoys. When you talk to them, they'll tell you each other is the worst piece of crap on the planet. What they will fail to tell you is they had an excellent relationship until—God, I didn't want to be fucking recorded—but James and the daughter had an affair, one that continues to this day. There's a child involved, too."

"How good of friends are you with James?" Burbridge asked.

Delao sighed. "You know, he's a pathological liar, so I'm simply someone he can use as his plan to make money. That's the honest-to-God truth right there."

"How did you end up in North Dakota?"

It was "James's recommendation," Delao said. The manager of Maheshu Energy "could not run the company," so James suggested to Tex that Delao take his place. Delao felt comfortable on the reservation, since his daughter's mother was a member of the Spokane Tribe of Indians. "I've dealt with tribal councils, and, you know, [James] thought that I might fit in, be able to speak the lingo. And it worked.

I did well, real well. I could relate to the Natives out there. I could go to the powwows, and at the same time, I'm not intimidated, so it was easy for me to organize the truckers."

"I talked with Tex. He's telling me there's over half a million dollars in fraud that went on, and [Tex is] talking with Homeland Security and the IRS."

"I understand. And you know what, if it goes to court, I will be happy to testify in my defense. I did not take anything from that man."

"What do you know about James and his criminal activity?"

"Well, his record's insane."

"I don't care about his record. I care about him right now."

"He's a pathological liar. He got involved in that disappearance with KC."

"Did you have anything to do with that?"

"No, hell no. Fuck no."

Burbridge sat up in his chair. He had dressed that day in a white button-down shirt, khaki pants, and hiking boots. "Can I get a DNA swab from you?" he said. "Won't hurt, just a little DNA swab on the inside of your cheek." Delao opened his mouth as Burbridge tore open a small package, leaned forward in his chair and, with the precision of a dentist, stuck a swab in Delao's mouth. Burbridge placed the swab in a plastic bag.

"Did you shoot Doug?" Burbridge asked.

Delao straightened. "No, I had nothing to do with it."

"I've got to tell you, I'm pretty sure James had everything to do with it."

"You know, I know it sounds bad, I'm his friend, but I don't think he did. I really don't think he did."

"Well there's no doubt Doug's involved in a whole ton of fraud back there," said Burbridge. "Let me tell you how this works. You've been involved in big business before, involving dope and other stuff. The big guy threatens everyone below to keep their mouth shut no matter what, but guess who's always the first one to talk."

"Yeah, he puts everyone away," said Delao.

"He puts everyone away. I'm letting you have a chance to get in front of this."

"That's why I'm telling you, honestly, I'm sure somebody is going to get caught, and you'll see, my name is not in this."

"Did he ever call you up and say, 'Hey, I need this guy taken care of'?"

"No. No. No."

"I got to tell you, you look scared to death."

"Look what we're talking about here!"

"Let's talk about the missing guy. If James didn't do it, who did?"

"I know something happened to him," said Delao. "Obviously. I never got to meet him, but everyone said he was a real charismatic guy. Real happy. Like how I am normally. Right now, I'm a nervous wreck. But normally I'm happy. I'm smiling. I'm all charm. I was told he was the same way. Somebody like that doesn't just disappear."

"Did James ever talk about how mad he was at the guy?"

"No, that's the thing. He told me they were friends, and he just went away. That was it. His wife says she doesn't know anything."

"Tell me about Sarah."

"How can I put it? Sheltered. The way she's described herself to me, she went to college. I believe it was something to do with hotels. And I know everything is in her name. I know that. Because she's the one with decent credit."

"Is she manipulative?"

"Of course. Yes. Like most females with charm, yes."

"How did you guys meet?"

"The gym. When I first met James, obviously he's on steroids, and he looked like he had his shit together. He works out, carries himself like he has millions, which he doesn't. So when I first met him, I was impressed. I said, if I can pick this guy's brain, I'll have it made. I honestly thought that by hooking up with him, I could possibly have the things he said he had."

"James talks a big time, but he's not big time," said Burbridge.

Delao nodded. "He's a pussy."

"He wants somebody dead, he knows somebody who knows dangerous people, right?"

"I know what you're getting at, but look at this: I cooperated"—with federal investigators in 2010. "I put away seventeen people."

"I'm aware of that," Burbridge said. "I want to make something clear. I'm not after you. I'm after the truth, and if you're caught up in my truth, I'm going to destroy you, but you want to be a friend and up-front, I'm willing to work with you."

"I know you think I'm in the loop, and I'm not," Delao said.

Burbridge leaned forward in his chair again, took off his glasses, rubbed his eyes, the movement so deliberate it appeared scripted. "I got to tell you, you look scared to death, my friend," he said. "I'm not kidding you. I think you're part of this. Minimum, James called and said, 'I need help,' and you hooked him up with somebody."

"No. Like I said, no."

"If that's what happened, and now you're like, 'Holy shit, he really did it,' you need to step forward on this and get yourself in front, because I guarantee you, I'm coming, and those people who did the shooting, they're going to roll back on everybody. If we get James first, I guarantee you he's going to shit his pants and puke his guts on the table for me when they start talking life and the death penalty."

"I know. I know," Delao said. "I've been through it, so I know."

THE INTERVIEW WAS PERHAPS MOST remarkable for the way Delao spoke about the oil fields, particularly about Fort Berthold. Even in the wake of the Carlile murder, as the sad fate of his life was becoming clear, the reservation seemed to contain for him a promise that after all the mistakes he had made, he would be redeemed. "Opportunities like that don't just come," Delao told Burbridge. "My only experience in life, really, is working for Tex Hall. Let's say I didn't have the oil field. What would I do? Sell cars? North Dakota is the only place in our country right now where somebody like me can go and make big money." His annual salary at Maheshu had been $75,000.

Later, Delao would insist under questioning that when he called James in January 2012, two months after his own release from prison, he had not wanted to go back to selling drugs. He wanted to go to the reservation, he explained, to make "an honest living."

In this respect, Delao was likely telling the truth, but the stories he would tell over the following months would lever open a gap between this truth and his ambitions. It would become obvious that Delao had found it harder than he expected to distance himself from crime. One could sense him trying in the way he described the oil fields: "You have these guys living in their trucks in the middle of nowhere. They're fighting depression on a daily basis, and now you're giving them six-figure salaries. So they're creating a breed of people, walking around with these false egos. They're causing problems. I wouldn't raise my kids there."

Whether or not Delao grasped the irony of his statements, it was obvious he had worked hard. He put in eighteen-hour days at Maheshu while also doing odd jobs at the chairman's ranch. "I knew all his fucking horses by name," Delao said. He considered Tex the gate-keeper to his own material success—a belief similar to the one that drew James and Sarah to Tex, and then drew the Carliles.

That same third week in December, Cestnik drove to Moses Lake, a town southwest of Spokane, where Elberta Carlile had gone to stay with her son after the murder. Seated in her son's living room, Elberta described for Cestnik a day that past July when she had gone with her husband to the reservation. They had met a tribal member, whose family allotment they intended to lease, at Better B's in New Town and then stopped at the Bureau of Indian Affairs office to place a bond—a requirement before their lease could be approved. "We were sitting there in the office, and there's a poster up on the wall of James and Sarah," Elberta told Cestnik. "I about fell over. I said, 'Doug, look at this.' There was something about criminal activity."

Cestnik brought up a copy of the flyer on his phone and handed it to Elberta. He had found a link to it on the Internet a day earlier while searching for information about James. The word BEWARE was

printed in large letters across the top. "Does that look familiar?" Cestnik asked. "Is that the one that was on the wall?"

"Yes," said Elberta. "They're saying a man disappeared and was
never found, and it was after he had an argument with James over
business and money. I'm saying, 'Doug, do you realize? This man?'
And he goes, 'We'll talk about it when we get out of here.' And I said,
'What are we doing?' I took the poster down so I could read it and
keep it and have proof of it. Doug just told me, 'I knew James had
problems, but I didn't know about this. I just wanted to give him a
second chance in life.' And I'm freaking out. We'd even stayed at their
house on that trip. So we go back to the house, and I just want to ask
them what's going on, and I'm not sure if I should."

"Did you ask them?"

"Yes, I did."

"What did they say?"

"They just looked at each other. They didn't hardly say anything.
They said, 'Well, part of that stuff is true.' So when I got home, I
started doing research, and I found out a lot of stuff that appeared to
be true."

Elberta spoke cautiously, constantly revising, fretfully wiping tears.
She was a tall, strong-looking woman, with thin hair that fell to her
waist. After she and Doug went home to Spokane, she explained, the
land deal fell apart. Their lease was approved, but by September, they
still had not found a loan to finance the drilling. One investor
demanded she be repaid in full even though the drilling had not yet
begun. Doug did not have the money. He worked constantly, but for
reasons Elberta did not understand, the truck operation acquired few
contracts. Bridgewater, Elberta said, never earned the Carliles a cent.
Doug spent much of that fall in North Dakota, while Elberta, disturbed by the flyer, did not follow him. They spoke every day. Doug
wanted to rent Tex's shop, or at least park his trucks there, since he
believed a relationship with Maheshu would lend Bridgewater, as it
had Blackstone, an advantage on the reservation. James warned Doug
not to reach out to Tex, but Doug ignored him. One day, as Elberta

recalled, Doug phoned Maheshu. "And you know who answers? Robert Delao. So, Doug tells him, 'I need to talk to Tex,' and Robert says, 'He's not in right now.' Doug wasn't off the phone ten minutes, and he's getting all these texts from James. James flew into this rage, and we didn't get it. *How did that happen?* Then we got it: Delao was a spy."

Delao entertained Doug's inquiry anyway. They texted regularly, and each time, Delao promised he would show Tex a contract, but he never did. Delao even met Doug once in Watford City, in a parking lot outside a cell phone store, where they discussed another contract that also never materialized.

Doug called Tex again later in the fall. "This time we got ahold of Tex's wife, girlfriend, whatever she is to him," Elberta told Cestnik. "We needed Tex on our side, because he's with the BIA and all that, but we knew he would either have nothing to do with us because we knew James or he would help us. So Doug told her, 'I'm going to be doing work over there, and I'd like to rent your shop.' She said, 'What do you know about Bridgewater?' And he thought, *Oh my gosh, they know.* So he said, 'I started Bridgewater. I got in with some despicable people, I didn't know what I was getting into, and I'm no longer part of that.' All the sudden Tex comes on the phone, and he said, 'Good thing you said that Doug, or I would have never spoken to you again. James embezzled $514,000 from me.' Doug told him, 'The strange thing is, last time I called your office, I got ahold of Robert Delao, and James started texting me.' That's when Tex realized Delao was a spy for James."

Elberta believed Doug had been scared but would not admit it. Even after the incident in which James held him by the collar of his shirt, Doug had not been deterred. "James said he was going to take him out if he didn't get out of the way," Elberta explained, and yet she and her husband had continued to believe the deal would work out in their favor. Doug assured her that once they got a loan, he would pay off or buy out their investors. The Carliles were deeply religious and believed that if they prayed, God would reward them. Whenever Doug ignored James's calls, James tried Elberta instead. Once, she texted James, "The Lord is in control. If God is for us, nobody can be against us."

James did not have patience for their proselytizing. "You need to pull your weight. I will not carry you, Doug," he texted one day.

"Someday grasshopper you will learn that friendship is worth more than money," Doug replied.

"Nothing is worth more than money, only my relationship with God and my wife," James wrote. "God, wife, money, friends."

The Carliles had one more option. Through a broker, Doug had found an investor in Dallas, Texas, who had a record of funding oil and gas production in Oklahoma, Louisiana, and the Appalachian Basin. The investor thought the lease looked promising. An Exxon subsidiary had successfully drilled land surrounding the lease, and from seismic data the investor estimated that if KDE drilled into the Bakken, as well as into a deeper formation called Three Forks, their wells would produce up to thirty-five million barrels of oil. In early December, the investor negotiated an agreement with Doug. When Doug shared the news, Elberta told Cestnik, "We were sitting on the couch holding hands. He said, 'I will know by Sunday about the money.'" Doug also told Elberta that he believed James was involved in criminal activity. After he got the money, Doug planned to go to the FBI.

"He never told you what he had on James?" Cestnik asked.

"No," Elberta said and began to cry. "We had a lot going for us, because we had God going for us, but we didn't have the money, and in this world, you have to have the money."

A SNOWSTORM WHIPPED ACROSS THE northern prairie on the day that the Spokane detectives, Mark Burbridge and Brian Cestnik, arrived in North Dakota. It was fifty degrees below zero with wind chill. They had stayed the night at a hotel in Montana, where, by morning, their tires had frozen, thumping loudly for the first hour of their drive. The wind blew so hard that everything became white. Twice they had to stop in the road to wait for the snowy curtains to part, and when they came to Watford City, night had fallen, gas flares casting everything in orange.

The next morning, they ate eggs in the lobby of the hotel, empty but for an eighteen-year-old with a bad windburn who had worked his first shift in the oil fields that night. Then they drove north on the main street. "There were guys everywhere," Cestnik would recall. "All the mom-and-pop stores were shut down, sold, and every business had to do with the oil field." Wherever the detectives stopped, they asked after James and Sarah. Many people claimed to have heard of them, including a bartender who said when Cestnik mentioned Sarah, "Oh, you mean 'Bentley'?" The woman knew Sarah from the gym and often spotted her driving an expensive car around town.

When they arrived at James and Sarah's house at the north end of Watford City, they noted it was larger than other houses in the neighborhood, with gray siding and a wide porch with a view of the road. Cestnik knocked; a woman answered. Delao was inside, mildly surprised to see them. James and Sarah were not home, Delao said, but would return to the house in an hour. The detectives chatted briefly with Delao, and indeed, when they returned, two matching pickup trucks were parked side by side in the driveway.

Burbridge later described the encounter: "We went in the breezeway area, through the garage. I saw the Bentley sitting on flat tires. That's one way to treat a car that beautiful. We knocked, and Sarah came to the door. She knew that we had been there already. She snarled at us, gave me the dirtiest look. She said, 'You want my husband. I'm not going to talk to you,' and stormed off. Didn't even say, 'Wait here.' Nothing polite. I'd never met her before. She was extremely aggressive. It didn't surprise me. I'm used to dealing with major, major bad guys. You don't give her anything, because you don't want her to read you. So it's thirty seconds, forty seconds, and James comes to the door. It's a screen door, and the inner door's cracked. He was a big son of a bitch. I'm a big guy. I used to be a major weight lifter in college, and it was clear to me that he can move some weight.

He benches five plus, probably. And he leaned out the door, and I introduced myself, and he slapped me on the shoulder. He said, 'Hey, too bad you drove all that way. My attorney told me not to talk to you.' That was the end of it. He shut the door in my face. I grew werewolf fangs. I wanted to rip that arm off that shoulder so bad. It was very clear to me at that point that he was my number one suspect."

IF IT OCCURRED TO BURBRIDGE to connect the murder of Carlile with the disappearance of Kristopher Clarke, he soon forgot about it. He did not remember Darrik Trudell, the young Homeland Security agent, calling the morning after the murder, though Trudell insisted he did. Burbridge did remember Lissa's calls—and remembered ignoring them. He would claim the first time he heard of Clarke was a week after Carlile was murdered, when Cestnik discovered the flyer. In any case, it was after Burbridge saw the flyer that he phoned the North Dakota Bureau of Criminal Investigations. Steve Gutknecht was out of the office; Burbridge was told to call Trudell. He called but would not remember what they spoke about. Neither Burbridge nor Cestnik told Trudell when they went to Watford City. Clarke was not his case, Burbridge said—"We're not searching for his evidence."

None of the evidence Burbridge gathered pointed clearly at James. It was only a hunch, a mass of accusations, that placed James at the top of his suspect list—hardly a sure bet, since on January 10, 2014, new evidence pointed at someone else.

Detectives had submitted the welding glove found in the Carlile's backyard for DNA analysis, and got a match: Timothy Suckow, a white male, fifty years old, with a record of burglary and assault. Burbridge had never heard of Suckow before. In a records search, he learned that Suckow lived with his wife on the east side of Spokane. Burbridge assigned officers to surveil the suspect's house, and on the thirteenth of January, officers followed Suckow to the offices of a company that cleaned up hazardous waste, where Suckow worked, and arrested him in the parking lot. While Suckow was detained at the police station, officers searched his house, where they found twenty guns, several black balaclavas, and a single welding glove. Meanwhile, the detective whom Burbridge had assigned to locate the van learned it belonged to the same company for which Suckow worked. Detectives searched the van and, in a center console, found a handwritten list on college-ruled paper:

glove?
badge
trenchcoat
2 boots
led lite
radios w

The appearance of a new suspect baffled Burbridge. In a month of interviews, no one had mentioned Suckow. None of the Carliles, nor Doug's partners, nor Tex had heard of or recognized him. In photos taken upon his arrest, Suckow's skin looked pale, his eyes sunken and dark. He had a shaved head and wide, muscular shoulders. Reporters suggested he was mentally ill, that he believed the world was coming to an imminent end, but no one could make sense of his involvement in the murder. Only one thing connected Suckow to the other suspects: James's number was listed in his phone.

Now Burbridge faced the same dilemma Gutknecht and Trudell had encountered before. While it seemed obvious that James was connected to Carlile's murder, the detective had hardly enough evidence to gain a warrant for James's arrest, let alone charge him with a violent crime. In the middle of January, Burbridge called Trudell, who offered an idea: Federal agents could use the evidence they had gathered while investigating James for fraud to obtain a warrant to search James's house. In December, a Blackstone employee had told Trudell that James had a gun safe, even though James's prior felony convictions prohibited him from keeping firearms. Burbridge accepted Trudell's offer, and on January 14, 2014, Trudell and his fellow agents executed the search warrant. As Sarah and James made their way home from Denver, officers raided their house, confiscating three handguns, two shotguns, and an AR-15. Over the following days, authorities monitored James, who fled to a Bismarck suburb where he stayed with Peyton Martin. On January 18, Trudell arrested him.

James did not "puke his guts on the table" as Burbridge had suggested to Delao he would. Rather, on the day of his arrest, James evaded Trudell's questions. In a video recording of the interrogation, he would appear stiff, his voice a strange, bending whisper as if he were letting air out of a balloon. "I guess nothing really happened," James offered. "There's something on the Internet, and then everybody starts to hate you." He changed the subject to Sarah.

"Let's talk about Washington, how you hired someone to have a guy killed," Trudell said.

James laughed. "No," he said. He mentioned Sarah again.

"What are we talking about there?" asked Trudell.

"Murder. They're going to take her out."

Trudell sounded annoyed. "Tell me what you want, and let's start there. You can't say that the boogeyman is going to get her, and we call witness protection. You give us something actionable. Why would someone want to kill Sarah?"

James did not answer the question.

It did not take long for investigators to realize that the case depended on Robert Delao and Timothy Suckow, the suspect whose DNA had been found on the welding glove. In January, Suckow was assigned a public defender, and by early March, he agreed to meet prosecutors for a "free talk" in which he would tell the whole story of the Carlile murder. Unless he lied, nothing he said could be used against him in court.

Trudell flew to Spokane for the talk, but almost as soon as he arrived, the deal fell apart. State and federal prosecutors were jockeying for jurisdiction in the case. In the meantime, Suckow had asked if he could get a better deal if he confessed to another murder. For the first time, it occurred to investigators that perhaps Suckow had also killed Kristopher Clarke.

The day after the talk fell through, Burbridge and Cestnik visited Delao at his house in Spokane. They told him he still had a chance to "beat Suckow to the table" and offered to find him an attorney. Delao agreed, and on March 2, 2014, he met with federal agents and an assistant U.S. attorney for the Eastern District of Washington.

The story Delao told on that day diverged from the one he had previously shared with Burbridge: In January 2012, when he called James looking for work, James had not, in fact, offered a job but rather asked Delao if he knew anyone who could beat a person up. Delao told James he would think about it. "The last thing I was trying to do is call my old friends, because I'd done this cooperation," Delao explained to prosecutors. He worried his friends would kill him, but he wanted the job, so he called a former cellmate who suggested Suckow. Delao once had worked for Suckow, stripping asbestos from buildings, and gave him a call. Suckow sounded interested. James bought him a train ticket to Williston.

In March 2012, a few weeks after Suckow returned from North Dakota, Delao met him at a bar in Spokane: "I said, 'So what did you think of North Dakota?' What I wanted was, 'Does James really have all the money he was talking about, and am I really going to be able to get a job out there?'" Suckow acted cagey with Delao and said he had done "more than he signed up for."

That same March, James told Delao he had more work, so Delao took a train to Williston. The work was not what Delao had hoped. James asked him to locate a kilo of heroin, which they would press into pills imitating the prescription opiate Oxycontin. A kilo of heroin could produce twenty thousand pills, which could sell for more than a hundred dollars apiece. Delao struggled to find a source, and after two weeks, James "fired" him. But that June, James asked Delao to return. Ryan Olness, the Blackstone investor from Arizona, met Delao in Williston. George Dennis and Justin Beeson, two truck drivers for the company, joined them. They drove to a drilling site serviced by Trust-land, the rival trucking company owned by the tribe's former lawyer, Steve Kelly. On James's orders, they vandalized storage tanks and opened valves, letting hundreds of barrels of oil spill out.

James never mentioned KC to Delao, though he often talked about wanting to kill other people—Steve Kelly, Ryan Olness, and Jed McClure, the investor who was suing James and Sarah. In July 2012, James made Delao a full-time employee at Blackstone. Delao's primary task—locating a source of heroin—remained the same, and he reached out to a friend in Spokane, Todd Bates, who said he had a hookup in Chicago. Meanwhile, James was having problems with a truck driver and solicited Bates to kill him. That November, Bates traveled to Watford City four times, and each time he failed to kill the driver, James grew more frustrated with Delao. Finally, in January 2013, Delao, Bates, James, and Peyton Martin, Tex Hall's stepdaughter, traveled to Chicago, where James purchased $20,000 worth of heroin. Their dealer was a former Vice Lord called "the Wiz." James asked Bates to ask the Wiz to murder Jed McClure. The Wiz agreed to do it for $25,000. In February, he met Bates at the Chicago airport, where Bates gave him a down payment of $9,500. The Wiz took the money and ran.

Around the same time, oil companies began dropping contracts with Blackstone. As BEWARE flyers appeared on the reservation, drivers went to work for other water haulers. Tex was losing confidence in James and Sarah, but after he ended their business partnership, he allowed Delao to remain at Maheshu. Some believed Delao was James's spy, but it was Peyton who "would tell James everything," Delao explained. "Peyton was James's inside guy. Anything that ever happens at Tex's house, Peyton reports to James, so James is always one step ahead of Tex." In fact, Delao rarely spoke to James, he said. "Tiffany told me I wasn't allowed to talk to him. It was because of the whole affair. She would constantly go through my phone to be sure I wasn't talking to James or her daughter. When Homeland Security"—Darrik Trudell—"and Mr. Gutknecht came to Tex's office to talk about the KC situation, I was rehearsed by Tiffiany Johnson. She said, 'When law enforcement comes, one, you cannot mention my daughter. Two, anything negative about Tex, clam up.'" Without telling Tiffiany, Delao still met James now and then at the gym in Watford City, where they conferred about Peyton, Suckow, and eventually Carlile.

Delao told the story eagerly, betraying none of his earlier reluctance, and so, in April 2014, when Suckow made his own confession, prosecutors were struck by the difference in the two witnesses' tones. In a recording of the confession, more than four hours long, it would be difficult to make out the hit man's words, which conveyed an immeasurable sadness. Suckow appeared unusually small in the video, sunken into his red jumpsuit. He spoke slowly, rocking back and forth, rattling his stomach chains, and when he cried, he cast his eyes toward the ceiling, his bottom lip quivering uncontrollably.

Before Suckow had gone to North Dakota in 2012, he had never killed anyone, he explained. As he understood it, James had hired him to "take care of" Steve Kelly, the owner of the rival trucking company, so that "he could have the whole rez to himself." Suckow had decided he would simply beat Kelly up. On February 21, 2012, he had taken the train to Williston, where James met him. They slept that night in Watford City. The next morning, James drove Suckow to Maheshu, and that was when James's request changed. "He started telling me about KC," Suckow said, "how he was threatening to leave the company and take some of the truckers with him. That's when he asked me to kill him. I didn't even think he was serious. When we got to the shop, he wanted to introduce me to everybody. I was like, I don't know about that shit.

"It was the morning," Suckow continued. "When we went into the shop it was empty except some garbage, some cans, recycling in the corner. He was telling me, 'I'll bring KC back here, and you just put a choke hold on him.' Even though I was a big guy, I didn't feel very comfortable about—I'm not a fighter. I'm not very confident about my strength. And he told me he carries a gun. I said, 'I'm not going to choke him out if he's going to carry a gun.' He said I could hit him with something. I looked around the shop, and all I could see was those floor jacks."

Suckow looked up. His lip quivered. His chin furrowed. His voice rose and began to shake. "I went back over by the door. I still remember. I didn't believe it was real. There was a part of me that just didn't believe it. And I stood by the door." Suckow began to cry. "I shook KC's hand. I didn't think—I didn't think—" He stopped, looked around the table. "I'm really not violent," he said.

PROSECUTORS SHARED THE STORY WITH Jill, leaving little out, and when Jill repeated the story to Lissa, they cried together on the phone. Suckow had known that KC was dead when his last hit "went soft," he said. He had emptied a garbage can and removed a plastic bag, which he wrapped around his victim's head, and pulled KC into a bathroom, where he left him while he mopped up the blood. When Suckow finished, he drove KC's truck to Watford City and returned to Maheshu with James and George Dennis, the truck driver with whom James seemed close. They stuffed KC into a cardboard box, which Suckow sealed with masking tape, while George backed up his truck to the garage. They drove, again, to Watford City and south into the badlands, turning west on a dirt road. George parked at the head of a ravine, and James and Suckow continued on foot. The ground was wet and soft. Suckow dug a hole as deep as his chest. It had begun to snow when he returned to the truck, and the box, damp, broke when he lifted it. He carried KC like a child, cradled in his arms.

Lissa sensed relief in Jill, but it was tempered by the fact that her son's body was still missing. The only evidence linking James to the first murder was circumstantial, one man's word against another, and without proof that KC was dead, the likelihood that they could prosecute James for KC's murder was alarmingly low.

In May 2014, investigators flew Suckow to North Dakota twice. Although he led them to what he believed was the burial area, he could not find KC's body. Trudell said Suckow had made an honest effort. Later, investigators returned to the site with dog teams and backhoes, but they could not find a body, either.

Lissa traded fewer messages with Trudell that spring. When she asked him if he knew where Sarah had gone, he told her he did not. Lissa assumed, correctly, that Sarah had been taken into protective custody. She missed Sarah—or perhaps it was something else she missed. After Sarah's silence, after James's arrest, after Robert's and Timothy's confessions, Lissa was no longer the keeper of secrets, the one who knew more than anyone else.

In the beginning, she was grateful that James would be prosecuted, and when she heard that investigators were preparing for a trial, she was moved nearly to tears. "Thank you from the bottom of my heart," she texted Trudell.

"No problem. Thanks," he replied.

The fear she had felt leaving her apartment dissipated without her noticing. In the winter and spring of 2014, she spent fewer weekends on the reservation, and when she went home to the apartment after work, she often fell into a deep, uninterrupted sleep. She felt exhausted, sick, but there was also a certain darkness that enveloped her during this time. One afternoon, Lissa woke to find the apartment empty. She called for her children, but they had gone out. She drove to the grocery store and thought, as she wandered the aisles, that even the people she knew looked unfamiliar: "Everybody moved on without me. I got so wrapped up in this case, and when I looked up, everybody was gone."

Lissa wondered if Shauna had been right—one addiction for another, the same person, only sober.

To feel unnecessary, cast off, made Lissa desperate, and she became strident, even boastful with investigators. Burbridge still did not return her calls and, once, when he accused her by email of leaking information to the press—falsely, it was Jill—Lissa replied angrily, "Focus on connecting James and his crew. I've been following this guy for nearly two years."

She did not speak with Steve Gutknecht, the Bureau of Criminal

Investigations agent, and knew of his work on the case only through
Jill. Then, in May, Lissa heard from a source on the reservation that
Suckow was in the badlands. She mentioned this to Jill, who mentioned it to Gutknecht, who called Lissa the next day. He wanted to
know how Lissa knew, but she would not tell him. "He thought someone in law enforcement was giving out the information," she later
recalled. "I said, 'You know what, I'm going to tell you something. I've
got eyes all over fucking Fort Berthold. Anytime shit goes down, I get
a private message about it, or people call. I know what the fuck is
going on.' He said, 'So you're not going to cooperate?' I said, 'No.'"
A few minutes later, Trudell texted Lissa, demanding that she call
him. When she did, Lissa thought she could hear Gutknecht in the
background. "I told Darrik, 'Fuck Steve Gutknecht.' Darrik was like,
'Well, I figured you'd talk to me.' I said, 'You know what? Tell him I
heard it from you. Tell him it was you.'"

That Lissa still received tips from people on the reservation was
true. She traded messages regularly with Tex, though he seemed to
evade her attempts to speak in person, and he rarely offered anything
of substance, remarking mostly on the weather and on an occasional
visit from investigators. Once, he told her to come by his house, but
when she did, no one answered the door. She circled the house, knock-
ing on windows, until at last Tiffany came out holding, in Lissa's
words, "some homely little-ass dog." Tiffany told Lissa that Tex was
not home and retreated inside.

In the spring, ice broke on the lake and lodged in the banks like
shards of glass. Rain fell. The roads thawed and cracked.

Lissa's joints ached. She wanted to sweat, to pray, and told this to
her friend who lived in Sanish, Tiny Crows Heart, who said he would
gather branches to build the lodge. Waylon, her cousin, said he would
join, since he knew the songs, as would Micah, since he still went
everywhere with his mother. They met at Tiny's trailer one afternoon
in May. A fire burned in a low, gray pit. Lissa changed into a cotton
dress and knelt by the lodge Tiny had constructed. With a thumb and
forefinger, she stripped sage from its stem, rolling the leaves between

the palms of her hands and packing them into her pipe. Then she lit another plug of sage, placed it in an abalone shell, and smudged the pipe and herself. She spun once around before entering the lodge. It was so small that she curled her back to fit, and when she emerged, she was soaked, stinking of medicine.

Sanish is on a high cliff at the north end of the lake, where the river pinches to its narrowest point. The slope is steep at first and then fans out onto grassy bluffs some hundred feet above the water. Lissa walked out onto one of the bluffs and sat. Micah, Waylon, and another companion spread out behind her, while Tiny tended the fire. From where she rested, Lissa could see the blinking colors of the casino, the pickup trucks parked on the beach, the dim lights of oil workers camped in the trees, the gleaming white yacht on its fateful perch, and the shadows of boats drifting in toward the marina. Darkness came. Flares brightened on the horizon like tiny rising suns. Waylon had forgotten his star quilt, so Lissa had given him hers. Now, as her sweat cooled and stiffened her dress, a chill sank into her. She had only her pipe, which she held in her lap, and two horse skulls, which she had placed on the ground next to her. The moon rose and shimmered on the lake. Lissa tried to pray. She found that when she focused on the words to the songs, she forgot the cold, but then Micah called out to her, and the cold returned, throbbing.

"Mom, are you okay?" he said.

"Shhht," she said, quieting him.

She thought of the sun dance. When dancers "entered the circle," it was said, they should be prepared to die. Now, as Lissa shivered, she prayed for her children, for Shauna, for the murdered and missing, and as she prayed, she heard footsteps breaking across the grass behind her. She wanted to turn around, but she gripped her pipe and remained still. Suddenly, Lissa was no longer in her body but watching herself from a hillside above. She saw she was flanked by two gray horses. Or were they people? Now the horses were gone, and a man and a woman were standing in their place, the woman bent to whisper in her ear. *We hear your prayers,* the woman said.

· · · · ·

Lissa heard a rattling breath and opened her eyes. Micah was
curled on the ground beside her. He had draped a quilt over her legs,
and when the sun rose, they hid themselves from the light, and when
they woke on the second morning, they were nestled in the quilt. The
colors of the casino still blinked. The trucks had not quit their groan-
ing. And beneath the Sanish cliffs, a body floated in the lake. A fisherman spotted it from the beach.

PART II

Bust

13

Us Against the World

THE DECLINE IN THE PRICE OF OIL COINCIDED WITH SOME UNSETTLING events on Fort Berthold—first, the reappearance of Daniel Mossett, a thirty-two-year-old tribal member who had been missing for months when, on the morning of May 19, 2014, a fisherman noticed his body floating in the lake. In the following weeks, the price of oil would fall below a hundred dollars a barrel and keep falling. The state medical examiner would determine that Mossett died of suicide and exposure, though it was rumored he was found with a bag bungeed around his head, which suggested he had been murdered. Lissa had taken an interest in his case and suspected his death was at least more complicated than the autopsy made it seem. And so his became another unresolved story whose fragments drifted like orphans amid the boom, clinging to other unfinished stories or disappearing altogether.

His funeral was held at the community center in Twin Buttes, where Mossett was from. As mourners followed his casket to the cemetery, the procession stalled on the edge of town where two oil workers had stopped in the road chatting, oblivious to the line of cars.

A mourner got out and spoke to them; the workers moved aside. Lissa at first felt angry with the workers, but then they took off their hats and bowed their heads, and the sight of this made her cry.

Tex Hall attended the funeral as well but left before Lissa could speak with him. Months earlier, news of another unsettling event had landed like a small bomb on the reservation—the murder of Doug Carlile.

For weeks after the murder, it had seemed that no one on the reservation except for Lissa and Tex knew of it. Then, in late January 2014, a federal court in Eastern Washington released a summary of interviews with investigators and witnesses regarding Carlile's case. On page eight of the report, Tex's name appeared. According to a detective, while Robert Delao worked for Tex's company, Maheshu, a Spokane resident, Todd Bates, had often visited Delao on the reservation. During one of these visits, a Blackstone employee overheard Bates talking to James about a "job [that would] pay the same as the last job." This employee "believed the last job was [Clarke], Henrikson's operations manager who has been missing since February 2012."

Lissa circulated the summary online as soon as it was released. Among the tribal members who read it was Damon Williams, a tall, boyish, bespectacled man who in 2008 had replaced Steve Kelly as attorney for the tribe. Williams printed the summary, marked it, and delivered it to the tribal council, recommending they suspend Tex for thirty days while they commissioned an independent investigation. The council voted against suspending the chairman but agreed to hire an investigator. Several days later, Williams flew to Missouri to meet a former U.S. attorney with expertise in corruption.

It was early February in 2014—shortly after the council meeting, ten months before I would meet Lissa for the first time—that news of the scandal burgeoning on the reservation reached me. It arrived as a single photograph on my Facebook feed: Tex Hall dressed in a Hawaiian shirt, standing and smiling with a group of people who appeared to have just finished eating. To his right was Tiffany Johnson, the woman I knew to be his partner, and beside Tiffany were two people I did not recognize—a tan, blond woman in a black tank top, her teeth strikingly white, and a white man with a bad sunburn, his pecs bulging under a T-shirt.

The photograph, taken in Hawaii over a year earlier, had been shared by a tribal member I knew, but the person who had originally posted the photograph was yet unfamiliar to me: Nadia Reinardy.

Over the following weeks, other tribal members I knew would repost the photograph. I would learn that the white man and woman were James Henrikson and Sarah Creveling, and when I looked up their names, sorting through the many articles that by then were emerging, I read, for the first time, about Kristopher Clarke.

Meanwhile, beneath the reposted photograph, comments by tribal members accrued:

I wonder if he is spending tribal money on his family's outings?

He flies first class. I seen him on my flight.

Chairman with a snake tongue. Shove his helicopter up his ass.

he living a more than comfortable life when we ppl frm our tribe struggling to survive n homeless . . . im sure that trip could have put someone in a home

Or even in a hotel. I hear all the time how it feels to be from one of the richest tribes. I just say we are one of the poorest. Idk how dude can live with himself.

I tried calling Tex at the tribal office, but no one answered. So I called Mark Fox, the tribe's tax director, with whom I had remained in touch since my first trip to the reservation three years earlier. "He's trying to say he's the victim, but people think he has his hands dirty," Mark told me. Mark was unsure what to believe, but he did not feel sympathy for Tex. "If you make a choice to partner with somebody, and you find out they have a questionable background, most people cut their ties and run like hell, because you don't want that to come back on your legitimate business." Mark had been hearing rumors about Clarke's disappearance for years and wondered about Tex's connection to James. The rumors were eroding people's trust in the chairman, Mark said, and he wondered if the Carlile murder was a tipping point: "Stories are going to come out. Anybody trying to put Tex on a pedestal better be careful, because that pedestal will be knocked out from under him, and he won't ever get back on it again."

I was surprised by Mark's bravado, given that he was part of the chairman's administration. It was only months later, when Mark announced his bid for chairman, that I suspected some opportunism. But Mark was right. On August 28, 2014, the woman I knew then only as Nadia Reinardy once again posted the photograph of Tex vacationing in Hawaii, this time captioning it, "Vote Tex Hall if you want lies, embezzlement, and continued exploitation. Pictured left to right: James Henrikson, Sarah Creveling, and your majesty, king TEX!"

On September 11, five days prior to the primary election for chairman, the firm that the tribal attorney, Damon Williams, enlisted to investigate Tex sent a sixty-six-page report to the tribe. When the council refused to release the report, some hundred tribal members protested outside the chambers, among them Mark, until Judy Brugh, the councilwoman, unlocked the doors, let the protesters in, and gave them a copy. That evening, the protesters scanned the report and posted it on Facebook.

Much of the information the report contained was known or at least rumored on the reservation already, such as Tex's partnership with Blackstone. But the report also contained some new findings. Allegedly, in the winter of 2012, Tex had authorized the tribe to hire Blackstone to spray roads with water to suppress dust. The job paid $500,000. Blackstone had been hired without the consent of the council, which, according to tribal law, should have solicited bids from Indian contractors before giving the job to non-Indians. Tex had never disclosed to the council that his own company profited from Blackstone. This appeared to be a conflict of interest, and it was not his first impropriety. In 2008, two years before Tex was elected chairman, he had worked as a consultant for an oil company called Spotted Hawk, soliciting leases from tribal members. Tex claimed the company owed him more than a million dollars, and after he became chairman in 2010, he had asked the Bureau of Indian Affairs to delay approval of a lease agreement between Spotted Hawk and the tribe. The Bureau delayed until August 2011. During that time, Tex tried and failed to win a settlement from Spotted Hawk. After the Bureau approved the lease, Tex continued to target the company, deriding Spotted Hawk in meetings with the Bureau and in council sessions. Such findings confirmed what some tribal members long suspected— Tex had tried to use his position as chairman to enrich himself.

While the report addressed some questions, it left many others unanswered: What was the nature of Tex's relationship with James Henrikson? How was Tex connected, if at all, to the murders? And where was Kristopher Clarke?

On September 16, 2014, Tex lost the primary election. Mark Fox and Damon Williams, the tribal lawyer, won the most votes, advancing to the general election in November. That same September day, Sarah Creveling testified before a grand jury in Bismarck, Robert Delao was arrested, and the U.S. attorney for the Eastern District of Washington charged James Henrikson with eleven counts—among them, conspiring to distribute heroin and soliciting the murder-for-hire of five men, two of whom were murdered.

No memory of the time I spent on the reservation is as clear to me as the night I returned that fall of 2014. It was October, cold. I crossed the border at dusk. Trucks crept toward a darker horizon, and soon everything was black except for the lights—the crawling red fenders, the flash of passing cars, the casino blinking larger than when I had left it, the flicker of grass fires I mistook for flares, the diamond beam of drilling rigs, and the moon that rose above it all, made orange by an invisible haze. The lights etched their brightness like sun scars on my eyes. In the morning, I would recognize the place again, but that night I felt unsettled, like a visitor in a vast, unknowable city.

In daylight, too, it was clear things had changed over the past year. Where before the highway had been marked with farmsteads, it had become an industrial corridor, with warehouses and stacks of pipe and, on a corner where the restaurant called the Scenic had stood alone, a new gas station and motel. One day, I stopped at the Scenic for lunch and found it full of white people like me. The inside was dingy and poorly lit, and when I looked out the window, which once had served a clear view of the lake, I noticed a new train depot and, arcing around it on a set of tracks, the matte-black tanks of an oil train.

If the place felt unfamiliar to me, I wondered how it felt to the thousands of tribal members who by then were returning home to vote in the November election. I had noticed that the casino, Better B's, and the grocery stores in New Town were full of people dressed in city clothes. They had come from Cleveland, New York, Atlanta, Denver, Minneapolis, Rapid City, Albuquerque, Phoenix, Seattle, Portland, San Francisco, and reservations across the West and Midwest. Since the tribe lacked absentee voting, if you wanted to vote, you came home. More tribal members would come home for this election than any one before it—3,500 out of 8,000 eligible voters, the tribe estimated—and as I interviewed members about their decision to return, many said that although they did not live on the reservation, they worried about it. They lamented the crime brought by the boom, the oil spills, the "mismanagement." When I asked one woman what concerned her most, she replied, "contamination." In July, a wastewater pipeline had burst, spilling twenty-five thousand barrels of chemical brine into a creek near the water intake for Mandaree. The woman had recently moved her family to Bismarck and doubted she would live on the reservation again. Her mother had been displaced by the flood. "She always said, 'I want to go home, but I can't,'" the woman told me. "Sometimes I think, *Are we going to be saying the same thing?*"

On my first morning back on the reservation, I met Mark Fox in his office. He was not as wiry as when I had last seen him, but he looked about the same in a pressed collared shirt and glasses. A new poster hung on his wall: *Never underestimate the power of stupid people in a large group.* "The gold rush mentality has hurt us greatly," he said. "You know that T-shirt people wear sometimes? *We treat this planet like we have another one to go to?* Well, we treat this reservation like we have another one to go to."

In the months since we had last spoken, Mark had cast himself as a populist and amassed a fervent following. He was campaigning on the promise to "slow the boom," which seemed to resonate with voters. He believed the tribe should levy a higher tax on oil producers, and he promised to lobby the Department of Interior to grant drilling permits less hastily and to consider environmental impacts more seriously. If the tribe had been more prepared for the boom, Mark argued, it would not have put so many lives at risk or wasted so much money. The council had spent haphazardly on infrastructure to keep up with development and on glamorous projects that did little to serve people's needs, he believed. Due in part to the rising rates of addiction, life expectancy on the reservation was fifty-seven, more than twenty years below the national average. Mark would allocate more money to law enforcement and drug treatment and make sure every tribal member had health insurance. "You think about, in the history of our people, how many of our ancestors died and bled and suffered to have what little we have left today," he said. "Suffered for hundreds of years! And now, in a matter of a few short years, our people are leaving, giving up our land, moving away. How crazy is that? Why? I'll be straight up. Greed. Money, money, money. That's where Mark Fox is saying, *Oh shit.* We're going to slow this down so that we'll have somewhere to live."

After I left his office, I wondered how realistic Mark was being.

What was there to do after more than a thousand oil wells had been drilled—after the boom was practically done? Still, I had been struck by how Mark and other tribal members now spoke of the boom. Before, I had sensed a reticence to curse it—a fear, I supposed, of sounding ungrateful for their fortune. Now that reticence was gone. Many tribal members were still careful, and when I asked them about Tex Hall, they rolled their eyes or spoke to me in whispers. But the words they used—*corruption, greed*—made clear to me that something had tipped the scales to bring them home to vote. I believed that something was the Clarke and Carlile murders. People had come home to see how these crimes had happened, and what they saw unsettled them. What they saw gave them reason to admit their discontent.

IN PAST ELECTION YEARS, THE month prior to voting day had been somewhat uneventful, but in 2014, on account of contributions from wealthy families, as well as a sense among the electorate that the stakes, this time, were particularly high, October would seem a never-ending run of campaign dinners and debates. Mark Fox and Damon Williams each planned a dinner in every segment of the reservation and together would meet for four debates, in Bismarck, White Shield, New Town, and Fargo.

While there were no political parties on the reservation, there were other more nuanced divisions within the tribe that influenced how citizens cast their votes. The clearest division could be traced to 1870, when a Hidatsa band led by Crow Flies High left the reservation over a disagreement and settled farther west until 1894, when soldiers returned them to Fort Berthold. When the descendants of this band later voted in opposition to their tribe's constitution under the Indian Reorganization Act, they became known as the "No's." After that, the IRA hardened divisions within the tribe between those who viewed the new system of governance as a step toward self-determination and those who saw it as a vessel for federal interest and would distrust any program the tribe administered. If the No's now aligned with a candidate, it was with Damon Williams.

Still, there was little difference between the candidates' platforms. Both claimed the tribe had lost control of the boom and promised to rein it in, and both blamed this loss on the chairman and councilmen, whom they believed the boom endowed with too much power. Among the solutions they proposed was constitutional reform. Ed Hall, the elderly man I had dined with on my first visit to the reservation, was already working on a blueprint for a new constitution. Damon had incorporated the plan into his platform, and Mark was suggesting similar changes. Since federal laws had undermined and displaced traditional ways of governance, tribal members had few ways to keep their council in check, nor did the constitution they adopted in 1936 offer a separation and balance of power. In 1975, when a new law allowed tribes to directly manage reservation services, many members saw this as a positive change, having long been victims of federal over-step or neglect. But others believed the act transferred a pattern of dependency fostered by federal agencies to the council while failing to restore or strengthen tribal institutions, lending councilmen unfair leverage over citizens. When Mark mentioned the problems with the constitution, he invoked *The Lord of the Rings*. "There's too much cen-tralization of power," he told me. "People change when they put on that ring: Suddenly everyone's coming to them, and they say, 'This is cool. I've got all this power.'" Mark would be like the hobbit Frodo, he said, an unlikely hero who destroys the ring.

"The chairman is only as powerful as his council lets him be," Judy Brugh told me one day in her office. The most senior member of the council, she was dressed in an elegant wool sweater. "That's where we went wrong," she explained. "We let him have too much power. It's sad, because he had a lot going for him." She paused, as if won-dering if she had meant it. "He's a really good speaker," she said.

I had dropped by tribal headquarters looking for Tex, but no one knew where he was. His press secretary would not return my mes-sages, and when I went by her office, I found it locked and dark. I had

asked another secretary, but she averted her eyes. It seemed Mark was
the only one who had seen Tex recently—weeks earlier, at an event in
Bismarck. Tex had told Mark he was doing "all right." He had been
in Arizona, where he and Tiffany owned another house, and where
Tex often went to play basketball.

I could think of one councilman who might lead me to the chairman, but when I found him at the Northern Lights building in New
Town one day, he also shook his head. He was seated at a table in the
lobby, at a celebration for a boy who had qualified to compete in the
Indian National Finals Rodeo. The councilman was not in the mood
to talk and suggested I interview his legislative assistant, a younger
man who had previously worked for a senator. "I'm concerned about
the shift we have to make in conscious thought from survival econom-
ics to long, sustaining economic planning," the man said. "We do
want to promote entrepreneurial endeavors. It's unfortunate that
money is just flowing by us. But our leaders should be stewards of it,
rather than participants in it. I think you have to be a government
official or a private citizen. There aren't enough safeguards to be
both."

Another man dressed in coveralls emblazoned with the Petro-
Hunt logo joined us at the table. "Where's Tex at?" he said.

The councilman laughed. "Good question! He didn't come to the
last meeting. Is that a sore loser or not?"

"I think he's embarrassed," the man replied.

Later that day, I interviewed a woman at the table who asked not
to be named. "It was foolish for Tex to think he could get away with
it," she said. "Three thousand to four thousand people get royalties,
but everyone has to put up with the traffic, the crime, the violence.
Then you see Tex's helicopter flying by. We've always been oppressed
by the government, but when it's your own who do it to you; it's a
double slam. There's a lot of anger. Tex is done. This is his legacy. This
is what he has to live with, because people won't remember the good
things he did in the beginning of his run. People are only going to
remember what he did in the end."

Nearly everyone I interviewed implied that Tex had done something wrong, but what exactly he had done was unclear. Many seemed to believe he was involved in the murders or, at the very least, guilty by association, but there was no evidence that, aside from Lissa's attempts to tell him, Tex had been aware of the violence, nor would such evidence emerge. The true nature of his relationship with James continued to elude me as well, and since I could not ask Tex myself, I had no way to confirm the rumors I heard. I had only what the public had—a copy of the report—which, apart from some email correspondence, contained little evidence. Tex's most obvious mistake, aside from enriching an alleged murderer, was soliciting payment from an oil company while urging the Bureau to delay the same company's drilling permit. Some tribal members were lobbying the Department of Justice to press charges, but when I asked a department spokesman if Tex was being investigated, he declined to comment, and when I asked a former U.S. attorney of North Dakota, he hedged. If it were his decision, he said, he would spend his limited resources on prosecuting the reservation's lengthening roster of violent and sexual crimes.

I had taken to asking tribal members what crimes they believed the chairman committed; answers varied. Charles Hudson, the son of the woman whose house I stayed in and who had come from Portland, Oregon, to vote, said that while he hoped Tex would be prosecuted, he believed the crimes alleged in the report were "pedestrian." What Tex did legally was more serious: By pushing the idea that the tribe could become "sovereign by the barrel," he had threatened what was guaranteed to tribes by treaty. "He did that without attending to the fact that the federal government took things from Native people and will always owe something in return," Hudson told me. "So to say 'we don't need appropriations' I think is highly irresponsible"—especially when because of and in spite of the boom, the tribe was short on police, teachers, doctors, and basic infrastructure.

Some went further to suggest that Tex's greatest sin was the boom itself. Indeed, it was Tex who had courted one of the first oil companies to lease reservation minerals; who lobbied Congress and federal agencies to rush the approval of drilling permits; who eschewed federal oversight when the tribe had few environmental codes of its own and limited means of enforcement; who bought a yacht before investing in public services. It was Tex who consorted with violent criminals. All this was true, so I understood the anger, though I also understood that the boom was not wholly his. Tex was not the only one who had gone door-to-door soliciting his relatives to lease land. "Think about it," Mark Fox said. "The oil companies knew what the value of that land was when they paid fifty bucks an acre, but at some point in time, to get it done, a tribal member had to say, 'I don't give a fuck about the tribe. I care about myself. I'll help you get that acreage. And when we flip it, we make millions.'"

I SUSPECTED MARK WAS REFERRING to someone in particular—to the casino manager, Spencer Wilkinson, Jr., who had leased a third of the reservation for fifty dollars an acre before flipping his acres to a larger oil company for two hundred times that amount. But I also knew Mark was speaking generally about the way colonization works. After the massacres, the boarding schools, the outright stealing of land, what lasted was the violence that got under a person's skin, inside a person's head. Shame became violence toward oneself and then violence toward one's own community. *I don't give a fuck about the tribe.* Greed was human nature, but it was hard not to see the taking advantage that went on within the tribe during the boom as the legacy of a centuries-old design.

Most efforts to separate Native people from their land have been elaborate and overt—the breaking of treaties by executive order, the sale of acreage to homesteaders, the taking of children from their families—while others have been subtler. Among the oldest strategies to acquire land and resources in America was marriage to Native people. In Oklahoma, where the Chickasaw Nation resettled after it was forcibly removed from the Southeast, it was so common for white men to marry Native women and for these men to then abandon their wives that the tribe passed laws revoking a white person's access to land and annuities if that person sought a divorce. In 1876, the tribe tightened its laws, requiring white suitors to reside within its boundaries for two years before marrying a tribal citizen. Still, the laws hardly dispelled the rumor that Native women and land were for the taking. "I understand that your tribe offered an inducement in money and land to good moral white men that would marry your young maidens," a preacher wrote to a leader of the Choctaw Nation, another tribe forcibly relocated to Oklahoma. Meanwhile, a Texas rancher wrote to the Chickasaw council that he "wanted to marry an Indian girl so he wouldn't have to pay the permit on a large herd of cattle." More infamously, in the 1920s, white men married into the Osage Nation and conspired to kill scores of tribal citizens who were beneficiaries of a vast oil fortune.

On the Fort Berthold Indian Reservation, many of the largest tribal families bear the names of the first white men who gained property in the region. These men were fur traders, interpreters, farmers, gold diggers, cattle rustlers, ranchers, and Indian agents assigned by the government to oversee the reservation. In the twentieth century, after Congress divided most Indian land into allotments, ranching became the sole industry on reservations across the Great Plains. Landowners leased their allotments to white ranchers if they could not afford the cattle to use the land themselves, so even most land belonging to tribal members was, in function, under white control. There were some exceptions—reservation families who managed not just to use their land but to acquire more of it. On Fort Berthold, it became a matter of conflict that families who fared better economically tended to be "mixed-blood" and have positions in government. As control of the land conferred on these families more wealth and political influence, it stratified the tribe. Before the oil kings of Fort Berthold, there had been cattle kings—descendants both of America's first people and of its first capitalists.

If colonization had begun the stratification of the reservation, the oil boom was finishing it. Many tribal members I spoke with lamented the widening gap between rich and poor and the sense that most money being earned from the boom was leaving the reservation. The consequences had remained local, while the benefits had dispersed. Corporations were earning the most money; then the men and women who serviced drillers, most of whom would leave when the boom was over. Tex Hall embodied both dilemmas in the eyes of his constituents: He had allowed non-Indians access to Indian resources in the interest of becoming rich himself.

Few seemed to recall that Tex had resisted the boom in its beginning for these very same reasons. I could think of one man who would remember, and that was Steve Kelly, the former lawyer for the tribe who facilitated a majority of the initial leases on the reservation before founding Trustland Oilfield Services, the company for which Kristopher Clarke, James Henrikson, and Sarah Creveling first worked. In the middle of October, I met Steve at his shop on the edge of New Town. The building, though relatively new, appeared to be falling apart. There was a faint smell of diesel inside, the hiss of a welder's torch. I made my way through a windowless corridor and climbed a set of metal stairs, emerging in a room decorated with three garish paintings—a bear, an eagle, and two white men on horseback pointing over a prairie. Steve was seated at a mission-style desk and offered me a leather chair. He was a corpulent man, with pale skin and a shrill, breathy voice. A television was on, muted.

I had not spoken to Steve since he called me about the story I had written more than a year ago, when he offered to explain the politics of the reservation. Now I wanted to understand how Tex had gone from once standing up to a Canadian oil company to willfully opening the reservation to outside interests.

When Steve took the job with the tribe in 2002, he said, "There was nothing going on" on Fort Berthold. "You could have shot a cannon down Main Street and not hit anything." So when oil companies approached the tribe in 2005 with offers to lease land, Steve encouraged Tex to make a deal. Tex had not been interested. He wanted the tribe to drill oil itself and keep more of the profit, as one tribe, the Southern Ute, in Colorado had done. Steve warned Tex against this. "I told him, 'If the tribe's going to run something, we're going to screw it up.'" When Steve negotiated the tribe's first oil deal, "Tex was pissed. Really pissed. I asked him, 'Tex, what's the big deal? We needed the money.'

"It's socialism versus capitalism," Steve told me. Tex wanted, essentially, to nationalize tribal resources, while Steve thought that by allowing corporations to compete for rights to drill on the reservation, landowners would earn higher bonuses and royalties and other tribal members would have more opportunities to own businesses. Steve believed in the free market. He also distrusted Tex. "Tex wanted control," Steve said. "You know, 'If you vote for me, I'll give you some oil wells. I'll make you a rich man, but you've got to stand behind me.'"

When James Henrikson called Steve in the early summer of 2011, Steve had been working privately in the.oil fields for more than four years. By that time, Trustland was the most successful business on the reservation in that it employed the most people and ran the most trucks, but Steve insisted it was far from the wealthiest. The companies earning the most money, he said, were those acting as shells, hiring other companies to do the work for them as Maheshu would do with Blackstone. Not long after James and Sarah began working for Trustland, Steve suspected they were going behind his back, arranging work for themselves. Steve ended their contract, and after they joined Maheshu, he considered submitting a complaint against Tex to the Tribal Employment Rights Office but decided against it: "I got to thinking, *I know how James is, and I know how Tex is. I'm not going to do anything to break that relationship up. I'll let those two do each other in.*"

Steve had been twirling a paper clip between his thumbs as we spoke. Now he set it down and gulped from a mug of cold coffee. I still did not understand what changed in Tex. Had money corrupted him? I asked.

"No," Steve said, reaching again for the paper clip. "He was already that way. There's a saying: *Money doesn't define who you are. It reveals who you are.* Listen. I don't want to personalize this. On the reservation, there wasn't anything here four years ago before the boom. The jobs, everything, came through the tribe. So you kept your mouth shut if you wanted a job. People didn't have the financial independence that they do today. They couldn't afford to speak their mind. Now, people can afford to speak."

Had Steve forgotten that a majority of tribal members earned no royalties at all?

He continued. "The thing is, on the rez, you have two very strong personalities—Tex Hall and Spencer Wilkinson. People are mad at Spencer because he got all these leases from the tribe, and he ended up flipping them. Everybody thinks he made a billion dollars. Well, he didn't make a billion, because he had to split that with his partners, but I'm sure he made a pretty handsome sum, in the neighborhood of twenty or thirty million. And people are mad. I understand that, but people had the same opportunity that he did. I think these same people that are bitching, if they would have done it, you wouldn't hear them bitching. I might be wrong about that, but I doubt it."

I had tried to interview Spencer over the years, but he eluded me. Once, I had spotted him at the casino—tall with short, slick hair. He gave me his card and said to call him, so I did. He chatted like he was eager to talk, and then, midsentence, he hung up. He never answered another call, but I found a full-page advertisement he had purchased in the *New Town News* in 2008, before he sold Dakota-3, in which he stated that no one on the tribal council was an owner of his company, that Dakota-3 "did not resell tribal acreage for a profit," and that his offer to the tribe had been "the best economic package" and was "approved by the Bureau of Indian Affairs." He added, "Free Enterprise is an opportunity that exists for all individuals on and off the reservation."

I mentioned an ongoing lawsuit landowners had filed against Spencer, as well as against the United States for failing to fulfill its trust responsibility.

"Here's what gets me," Steve said. "They really want to go after

Spencer, but they're not doing shit about Tex. You have people in Tex's camp that hate Spencer, and Spencer hates Tex's camp. Thing is, everyone has good qualities. Tex is a very hard worker and very intelligent. He's a good advocate. A strong advocate—sometimes too strong. And Spencer is probably the most politically astute person on the rez."

"Really?" I said.

Steve chuckled. "That guy covers his bases like no other. He was casino manager here for fourteen years, which is unheard of. You know how many different bosses he's had in fourteen years? You've got to keep the council happy, which is hard. And he does. He's kept them happy."

"How does he do that?"

"You'll have to ask Spencer that one. All I can say is, they haven't fired him. Not even Tex fired him."

"Why not?"

"That is the question, isn't it. Especially when he promised everybody he would." Steve chuckled again. "I'm not being coy, here. I've always wondered."

STEVE WAS NOT THE ONLY one who saw the politics of the reservation as a struggle between Spencer and Tex or the election as a culmination of this struggle. Mark had told me he believed Spencer was funding Damon. "This is an economic war between Spencer's people and Tex's people," he had said, holding his hands as if palming two basketballs. "I'm the guy coming up in the middle who has no oil business of my own. I'm the guy they need to get rid of."

Damon, meanwhile, was suggesting that Tex had funded Mark. "He's smearing me hard out there," Damon said of Mark one night while eating dinner with supporters at a Mexican restaurant in Parshall. Damon's grandmother was a Wilkinson, but "I didn't even meet Spencer until I went to work for the tribe," Damon said.

"You can say that, right, if Mark challenges you on it, that you're not taking any oil money?" a man asked. Damon assured the man he was not.

A few days later, I met Damon at a hotel in Bismarck. The lobby was carpeted, quiet. Morning light filtered through the slats of closed shutters. Damon had woken with a cold but looked sharp, in dark jeans and lime-green sneakers, clasping a new Moleskine notebook.

"Mark is Tex's candidate," Damon said. "He didn't say boo to anything Tex did for four years, and now he wants to claim credit, but all he's done is take one step over the goal line and make the play." I asked how he knew Tex supported Mark. "That's who Tex has to support," Damon said. "That's who his people have to support. Mark was part of Tex's team, so everyone is worried that if it shifts the other way, they're out in the cold. The people working in appointee jobs have to go with Mark because they'll keep their jobs."

Damon had grown up in Parshall like Mark but was eight years younger. In 2007, he had been negotiating water rights and gaming deals for the Kickapoo Tribe in Kansas when he called a cousin on the council to ask if the MHA Nation was hiring. As soon as Damon arrived on Fort Berthold, he arranged leases of remaining tribal minerals. "We had reached the bottom of our borrowing at that point," he told me. Once, he and the tribe's energy director sold leases just to make payroll. "We were on the road, and we negotiated an up-front payment. That scattered acreage was the only thing we had."

The trouble with the tribe, Damon explained, was that after having lost power to the federal government, it had tried to reassert its sovereignty by controlling all aspects of reservation life. He believed this was what set him apart from Mark. "People like Mark—they want the tribe to own everything because the tribe has given them everything they have, and while that's good, providing for your people, we're just continuing this level of dependence. We have to create more independence while still recognizing that we're part of this tribe. I recognize the authority of the tribe to regulate within its own province, but you have to give the tribal members a remedy if you wrong them. It's a dictatorship. I can kick you out of your house if you're renting from the tribe, and you have no recourse. I've seen that every election." The argument echoed Steve Kelly with one exception: Damon was not wooed by the capitalist promises of the boom. "We were always forward thinking, progressive, highly educated, and when we were flooded out, we lost a lot of that," he continued. "Money has really changed us. We've got people aspiring to be on the council who have probably never really made any money in their lives, and all of a sudden, they're making a salary of a hundred and some thousand dollars. Everybody in the country who wants to do business with the tribe is coming and putting them on a pedestal, wining and dining them." I suggested this was not so different from times prior to the boom, when white ranchers courted Indian landowners for access to their pastures. It was similar, Damon acknowledged, but the stakes were higher now. "It's not about hay bales and range units anymore," he said. The difference was millions of dollars.

That evening, I drove to White Shield to attend a debate. I had not been to the segment since my ride with the tribal officer, but I recognized the steep roof of the community complex and the pow-wow grounds, now quiet, just beyond it. The complex smelled clean inside, like a cafeteria in the morning. A line had formed for the buffet, and at tables and along the walls, men and women ate from paper plates.

The crowd hushed when a man flipped a coin. Damon began. Earlier that day, he had seemed confident, even cocky, but now his words stiffened, calcified by repetition. He had told me he believed his weakness was that voters perceived him to be an outsider, and as I watched Damon, I saw what he meant. He was more polished than Mark in his manner and dress, but he spoke at a knowing distance, like an ambassador from another country. When asked to define sovereignty, his answer was dense and cerebral, the stuff of academic texts, and when he explained why poverty persisted and addiction worsened in spite of the boom, he was reluctant to blame the drug dealers for their opportunism, the tribal council for its lack of support, or the federal government for the trauma it had long inflicted. Instead, he implied the problem was cultural: "Why are the drugs coming in? Because mom, dad, grandma, and grandpa have more money now. We have to get away from this enabling that's so awesome about Indian people. We protect our own, but we have to move past that." The argument sounded dangerously simple. I glanced around the room. Everyone was still.

When Mark stood to speak, he moved like a preacher, throwing open his hands, bending his knees, rocking on his toes. "The corruption on our council is rampant," he declared. "If you think the fact that we just had a primary election in which the former chairman's no longer going to be in power ends corruption and self-dealing, you're living in a fairyland. The problem that we have is that we've relied on the federal government to come back and save us, when they're the ones that made us to be unhealthy by taking away our economy, our way of living, putting us on commodities, isolating us, pushing us into unhealthy lifestyles, subjugating us through federal policy. But if you think at some point in time the federal government's going to say, 'Darn, we shouldn't have done that to those Indian people, let's get in there and fix it, make it the way it was, again, you're living in a fairy world. The federal government will never live up to its obligations of what it did to us, what it took away from us. The only ones that are going to live up to that obligation is us."

WHEN I WASN'T ATTENDING CAMPAIGN events or searching for Tex Hall, I sometimes joined a tribal member, Jason Morsette, on drives around the reservation. Jason did not own a car, so I would pick him up in New Town. He was forty years old and had no oil income of his own. He worked in the tribal tourism office, drumming and singing at dances and funerals, accompanying industry men and various dignitaries to the earth lodges on the edge of town. The lodges were replicas, made with cedar instead of cottonwood, but they were large and left an impression. Jason earned eighteen dollars an hour. He rented a trailer in a park north of New Town, beside other trailers where oil workers lived. He was proud of the place—"It's nice," he said, when he showed it to me—and indeed it was cozy, with wood paneling and heaps of blankets in all the rooms. Jason shared it with four cousins. He paid the bills, and though he complained about their tussles with sobriety, he would never throw his relatives out. Jason was "traditional," he said—family meant everything.

He was from the segment of the reservation called Twin Buttes, separated from the rest of Fort Berthold by the lake, so that to reach it one had to leave the reservation, drive south and east again. Twin Buttes felt different from other segments, quieter and more remote, although it had not been spared by the boom. Toward the shore of the lake, the land broke into canyons and narrow clay ridges and plateaus pricked with oil wells. One afternoon, Jason and I drove across several dry creek beds and then got out to walk. The day was warm and bright. We could see a bend in the lake where the bottomland village of Elbowoods had been, and in a canyon below, a porcupine clung to a cottonwood tree. "Anyone told you how to pluck its quills?" Jason said. "You get a tire iron, knock it on the head—not too hard— and when you're done you make sure it wakes up."

Jason often seemed intent on teaching me a lesson, and so it was hard to tell when he was bullshitting me. Earlier that day, as we were leaving New Town, we had passed four men from another tribe whom Jason knew from powwows. "Those are my relatives!" he had cried and told me to turn around. The men ran at us, opened the doors, crammed themselves in the back. Only then had they noticed me, a white woman driving, but Jason acted as if nothing were odd. The men were on their way to a powwow in Minneapolis and thankful for the ride. By the time we dropped them off back in New Town, Jason was beaming. "What do you think of that?" he said. "White people are always in a rush, but us Natives have time for our relatives."

Now we were on our way to visit Jason's uncle, Roy Morsette, who lived in Twin Buttes in a house perched on stilts. The house was small and clean, furnished with oak cabinets and upholstered chairs. Roy had worked for thirty-two years as a janitor at the local school. He had never worked for the tribe. "If you have a tribal job, you can't speak up," he told me. The councilmen were "putting money in their own pockets," he believed, "trying to make themselves millionaires." Roy did not think highly of Tex, whom he called "a thief."

Before the flood, the Morsette family owned property in the bottomlands, in the village of Beaver Creek. They had worked for other farmers, chopping wood to make fence posts. Roy was six when the flood came and the family left their house for the site where he and his wife now lived. They moved their furniture by wagon; Roy rode on the shoulders of a horse. "Whatever you couldn't get, you lost it down the river," he told me. Among the things the Morsettes lost were their mineral rights. The government returned these rights to the tribe eventually, but the tribe never gave the rights back to the original allottees. Roy would vote for whichever candidate returned his minerals. What would he do with the money? I asked. "Spend it on things I never had before," he said.

That evening, at a campaign dinner in Twin Buttes, Mark won over the Morsette family. As Roy explained his predicament, Mark listened carefully and promised to bring the issue to the council. He looked tired but buoyant. Since 2008, Mark explained to the crowd, the tribe had earned a billion dollars and given $20 million directly to tribal members. "Does anyone think they've gotten $980 million worth of services from the tribe?" he said. The Morsettes laughed. "With what's going on in the world market right now, this boom could bust," Mark continued. "That's why this is so important." On a sheet of paper, he scribbled "R-O-I."—"Return on investment. We don't know that term yet, because every dime we get, we spend."

As we returned to New Town that night, Jason called a cousin who'd attended the dinner. "It's good, right?" he repeated into the phone. He was pleased with what Mark told his uncle, and he took it as a sign that Mark might grant him another favor: A real estate broker Jason knew through the tourism office had promised Jason a cut if he could convince the council to permit a new hotel. It was the first time I had heard of the hotel, and when Jason hung up, I asked about it. He told me he hoped the project would earn him a lot of money. I was confused. Just that morning, we had passed a large, new house belonging to a councilman's brother, and Jason had remarked bitterly, "What's he going to do with that when he dies?" Now I saw that the boom had sowed in him, as it had in his uncle, both a disdain for wealth and a desire for it.

We made our way through Mandaree, and Jason pointed to a rig in a field behind the house where Tex had grown up. The house was in shadow, lit by a solitary streetlight, but beyond it, the rig glowed like a cluster of stars. "Look at that," Jason said in awe. "Now you think he's getting some money for that?"

"Do you know him?" I said.

"He's my relative."

"You don't feel betrayed by him?"

"Why would I feel betrayed? He didn't do nothing to me. Not like Spencer. Spencer stole money. It's a fact. The murder—it's just allegations."

"I'm looking for Tex," I said.

Jason nodded, serious. "Well, if you find him, tell him from me, it's been a good run."

TEX DID NOT ATTEND HIS last council meeting as chairman. At noon on October 16, a man entered the chambers with a drum and led a round dance to honor Judy Brugh, who was retiring from the council that day. Friends and family clasped her hands and draped star quilts on her shoulders, and when the dancing was through, a squad of secretaries entered with plates of turkey, corn, and mashed potatoes. I stood beside a white man in a red shirt with a logo embroidered on his chest pocket. He sold natural gas compressors. "We've lined up the entire supply chain," he told me excitedly. "We could be pumping tomorrow if the tribe wanted."

Over the course of the meeting, the council allocated $87,865,000 toward the renovation of the casino and an expansion of Mandaree

Village, among other projects. The village expansion would include dozens of homes, new powwow grounds with RV hookups, a community center with a pool and water slide, an indoor basketball court for tournaments and funerals, a clinic with a dialysis unit and a helicopter pad, a twenty-bed veterans' facility, a wastewater disposal area, and a truck stop with a drive-through restaurant. The council gave $15,000 to a man with a medical emergency and $1 million to each segment to build homes. Then an elder from Twin Buttes asked the council for a grant to repair her house. "We're kind of tired of waiting," she said. "We don't have oil kings down there to help us." The council allocated another $500,000 to each segment for home repair.

After hours passed like this, a white man with hair slicked behind his ears stood to speak. He introduced himself as Jim Glenn and apologized for interrupting. The price of oil had dropped 25 percent in the past month and was expected to drop more, he said. Companies were waiting on permits to drill, and rights-of-way. Glenn asked the council to urge the federal government to move faster.

What Glenn said was true. After oil prices fell below a hundred dollars a barrel in August 2014, they had gone on falling. By November, the price would be seventy-nine dollars; by February 2015, thirty-five. Economists were blaming the fall on global demand, on faltering economies and the efforts of some nations to abandon oil for other fuels, but the problem was largely a matter of supply. Due in no small part to the drilling of the Bakken, the industry had flooded its own market.

I followed Glenn out when he left the meeting and asked if we could talk. We sat on a bench by the chamber doors. Glenn lived in Denver and represented Halcon Resources, which operated three drilling rigs on the reservation. He wanted to bring in more rigs but was concerned by the falling oil prices. I asked if the election worried him, as well. Recently, the North Dakota director of mineral resources had told a gathering of reporters that oil companies were alarmed by the tribal election, since both candidates were "less friendly to rapid development" than Tex's administration. Glenn was not concerned.

"You saw all that money," he said. "And what's funding it? Ninety-nine percent is oil and gas. They have a cash flow commitment that's funded by oil and gas. The last thing [a new chairman] needs is a drop in production." I asked again: What Mark Fox said about slowing the boom did not worry him? "No," Glenn said. "I think some of his constituents may want to hear that, but the ones using that community center aren't going to want to hear it, and the ones using the roads, and the hotels."

He stood. "Time for a beer?" he said to a man beside him. The meeting was not over, and Glenn motioned toward the council. "Bottom line is, I think they're happy that Mother Nature put these rocks here. I don't care who the chairman is."

IN THE LAST DAYS OF October, a cold rain soaked the reservation. One evening, Tex's press secretary called. The chairman had agreed to meet with me at his Maheshu office, so, a day before the election, I drove to Mandaree.

I remember the strange emptiness of the shop—the beige metal siding, the near-windowless interior that echoed as if abandoned. The lights were turned off, the furniture reduced to silhouettes. The lobby, a wall away from where Kristopher Clarke had been murdered, contained a play area for a child, with a shag rug, a painting of a peacock feather, and a flat-screen television mounted on the wall. I called out, but no one answered. I followed a hallway to the end of the building, where hundreds of basketball trophies were displayed against a wall. There, propped amid the army of tiny metal bodies, was a photograph of Tex with Hillary Clinton.

Suddenly, Tex appeared in the hallway, grayer than when I had last seen him. He wore a jacket, sweatpants, and a pair of dirty sneakers. His hair was drawn in a loose ponytail, his eyebrows still wild. He led me into an office and offered me a chair made of fur and turquoise leather. His own chair rocked and had a zebra-skin back. There was a wooden desk on which the light from a window illuminated a layer of dust, and on which rested a calculator, a cell phone, an abalone shell containing a small wad of sage, and a dollar bill. In the corner hung a warbonnet, and beside that a crumpled map of the reservation was pinned to the wall.

His manner was as I remembered it, at ease if a little less confident. I wanted to know how he had gone from seeming so wary of the oil boom to embracing it, so I asked him to recall a day in 2007, a year after he lost his bid for a third term as chairman.

That October, he said, several white men in suits appeared at his house in Mandaree. Among these men had been Jack Vaughn, the CEO of Peak Energy, an oil company based in Durango, Colorado. Vaughn had experience leasing Indian land and asked Tex to help him acquire acreage on Fort Berthold. "Jack said, 'Tex, you were the chairman, and everybody we talk to says you've got credibility, and people will listen to you, and we want to get a big footprint,'" Tex recalled. Tex told Vaughn he would consider it. "I said, 'You know, Jack, you don't know me, and I don't know you, but I never wore a suit in my life, and I don't care for guys in empty suits.'" Vaughn wore a cowboy hat the next time he visited Tex's house.

I had interviewed Vaughn three years earlier when I first heard of Tex's work for Peak. "Tex could talk to anyone," Vaughn had told me. "Tex could pull the strings." Now Tex said that he had taken Vaughn's offer because he needed a job. He had also realized, upon his failed bid for chairman, that it was too late for the tribe to drill its own oil. By the time Vaughn approached Tex, the council had struck a deal with Spencer Wilkinson, Jr., leasing much of its acreage to Dakota-3, and Spencer had made similar offers to individual landowners. The offers were deviously low, Tex thought, and he wondered if he could convince Vaughn to offer more. "I told him, 'Jack, you're coming to the game late. You can't come here with no small offer.'" Vaughn offered landowners $500 per acre and 21 percent royalties, the highest rates on the reservation at the time. Tex formed Maheshu Energy to facilitate the leases and helped Vaughn acquire fifty-two thousand acres. He also formed a landowners' association, through which many reservation families leased their acreage to Peak. The company drilled some wells but eventually flipped the leases for profit, as other companies had done. Tex took no issue with this. He believed Peak, through his cajoling, offered a fair price, while Dakota-3 had swindled people. Tex won the next election. "I saw how things were running away, and so people elected me to rein it in," he said.

Before he became chairman again in 2010, Tex visited Vaughn in Colorado. He recalled sitting in Peak's "war room" as Vaughn pointed to a map of the oil fields. "I wanted to know more about the oil play, and so he showed me all the geology," Tex told me. Vaughn likened the Bakken to a bowl, the reservation hovering on the surface in the center where the vessel was deepest. It occurred to Tex that the tribe would never have a chance like this again. For all his life, the tribe had depended on the federal government, often with dire consequences. "We entered into treaties, and the BIA said as long as the grass grows and the wind blows and the water flows, we'll provide for your health, education, and welfare," Tex told me. "We fought from then to make the government fulfill its treaty obligations. And we still need to do that. But if your budget is fifty million, and 90 percent of it is federal money, you're in trouble. Because when there are cutbacks, where are you going to get that money? Somebody's going to go hungry. Somebody's road is not going to get built. Somebody's house is not going to get renovated. Somebody's not going to get proper medicine, or some child is not going to have a computer or even a new textbook. Somebody is not going to have a new pair of shoes or a warm winter coat. It makes our people really vulnerable." The oil, he believed, offered a solution.

If he could not keep oil companies off the reservation, Tex had decided he would try to control them. He forced companies to pay for road repairs, threatened to close roads he deemed unsafe, and pledged to banish drivers he caught dumping wastewater. Some companies were leery of his involvement in their daily affairs but also benefited from this intimacy. Once a month, Tex met with company men to field their questions and address their concerns. He urged federal officials to expedite drilling permits, believing it was his personal responsibility to keep the boom moving without a hitch. The faster the boom grew, the sooner his tribe would be less vulnerable.

We had been talking for several hours when, in a distant room, a door slammed. Tex paused, frowned. "Hello," he called. Then again: "Hello?" There was no answer.

He rose to his feet, walked stiffly to the door. Perhaps it was a secretary from the tribe, I thought—Tex rarely went to the tribal headquarters anymore, so his assistants delivered his papers to the shop—but the hallway was empty. "Somebody else here?" he called. There was a scuff of feet on linoleum, the static of a television flicked on. It was his daughter, Peyton Martin. Tex settled back into his chair, and then from the hallway came a softer noise, a child padding through the open door.

"Hey, Boo. Hey, baby," Tex cooed. The boy rose on shaky legs and stumbled toward the chairman. "He's going to be one year old on the eighth. He sure is." The boy climbed into his grandfather's lap and reached for the dollar bill. Then he reached for the phone and handed it to Tex. "Hello!" Tex called, clutching the phone to his ear. "Hello, Boo! Is that you?"

I stared at the boy and then looked away. I thought of the photo I had seen on Facebook of James Henrikson vacationing with Tex in Hawaii. The resemblance was unmistakable; the boy was James's son.

I had been waiting to ask about James. Now Tex began without my prodding. In November 2011, he said, James had knocked on his door claiming he had run out of gas. "I didn't even think to ask his name," Tex recalled. "I said, 'What do you need?' He said, 'I need ten gallons if you got it,' so I gave him two five-gallon cans. I didn't think he'd bring them back, but he brought them back the next day, introduced himself, wanted to know if I'd be interested in doing any work with him. I said, 'Well I don't know who you are. Are you doing any business here now?' He said, 'Yeah, I'm working with Steve Kelly at Trustland.' Steve is a tribal member, so I said, 'Oh, okay. I don't know. Maybe. Why don't you write something up, and I'll look at it.' The agreement was just that he'd be a subleaser and help haul salt water. That was December and January."

On January 17, 2012, after James and his crew moved into the Maheshu shop, Tex's gallbladder burst. Tex spent several months in hospitals, and that February, James brought him a contract to partner with Maheshu. "He said, 'My company's called Blackstone.' I said, 'Where did you come from?' 'Texas.' I can't remember who I called, one of my friends, and they said they did a search, and he wasn't the owner. It was his wife, Sarah. So he come back [to the hospital] and I said, 'You're not the owner. Your wife is.' He said, 'Yeah, yeah, well you know, we're one and the same.'" Sarah added her name to the contract, and Tex signed it.

After four months in the hospital, Tex returned to the reservation. He knew something was wrong almost immediately, he said. In bank statements, he noticed names of companies that he supposedly had paid but had never heard of. "Blackstone Crude. Geneva World Investments. I was like, 'Sarah, who the hell is Geneva World Investments?'" Sarah tried to explain, but over the following months, Tex lost trust in both her and James. One day early in 2013, Tex kicked James out of the Maheshu shop. "I said, 'You're stealing from me. You get your ass out of this place and never show up again.' Right out here in the yard, I confronted him."

"And what did James say?" I asked.

"He was always acting like a tough guy. Always smiling. A real damn con artist. He had a beanie on, short sleeves, a vest. It'd be January, and he'd have short sleeves and that vest on. He liked to lift weights, and he was kind of pumped up. He always drove a great big truck, so he jumped out of the pickup, and I waved him over. Big smile. I told him, 'I want you to eff off this property.' He was trying to talk me out of it: 'Things are going to turn the corner.' I said, 'Bullshit. You're stealing from me.' I held up my bank statement. Sarah—she was a con artist too. She called me and tried to smooth it over. I said, 'There's no explaining.' So we signed a settlement."

The boy squirmed in his grandfather's lap and stumbled to the floor and into the hallway. Tex rocked in the zebra chair. "See, my family were the victims," he said. "Now these guys say, 'Oh, Tex stole money. He did wrong.' And Spencer's still lurking in the background."

"Did you try to fire Spencer?" I asked.

"Yeah."

"Why weren't you able to?"

Tex blushed, startled by the question. He looked away. "I was able to get him demoted," he said. He paused, added, "He needed to keep his health insurance. He still had his kids in school, needed his job."

"That's what he told you?"

"Yeah. I knew it was hocus-pocus, but he's also got votes on that council, so it was a compromise deal. I'm no fan of his. He's a taker. He got a huge payoff and still draws a full paycheck from the tribe."

But Spencer was hired, not elected. Wasn't there a difference between Spencer's position and that of the chairman?

"I didn't break an ethics code," Tex said. "The code didn't prohibit me from owning a business. I had this business when I was elected. It would be a violation if I did work for the tribal oil company, but I hauled water for Marathon." All the information contained in the investigative report was just "a smear," he said. "If I broke the law, why would the feds taint their case by using me as a government witness? They know it was a smear. We were the victims.

"If I hadn't kept my ranch, kept my cattle, kept this business, I'd have been shit-out-of-luck. If both my feet were with the tribe, I'd have had nothing. The direction our tribe is going is not good. When individual families have wealth because of oil, when their parents die, they're fighting each other. When the tribe has wealth, and people don't like the way the chairman or council is doing things, they smear them. There's no respect at all. There's no respect for what I've done or accomplished. Now they'll learn. It's not easy. You can't say, 'There was a pipeline spill. It was Tex's fault.' 'The roads department never plowed that elder's home. It's Tex's fault.' Our people have to take responsibility. The chairman is going to have to say no, because if you say yes to everything, only those that are hanging around the fort will get the money.

"Our people can get really jealous," Tex continued. "When I became chairman, my dad said, 'They're going to be jealous of you, because you're going to be successful. You're going to win again, but a lot of people you thought you knew are going to turn on you. So you just have to keep grounded and know in your heart what needs to be done.' I seen it back in the sixties. He would get a new car and have to hide it. I'd say, 'Mom, why is he buying a new car, and we're hiding it in the garage?' 'Well, son, your dad's in politics, and in politics people get jealous, and they won't vote for him if they're jealous.' People are real funny. If they think that you're higher than them or you've got more money, they're not going to vote for you. I didn't know that it'd come from my relatives."

"Do you think the candidates can slow the boom?" I said.

Tex laughed. "How are they going to do that? A lease is a legal contract to drill on your land. If you and I have a lease with Marathon, and it's a five-year lease, and we're in year five, how are you going to slow them down? There's nothing you can do. All these lands are leased, Sierra." Besides, he said, the boom was over.

He rocked back in his zebra chair. It was five o'clock. We had spoken for five hours, and his secretary had not come.

"My goal was full sovereignty. You grow your own food. You utilize your own energy. You do intertribal trade to help those that are less fortunate. That's the direction I was going. I grew up with no running water, no electricity, no TV, no telephone. I grew up feeding cows and horses in thirty, forty below. We'd haul our water in cream cans from the spring. This is what it's all about—good water, a decent home, decent health care. We didn't ask for the moon. We just wanted a sliver. And then the oil came."

I noticed in a corner of his office, leaning against the wall, the photograph taken on the day the federal government took the bottomlands, the chairman weeping into his hand. Tex was born two years after the flood, so his earliest memories were colored by its aftermath. He remembered one particular gathering in 1960, when he was five years old. "We were in an old building east of here about fifteen miles, a community center called Water Chief Hall," he said. "It was brought up from the bottomlands before the flood. It had a potbelly stove, and my grandfather was chairman, and my father was a councilman, and they were standing up in front and talking Indian about the dam. 'The government hasn't built us a hospital. They haven't built us a school.' It was cold. My grandmother was feeding the people, and the women had scarves and blankets covering them. Kids were playing. I went to go play with the kids, and that's when my grandfather told me in Indian to come back, sit down, pay attention. 'Some day you might have to lead your tribe.' So I grew up listening. 'Don't trust the government. Take care of the people, first.'

"That's why I keep that picture," Tex said, nodding toward the corner. "In that old, cold building, it was us against the world. It's sad, in a way, that we seem to have lost where we came from when we had nothing. It's almost like I wish we had nothing. It was clear, before, what we were fighting for, and it was to make the tribe whole again, and now it's a fight over money."

THE DAY OF THE ELECTION, November 4, 2014, a bitter wind turned the rain to snow. That morning, I dropped by the offices of the tribal newspaper, in the old clapboard house by the lake, to say hello to the editor, who mentioned she had a source for me. The editor offered to arrange an interview that evening. So, as officials delivered ballots to the casino—Mark Fox won—I returned to the newspaper offices and waited, shivering, for Lissa to come.

14

The Badlands

LISSA TOLD ME THAT TO FIND A BODY IN THE BADLANDS, I WOULD HAVE TO know the landscape in all seasons. I should be there when the snow melted in April, and when the heavy rain in May carved rivulets in the gumbo and washed sediment into the channels that cut around the buttes. I should see the cottonwoods bud in the late spring and, in the summertime, watch the cockleburs grow thick in the coulees. The foliage would not last long, Lissa said. By late summer, the brush would turn brittle, so that a cigarette flicked out a car window might cause it to burn for days. In the fall, the rain would come again, and this, too, I should see: how the bentonite clay would glisten like whale skin, evening its own surface, filling the tracks of animals imprinted during the summer and fall before. The winter was also important, when the snow would bring the land into full relief, and I would notice shapes that in other seasons I had overlooked. The badlands were never the same, Lissa said. They were always slumping, folding in on themselves. The land would reveal what it wanted to us. The point was not to force the land to give up the body but to be there when it did.

·····

I visited Lissa regularly in the years after we met. I would fly to Fargo, where she would pick me up at the airport, and where I would spend weeks at a time tracing the paper trail of her life. That first winter and spring of 2015, I stayed with Lindsay or slept on the floor of Lissa's apartment. Then summer came, Obie moved out, and Micah repainted the spare room for me. In the fall, Lindsay moved back in, and I returned to the floor. CJ found a girlfriend, who also slept on the floor awhile; and Obie came home with a girlfriend, too, and they shared a room with Micah. By then I had decided the apartment was full and rented a room of my own.

I accompanied Lissa to the reservation for the first time in April 2015. We met in Fargo, where I helped pack the car with tents, blankets, changes of clothes, flashlights, Coleman lanterns, Band-Aids, phone chargers, and a set of camouflage radios. We left the following morning after dawn. There was hardly room for Micah or Waylon, Lissa's cousin, who rode on a mound of Pendletons in the back. Waylon was so skinny his cheeks caved in. He had spent the recent months in jail, and Lissa thought this had done him good. His skin had color, she noted approvingly, and he was sober, praying a lot. He had spent the night before we left binding a fan of sparrow hawk feathers with a strap of leather that belonged to his late mother. "Everything I have of hers I'm slowly giving away," he told me. He had gifted the fan to Lissa, who stuck it in her visor like a toll ticket. It quivered angelically above her head.

The trees were budding, a green blush along the edges of the highway. Waylon tapped on a drum and now and then burst into song, Lissa murmuring the words. I would soon learn that driving to the reservation put Lissa in her best mood. She told more jokes, smoked fewer cigarettes. "You'll see," she said. "I think there's this nervousness, all this energy. It feels like my insides are tuning up to a higher frequency, so when I get there, I'll notice things. It'll happen to you. All these things we're driving by, they'll come into focus, and you'll think, *Wow, there's a million places this kid could be.*" She turned to Waylon. "I brought some of that smudge so we can get that evil off you," she said. Jails were full of bad spirits, and she didn't want any tagging along.

Waylon nodded and pointed out the window to an embankment. "Look at all those sweat rocks, Cuz! Load 'er up." He was always collecting from roadsides, he said. Wood. Feathers. The quills of flattened porcupines.

"Have you ever knocked one out with a tire iron?" I asked.

Waylon cackled. "Nah. That's funny though. Wake up and find out they've been rolled for their quills."

WE BEGAN BY THE LITTLE Missouri River, where the bridge crossed north of Killdeer into the badlands of Mandaree. There was a cattle guard at the entrance to the allotment and a red gate fastened with a chain. Lissa woke Micah, who opened the gate and followed us on foot to the riverbank. A dry winter had reduced the river to a trickle. We walked over sand and silt, through grass and the winter skeletons of chokecherry bushes, to where the river parted like loose strands of a braid. There, in a clearing, was a set of wooden pallets, the ground littered with bullet casings. A target had been nailed to one of the pallets and shot through a couple dozen times.

"Oil workers?" I asked. A rig was perched on the cliff above.

"Yeah, probably," Lissa replied. "Or rez kids playing around."

She walked the perimeter of the clearing and then cut through the brush into a small grove. I followed and saw that she had paused. "Oh, come look," she said. At the trunk of a tree were two coyotes, shot and laid like dogs in the shade. They had small wounds above their front legs, each crusted with maggots, but otherwise, they might have been alive. Their coats were glossy and thick, and they lay to opposite sides, their legs extended toward the river so that the spaces between their eyes were touching. Had they arranged themselves to die this way, or had the hunter put them there, I wondered?

We spent the whole afternoon like this, no pattern to our searching.

Lissa seemed guided by whim, and then by instinct, and then by some mysterious calculation. She dug her boots into the ground to test its softness. She pulled up deadwood to see what was beneath. When she came to a clearing or a coulee, she paused and said, "This isn't right," or, "This is the kind of ravine I was telling you about, where the ground is easy to dig." She was always pointing to anomalies in the land—sunken patches of earth, sticks unnaturally piled so that they had to have been laid by humans. We left the riverbank and climbed a series of draws toward the cliffs, where the silt became clay and the ground hardened. A creek cut around a plateau, forming a ravine into which Lissa descended. She was hardly graceful. Her feet stabbed the dirt like anvils, and she wobbled on steep terrain, but she was quick. I followed her along the creek through a mess of cattails, leaping over mud onto islands of sand. The ground was scored with the tracks of foxes, rabbits, ermine, and raccoons, and the brush along the channel was garnished with bits of fur. It struck me that KC, if buried here, was hardly alone. To the side of the channel, beavers had built and abandoned a lodge, which had sunken into the hill like a grave.

By dark we had covered four or five miles and seen no signs of a body. I had not expected to find KC, but I was surprised that the process soothed me, an enormous task reduced to small movements. It seemed to have a similar effect on Lissa. She was quiet on the drive that evening, pulling thoughtfully on her cigarettes. We stayed the night at the casino, where I made a bed for myself on the floor of our hotel room. Waylon and Lissa were gone most of the night, gambling their free players' cash and chatting with the guards, and when I woke in the morning, Micah was cocooned in the sheets of one bed and Lissa was fully clothed, lying prone on the quilt of the other. Waylon had not slept at all. After we had awakened, he announced proudly that one of the guards happened to be his cousin and had hooked us up with breakfast at the casino buffet. Waylon ate three steaks and fell asleep in the car.

Snow had fallen overnight. As we drove south along the lake, through rangeland toward the Little Missouri, the sun lifted and the snow vanished. The noise of the casino had fallen away—a couple had been arguing in the room next door. We wound on a dirt road through a shallow valley and came to a bluff overlooking the river.

We walked most of that day, up and down the bluff and through ravines that narrowed toward the cliffs. Micah found a puffball, which he gave to his mother to use at sun dance as a coagulant to heal from piercings. Lissa found a patch of bitterroot on the river's edge, which she harvested by plunging her arm into the muck. Waylon gathered feathers. His traditional name was Picks Up the Feather, and Lissa liked to call him by variations on the theme. "Hey, Eats Ham Sandwich," I heard her say at lunch in her lowest medicine man voice. Waylon did not always play along, but this time he taunted in reply, "Shops with Credit Card," and Lissa laughed. Waylon did not have a bank account, let alone a credit card.

That evening, as we returned to New Town, I asked Lissa if she had ever seen a dead body apart from those of friends and relatives at funerals.

"Yeah," she said. Briefly, in college, she had enrolled in a program to prepare for medical school, and in class, she dissected a cadaver. "There was this one woman who committed suicide. She drank Drano. Can you imagine? She still had nail polish on her fingers and toes. We weren't supposed to take the shroud off their faces, but one day I couldn't stop myself. I brought sage in and wiped her down and thanked her. It was such an intimate thing, you know? I'm going to let you dig through my stomach, through my reproductive system, through my brain matter."

"What did you think when you saw her face?" I said.

"I remember looking at her and thinking, 'Why did you do that? What could be so bad in this life?' You read that someone killed herself with Drano, and you think that behind that shroud you're going to see this horrible face—twisted, eyes swollen from crying twenty years. You think it's going to be this terrible life written on a face, and then you lift it up, and it just looks normal."

Lissa drove slowly, peering past me into the woods alongside the road. The trees grew thickly here, trunks tangled, buds sprouting new green. Every landmark reminded Lissa of something she wanted to tell me: discolorations in the soil, where water collected and evaporated to salt; the year-old tracks of an excavator pressed like fossils into clay; bones, bleached white, of various animals. "If you ever need to clean a bison skull quick, just put it on a hill of fire ants," she said.

Waylon and Micah had fallen quiet in the backseat. I heard Micah sigh. "Oh my God, Mom. I just want a freaking flush toilet," he muttered.

Lissa sat up, pinched her eyes in such a way that I knew she was thinking.

"Hey, Mom," said Micah.

"What?"

"Why's the lake named Sakakawea?"

"You know who that is."

"That wasn't my question."

"She helped Lewis and Clark, remember?"

"Was she Arikara?"

"I think she was from further East," I said. "She was kidnapped by Hidatsas."

Micah stared at me, his face unexpressive. "Who taught you history?" he said.

"Then she had a baby with Lewis and Clark," added Waylon.

"Which one was it?" asked Micah.

"I don't know. Both?" Waylon said.

Lissa laughed. "And that was when human trafficking all began on the Fort Berthold Indian Reservation."*

"Ayyyee!" Waylon cried.

---

* We were all a bit off. Sakakawea, or "Sacagawea," was Lemhi Shoshone from present-day Idaho. She was captured by a Hidatsa war party when she was about twelve years old and sold to the trader Toussaint Charbonneau as his slave and wife. Two months after she gave birth to their son, Jean Baptiste, Sakakawea and Charbonneau joined the Lewis and Clark expedition, on which she served as an interpreter and communicated to tribes through her and her son's presence that their party was peaceful.

I was laughing now, too. Micah held his head in his hands. Lissa's cigarette jittered between her lips. We were still laughing when we turned a corner and saw a car ambling toward us—two men, both tribal members, the passenger holding a gun. Lissa slowed to watch the men pass. She lowered her chin, narrowed her eyes at the driver.

"Mom. The toilet," Micah said.

OUR TIME TOGETHER WAS OFTEN like this. Lissa would say something that made us laugh so hard our bellies hurt, and then she would go quiet, reproachful, as if we had stumbled into danger. Driving with Lissa on the reservation made me feel electrified. Her moods shifted wildly. I rarely knew where we were going, or why we went to the places we did. If I asked, Lissa often would not tell me. She would act as if I should have known, or as if she had said it already. I started asking fewer questions. I stared out the window, answered her demands. "Find my lighter," she would say, or, "Do I have any more cigarettes?" and I would go rooting through the console, through instant coffee and pill bottles and phone chargers and sage, until I found what she was looking for. With anyone else, I would have felt annoyed, but with Lissa, I felt like a wingman. She made every task seem important, as if we were on some covert mission, which, in a sense, we were.

By then her efforts to find KC were well known on the reservation, and it seemed to Lissa that more people than before were willing to help by joining searches and reposting her announcements on Facebook. She owed this willingness to the fact that James was in custody and Tex no longer in office, but there was, perhaps, another reason: Many families were desperate for the sort of help Lissa could provide, and word of her benevolence had spread.

The winter before I met Lissa, a tribal member named Robin Fox had gone missing, abandoned on a snowy night by a companion. A domestic violence advocate on the reservation had asked Lissa for help, and so Lissa organized a search party. The woman was discovered in a farmer's garage, not far from the bar where she last was seen. She had climbed into a vehicle, found a key in the ignition, and turned it on, perhaps to stay warm. She died of carbon monoxide poisoning.

Soon afterward, Lissa had founded a nonprofit, which she named Sahnish Scouts. Other families from tribes and cities across the West and Midwest began to contact her, many of them missing their sons or daughters. Though federal agencies collected no reliable statistics, it seemed likely, based on available data, that Native American women disappeared at higher rates than women in any other demographic. In February 2015, the Fargo Native American Commission hosted a forum on missing Indigenous women and invited Lissa to speak. When I met Lissa, she had just begun to develop a public persona, but while she spoke openly about missing person cases, there remained an aspect of her work that most people never saw. In the time I spent with her, I would never hear her tell anyone else about the BEWARE flyers, nor about the messages she traded with Sarah Creveling. Even with loyal volunteers, Lissa shared very little. She compartmentalized her relationships. Often, she would glare at me if I publicly referenced something she did not want others to know. I learned to ask questions in private or in the company of only her children, whom she trusted more than anyone. I knew when she was withholding information from me as well, or waiting to tell me certain things. I listened carefully. Sometimes, she would answer a question with silence and, weeks later, pick it up again, as if no time had passed.

Her secrecy was in deference to her sources, many of whom were fearful. Lissa was in touch not only with victims' relatives but also with the relatives of an expanding cast of perpetrators. One night, I was riding with Lissa when she received an unexpected call from the step-mother of an accomplice to KC's murder. The woman had seen Lissa mentioned in an article about the case. She did not understand how her stepson could have done such a thing and sobbed for hours into the phone as Lissa tried to console her.

People told things to Lissa they would not have told police. This was particularly true on the reservation, where there remained a deep distrust of outside law enforcement. Once, in the spring of 2014, an elder had called Lissa with a tip. He refused to share his tip over the phone and insisted on meeting Lissa in person, so they met at a gas station an hour north of Fargo. "You know how Indians are," Lissa later told me. "We're going to sidestep what we're really there for and go all the way around the bush and then come back to the point." The elder finally told her that he had a nephew in Mandaree who drank and used meth. One night, when the nephew was drunk, he had confessed to his father that he had reburied a person's body.

Lissa tried to contact the nephew, but he had deleted his Facebook account, and when his relatives asked about the body again, he denied every part of his story. Lissa began leaving notes for him at the Mandaree store; he never got in touch. She did not press it, but she began to take seriously the possibility that KC had been moved from his original burial site. Case investigators thought this was unlikely— James was far too lazy, they said—but Lissa had not ruled it out. According to a document filed in advance of the trial, Suckow returned to the reservation two weeks after he murdered KC and told James he wanted to rebury the body. "Don't sweat it," James had said. Either James did not want to disturb the burial site, Lissa thought, or he had arranged for the body to be moved by someone else.

In the spring of 2015, on another trip to the reservation with Lissa, we stopped at the Mandaree store, where she met with a tribal member. The member had been among the first informants to speak with Steve Gutknecht, the Bureau of Criminal Investigations agent, in July 2012 regarding KC's disappearance. He had worked with KC in the oil fields and, in his interview, suggested KC was buried in a cattle bone pile near Maheshu. Around the time KC disappeared, the informant had been driving by the shop late at night when he noticed a backhoe digging in a nearby field. Lissa had been trying to meet with the informant for months. I waited with Waylon and Micah in the car while they spoke, and when they were done, Lissa brought the informant—a short, nervous man—to greet us.

"You packing arms?" he asked.

"No," Lissa said. "I'm a felon."

Waylon pointed to an eagle feather dangling from the rearview mirror. "We've got this for protection," he said. The informant scoffed.

As we left Mandaree, Waylon shook his head. "These nontraditional Indians," he complained. "They get scared when they see an eagle feather."

I laughed, but the man's fear made sense to me. While James was in custody, not everyone allegedly involved in his schemes had been arrested. There was still George Dennis, who had delivered KC's body to the burial site; and Justin Beeson, who had watched the door of the shop while KC lay inside. Recently, it had emerged in court records that Ryan Olness, the Blackstone investor from Arizona, was at the shop on the day KC was murdered and had known about it. And there was the hit man James solicited for other unsuccessful murders. When a portrait of this man, Todd Bates, appeared in the news, Lissa recognized him instantly. He was the man she had spotted watching from his car in the Maheshu lot on the day she went with Rick, Jill, and Jill's husband. Lissa showed me the photograph she took that day alongside the portrait, and, indeed, the man appeared to be the same person.

I felt unsettled that so many men had participated in the murders and not one, in two years, had mentioned it to authorities. But strangely I did not feel afraid. I could not feel afraid with Lissa, whom I believe infected me with her confidence. It was not that she considered herself safe; it was that she considered herself invincible. I knew she did not have the same confidence in me. She insisted that my eyes were not wide enough, that I could not see what was happening around me. After I started spending time with her, I found myself looking more often in car mirrors, memorizing license plates, glancing around to see if anyone was following. I wondered if Lissa was paranoid, her caution a residual effect of the years she spent evading social workers and police, but then something happened that made me sorry for doubting her. One evening, when we stopped in Bismarck for gas, Lissa spotted two white men in an SUV staring at us from across the road. I saw the men and thought nothing of them, but as we prepared to leave, they came and parked behind us. They followed us closely for several minutes, and when at last I turned to look back at them, they fled. "You see!" Lissa said. "And you think I make this shit up." I never suggested she made shit up, but I knew what she was getting at.

On the days I spent in Fargo, Lissa would leave for the welding shop, and Micah and Obie for school, and CJ for various construction jobs, and I would be left alone in the apartment. It was dim and quiet inside. Hours passed without my noticing. I sat in the living room, in front of a television I had never seen on, amid stacks of clean towels and clothing piled in the space between two couches that CJ had claimed as a makeshift closet. On a side table sat a bottle of cologne, which CJ applied liberally each night after he showered. "Take that shit outside," his mother complained, but he never listened. There was something mindless, sweet in the way they fought—not bitter like Lissa's arguments with Obie.

By the summer I had sorted through the documents on her computer and moved on to some crates she had also shared with me, which she kept in the garage. Lissa had two of these crates from the storage unit she rented while in prison, containing every record she had saved since the nineties. Here were the police reports from the morning OJ almost killed her, and the transcripts, arrest records, and affidavits that trailed her own slip into crime.

About a year after Lissa survived OJ's attack, she had finally left Minneapolis. Shauna had been on the run for two months when, in September 2000, she appeared in school. Irene, who was on her way home from a conference, collected Shauna and brought her back to the reservation. That winter, Lissa followed, staying with her grandmother in White Shield and then in a shelter with Micah and Obie, who were one and two years old. In 2001, Lissa rented a house near her mother's in Minot. That was where she was living on January 17, 2002, when the train hauling anhydrous ammonia gas derailed. Thirteen people were hospitalized. While Micah suffered damage to his lungs, Obie began to have seizures. Lissa often sat awake at night, afraid her sons would stop breathing. It was their near death, she had told me, that triggered her second addiction. By then, her mother had convinced her to see a psychologist, who diagnosed Lissa with a variety of disorders and prescribed Adderall to treat her ADHD. Something about the Adderall worked, and Lissa had stopped using crack, but after the train derailed, she lost control again. One morning, as she prepared to leave for her job—construction at the time—she noticed her Adderall was missing. Her new boyfriend had taken it. He gave her meth to use instead until she could refill the prescription.

Lissa's arrest record began the following September, in 2002, when she shattered a friend's car windshield with a tire iron and attacked another friend with her keys. In a statement, Lissa explained that the second friend had taken CJ to her own house without Lissa's permission. Two days later, Irene submitted an affidavit:

> *Lissa seems to have lost interest in caring for herself. She is wearing the same clothes for days, does not take baths, sleeps all day, uses profanities toward the kids. I heard from Shauna that Lissa may be using meth and drugs like that. There is a history of addiction and I think Lissa has been in treatment before but it was in Minneapolis. She . . . is falling back into a major relapse. I feel she needs long-term psychiatric and addiction treatment and this is the critical time. Lissa is college educated, quite manipulative. It has been very difficult for her to stay on the right track with her children.*

Lissa did not go to treatment. That December, she attacked the second friend again, with a baseball bat. When officers found Lissa, she was drunk, screaming obscenities. She spent weeks in jail. Upon her release, Irene arranged to have Lissa arrested again and sent to an addiction treatment facility. Legally, her blood had to be drawn and tested first, but nurses could not get a needle in, her veins collapsing from her drug use. They let her go.

Lissa was arrested many times after that for minor violations, but it was not until the summer of 2005 that she was caught possessing drugs. That July, Irene spoke with an investigator in the sheriff's department and relayed what Shauna had told her—that Lissa was "not 'with it' or coherent"; that she left needles lying where her young kids played; that she had lost weight; that she had sores on her body and face; that strangers were always coming to the house. For three days, officers surveilled Lissa, and on July 22, they arrested her. She was let out on bond. The following March, she was arrested, again, for drug possession, and on January 11, 2007, she was sent to prison.

I had acquired the transcript of her trial from a courthouse in Bismarck, and when I saw her mug shot on the top page, I had hardly recognized Lissa. Her hair was thin, her skin pocked with sores. "Where is she now?" the clerk had asked when she gave me the file, and I replied that she was well and sober. The clerk seemed surprised. "You don't really hear stories like that," she said.

Now, as I sorted through the files in the garage, I thought of what the clerk said. Lissa's sobriety seemed so certain to me, and indeed, enough years had passed since her recovery that others who knew her were similarly confident. "I think nothing is going to make her use," an addiction counselor who knew Lissa at the halfway house had told me. "In the community we say, 'You don't listen to what people say. You watch what they do.'"

But as I read the police reports, my confidence in Lissa waned. I saw that addiction had driven her to violence, and yet I recognized her in the reports—her rage, her disdain for authority, her cleverness and knack for manipulation. It was all there, in the documents and in her, it had been there and always would be, and for the first time, it became obvious to me that the line separating Lissa's past from her present was porous. Sobriety was not a dam. It could not hold back her pain. The fact of her sobriety seemed miraculous, fragile. What had changed in her? I wondered. I thought of all the people I had met through Lissa—cousins, uncles, oil-field workers—who, in the short time I knew them, had relapsed. I wondered if Lissa ever felt lonely, all these people falling down around her, and I realized that the person least certain of her sobriety was, perhaps, Lissa herself. Later, I would mention this to her, and she would reply, "Every day I wake up an addict. It's something I can't shake, just like being Indian."

I had begun to notice a certain vigilance Lissa applied to her daily life. She rarely went more than a few days without taking Adderall, making exceptions only for ceremonies and searches, since the drug, she believed, interfered with her spiritual sensibilities. If she ever felt she was spinning out of control, she visited the sweat lodge or closed herself in her bedroom and slept. She had tricks to contain her anger. Once, she called me from an airport, where she had come "this close," she explained, to punching a customer service agent, but she had taken a deep breath, mustered the funniest story she could think of, and burst into laughter. She was particularly careful about whose company she kept and allowed few people in her apartment. It was no accident she was still single. Among the documents in the garage, I came across a letter from an old friend, Billy, whose windshield she had smashed with the tire iron. He had written to Lissa when she was at the halfway house and visited her when she got out. During his visit, Billy was caught on security camera stealing a jacket from a store and leaving in Lissa's car. Lissa found this out only when her parole officer called. Lissa called Billy, who posed as his brother and called the store, promising to mail the jacket back. Shortly after that, Obie and Micah delivered a lecture to their mother on "relation-shits." Lissa filmed their speech, giggling, but her sons meant it. "Boyfriends are out of the question," Micah told me. "I just don't trust guys. Guys are assholes."

Lissa could not control everything—least of all, her children. One evening, I was sitting with her in the kitchen of the apartment when voices rose in a far bedroom. Lissa remained still for a moment, listening, and then got up and knocked on the bedroom door. No one answered. "Open the door," she commanded, and the door swung open.

Obie and his girlfriend, Caitlin, were fighting. Obie had tried to leave the room; Caitlin had tried to stop him. "I feel like everyone's obstructing what I'm trying to do," Obie told his mother. "I'm trying to get some space. I don't know how that's not clear."

Caitlin was crying. "I just wanted to talk to him," she said. "I've had a long day. I just wanted to lay with you and talk to you."

"We did. We were laying down. Then you started watching TV. You can't be selfish. You can't just control me."

"You always talk about breaking up whenever you're mad at me," Caitlin said.

Lissa took a deep breath. "Listen up, Obie," she said. "You need to quit making this ultimatum that it's over, because it's traumatic to her. I can hear it. Okay? If you guys are going to fight, fight right, or don't fight at all. You need to be more respectful. I don't want any physical shit in here. Caitlin, you need to stop standing in the way, because if he wants to leave this room, he's going to leave this room. Let him go. But, Obie, don't put more fear on top of her fear by saying, 'Fuck it, we're done.'"

"I need to get out. I need my space," Obie muttered.

"So when are you coming back?" Lissa said. "Give her a time. How long are you going to be gone? An hour?"

"I was going to wander to the movies. I have no plans."

"Can you come back in an hour or two?"

"I don't know."

"Two hours."

"Yes," Obie said.

Lissa turned to Caitlin. "You going to be okay?" she said. Then she shut the door.

On another evening in Fargo, just before Lissa, Micah, and I were to leave for the reservation, Obie and Lissa got in a fight. She wanted to take him out to dinner before we left, but when she asked where he wanted to go, he suggested an expensive steakhouse. Lissa said she could not afford it. Obie became angry. She was always leaving, he said, and she never did anything he asked. We were sitting in the living room, Obie and Caitlin side by side on the couch. Lissa rose silently and walked out the door. I followed, but as soon as we had left the building, Caitlin caught up with us. Obie had pushed her, told her to get out of his way, and fled through the sliding doors. Now we could see him sprinting down the sidewalk, the hood of his sweatshirt flapping as he ran.

Obie moved out of the apartment a few weeks later to live with Caitlin and her family. His departure saddened Lissa. Micah, who sensed his mother's loss, tried to fill the void. He teased her to make her laugh. One night, in the living room, Lissa asked Micah to show me "that thing with the purse."

"What, you've never seen her man purse?" he asked me. He lifted a red canvas tool bag from a chair in the kitchen, slung it over his forearm, and began to strut. "She'll walk into Walmart like—" He shot his mother a coy look. Lissa giggled. "She tries to make it look all fancy, too. Then she gets to the register, and the thing's so unorganized, she pours it out." Micah dumped the contents onto the carpet, held the bag up to the light. "If she angles it just right—" Lissa was laughing hard now, her cheeks streaked with tears. "Then she tries to sweep it back—" Micah mimed shoveling the contents with one arm while causing them to scatter.

"I hate teenagers," Lissa said.

"Tobacco, keys, pills, kinnikinnick." Micah held up a sprig of sage. "Once she finds this, it's smooth sailing."

"Shit," Lissa said, pulling her son into a hug. "Come here. You've made me cry, so that's going to cost you."

Later, Micah told me, "People use your past as a weapon, but I can see what she's been through. There's been times where we got separated, and she was like, 'I promise that won't happen again.' Some of the times haunt me. I remember the first day I saw my mom in jail. She was sitting in that white and black pinstripe. It was fucking upsetting. She's like, 'Everything's going to be okay, honey.' Another time, I came home, and there was a cop sitting outside the house. He said, 'You guys are coming with me,' and I was like, 'Oh my fucking God, again?' We jump in the car with this guy, and he passed us all a piece of green-apple gum. We went to a house that night, and the whole night I cried. Nothing compares to the parent bond. It's like a heartbreak. You don't want to wake up. You can't go to sleep. Just, every day, you live second by second. I can still remember the pain.

"I don't know who my dad is. On Father's Day, I'll say, 'Happy Father's Day, Mom. You were by my side through it all.' Even if she wasn't here, she would write to me. I remember when my mom got out of prison. She worked two jobs. The only day she had off was Sunday. She would bike all the way from Centre"—the halfway house—"to the Ridge, where I was with Grandpa Dennis. She'd always go out of her way to come visit. She's always supported me no matter what. She's like, 'You're capable of doing anything you want.' My mom is a big inspiration for me. I tell her this: 'It's crazy, Mom, people can call you what they want, but you went from selling drugs, using drugs, and completely switched it around.' I think my mom is one of the most intelligent people I know. Intelligence is something that can't be measured. You have to be open-minded, and I feel like what my mom has been through has allowed her to be open-minded, which allows her to do what she does."

LISSA HAD A TERM FOR things outside her control—"spiritual warfare," she called it. I wasn't sure what she meant at first so I looked up the term on the Internet. I learned it had roots in Catholicism but was popular among evangelical Christians, who use it in describing their prayers as combat against a myriad of evil forces. Lissa had never been inside an evangelical church, skeptical as she was of "white people religion," and when I asked her where she heard the term, she could not remember. The first time she used it with me was on the day she fought with Obie and he ran away. After we had seen him sprinting down the sidewalk, Lissa had climbed into her car and sat there for a long time. "This is what I was telling you about," she said finally. "This is that spiritual warfare."

I came to think of spiritual warfare as something that could be dislodged inside of us, that could drift from our guts into others' guts, that could shake us like the flu. It was all our pain in spirit form, marauding invisibly among us. If there was ever a time I saw it myself, it was that first spring I began accompanying Lissa to the reservation.

I remember the night clearly. We had arrived at Tiny Crows Heart's place, a single-wide trailer on the Sanish bluffs flanked by old bed frames, some lawn mowers, and a boat. It was dark, the lights of trucks flickering on the road below. Micah and Waylon had gone inside while I lingered in the car with Lissa, who was finishing a cigarette. We were talking when, suddenly, Lissa looked away. I asked what the matter was. She shook her head. "It was probably just the light," she said. "I saw blood coming out of your nose."

Inside Tiny's trailer, Lissa burned sage in a cast-iron skillet, fanned the smoke across her body, and ordered me to do the same. Then she sat at the kitchen table and lit another cigarette. The trailer was sparsely furnished but felt crowded. There were two leather couches in a V by a window, a jug of water—the utilities were shut off—a table strewn with books and papers, a radio tuned to country, a propane heater that screamed like a blowtorch, and a hologram tacked to the wall of an eagle, which flapped its wings when you moved your head back and forth. Micah and Waylon were asleep. Tiny was telling a story about a time he jumped off the bridge into the lake. He had not intended to jump, he said. He had been walking on the bridge when it just happened. In the air, he had straightened himself into a dive, and when his body pierced the water, he sank so deep that he brushed the bottom with his fingertips. When he resurfaced, he swam to shore, but in those moments that Tiny was underwater, he had felt himself entering a world beyond this world. He had felt himself die and come back to life.

The air in the trailer was thick with loud heat and smoke from idle cigarettes. I excused myself and went to a back bedroom. I believe I fell asleep, and when I woke, I could not breathe. Something was hovering over me, weighing on my chest. I ran to a window to open it, but it was sealed with plastic and duct tape. I took my bedroll and went outside and lay down on the grass. There was a pit dug in the yard, where, a year earlier, Tiny had built the sweat lodge in which Lissa, Waylon, and Micah prayed. I could breathe again, but I could not sleep. I stared out at the blackness of the lake and at two houses perched on the edge of the bluffs not far from where I lay. I had been to these houses. Once, Jason Morsette, the tribal member I sometimes drove with around the reservation, had taken me there. His aunt lived by herself in the first house, since her grandson, whom she had raised, was in prison. Auntie, Jason called her. She earned oil royalties, but there had been no sign of wealth in her house. As we sat in her kitchen, she had chain-smoked cigarettes and told stories about the spirits who lived on the bluffs. Then Jason had said there was something he wanted to show me, and I had followed him outside. We stood on the porch of the other house, staring down at the lake. Blankets covered the windows. I asked who lived inside. No one lived in the house anymore, Jason said—it was haunted with bad spirits—but only when we returned to Auntie's kitchen did I realize what he meant. I stepped close to a portrait of her grandson that hung on the wall and recognized his name. He was in prison for prostituting girls, for raping them inside that other house. "He told me his relative did the same thing to him," was the only thing Auntie said about it. I remember, when she said it, how grief drifted intangibly between us.

LISSA WOULD TELL ME THERE was something strange about Tiny's trailer that night—that a spirit had been restless or angry, perhaps. Micah and Waylon noticed it too. But months later, when I mentioned the incident in the car to Lissa, she barely remembered it. I still thought of it often; it scared me; and now that it was obvious it meant nothing to her, I felt incredulous. Had she actually seen blood? Was it a trick of the light? Or had she been testing me, in the way—I was beginning to learn—she had tested Sarah?

As I came to know many of her relatives that year, some would express a similar confusion about Lissa's spiritual insights and beliefs. "Sometimes it's like, 'I don't know about that one, Lisa. That's maybe a stretch,'" Irene said. A cousin with whom Lissa was close, Tony, was even more skeptical: "I'll be honest, sometimes I think those drugs destroyed her brain, man, because she'll be saying some crazy shit where it doesn't make sense."

Still, everyone in her family would admit there had been times when Lissa was right. Once, she told Tony about a wolf that appeared in her dreams. "She said, 'This wolf come, and he jumped over the top of us, and he was running in your direction,'" Tony recalled. "She said, 'I think something's coming, little brother. It's going to be bad, but you have to be strong.' I was like, 'Damn, that's too much. You might have messed your brain up.' I tell you, six or eight months later, my girlfriend miscarried our baby."

Her relatives listened whether they believed her or not. "I tease her about it," Irene told me, "but everyone sees things differently." Irene was quieter than Lissa about her spirituality but held many similar beliefs: "My grandmother, Nellie, when I was a little girl, told me that you could speak to the spirits and ask them questions. I trusted what she told me, so I would talk to the spirits. I grew up believing in it. Different things would appear to me. Sometimes, I would tell my mother when I would get scared, and my grandpa would stop by, and she'd say, 'Tell your grandpa what you dreamt.' And so I'd tell him. I told him once that somebody had died. There had been a burial. He said, 'Well, it sounds like somebody is going to die.' Here, his brother died."

Irene later suppressed the dreams, but sometimes certain feelings returned to her, and she knew they were spirits. One day, after her brother Chucky died, she had been washing dishes in Madeleine's kitchen when she sensed someone behind her. "You know who that is, because your mind tells you," she explained. "I think Chucky saw spirits, too. He always seemed to know something would happen before it happened. I think that's why he drank. It bothered him. A lot in our family seem to have that ability."

. . . . .

I DID NOT HAVE THAT ability, nor could I explain what came over me that night in Sanish. At the beginning of the next winter, Tiny Crows Heart died in his trailer, asphyxiated by a propane leak, Lissa was told. When she called me with the news, Lissa would mention the night we spent there and how the spirits had been angry.

Only once more would I feel something similar, when, one morning, Lissa sent me a message: "You should smudge! I had a dream about you and woke up in tears."

"What was the dream?" I asked, but Lissa did not reply.

I forgot about the dream. I did not smudge. I never smudged, unless I was with Lissa.

The following week, I cried harder than I have ever cried. There was no reason for me to cry. It came suddenly, violently. I lost control of my body. When it was over, I went into my bedroom and found some sage a man had given me the year before in Browning, Montana. It was old and crumbled in my palms, but I put it on a plate and burned it anyway.

15

Trial

A DATE FOR THE TRIAL OF JAMES HENRIKSON WAS SET, AND MOVED, AND moved again. James pled guilty and then retracted his plea, claiming he had misunderstood the terms. By the summer of 2015, it was becoming clear he had no interest in leading authorities to KC, which left only Timothy Suckow, the hit man, and George Dennis, who drove James and Suckow to the burial area, to locate KC's body in time for trial.

Darrik Trudell accompanied Suckow twice and George once into the badlands, but the men identified two different sites, roughly a mile apart. Trudell visited both sites dozens of times, accompanied by Steve Gutknecht and squads of officers. They brought dog teams and backhoes and marked spots with flags. "We had one spot where the canines hit," Gutknecht later told me. "We dug the whole area by hand." Trudell spotted a piece of paper and leapt excitedly into the hole—criminals often left trash behind—but it was only the label from his own shovel, worn off from all his digging.

The longer they searched, the more baffled they became. No one appeared more frustrated than Suckow, who had been confident in the beginning that he would find KC. "He could walk all day long," Gutknecht said. "We had to take shifts just to follow him around. You could see him trying to remember. He'd look at the horizon, this way and that way. You don't realize how big that country is until you're out there, in it."

On August 31, 2015, Aine Ahmed and Scott Jones, the assistant U.S. attorneys assigned to prosecute the case, met investigators to tour the area Suckow and George had identified. "We scoured it for everything," Ahmed told me. "We found a sock. We found bones, a cow or something. It was a scary place. We got separated, and I was a little nervous, because you lose sense of direction." Ahmed thought they might "get lucky and find a body" but soon realized how impossible this would be. The only other way they would find KC was now seeming to Ahmed equally impossible: "I wonder why James is such a cold-ass bastard that he won't tell me where he buried him."

When the trial was at last set for January 2016, Ahmed still hoped James would plead guilty. But as the date approached, it became even clearer that James had no interest in acknowledging his guilt, let alone ingratiating himself to the court. One morning, staff at the Spokane County Jail, where James was being held, spotted a rope woven from bedsheets dangling from a top-floor window. James was trying to escape.

THE AREA TO WHICH SUCKOW and George led investigators was off the reservation, roughly twenty miles up the Little Missouri River from the spot Lissa had spent much of her time searching. Investigators refused to share the location with Lissa, but she figured it out anyway in the summer of 2015, when, one day, she was scrolling across the badlands on Google Earth and noticed an area that appeared to have once contained a pond. The pond had dried up, indicating that the soil would be easy to dig. Lissa realized she had once visited the area, after a man committed suicide there in 2013. It was a good place to not be found, she thought, carved by coulees and canyons and steep ravines. The following weekend, Lissa located the pond with some volunteers and, in the same area, noticed some freshly dug holes. Investigators had been searching there for KC.

One day in September, Lissa was at work when she glanced at her phone and saw six missed calls from an unknown number. The phone rang again; Lissa answered. The caller had a stern, formal manner. He refused to identify himself. He ordered Lissa to open Google Earth and acted annoyed when she told him she could not. "I wanted to say, 'Who is this?' but I was like, *I'm not going to be overexcited*," Lissa told me a couple of days later. "So I said, 'I just got off work.' He said, 'Well, can you get it on your phone?' 'No, I can't. I'm talking to you.' And he said, 'I want to pinpoint the location of a body.' I said, 'You want to pinpoint the location of "a body"? Or do you want to pinpoint the location of KC's body?' I found it interesting that he would disconnect from KC as a human being. I wanted to make him say it. He said, 'I want to pinpoint the location of KC's body.' I said, 'Well if you let me dig in my car for a while, because I basically live out of my car and it's a freaking mess, you could give me the GPS coordinates, and I'll write the numbers down." The man did not give her the coordinates, but he described the burial area to her over the phone. The next weekend, Lissa followed his directions with the help, again, of some volunteers. They located the spot the man spoke of and dug a hole. There was no sign of KC.

On the Tuesday after she returned to Fargo, the man called her again. Lissa and I talked that night. "He said, 'You guys are walking right over him,'" she told me. "I think he has someone watching us."

"Who?" I asked.

Lissa didn't know but had a feeling that whoever was calling was connected to George Dennis, the driver. Perhaps George had hired a private investigator to find KC so he could secure for himself a kinder sentence. "I said to him, 'What if James had someone move the body? This guy's not stupid. This is the only leverage Tim Suckow has for a plea deal. Tim's only weapon is to lead him to the fucking body. So what if James took that away from him?' It went back and forth. I said, 'Who are you? What is your stake in the matter? If you really wanted him found, you would come out here and show me where he is.' He said, 'I can't do that.' 'Why can't you? Obviously you've been watching me, so you should know by now that I'm not going to tell who you are. That's not what my interest is. I'm interested in recovering KC, so I can move on with my life.' He said, 'What do you need to know?' I said, 'Well, since you seem to know so much, people are stupid and always leave dirt right next to the burial spot. Am I looking for that as a landmark?' That's when I heard him talking to somebody. He said, 'No. They scooped up the excess dirt, put it on a tarp, and threw it in the back of the truck.' I kept asking questions, and I could tell he was turning his head. Either the person was there, or he was talking into another phone."

Lissa returned to the burial area once more that September. She found a bedroll containing a battery charger, a map of South Dakota, a peanut can packed with freeze-dried broccoli, a Veterans Administration card, and a set of dentures, the pearly molars hardly worn. She found no sign of KC, and when the man called again, he sounded frustrated. That was the last Lissa heard from him.

I expected her to continue searching until winter, so I arranged to stay on the reservation through the fall. Lissa never came. She would not return my calls.

In early October, I went to the burial area alone. I drove along a bluff past a set of steep ravines that cut to the south, and then I turned north through a stretch of pasture toward a shallow draw. It was evening, the light low. I parked by an ephemeral creek and followed the old watermark to the bottom of the draw, where I sat for a while in the grass. It was cooler here. I had scared a coyote, who kept stopping and running and stopping to look back.

ONE NIGHT IN LATE OCTOBER, I called Lissa, and she answered. Her life was a mess, she said. CJ and Micah had wrecked their cars, and then a man had backed into her own car, tore off the bumper, and fled. Lissa would have to miss work, but she had missed too much work already. She should have earned $37,000 that year, but she had taken off so much time to search that she would earn only $20,000. She owed $2,000 on a credit card and had bounced twelve checks in the same week. She longed for her grandchildren. Shauna had let Lissa see them again but still refused to speak to her. "I started thinking about all the birthdays I've missed," Lissa told me. "How did I let it get this bad? I'm like, *What am I going to do?*" I said I wished I could think of something that would make her money fast. Lissa laughed. "I can think of some things, but I'm not going to do them." After we hung up, I sent her a hundred dollars. She must have paid the debt, because she never mentioned it again.

A few days later, Lissa received a call from Dennis Banks, an Ojibwe elder and a leader of the American Indian Movement. His granddaughter, Rose Downwind, had gone missing from her home in northern Minnesota. He asked Lissa to organize a search.

The next weekend, I accompanied Lissa to Minnesota. She was doing better than when we had talked. She was spending more time with Obie, she said, who had moved back into the apartment. He had even joined her on a search in the late summer—they had camped at a state park not far from the burial area and spent most of their days walking the ridges above the ravine where the caller had insisted KC was buried. Lissa taught Obie how to identify the bones of deer and bighorn sheep. "He was more excited than Micah ever was," Lissa told me. "He saw the beauty. I said, 'Hey. Obie, this is where we're from,' because he's always kind of denied his Native side. He seemed really impressed. He said, 'Now I see why you do what you do.' It was such a relief for me. I felt like crying, because I was like, *It's okay now.*"

I talked to Obie a few weeks later. He told me that living with another family had made him realize his was not the only one with problems. He had seen his girlfriend fight with her parents and decided he no longer wanted to fight with his mother. He had agreed to go on a search because he knew it would make Lissa happy. "It wasn't really searching. It was more of a bonding experience," he said. "On our way there, I played a few songs that kind of make me remember all the resentment I had, because I held a lot for my mom, but I always wanted to be in a good relationship. I was trying to show her my feelings.

"When we got there my mom was making sure I had a good place to sleep. She kept asking, 'Are you hungry? Are you thirsty?' I said, 'No, Mom, I'm fine. I'm just happy I'm here,' and she'd be like, 'I'm so happy you came.' Then she started telling me everything about KC. We were walking, and I was sliding down all these hills. This one spot I slid into, when I moved these trees open, I swear to God it was the most amazing moment ever. It was a clear sky, and the sun was pointing at me, and so when I moved these trees, the sun came through. I said, 'Mom, I feel so good. I feel like if we just kept doing this, we would get somewhere.' I said, 'What if we did find him? Are you going to stop?' and she said, 'No, I'm going to keep coming out.' We talked about getting a place out on her land, building a micro-home, farming and whatnot."

After they returned to Fargo, Obie told me, it had seemed his mother paid more attention to him. One weekend afternoon, when he still had not woken, she burst into his room with a drum, wailing an Indian song.

THE TRIAL TESTIMONY BEGAN ON January 29, 2016, in Richland, Washington, two hours south of Spokane. A flat, residential city with no downtown to speak of, Richland's most defining feature was a seven-story concrete cube that served as the federal courthouse. The building had been secured for the occasion. The morning I arrived, before Suckow took the stand, officers searched the perimeter for bombs, and I passed two security checkpoints on my way to the courtroom, which was guarded by a U.S. marshal. The man, kindly but stone-faced, let me through into a bright, cavernous room where the judge presided from the far end. He was flanked on his left by the witness stand and on his right by the court reporter. The jurors were arranged in rows against a wall to his left, and facing the jury from a table in the center of the room were the assistant U.S. attorneys, Aine Ahmed and Scott Jones, dressed in similar black suits. At the end of the table sat Darrik Trudell and an FBI agent, Eric Barker, and at the table to their left was James Henrikson, his feet chained to the floor, hands and torso free. He was smaller than I had expected, pale but not sickly, with cropped hair and mild features that lent him the look of a cocky schoolboy. He had the gestures of one, too, twirling a pencil and taking notes, leaning casually toward his counsel to whisper in their ears. He was better dressed than both his lawyers, in a lavender button-down shirt and a fitted gray jacket.

Suckow entered the room, crossed from left to right, paused for a guard to undo his handcuffs. A deputy read the oath, and Suckow raised his right hand. Then he lowered himself to the witness stand, where the deputy poured him a glass of water. His head swayed back and forth. His gray hair was overgrown. He wore a white T-shirt, and loose jeans, and thick glasses with dark rims. He did not look at James, though James looked at him, eyes wide and hardly blinking.

Suckow told the story from beginning to end as he had on the day of his confession, answering each question as if lifting a heavy weight, pausing before he spoke. The details of his story remained the same, but his emphasis had shifted. Ahmed was less interested in Suckow's guilt than in James's, and moved quickly to establish that the witness would not have acted alone. Suckow had no reason to kill KC, nor even Carlile. In fact, he had never intended to kill either man, and when he realized James wanted him to kill Steve Kelly, the rival tribal businessman, Suckow had tried to talk James out of it, suggesting they "take care of his problem legally." But James had seemed intent on murder. It was only after Suckow arrived in North Dakota that James had mentioned KC. As James drove Suckow to the shop the morning after Suckow arrived from Spokane, he told Suckow he was "upset about somebody" who was leaving the company and taking Black-stone drivers with him. James spent much of their drive on the phone.

"All I remember is when he got off the phone on the way to the shop, he was mad," Suckow recalled for Ahmed. "We were talking about KC prior to that, and when he got off the phone, that's when he was like, 'I want you to kill the guy.' You know how people get mad sometimes—'I'm going to kill you.' That's what I thought it was. But I wasn't sure, you know?"

"Did you say anything to him?" Ahmed inquired.

"No. I was—I was stunned, really. I didn't know what to say."

"Did he at any point say, 'Whoa, I just meant to beat him up, not to kill him?'"

"No."

"[At] what point did you indicate that you agreed to do this?"

"Probably when we were standing in the shop is when I realized things were actually going to happen," Suckow said.

Ahmed would later tell me that the night before the trial began, he had visited Suckow in his cell and found the witness curled in the fetal position on the floor. Ahmed knew Suckow took antidepressants, and when he asked the jail staff if they had treated the witness, they explained they did not have his medication. Ahmed demanded the staff call a doctor, who wrote a prescription that night. He worried the witness would be too ill to testify, but the next morning, Ahmed found Suckow upright, speaking again.

The hit man was not their most important witness—Robert Delao was—but as Ahmed coaxed Suckow through his story, I wondered if he offered something Delao could not. Suckow did not tremble like he had during his confession, nor did he cry in the opening hours of testimony. He delivered his lines numbly, as if reading from a script, and it was only when he came to the murder that his voice cracked. His shoulders tensed. His mouth went slack. His tone crept into a high, whispered pitch, as if someone were clasping their hands around his neck. Through all this, James had no expression at all, tracing the shape of his right eyebrow with the pad of his index finger.

"Where was the defendant standing when you were striking Mr. Clarke in the head?" Ahmed asked.

"Five to six feet away," Suckow said.

"At any point during your four strikes to KC Clarke's head, did the defendant tell you to stop?"

"No."

"What did he say?"

Suckow paused, remembering, " 'We need' . . . " 'we need to stop the bleeding on the floor,' " he finally said.

Although George Dennis drove them to the badlands that day, it was James who told George where to go. When they came to the ravine James had chosen, James and Suckow got out of the truck and fought their way through brush to the bottom. There, as Suckow dug, James did not offer help. They had not yet negotiated Suckow's fee, and when James asked how much the job would cost him, Suckow replied, "Twenty thousand dollars."

"What was his reaction?" Ahmed asked.

"He choked and said, 'Twenty thousand dollars?' " Suckow answered. "And I, uh—I turned around, and I looked at him, and I said, 'It's first-degree murder. It's the death penalty.' I said, 'Do me a favor. Don't shoot me in the back while I'm digging this hole.' "

That night, George drove them to the cabins, where Suckow changed his clothes, and to Williston, where they parked KC's truck on a random street. From the truck, Suckow removed a cell phone and a money clip, which he would destroy, and a handgun, which he would keep. He found a pair of dirty shorts, which he sprayed with WD-40 and used to erase his fingerprints. He left the keys in the ignition, "hoping some kid would steal the truck." Then he rode with George and James to a gas station, where he filled two jerricans, and to a well site where George worked. There, in a barren lot, Suckow burned the evidence.

In court the next day, Suckow still on the witness stand, Ahmed asked the judge for an exhibit to be admitted and, stepping toward a cart stocked with evidence, lifted a clear plastic bag containing several tiny objects. "Mr. Suckow, if you could step over here with me," Ahmed said.

Suckow rose stiffly from the stand.

"Do you see this item?" Ahmed placed the bag beneath a projector.

"It looks like cardboard," Suckow said when Ahmed pointed to an object. Then: "a loop from a hoodie"; "grommets from the tarp"; "loops from the top of my boots"; "the top button of my Carhartts"; and, at last, the remains of a money clip.

By the third day of trial, Suckow was exhausted, and when a tall, flappable defense attorney, Mark Vovos, questioned him, Suckow answered impatiently. Vovos was from Spokane and once had won a case against Ahmed, but he stumbled to discredit the witness, who now seemed utterly unwilling to defend himself. As Vovos rattled off Suckow's past crimes—a vehicle stolen in California in 1989; another stolen in New Mexico; a car chase that ended with Suckow lying in roadside weeds, clutching a pistol—Suckow acknowledged each one gravely, and when Vovos noted that Suckow once had claimed he "hated cops" and threatened to kill one, Suckow admitted to this, too.

Vovos doubted that Suckow never intended to murder Clarke or Carlile—Suckow said he hoped to burglarize and frighten the older man, not kill him—but even this line of questioning fell flat.

"Was he scared?" Vovos asked about Carlile.

"Probably as much as I was," Suckow replied.

"So you panicked."

"Yes, I did."

"And you fired."

"Yes, I did."

"You didn't mean to kill him."

"I didn't want to."

"Was your memory good?" Vovos asked.

This time, Suckow did not pause: "It haunts me every day."

FOR THE FIRST WEEK OF testimony, I shared a room with Lissa in a large, empty chain hotel. She took the bed closest to the hallway; I took the one near a set of glass doors that led outside to a parking lot. Every morning, Lissa would rise an hour before trial, open the doors, and smoke a cigarette. Then she would shower, wash and comb her hair, and put on a pair of black pants and a cotton blouse, which she had purchased for the occasion. I had never seen her dress so nicely and was surprised when she emerged from the bathroom that first morning. She did not eat breakfast. She drank coffee and lit another cigarette, which she smoked in her car with the window down, waiting for me to come.

She insisted we arrive early to listen in on the conversations between the parties. Each day, before trial began, the attorneys discussed information they agreed to exclude from questioning, such as the failed hits James allegedly solicited on Jill Williams, Tex Hall, Robert Delao, and James's wife, Sarah Creveling.

It was on these mornings that Lissa mingled with other attendees. The courtroom was never full. A reporter from Spokane came now and then, as well as some locals who had followed the case. But apart from Lissa and me, the only regular attendees were the Carliles—and usually only Elberta, a kind, fretful woman who watched quietly from the row in front of ours. One day, Elberta asked Lissa about Jill, who had come but left after a few days. Lissa felt Jill was making excuses, claiming she did not have money to attend while in fact the Department of Justice would have covered her expenses, but she did not share this with Elberta.

Our presence was obvious. James cast frequent glances at Lissa. At first, he seemed not to know who she was, and then, one day, he began smiling at her. "It's weird," Lissa whispered to me. "It's like I'm still talking to Sarah and he thinks we're on the same team." In fact, James was among few in the courtroom who acknowledged Lissa. Several times, federal officials turned to survey their audience, but only Trudell spoke to Lissa—once, in the hallway. I did not see their interaction. Later, Lissa told me Trudell had seemed surprised that she would miss work for the trial and had asked how long she intended to stay. She told him she would leave after Tex Hall testified. Trudell abruptly ended the conversation.

I sensed Lissa was frustrated with Trudell, though she was more frustrated with Jill, who, by the end of Suckow's testimony, still had not appeared. One morning, Jill called while Lissa and I were out getting coffee. "You know, if it's any comfort, Timothy really seems remorseful," Lissa said.

"I know," said Jill.

"It's like they found the perfect vulnerable adult to carry out their mission."

"I know," Jill said again. "It just makes me hate James and Robert more."

For a while we sat in the café parking lot as Jill sobbed quietly into the phone. Lissa asked Jill when she was coming back. Jill said she did not know.

"You need to be here, Jill," Lissa said.

"I know," Jill said. "I know."

Lissa wanted Jill to find closure in attending the trial, but more than this, she believed Jill's presence would send an important message. KC's grandfather was dead. The only person who could sit in a courtroom with the murderers and remind them of the pain they had inflicted was Jill. Guilt, more than prison time, made criminals suffer, Lissa believed, and she resented Jill for letting them off the hook. She worried, too, what the jury saw. Did they think no one loved KC? Did they wonder if he had been less innocent than his story made him seem?

Lissa was losing confidence in the case. Each evening when we returned to the hotel, she opened the doors, lit a cigarette, and mulled over the day's proceedings.

"It's like they're just going through the motions," she complained one night. The prosecutors struck her as too assured, while their evidence in KC's case was mostly circumstantial. That day, Ahmed had called Delao to the witness stand, and it had soon become clear that the case depended on his testimony. This made Lissa nervous, since Delao was an easy target. The defense could list his crimes, including a murder, and say that he had cooperated with the government before, that he "knew how to play the game." They could cast him as an opportunist, talking his way in and out of his own mistakes. Certainly, Delao had a knack for telling people what they wanted to hear. In front of the jury, he assumed the bearing of a beloved high school teacher, gesticulating with his hands, defining his terms, pausing to be sure his audience understood.

In certain ways, Delao reminded Lissa of herself. He was smart, charming. She believed him when he said that he had gone to North Dakota in hope of escaping a life of crime. "This is where the criminal justice system fails people," she said. "He gets out of prison, hears James is doing good. He just wanted to be legit, on top. It was the dream. *I can do this without going to prison.* But James already decided what his function was going to be because of his past. He exploited Robert just like he exploited Timothy. I can see why the state continues to make deals with Robert. They owe him. They've shortchanged him from the beginning. I would guess he comes from a single-parent, migratory family and all the bullshit that comes with it. And he's been in the system most of his life, but he's never been rehabbed. He's never had a fair shake."

Lissa dragged on her cigarette and shook her head. "I don't know," she said. Her sympathy extended only so far. Delao did not seem as remorseful as Suckow. "I think he's too fucking happy about this shit. Did you see the way James looked at me?"

I had. Not long after Delao entered the room, James had locked eyes with Lissa for a length of time that seemed more than accidental.

Lissa stamped out her cigarette, pleased with herself. "Remember I told him, 'Aren't you worried Robert's going to snitch on you?'" She smiled. "I was thinking, *I told you this day was going to come.*"

THE BLUEPRINT ON WHICH THE prosecutors built their story came from a collection of more than ninety thousand text messages, which the FBI agent, Eric Barker, had recovered from Delao's and Henrikson's phones, as well as the emails traded between Delao and Suckow in the months prior to the Carlile murder. Barker would later describe to me how he sorted the data, which had come to him in one file containing, in chronological order, every message the phones delivered or received. First, he deleted conversations he deemed unimportant to the case; then, he copied the remaining conversations into spreadsheets corresponding with each alleged crime. "These guys lived on their phones, so there was just a ton of data," he told me. He read every message. "Not that I'm a control freak, but I wanted to know exactly what was in there, so that if I had to explain this on the stand, I could."

In fact, Barker admitted, he was a bit of a control freak. A former chief lending officer, he had just spent four years investigating corruption in Texas when he arrived at the FBI office in Spokane and was immediately assigned the Henrikson case. His father had been a truck driver in the oil fields of Wyoming, where Barker was from, and as he read the messages, Barker recognized the industry language. It had not taken him long to realize that this language was a code.

"When you want to send out roust crew?" Delao had written to James one night. Roustabouts were the workers who cleaned up sites after a company finished drilling, but Delao was referring to Todd Bates, the hit man, and another accomplice whom James had solicited to kill an employee the next day. "Get a good night sleep," Delao wrote Bates. "Tomorrow afternoon you start work."

The messages Barker sorted were so dense with innuendo that even the authors sometimes confused legitimate work with violence. "Welder will meet me for orientation tomorrow," Delao had updated James. "Should I send welders to the 1st job while I do work on the second?" These messages, Delao explained to the court, referred to their preparations for a hit. When Delao later texted James about an actual welding job, he wrote, "We need welders. Real welders."

Ahmed spent days deciphering the messages, and if ever the meaning of one was unclear, he asked Delao to enlighten the jury. Most of the messages concerned the heroin deals, for which the criminals used a different code. "Chinese food" was China white heroin. "Virgin black girls," black tar heroin. "Spanish brown sugar cake" meant heroin from Mexico. Delao answered as eagerly as ever, lapsing into long explanations. "He's basically offering translation services from the hood to the privileged," Lissa said.

It was impossible to overlook the importance of the messages. While the Carlile murder file was thick with evidence—a gun, bullets, handwritten notes, a body, the welding glove—the Clarke file was comparatively thin. There was no body, no DNA, no weapon, no proof that a murder had even occurred. Later, Barker would say that KC's murder might have been impossible to prove were it not for two pieces of evidence he discovered among the text messages—first, an exchange between Delao and Suckow on July 31, 2012:

> RD: *When you're bored, look up missing Blackstone driver on the computer.*
> TS: *Sounds serious. Everything alright?*
> RD: *It's all cool.*
> TS: *Good, don't make me worry about u.*
> RD: *Heck no. That incident was before my time and it's a North Dakota mystery lol Just sharing info as it passes to me. Drivers are comfortable with me now and asking me if I knew that guy*
> TS: *Good, I don't like 2 b worried. Lol*

The second piece of evidence was a photograph of KC's gun. Suckow had sent the photo to Delao in early August, shortly after James met with Steve Gutknecht, the Bureau of Criminal Investigations agent in Williston, and Gutknecht mentioned to James that KC's gun was missing. James contacted Delao, who asked Suckow about the gun. Suckow admitted he had taken it. At work the next day, Suckow placed the gun in a vise, cut it in half, wrapped the pieces in duct tape, and tossed them into a dumpster. He sent the photo to Delao to prove he destroyed the gun.

AFTER DELAO CAME STEVE KELLY, Rick Arey, Judd Parker, Justin Beeson, George Dennis, Ryan Olness, Jed McClure, and Peyton Martin.

None of the testimonies would seem as important as Suckow's or Delao's, but they had, altogether, an impressive effect, as if the witnesses had been drawn into the same centrifugal epic and now were emerging, their lives forever altered. In the story the government crafted, James was a lonely villain, weaving the web in which the witnesses had been trapped. It was a simpler story than the one Lissa believed. It was the story, I supposed, that prosecutors had to tell. Later, I would ask federal officials if they felt sympathy for some victims or perpetrators more than others. Ahmed said he felt most sorry for Clarke, whom he considered a truly innocent victim. Certainly no one deserved to die, Brian Cestnik added, but "they're all con men, all conning each other." The only outlier in this morass of deceit seemed to be the hit man. Several officials told me they felt most sorry for Suckow, who seemed more aware of his crimes than anyone and expressed the most remorse.

In this spectrum of guilt and innocence, I wondered where Sarah Creveling fit in. According to a report detailing the justification for James's arrest, a few days after investigators raided James's and Sarah's house, Sarah and her lawyer called law enforcement and arranged a meeting with investigators in Minot. In this meeting, Sarah admitted she and James routinely defrauded their investors. She also admitted she had purchased, at her husband's direction, most of the guns found in her home.

Every investigator had a theory about Sarah. One would tell me that he had been struck by her intelligence and could not help but wonder if she had been the mastermind behind it all. Another was certain of her innocence: "She was consistent with her story," he told me. "I don't know how many times we interviewed her. It was a lot, and her story didn't waver."

In the story Sarah told investigators, she had cast herself as another victim of her husband. She never had any reason to believe James murdered KC, and it was not until she was taken into protective custody that she realized he was capable of murder, she said. But while Sarah told a consistent story, there were parts of her account that confused investigators. A few months prior to the trial, the U.S.

attorney of North Dakota had indicted Sarah for defrauding Blackstone investors, based on evidence Trudell and others collected. Although Sarah was the owner of Blackstone, and although she was responsible for keeping the books, in interviews she distanced herself from her company's financial malfeasance. She raised suspicions in other ways, as well: Some Blackstone employees believed Sarah had known about the murders all along. According to Ryan Olness, the investor from Arizona, Sarah had asked him to speak to her in private shortly after KC disappeared, and she had acted so nervous that he felt certain she knew KC was murdered. Sarah denied the story. Nor did she remember meeting Suckow, but according to both Suckow and Olness, James and Sarah had driven Suckow to Williston the morning after the murder. James had forgotten to pay Suckow and called Olness, who took ten thousand dollars from his personal safe, stuffed the money in an empty Cheez-It box, and delivered it to James, Sarah, and Suckow in a pullout on the side of the road. Later, Sarah wrote two checks to reimburse Olness. "And she remembers none of this?" Mark Burbridge, the Spokane detective told me. "Come on. She spent probably two to three hours with Tim. He's a dangerous, scary-looking guy. And you don't remember that? My ass."

When Sarah entered the courtroom on the thirteenth day of trial, she had the poise of a funeral-goer. She did not appear to walk so much as float, her hips moving slightly, her shoulders entirely motionless. She wore black flats, dark gray pants, and a long coat fitted to her slim figure. Her hair was dark at its roots, tied in a bun.

She noticed Lissa only after she had taken her seat on the witness stand. Her eyes flickered and looked away. She would not glance at James, who did not look at Sarah, either. Where, before, James had stared aggressively at every witness, now his face flushed, and he looked like he might cry—the only emotion I had seen him express in the days he had been on trial.

Sarah's voice was sweet and firm.

"Did you ever ask the defendant about KC's disappearance?" Scott Jones asked.

"Yes," Sarah replied.

"How many times?"

"Maybe a handful."

"On any of those occasions, did he have a physical response to the question?"

"Once. He went pale and completely quiet."

"At some point in time, [did you see a] Facebook posting indicating that KC's body might have been found?"

"Yes."

"Where were you?"

"In the vehicle with James."

"Can you please describe his physical reaction?"

"He looked like he'd seen a ghost. He went completely white and started asking me questions."

A half hour had passed when Jones showed Sarah a copy of the flyer. Suddenly, her still exterior cracked. She glanced at Lissa and began to cry. Lissa looked surprised. "Do you think she knows you made those flyers?" I murmured.

"No," Lissa said. "She has no clue."

The next morning, a defense attorney would suggest inconsistencies in her story, but Sarah would not soften under his questioning. She would correct his dates, his mixed-up facts. She would interrupt to clarify what he had asked. I would notice Lissa smiling, as if in approval of Sarah. She tore a sheet from her journal and composed a note. She was glad Sarah was safe, she wrote, and when we broke for lunch, I watched Lissa hand the note to a slender woman with curly gray hair, whom I recognized as Sarah's mother. Later, when we returned to the courtroom, the woman bent to whisper in Lissa's ear.

"What did she say?" I asked.

"She said, 'Thank you,'" Lissa replied.

WE ROOMED TOGETHER FOR A little over a week, until a friend joined Lissa from North Dakota, and I rented my own place. I don't think I could have lasted another night with her, and I don't think Lissa could have lasted with me, either. She was hardly sleeping. I had taken to shutting off the lights to see if she would go to bed, and still she would lie on the covers in her court clothes, scrolling through news long past midnight. Later, we would laugh about this—Lissa liked to mock my sleep habits, which she considered excessive and dogmatic—but, at the time, nothing seemed very humorous. As she had expected, the defense was undermining Delao's credibility, calling for his impeachment, which could exclude his testimony from the jury's consideration and result in a mistrial. Coincidentally, the judge was presiding at the same time over another case involving Delao: Years earlier, the witness had been accused by a defense team of giving false testimony to a jury regarding his involvement in the attempted robbery of an elderly woman. Two weeks into the Henrikson trial, the judge ruled Delao had, indeed, lied in the robbery case, but he chose not to inform the Henrikson jury of this ruling.

Ahmed was livid, especially when the *Spokesman-Review* printed an article before the Henrikson trial was over about Delao lying in that other case. "I'm not being critical of the judge," he later told me. "I am being critical of the timing of it."

At trial, the parties began to bicker, which Lissa took as a sign that the prosecutors were getting nervous. "I'm sorry, but I could do better than that," she bragged to me one morning. I had begun to suspect the distrust was mutual. In the first week of trial, Lissa had gone looking for Jill on a lower floor of the courthouse when someone yelled her name. She had turned to find herself face-to-face with an agitated guard. She was not allowed on the floor, the guard had said, and Lissa complied, but it was the way the guard called her attention that rattled her: "He knew my name," she told me—not "Lissa," but "Yellow Bird."

She had noticed other things, too—the way Trudell avoided her after their encounter in the hallway, the way the guards watched her whenever she went out to smoke. After Mark Burbridge, the Spokane detective, gave his testimony, we both saw him roll his eyes at her.

Then, one afternoon, as I rode with Lissa to her hotel, a cop trailed us most of the way. When we got to the room, I sat at the desk, turned on my recorder, and asked Lissa to repeat the story of the flyers. "So I came home to switch Percy's bandages one day," she said, "and he was like, 'Sis, your packages are here,' and I looked, and they were all piled up—" Lissa pulled a cigarette from her pocket and slid open the glass doors. "And I—" She stopped. "The fucking cops are here," she said.

"What?" I rose to the doors.

"They're taking my license number and shit."

Indeed, a cop had parked behind her rental car—one of only two in the lot—and was pointing some sort of device at her license plate. He looked up at us and drove off.

Suddenly, Lissa was laughing, folding over, choking on her cigarette smoke.

"That's some covert shit up in this bitch," she said. "See him take off as soon as he seen me? That door surprised him. I looked right at him. He was sitting there behind that license plate."

I watched Lissa. She was laughing still, her eyes blinking tears. She swallowed her breath, wiped her eyes. "That's not my imagination, girl," she said. "I'm telling you. That's why I say, 'Be alert. Don't fuck around.' Because nobody knows whose team you're on. I'm perceived as an enemy of the state. I'm a threat." Lissa pulled on her cigarette. She coughed, a loose rattle. "And it's like, they don't know what I've been through. I'm here because I have a right to be here. I know my rights. Try to tell me I can't be here." Her cigarette had gone out, and when she relit it, I noticed that her hand was trembling. "I'm telling you. I live like that all the time. All the time. All the time," she said.

I NEVER FOUND OUT WHY the cop followed us. Lissa suspected it had to do with the trial, but as for who would have given him the order, she did not know. "I feel so far from home," she told me. Three weeks into the trial, she bought a return flight to Fargo. I agreed to drive her to the airport, but when I called to make plans the evening before her departure, Lissa did not answer. At last, she called. I asked how her night was going. "I don't want to talk about it," she said. "I just need to get my ass home."

She was smoking a cigarette when I found her the next morning. For a while, we drove in silence. Finally, she said, "I've been thinking, and I'm kind of at the point where maybe he's better off if we leave his ass out there."

"What makes you say that?"

"Do you remember when I was out there with Obie? There was this really steep incline, and my pelvis was hurting, so I couldn't go down there, but I told Obie, 'When you go down, it's a drop, about sixty feet, and there are trees, and if you start going, those trees aren't going to stop you.' I told him, 'If you start going, just drop back and grab those bushes.' He didn't believe me. He got maybe a quarter of the way down, and gravity started taking over. He did exactly like I told him. He grabbed those bushes. Then he kind of tumbled down some more, because gravity kept pulling him, and he ended up in this tiny grove, and there was an opening in the shrubs there. He landed on his feet. And he said, 'Oh my God, Mom. I wish you could see this.' He said, 'You're not going to believe how beautiful it looks from here.'"

"It is a beautiful place," I said.

"That's what I'm thinking. He's buried in a beautiful place."

16

The Body

THERE WERE TWO WEEKS REMAINING IN THE TRIAL WHEN LISSA LEFT. I called her the night Tex Hall took the stand and again on the day of the verdict, but she did not answer. The jury convicted James Henrikson on all eleven counts, including both murders-for-hire, four attempted hits, and the conspiracy to distribute heroin. Later, the judge would hand him two life sentences—one for killing Doug Carlile and the other for Kristopher Clarke.

As I watched the trial alone, I had the strange sensation that Lissa was nowhere and everywhere at once. No attorney or witness mentioned her name, though signs of her glared out at me. The flyer appeared many times throughout the trial, the most essential prop in the story the government had crafted and a symbol of the ruin of Blackstone's reputation, since it had forced James and Sarah to flee Fort Berthold and seek another front man in Carlile. This version of the story was true except on one point: According to prosecutors, it was Jed McClure, the investor, who acted alone to distribute the flyer—McClure who had been intent on forcing Blackstone off the reservation. And this was not the government's only omission. When Scott Jones questioned Sarah Creveling about the "Facebook posting" suggesting Clarke's body had been found, he was likely asking about a text message Lissa sent to Sarah in the summer of 2013. Indeed, a body had been found, but Lissa knew it was not KC's; rather, it belonged to a rancher murdered on his property near Williston. Lissa had sent the message to see how Sarah would react, and in the days afterward, Sarah asked Lissa about the body multiple times, wondering if anyone identified it. Later, when I asked officials what made them believe Sarah knew about KC's murder, they mentioned this moment when Sarah told James a body had been found, and James, in her words, "went pale and completely quiet."

I suspected prosecutors left Lissa out of their story because they did not know the depth of her involvement. If Sarah or Jed mentioned her in interviews, each would have known only a small piece of the role Lissa played in the case. Trudell knew that Lissa had spoken frequently to Sarah, but none knew the extent of their communication. Even I found it difficult to define what Lissa had done. It was easier to say what might never have occurred had she not been involved in the case: James might not have been forced off the reservation; Carlile might not have been killed; KC's murder might not have been solved; and Tex might have remained chairman of the tribe.

I also suspected that investigators left her out because they distrusted her. Aine Ahmed, the federal prosecutor, told me that after Suckow brought investigators to the burial area, they had tried to keep the site a secret, because, "We felt that if Yellow Bird or anyone else found the body, now we have issues with forensics. I just didn't want a thousand people at that scene, looking for a body, when we had expended all those resources."

Other investigators seemed suspicious of Lissa's motives. "I want to be careful what I say," Burbridge told me. "She's a cop wannabe who forms theories based on theories without evidence, without any real knowledge of how bad guys work, and she can cause problems. You can get off on a tangent and get lost if you start going down some of those roads." Even Mike Marchus, whom Lissa considered a friend, made clear to me that he did not reciprocate the feeling: "She's a smart gal. I think she always wanted to be in law enforcement." Police have a word for this—"We call them 'holster sniffers.'" Before Lissa went to prison, Marchus told me, "I didn't like dealing with her. She was a pain in the ass. Then, after she got out, I'd hear from her. Then I wouldn't hear from her. I just always assumed she was going through that cycle, you know?" He meant that he assumed she was still using drugs and was surprised when I told him Lissa was sober.

When I recalled the conversation for Lissa, she told me that Marchus was playing down how friendly they once had been. She was more bothered that he thought she was still using. "Maybe it's because these guys in law enforcement don't often see addicts get sober?" I suggested.

"No," she said. "I think it's just easiest for them to think of us as throwaways. Being an addict is unsightly. It's unattractive."

Burbridge's comment stayed longer with Lissa. *No real knowledge of how bad guys work.* "They're so set on labeling people," she told me. "I *am* the bad guy. They put this veil between themselves and what they project to believe is a bad guy."

The investigator who had the clearest sense of her involvement in the Clarke case was Darrik Trudell. Though the Department of Homeland Security would not allow me to interview him on the record, I sensed Trudell was also wary of Lissa, if not confused by her. Lissa sensed his wariness too. "I'm not trying to put a feather in my hat," she told me when I visited her after the trial. "But what if I didn't call up to Washington and say, 'You need to call Darrik'? What if I didn't call Darrik and say, 'You need to call up to Washington'? What if Darrik didn't call them and say, 'Hey, you need to ask about KC Clarke'? There were just so many things that could have happened that would have let these guys off. Tim Suckow could have gone down for the Carlile deal, kept his mouth shut, and all those people would be walking out in the free world, conjuring up their next con game on some other unsuspecting victim."

Lissa and Trudell had recently spoken by phone. She congratulated him on the verdict and mentioned Tex Hall again, suggesting he was less of a victim than he had made himself seem. Trudell defended Tex, having no reason to believe Tex acted nefariously. This made Lissa angry with Trudell all over again.

"Darrik thinks I have an agenda," she told me. "Of course I have an agenda, but Darrik is so young and green that he can't even understand it. This is a spiritual journey for me. This is beyond Darrik's comprehension. He made this clear in Washington, when he asked, 'You're missing work and losing pay? Why?' You have no soul, Darrik. You can't put this kind of shit on paper. He may be well trained by the book, but when it comes to spirit or compassion, he's a flunky. A lot of Indians say, 'That's a white thing. They're not really taught from birth how to have these experiences.' Maybe something drastic will have to happen, something like I went through with Shauna, or with prison, but one day, the fucking light's going to go off, and he'll be like, 'That's why. I get it.'"

Lissa was getting worked up. "He's got his feather. I don't know why he's worried about me. I must be pretty goddamn important. God, I'd just like to meet that fucker at the bar," she said. "*Yup, you got your ass kicked by a fat little Indian chick.*"

A week later, when I called Lissa, she had forgiven Trudell. "If it wasn't for him, this case would still be sitting on Gutknecht's desk," she said. "My goal was to get justice for KC, and if it weren't for Darrik, I would have never gotten that. What I wanted to happen happened. I've got to give him a little chicken feather for that. He did listen. He did take the time to meet with me. All that Tex Hall bullshit aside, I think he should get credit, because one person out of all these people listened. Just because somebody doesn't have a badge doesn't mean their story's not worth listening to."

In June 2016, after receiving federal permission, Trudell invited Lissa and Rick Arey into the badlands to give them a tour of the burial area to which Suckow and George Dennis had led him. The Clarke case was officially closed, but Trudell suspected Lissa would want to keep on searching even after investigators had given up.

Lissa accepted the offer. Indeed, she was not done looking for KC, she decided. She chose not to tell Trudell that she had already seen the area, and she invited me along. One weekend, she picked me up in Bismarck, and together we drove west into the badlands.

We met Trudell and Rick at a pull-off past a gate, climbed into Trudell's dark SUV, and headed north. The grass was high and gone to seed. Trudell was wearing hiking boots, jeans, a gray T-shirt, and wraparound sunglasses. He kept sighing, as if he wanted to get the day over with as quickly as he could.

We came to a bend in the road, and Trudell pointed out a window to a small, desiccated pond. When he first asked Suckow to look at a map and identify the burial site, Suckow had chosen this pond as a landmark, but when agents brought the hit man into the badlands, Suckow had led them farther south, to the bottom of a ravine. Now Trudell showed us this ravine, dense with brush.

"Did he say anything about it being relatively flat until he got to that ravine?" Lissa asked. Her face was darkening, crinkling in the dry sun.

"Yeah," said Trudell. "It was flat, and he walked through some brush, and then he dropped down, and it just opened up, and he said, 'This is the perfect spot.' He'd never been out there before. That's why I think it's so odd that we can't find it. I mean, how can they just walk off the road, and we can't find that body? It's so frustrating."

"So, you're sure KC's out here?" Rick said. "Like, he's within a thousand feet?"

"I wouldn't say a thousand feet," Trudell said. "But I'm confident he's along this pass somewhere."

Trudell also wanted to show Lissa the site George had identified, so we returned south, parked, and followed him on foot down another ravine, steeper and less wooded. "George said he turned the truck around," Trudell explained. "He saw them go behind a juniper, and that's when he lost sight of them. It's behind here." He pointed to a tree. Trudell approached the tree, looked at the ground, and paused. At the base was a large hole. For a moment, Trudell seemed confused. Then he looked at Lissa. "How did you know it was here?" Lissa shrugged; Trudell sighed. Now he really seemed ready to go. "You know," he said, "sometimes I was like, *Why did I get involved with this?* But I just knew from the beginning when I heard about the case from Mike Marchus that there was something to it. Everybody knew James did it. Everybody knew. It was just, How do you prove it? That's what piqued my curiosity, the challenge of not letting him get away with it. I knew there were frustrating times, because I took the phone calls. 'You're moving so slow. Aren't you guys going to do anything?' And I told you guys, it takes time. If it had been easy, it would have been done a long time ago."

"Dude," Rick said. He was wearing a fisherman's hat and a T-shirt scrawled with the words VIVA LA REVOLUCIÓN. "Everything that James chose not to feel in this life is going to hit him like a fucking ton of bricks in the next one. But knowing James is where he's supposed to be, and KC is here, I will sleep at night."

Trudell nodded. "You guys did a great job keeping it on the forefront." He glanced at Lissa again. "Those posters were brilliant."

"Look what we got in the end," said Rick. "The justice system worked."

"It took a while to get there," said Trudell.

"A long-ass haul," Lissa said.

WE STAYED THE NIGHT, LISSA, Rick, and I, in a man camp that had emptied out since the bust. It cost ninety dollars to rent a trailer for a night. Rick, who had driven up from Wyoming, fell asleep early, while Lissa and I returned to the burial area.

We drove with the windows down, letting in the cool, damp evening air and mosquitoes that bounced on the inside of the windshield. We parked a mile past the gate, and I followed Lissa on foot. Her steps were clumsy, quick. She hadn't taken her medication that day, and her mind leapt across the landscape. "Is that spearmint?" I heard her say. And: "Some of these paths are growing over." And: "Did you know a lot of Indians used to drive out here? My uncle Dennis came to hunt. I think with the oil they quit coming around."

I stumbled after her. Thunderheads had gathered on the northern horizon. The wild turnips were blooming.

17

Shauna

IN THE SUMMER OF 2016, LISSA WAS INVITED TO SPEAK ABOUT CITIZEN engagement in missing person cases at a Department of Justice conference in Atlanta, Georgia. She called me as soon as she received the invitation, sounding uncharacteristically nervous. Organizers of the conference had asked her to send a résumé so that they could compose a biography for the program, but Lissa had not made a résumé since college. "I was thinking, *Where do stripper, bondswoman, drug dealer, and welder fit into this?*" Lissa told me. "I said, 'Can we skip the résumé?'" She asked if I would write the biography, and I agreed.

It was her third speaking engagement. Her first had been at a gala for the North Dakota Human Rights Coalition, in Fargo. Obie accompanied her. "My mom bought me some nice clothes," he told me. "We got there, and I was like, 'Wow, you're not my crowd.' These people were high-class. This one chick had a totally white dress on. Her hair was well-conditioned."

Lissa spoke, and then, to her surprise, the Coalition honored her with its annual Arc of Justice Award. "I wasn't going to stay," she recalled, "but a woman said, 'You know, Lissa, we'd really like you to stay and eat.' Obie grabbed a plate and said, 'Come on, Mom.' He made me stay. We were eating, and they were giving awards. They said my name, and Obie's like, 'Hell, yeah!' And—oh my God, this kid—he was hitting me on the back. 'You go, Mom!' I was sitting there in shock. He said, 'Get up! Get up!'"

"She was crying," Obie said. "I was like, Wow, my mom *really* likes what she does. Then the newspaper wrote an article, and in the picture I was kneeling next to her. My teachers were like, 'Is that your mom? Tell her to keep it up.'"

When Lissa told me about the award, I knew she was proud. Still, I wondered if she wished investigators had in some way recognized her effort as well. I asked her one night while we were sitting in the apartment. It was February 2017—seven months since Trudell showed Lissa the burial area.

"I think I'm just used to it," she said. "I mean, if it was all about getting a pat on the back, then that sort of person would have expectations that someone would respect what they had to say. Do you think a person used to that entitlement would still be looking for a body five years later? I don't have to have those pats on the back to go where I go. I don't need that from anybody. I've learned not to need what a lot of people get."

"You can't think of any time in your life that you've wished for affirmation?" I asked.

Lissa thought for a while. "One of the times would be with Shauna after I was paroled," she said. "I remember her sitting on that couch right there, holding a new baby, crying, saying, 'What am I going to do? I can't get a job.' I said, 'First you need to have faith.' I told her the mustard seed story"—from the Gospel of Matthew, about how "the Kingdom of Heaven is like a grain of mustard seed, which a man took, and sowed in his field," which grew so large "that the birds of the air come and lodge in its branches." Shauna had not been convinced. Since her dismissed charges had lingered on her record, no one seemed to want to hire her. "I said, 'You explain. You humble yourself,'" Lissa recalled, "and she did, and when she got a job, she said, 'They got tuition reimbursement.' 'Well, you better get in school part time, because it's free money.' And now look at her. That would be one time. She won't give it to me, and that's fine. I give it to me just by watching her."

"She told me that story," I said.

Lissa laughed. She didn't believe me, but it was true. I had it recorded.

THEIR RECONCILIATION HAD BEGUN ONE night the previous summer. Three years after Shauna stopped talking to her mother, she sent Lissa a string of messages:

> *Sometimes it's important that children know and accept that they can never love as much as their parents love them. I now know. You have those moments thinking, 'I'm NEVER going to be like her.' Then you become just like her. I have a daughter that I've tried to be the best mom to, all for her to resent me at times. I looked at an old conversation you wrote years ago (obviously). No response or acknowledgment on my part as you poured your heart out. How horrible that must've felt. I'm so sorry for that.*

When Lissa saw the messages, she cried. "It's okay," she replied. "I saw you read it and knew someday you would reflect on that. I prayed for it, sun danced over it for many years now and prayers answered! It was and always will be okay! . . . I love you guys so much!"

That summer and fall, Lissa did not search for KC. In August, a video circulated online showing dozens of tribal members from the Standing Rock Indian Reservation, three hours south of Fort Berthold, in a peaceful confrontation with police. They had gathered to stop the construction of a pipeline that would transport oil from the Bakken to a terminal in Iowa, cutting across the Missouri River north of their reservation. The company building the pipeline originally planned to cross the river above Bismarck, but the city protested, and although the Standing Rock Sioux Tribe opposed the new route, the company ignored its complaint. A group of Standing Rock and Cheyenne River youth ran more than five hundred miles to deliver a petition to the Army Corps office in Omaha, Nebraska, and when the colonel refused to see them, they ran to the White House in Washington, D.C. On July 26, 2016, the Standing Rock Sioux Tribe filed a complaint in federal court. Three weeks later was the peaceful confrontation with police, during which the tribal chairman, David Archambault, was arrested. In the weeks that followed, delegations from hundreds of tribes, including the MHA Nation, appeared at Standing Rock in solidarity, and thousands of Native Americans from around the country joined, erecting an encampment not far from the pipeline construction site. Soon it was the largest demonstration for Native American rights since the 1973 occupation of Wounded Knee. Lissa went every Friday after work. She built two snug wooden shelters outfitted with cots, heaters, and racks to hang clothing on, where several Yellow Birds joined her. Irene and Madeleine would not stay the night but delivered donations to the encampment. I visited a few times, as did Rick Arey, who would happen to be there with Lissa on the day that the pipeline company's security sicced dogs on demonstrators.

Then, one day, Shauna visited as well. Lissa sent me a black-and-white photograph she took that weekend: her daughter against a backdrop of snow and smoke rising from a circle of tipis. Shauna was flanked by her children, clutching a swaddled baby, staring stoically into the camera.

I visited Shauna that same winter at her house in Eagan, Minnesota, just south of Minneapolis. I arrived on a Monday evening. One of her sons answered the door and led me up a flight of stairs into a living room furnished with a plush couch and a television mounted over a fireplace. A playpen blocked the entry to keep her youngest child, a year old, from escaping. Shauna did not rise when I came in. She was seated on the couch with a laptop, her hair knotted above her neck. She wore soft black pants, the pockets turned out. "I have to finish something for work," she said, so I sat quietly until she was done.

We were the same age, twenty-nine, born five days apart. Her face was shaped like her mother's—wide with high cheekbones, full lips, and a small chin—but in other ways she seemed different. When she spoke, her words were calm, measured, and when she listened, she pressed her lips together, as if her mouth were a small cage.

"I had to do my own healing to move on," Shauna told me. "Now I'm trying to look at my situation through my own kids. My kids always ask me, 'Have you told her you love her? Have you talked to her lately?' It means a lot to them. I don't want them to think it's okay to hold on to those resentments, because I don't want them to do that to me. Even if it's a surface-level relationship with my mom, anything is better than nothing. I feel better now. I feel like I have more control over myself, over what I'm willing to enjoy or when enough is enough and I can walk away."

The baby cried sharply, and Shauna lifted her, rose from the couch, and lowered to her knees. In one swift movement, she removed an old diaper and slipped on a new one. "We don't really talk about personal stuff yet," she continued. "It's, check in, check out. The hardest things we talk about are parenting—the struggles I have with my kids and how she feels guilt for that."

"She says she feels guilty?" I asked.

Shauna nodded. "I used to take care of my brothers a lot while she worked several jobs to try to make ends meet, and once in a while I'd come home to a letter on the table and a couple of brand-new CDs. There were times like that when she showed appreciation. But other times I'd find a letter after something bad happened. She'd try to talk about her addiction, and I'd be like, 'What you did was wrong. I don't care what your excuse is.' I tried not to get emotionally attached to her words. I felt loved, but I also felt that she was dependent on me, and I didn't really have a choice in that matter."

She rose from the floor. "Do you want dinner?" she said, and I followed her into the kitchen and sat at a tall wooden table. Her oldest son was doing homework. He was ten, born on the day Lissa was arrested in Bismarck. I knew this because I had read it in the transcript of the testimony Shauna gave in her mother's defense:

> Q: *How old are you?*
> A: *Nineteen.*
> Q: *Do you know the lady next to me at this table?*
> A: *Yes.*
> Q: *Who is she?*
> A: *My mom.*

Had I only read the testimony, I might have assumed Shauna hoped to spare her mother from prison, but Lissa had suggested otherwise: It was Shauna, she told me, who put her there, on trial, in the first place.

"Yeah, not that she was doing or selling drugs of her own accord," Shauna said, rolling her eyes, when I mentioned this to her. But what her mother had said was partly true. Though Shauna had never seen Lissa use drugs, in the summer of 2005, when Shauna was almost eighteen, she began to notice new signs: needles and other paraphernalia scattered around the house, her mother disappeared into a bedroom. "I was trying to keep some order, but I could see the transition," Shauna said. "My mom became very aggressive. My grandma would commit her, and my mom's smart, so she would get through to people that she didn't need treatment, and they'd let her go. There was no helping her. She could con her way out of everything." Shauna told Irene what she had been seeing, and Irene told the police.

Shauna placed a warm sausage on a plate and set the plate in front of me. "Sweet tea?" she said. She strapped the baby in a high chair and called for her other children.

"We went through some really bad times," she said. "I don't let that dictate how I live my life, but I look at it as missed opportunities. That's what I hold on to. *You missed it.* There were critical moments that could have changed any of us."

"What kind of mom were you wishing for?" I asked.

"Oh, you know, the typical sit at home and cook dinner and wash your laundry and iron your clothes and take you to school and show up at conferences. The PTA mom. Whatever they show on TV. Who doesn't want that mom? But as I grew up I realized I learned a lot of things that not a lot of other people learned because of the struggles that I went through. No matter what, I'm still okay today. I have to give that credit to her. In the worst of times, she still made sure that we had somewhere to sleep. She still made sure we ate. We may have gone without a mom, but we didn't go without our other needs. I value that. I feel like it gave me strength and resilience in the end, and that's why I'm at where I'm at today, and I'm okay with where I'm at."

Shauna collected the dishes from the table and rose to wash them in the sink. "I grew up with somebody that I really didn't know," she said. "I didn't have the desire to know. All I saw was an absent parent. Now I want to know. Who is she? What are her passions? Why? I don't know a lot about her past. I think it's been a long journey for her. I think there's a lot more darkness than she's revealed. Things that she just feels aren't worth resurfacing. I don't know if it's being neglected, being lonely, or somebody hurt her. I just think she's been through a lot. I think she wants to move on. I think that's why she tries to make that impact on other people."

Shauna smiled, her lips closed tight, her eyes intent and blinking. I could not tell what she was feeling. I asked if she ever cried, and she laughed, rinsed another dish. "It takes a lot to make me cry," she said. "I used to when I was younger. You could look at me funny and I would cry, but I think I learned that crying gets you nowhere. I don't really cry anymore, maybe once every five years. My grandma's like that, too."

I had seen Irene cry once. It had been the first night we met, in a restaurant in Minot. She was telling me about one of Lissa's arrests. After the arrest, Irene had attended a pretrial hearing at which she approached Lissa's boyfriend in a hallway outside the courtroom. She grabbed him by the arm. *If anything ever happens to my daughter, I'm coming after you,* she had said. As Irene told me this story, she had begun to cry. "I really was going to," she said. "I was so afraid. I was so afraid she was going to die."

I told this story to Shauna. The baby squealed, and Shauna rose to lift her daughter from the high chair, pressing her to her hip. "I'm surprised," she said. She, too, had seen Irene cry only once. "We were talking about the things my brother went through in foster care," Shauna explained. "Our foster mother used to pick up my brother and throw him like a ball into the wall. She used to hold his head under toilet water, to the point of him almost giving up. We'd sit at the dinner table, and he had a speech impediment, so he couldn't speak clearly. If he couldn't say the word she wanted him to say, she wouldn't give him food. I felt really guilty, because I was in second grade, and I would have to leave him when I went to school. And being so conditioned—don't talk, don't tell, don't trust anybody, keep a secret—I never said anything, and so I carry a lot of that guilt. And those are only the things that I saw. There's no telling what I didn't see when I wasn't there. It's really hard for me to think about a lot of the things he went through. I look at him sometimes, and I'm just like, Could I have saved you? What more could I have done? I was old enough to convey that to somebody, and I didn't." When a foster father later molested Shauna, she had not said anything about this either, reasoning that at least her brother was safe.

Shauna set her daughter back down, returned to the sink, and soaped a glass with a sponge.

"I've seen my mom cry more times since prison than I did in my whole life," she said. "She was always in control. You would think someone struggling with addiction would be out of control. But I still felt she could put down the pipe whenever she felt like it. As odd as it sounds, I always felt that she was in control of herself, but I also felt that she didn't know how to find the answers she needed to move on with her life. She resorted to drugs as a kind of mask, but she always knew the truth."

"What truth?" I asked.

"Just that life was a certain kind of way. Nothing was going to change. That *she* needed to find who she was." Shauna rinsed the last dish, dried her hands, and came to sit. Her kids had gone to the living room, her baby fallen asleep. "I truly believe that going to prison helped save her," she said. "I wasn't regretful. A lot of people call me a snitch, but I didn't look at it that way. I knew that if she continued on that path, she might die, and I'd much rather my mom go to jail than die.

"I remember my mom always said, 'I'm not going to get old. I'm going to die young.' Her time was always in the near future. It's crazy to see that she's, what, forty-nine this year? I'm like, *Huh, you actually are getting old*. I always wonder with all the dangerous things she does, when is it ever going to catch her? And then sometimes I think she's untouchable. Sometimes I think she'll never die. She really is such a free spirit. Trapped within herself, but a free spirit. I do believe she's got a purpose in this world. I do believe that although she may not have been the ideal mom, her purpose is beyond being a mom."

THERE WERE MANY THINGS I still did not know about Lissa, although it had taken me some time to realize this. For a period, I had thought I knew her better than anyone I had ever known, and while this remained true—while even people I knew my entire life had never revealed themselves to me so intimately—I knew now there were doors I had overlooked, doors that had never been open to me. I had stumbled upon these doors by accident, in conversations with Lissa and her family. Most I chose not to open. Everyone should have their secrets, I thought, though on a few occasions I had made the mistake of stepping too close. Once, I angered Lissa for this reason. Later, she would say she had felt "like a little dog, barking" at me to step away. I believe this was the only time Lissa knowingly lied to me. The secret came out anyway: Shauna found her father.

For a while, I had thought Lissa's trick was to blind you with honesty so that you could not see what hurt her. Then I realized that even

Lissa was unsure of what had hurt her. Just as there were doors in her life closed to her children and to me, there were doors in her mother's and grandmother's lives closed to her as well. All her life Lissa had heard rumors, so she had a vague sense of where her family's pain came from. But it was not the precise events that mattered to Lissa. "You know people talk about how your DNA remembers from previous generations," she told me. "I wonder what role that played with me, because my whole life, I've never been a stable person. I could walk out of my life with young kids and everything. I could walk out of my life and not care. And I think about my mom, born in Elbowoods, a product of relocation. She was made to feel ashamed of who she was. She disconnected from her people, from me. I wonder, did that contribute to my inability to find the right path? I'm okay with my path, now. I can be accountable. But I want to have an understanding why, because somewhere I really lost my way."

I was surprised to hear Lissa say this. Rarely in the time I spent with her had I heard her wonder about herself. She was tired of people asking why she cared so much about finding KC. She found it easier now just to say why she cared for finding missing people at all. There was the fact that, years ago, she easily could have gone missing herself. She also believed she was paying a debt to society, making up for harm *she* had caused. "You know, this makes me happy," she told me once. "It makes me happy to help these people that have no hope left in this world."

Over the years, her relatives had speculated to me on Lissa's motivations. Obie said simply, "She does it because she wants to do it," while Madeleine supposed her granddaughter had finally found "something that fulfills her." Percy told me, "She's just that kind of person who sets her mind on something, you know what I mean?" Her uncle Michael explained, "When Lissa first started, I was like, *What are you looking for? Are you searching for yourself? Why are you doing this for strangers?* But I watched her, and after a while, I realized her passion was back. People discover their purpose."

I, too, speculated on Lissa's reasons. The more time I spent with her, the more I realized that in certain ways we were not all that different. It was possible that what drew her into the lives of people she searched for was the same as what drew me into hers: We wanted to know what others knew, to feel what others felt.

"You want to know what drives Lisa?" her uncle Loren asked me once. I had asked him because I knew that among her relatives, Lissa felt particularly close to Loren. They were the same age and had spent much of their childhoods together; in adulthood, they shared similar hardships. "It's her spirit, her determination to know," Loren said. He could think of few people who had lived as fully as Lissa had. "She wants to understand, to have a good time, to laugh about it, to cry."

Loren saw little difference between the woman his niece had been when she used drugs and the woman she was now. Once, years ago, she had brought him a gift—a jacket for his son. "She was on the run," Loren recalled. "She was tweaking, and she said, 'I got this for him.' I said, 'You hungry?' She said, 'No, I gotta go.'"

The point, Loren explained, was that even in the midst of her addiction, Lissa had thought of others. The drugs had never changed this part of who she was.

But now Loren pressed me to go further. He believed there was an answer neither of us had considered yet. "You want to know what drives Lissa?" he asked again. "What would make you do something that you didn't have to do? What's your breaking point? Maybe that's what you should look at with her. Maybe she hit a breaking point. You know, when I look at what she's been through, she had nobody to stand there, to pull her aside, to walk with her, to guide her. She had to find that within herself. And I prayed. I love her. I really do. You don't even know how deep that love is. But when she was in that dark place, I couldn't reach over and help her. I think that's why people come to her now, because she knows—that, at some point, nobody is going to be there. Nobody. Nobody will be there. You're going to be all by yourself."

. . . . .

WHAT WAS HER BREAKING POINT—THE moment at which she felt most alone? Two stories Lissa had told me came to mind.

In the first story, she had been in a coma, in a hospital room in Minot. She had swallowed a bottle of pills after her sons were taken from her and placed in foster care. This was her "overdose," her attempt at suicide, which I had read about in her journal, but later she had shared with me a dream she had that day. She had dreamed of a room, of the walls glowing red, of people gathered on a set of risers. She stepped closer to the people and saw they were her relatives. Her grandfather was there, and a cousin who had died, and then, from behind them all, her great-grandmother appeared. *Hey, this one,* Nellie scolded, shooing Lissa away as she always did. *What are you doing here? Go on. You don't belong here.* And suddenly Lissa had felt pain—a deep, old, shuddering pain—yanking her back to life.

The second story was not a dream. It was some years later, the summer before her trial. Lissa was out on bail, facing years in prison. She had decided Shauna would be fine on her own; CJ would live with his dad; but no one had yet offered to take Micah and Obie, who were six and seven years old. Lissa feared they would go to live with a strange family, where they would be shamed and touched, tossed headfirst into walls. Where they would lose their breath into toilet water, or, if they were lucky, be loved. There was one more option Lissa thought of. She gave her sons a choice: Either they would go to foster care, or she would kill them and herself. Micah wanted to join his mother. Obie was not sure. But it was Shauna who stopped them all. Shauna who heard them talking. Shauna who begged Irene, who asked Dennis to take the boys. Shauna who kept her mother alive once more—who kept her mother from becoming a murderer.

Now I understood: Her breaking point was her children. It was their living that made Lissa want to live, their loss that made her lose herself. Did she regret the suicide pact, I asked her once? It took her a long time to respond. Finally, Lissa said, "I regret putting my kids mentally through it, but I don't regret the decision, and I would

probably make that decision again if it were put in front of me." To
kill her children would have been unspeakable, an act of cowardice
and madness and love, but Lissa would have wanted people to speak
it. She would have wanted people to say, "A mother murdered her
children," and she would have wanted people to wonder why, and in
that wondering, she would have hoped they considered what she saw
at that time: that she could not bear the possibility that her children be
tortured by tortured people. That she had wanted only to save them
from the violence that went on and on and on.

Surviving and living are different things. I learned this from Lissa.
It was after Lissa survived that she chose to live, and it was when she
chose to live that she emptied her body of her pain, and in its absence
was so large a chasm that she could fit the grief of the world inside,
become the keeper of others' pain.

Not everyone was capable of healing themselves, she told me.
There was, for one, her uncle Chucky. He had wanted to get better,
had read all the self-help books, the latest theories and science. Sometimes he had made his nieces and younger siblings sit with him as he
listened to cassette tapes. Adult Children of Alcoholics, the series was
called. *You see*, Chucky seemed to be saying. *There* is *a reason I am this
way*. But maybe that was his trouble, Lissa thought. He clung to his
pain, his explanation. He would not let it go. This was the paradox of
trauma: To heal from it, you had to know where it came from and
then, in a sense, disbelieve it. You had to trust you were more than the
damage done to you. No matter how much others made you suffer,
you had to cease seeing yourself as a victim.

Lissa did not blame Chucky for this. "At some point, we're going
to have to realize that there are some people that are not going to
recover, so for us to expect that is unreasonable," she told me. The
morning Chucky died, he had shared with her the source of his grief.
He had chosen to tell her, he explained, because he knew that it would

not change the way she thought about their family. He knew she would go on loving their relatives nonetheless.

It was the ugliness Chucky wanted her to carry. Everyone would see the beauty after he was gone. "There was a lot of good things about Chucky," Lissa told me. "We all knew that part. Let's talk about the time he was laying in the ditch with pissy pants, and nobody wanted to touch him. Let's talk about that time, because we should learn to love each other enough that that doesn't make a difference. If you've got to change pissy pants thirty to forty to two hundred times to see that person out of this miserable life and transition them to another place, then so be it. I want to learn something from that. I want everyone to learn something from that. I don't want to just glorify Chucky, who he was at his good times. There's a whole lifetime of hurt that he carried, and I heard about that in those last moments of his life. Let's not forget that part. Let's not forget the pain he carried a whole lifetime that ultimately got the best of him. He saw no way out. Why? Let's talk about how we could make somebody else's life better. He would have wanted it that way. That's why I told him, *Uncle, I don't want you to die alone.* Pissy pants is nothing. Laying in the ditch—that's nothing. All that can be cleaned up. *I want to sit there with you, because there's something to be learned from this. I want to share that pain with you, because when you leave this earthly physical being, I don't want you to feel like you're the only one.*"

18

What They Say We Loved

THE BOOM WAS OVER. IN THE EARLY MONTHS OF 2016, THE PRICE OF OIL still did not rise above fifty dollars a barrel, and although state officials were hopeful it would, anyone I spoke to inside the industry told me the pace of development would never be what it had been before. The royalties landowners earned would grow and shrink as the price of oil rose and fell, but drillers no longer needed as many workers. Most wells were drilled, and companies had become efficient in their hiring. Booms, I learned, are inherently wasteful. They come to an end, in part, because companies catch up to them—learn to do more with less.

That winter, I noticed that a man camp on the outskirts of Parshall, the town where I often stayed, had vanished. Before, there had been hundreds of trailers. Now there were fewer than a dozen, and they appeared abandoned.

"Where did they go?" I asked Ed Hall, the elderly man I had met five years earlier on my first visit to the reservation.

"Home," he replied.

Some nights later, Ed called me. Had I seen the evening news? A junkyard to the north of the reservation was collecting trailers and feeding them into a crusher. I went to my computer and found the video. The trailers looked brittle. They broke like eggs.

One spring, Ed invited me to see the old Congregational church that had been carried up from the bottomlands. It had a new fence, for which he had raised the money. On a Friday evening before sunset, I walked to Ed's house and rode with him to the church.

He was dressed in jeans and a blue nylon jacket. Merle Haggard was playing on the radio. We passed Lucky Mound Creek, where Ed's mother taught school before the flood, and wheat fields, and a few trees. I asked Ed to tell me the story of the bones, again—of how he dug them up from the bottomlands and reburied them in the new churchyard. "I had to do it to eat," he said. "There weren't too many jobs those days." He did not seem to want to talk about it, and changed the subject.

"The pheasants are getting thick. We'll have a good crop this year," he said, and indeed, the birds were rising from the sloughs, skidding along the sides of the road. When we came to the church, I followed Ed through a gate and up stone steps that had pulled away from the foundation. It was quiet inside, except for the wind. A heart had been painted on some plywood boarding a window, and by the door was an alcove where a rope once hung to ring a bell.

"Did you ever ring it?" I asked Ed.

"Oh, lots of times," he said, and reached with his hand to pull the invisible rope.

Outside, the sky was thick with clouds. A meadowlark sang. Wind combed the grass. We wandered the graves, of which ground squirrels had made a mess, causing Ed to curse. The cemetery was scattered with colorful objects—crosses and cigarette butts, ball caps and undrunk Coca-Colas. There were pocketknives, their blades snapped. A snow globe. Flowers tipped and blown from the graves, gathered against the masonry of the church.

I did not touch the objects. I thought of what Lissa told me about the way spirits moved from hand to object, object to lips, skin to skin, skin to bone.

A car passed, fast and carelessly. Ed was waiting for me at the gate. He let me through, latched it, and for a moment, we studied the new fence. It looked nice, I thought, and I told him so. Then we returned to the car.

That was when I asked about Lissa, whom Ed had raised until her mother took her back.

"Who, Lisa? Lisa Yellow Bird? Oh, she was a real cuddly little girl. She always wanted to be held, and so I held her." Ed smiled, a look of love. That was all he said.

In January 2017, the new president signed an executive order instructing the Army Corps of Engineers to grant the easements to build the Dakota Access Pipeline across the Missouri River. Two weeks later, the Corps did so, and the Standing Rock encampment was disbanded. Lissa resumed her search for KC. More than a year had passed since she last had spoken to Jill. "Every family handles their missing a different kind of way," she told me. "Some families, it seems, have totally accepted the fact that they're not going to find their loved one. It's like they almost find more peace in knowing that we're out there, looking. Even though they don't come anymore. Not that they don't care. It's that they had to move on. It was taking away from their living. Where, for me, I don't feel it's taking away anything. It's a part of my life. I'm okay with what I do, and I think my friends and family have pretty much accepted this. *She's always been that way.*"

By now her searching had taken on an even more personal meaning. In August 2016, her own relative had disappeared—Chucky's daughter, Carla Yellow Bird. Carla had been gone for two weeks when Lissa heard her family mention it. Carla was two decades younger than Lissa, who knew her as "a real giddy girl, one of those weirdo kids. She had a lot of confidence, and she pulled it off." Carla, Lissa said, was "the kind of girl who would come in and wouldn't even introduce herself. She'd find a phone, jam it in, play music when you're trying to talk. Then she'd go, 'Oh, hi, I'm Carla.' She'd be in the kitchen dancing to this song, turning it up even more. Then she'd whiz out the door, and you'd be like, 'Thank God.'"

She was addicted to meth. At first, her family assumed she was out on a binge, but when three weeks passed and she still had not appeared, they began to worry. After four weeks, Lissa called every relative she could think of who might know where her cousin had gone. Around the time Carla disappeared, Lissa learned, she had been riding to the Spirit Lake Indian Reservation, east of Fort Berthold, with a Sisseton-Wahpeton man. Lissa posted the man's name on Facebook. Within a day, he called her and asked her to take it down. At first, he denied knowing where Carla had gone, but Lissa pressed him, and after they had spoken for hours, the man confessed: Carla had been selling meth on Spirit Lake when another dealer they were riding with shot and robbed her. The next day, the man led the FBI and Lissa to Carla's body, and Lissa identified her.

In 2017 and 2018, Lissa worked on dozens of cases of Native American men and women who had gone missing. There was Alex Vasquez, a twenty-four-year-old Lakota man who disappeared from the Pine Ridge Indian Reservation in October 2015 and whose rumored murder was still unsolved. And there was Jason Azure, from the Fort Peck Indian Reservation in Montana, who, in April 2018, leapt into the Missouri River to save a boy from drowning and drowned himself. Lissa found Jason with a sonar system she had attached to her boat, and with his family's blessing, tried to fish him out with a giant treble hook, but his body would not catch. Authorities offered little to no help, and when winter came, Jason remained in the river.

Lissa coordinated searches with law enforcement when officials were willing, but in most cases, families came to her because officials had so far done nothing. Among these cases was that of Damon Boyd, an Ojibwe man from Leech Lake, Minnesota, twenty-nine when he disappeared. Damon had been homeless when he last was spotted in

Grand Forks in April 2014, which made him difficult to track, but Lissa suspected his medical records might contain some clues. This presented another obstacle: Only a legal guardian could see the records, but Damon's mother and father were dead. His grandfather, Louis, was sickly. Still, Lissa found a loophole: The Leech Lake Tribe, with Louis's approval, exercised its sovereignty to appoint Lissa as Damon's guardian. "Don't wait for law enforcement," Lissa took to advising families. When a person went missing, she warned, authorities did three things: "Wait for the person to walk through the door, wait for the person to end up in jail, or wait for their body to surface."

While Lissa searched for Damon, another case came to her attention. On August 19, 2017, a twenty-two-year-old woman by the name of Savanna Greywind disappeared from her apartment in Fargo. A spokesman for the family contacted Lissa, who visited them at the apartment the next day. No one had seen Savanna, who was eight months pregnant, leave the building; she had left her phone behind. As Lissa visited with the family, police officers searched an apartment upstairs, where a white woman and her white boyfriend lived, but found nothing. Five days later, at the family's insistence, officers searched upstairs again and discovered Savanna's baby, alive. Meanwhile, Lissa helped organize search parties. Eight days after Savanna disappeared, volunteer searchers found her body wrapped in plastic, caught in a tree near the bank of the Red River.

It was the first case of a murdered Native American woman to make the national news, due in part to the horror of the story: The white woman who lived upstairs had cut the baby out of Savanna. *People* magazine published an article. Gloria Allred, the celebrity lawyer representing women who had been sexually assaulted by Bill Cosby, provided legal counsel to the Greywind family. Lissa was invited to speak at conferences all over the country about the high rates at which Indigenous women, men, and children went missing and how often their cases went unsolved. In the fall of 2017, she quit her welding job after her boss said he could no longer allow her absences. By then, another woman had disappeared—Olivia Lone

Bear, a thirty-two-year-old member of the Mandan, Hidatsa, and Arikara Nation.

Olivia had last been seen in late October, driving west from a bar in New Town to her home on Sanish Bay. Some suspected she made it home, since her cell phone, wallet, and the jacket she had been wearing were found inside her house. But the truck she drove—a Chevy Silverado borrowed from a friend, an oil worker—was missing. For months after Olivia disappeared, her family and teams of volunteers hunted for the truck. Lissa helped in the beginning but, after an argument with some members of Olivia's family, moved on to other cases.

Still, the disappearance tormented Lissa. "You know the feeling I had with KC?" she told me one night on the phone. "It's the same thing with Olivia." The woman's family had been searching for her all over the country, but Lissa suspected Olivia's body was not far from her house, submerged in Sanish Bay. In July 2018, after she spoke at a forum on Fort Berthold, Lissa launched her boat from a marina near the bay and, with a friend and young relative, motored out into the lake. They had been drifting hardly ten minutes when her relative spotted an odd shape with Lissa's sonar. Lissa took a photograph of the sonar image and texted it to Darrik Trudell, a local deputy, tribal chairman Mark Fox, and me.

I called Lissa. "What is it?" I said. She sighed at my cluelessness.

Four nights later, she called me from Crow Flies High Butte, overlooking the lake, as authorities towed a pickup truck from the water. Olivia's body was inside.

"What are you going to do now?" I asked.

"Go see my mom and grandma," Lissa said. "I think they miss me." The wind crackled from her phone. After we hung up, she forwarded me the text messages she exchanged with Trudell. How had she known where to find the truck, he had wondered. It was something "spiritual," she wrote. "You probably don't understand."

"10-4," Trudell replied. Understood.

......

FOR THE FIRST TIME SINCE Lissa's parole, her kids moved out of the apartment. Micah went to Minneapolis, where he enrolled in college, while Obie and Caitlin got pregnant, and they rented an apartment of their own. When Lissa was not working on a case, she visited Shauna and spent more time with her grandchildren, who often came to stay with her in Fargo. After Obie's son was born, OJ, who wanted to meet his grandson, stayed two weeks in Lissa's spare bedroom. She mentioned the visit to me only after OJ had left. I told her I thought it was the craziest thing she had done in the years that I had known her, but she promised their time together had been cordial and platonic. She had put OJ to work attaching flyers for a missing woman to lamp-posts around Fargo.

One spring, I spent a month in Fargo. Lissa had resurrected her interest in plants, and when I arrived, there were seed trays scattered around the apartment, stalks sprouting in ceramic pots. We spent most of the month on her patio. A family of rabbits lived by a fence separating the apartment building from another, and each morning as we drank our coffee, we watched them graze in the yard.

Tex Hall had appeared in the news again. According to an article in *The Bismarck Tribune,* he had partnered with a marijuana grower to bring the industry to reservations. He believed tribes, with all the land they owned, had an opportunity to corner the market. Lissa was not opposed to medical marijuana, but she was not keen on any attempt by Tex to resurrect himself. She was bothered that he had never been held legally accountable for the corruption alleged in the investigative report. Soon, Sarah Creveling would plead guilty to "conspiracy to commit mail fraud." According to her indictment, she, with James's help, had "diverted or embezzled approximately $1,720,835.11" from investors. Meanwhile, George Dennis would be charged for conceal-ing the fact that he had aided in the "disposal of the victim's body," and his charges would be dismissed after he completed eighteen months of supervised probation. Neither he nor Sarah would serve prison time. And what had Tex suffered? Lissa wondered. In one sense, she resented him more than she did James: James killed two people, but Tex, in welcoming the oil industry, had threatened the lives of thousands. "I'm not trying to minimize James's deeds," she told me, "but when you talk about Tex's crime, you're talking about what he did to his own people. When you look at our culture, one of the things we pride ourselves in is our warriors, the ones who delivered our people out of hard times when all the odds were against them. Tex had a choice, and what did he bring? Pain. Conflict. Hatred amongst his own people."

Lissa believed Tex had traded the suffering of his community for the enrichment of a few. His crime was greed, but also denial, and in this way, she said, he was not all that unlike Sarah Creveling: "Even she was blinded by greed. She didn't want to believe her husband was a murderer. She wanted to believe this false story, this storybook. But that's not storybook—not when somebody's missing, presumably murdered. She was not even willing to consider the fact that her husband was involved. Let's not be stupid. She had to question some of this. She didn't *want* to believe it. If she had been forced to believe something like that, which she eventually was, then her little fairy tale would go away."

I understood that it was easy to blame the story on James. Was it really just greed, many people asked me, that had driven him to hire the murders? Was he really that cold-blooded? There was something unknowable about him. I, too, had searched for other explanations. I had wondered if the trial might reveal some trauma he suffered in his past, some other reason why he hurt people, but I had learned nothing more about him, and with no story, I had been left thinking that James was fundamentally lacking in empathy—that he was a sociopath. But what *made* him a sociopath, I still wondered. He had placed material profit and human life on the same scale. Was that a definition of a sociopath? If the oil industry were a man, would we call him a sociopath? If our governments, which systematically took Indigenous lives, were men, would we call them sociopaths? Was a sociopath just the man himself or also the society that enabled him?

What Lissa had seen in this story, which many had not, was the complicity of a whole community that had willfully believed in the promise of the boom, in the saving power of wealth. The violence was all around them. They just chose not to look. Everyone was both victim and perpetrator, Lissa thought, and their crime was their unwillingness to see this. The injustice of the boom was not the money they lost, nor the opportunity they missed, but the forgetting that made space for the story they had told themselves: "They say, 'We're tired of being poor.' This is how they justify losing what they say we loved."

A FEW TIMES THAT SPRING I visited Ed Hall at his house in Parshall, in his office on a lower floor where he kept portraits of his late wife and art he had collected in the years he lived in Albuquerque. Ed had three desks stacked with reports and newspaper clippings. He was at work on a new report. It would take him a year, he told me, and it would be his last. The topic was "intergenerational trauma," a term he had heard before but that he had never given much thought.

In the 1980s, a Lakota sociologist, Maria Yellow Horse Brave Heart, had developed a theory of "historical unresolved grief." She believed that the depression, suicide, addiction, and child and domestic abuse in Native American communities could be traced to periods of trauma: first to genocide, to disease and alcoholism upon contact with white immigrants; then to subjugation by the government, when Indigenous people were confined to reservations and forced into dependency on their oppressors; then boarding schools, which broke apart families, and where children were beaten for speaking their language and in many cases raped; and, at last, relocation, when people left their reservations for cities, where they were treated as second-class citizens, and some abandoned their culture altogether.

In the years since Brave Heart published her theory, many sociologists, as well as geneticists, had supported similar hypotheses through other methods. In 1998, the Centers for Disease Control and Prevention and Kaiser Permanente published an Adverse Childhood

Experiences Study, which found that people who experienced more stress as children were at higher risk of developing depression, diabetes, and addiction, and of experiencing intimate partner violence and suicide. Scientists were beginning to understand why this might be. In the burgeoning field of epigenetics, studies had shown that trauma and stress cause the body to produce hormones that alter the way our genes are expressed, turning these genes on or off, and that changes to our DNA might be passed from generation to generation.

"I never paid much attention before," Ed told me. "But I can kind of see it. Why do we take advantage of our own people for money? We have a word for that in Hidatsa: '*Gírashaaci.*' *You're pitiful. You're poor.* Before we had dollar bills, *gírashaaci* meant you're poor because you've lost your culture. How did that historical trauma make us forget our cultural values?"

Many people on the reservation told me they considered the oil boom another layer in their tribe's traumatic history. Years from now, they said, their children would talk about the boom just as their elders talked about the flood.

"It created pain, but it reactivated a lot of it, too," Nathan Sanchez, the tribal officer, said when I visited him another day that spring. He had quit the police force not long after I rode along with him. One call he responded to haunted him in particular: A family of tribal members he knew collided with an oil truck, and all of them died. After the accident, Sanchez had not been able to touch his own son; when he looked at the boy, he saw the face of a dead child. "I started having these anxiety attacks, these weird dreams and thoughts," he told me. He quit and took a job dispatching trucks for Tesha Fredericks, the same woman for whom KC intended to work when he left Blackstone. Fredericks often pleaded with Sanchez for information regarding KC, but he had none. "It was a relief to get away from being a cop for a while," he told me. "But I still knew. I drive these highways, and I remember that accident or that house where someone was murdered or raped. It always comes back. I guess for a guy driving to work, that's just a fence post, but to me, that's where so-and-so died. People don't realize how much death and suffering this oil brought."

Now Sanchez worked at the juvenile detention center in New Town. He was happier in this job. He played basketball with the kids every day, and they had planted a garden behind the jail. "One kid's growing tomatoes. We have potatoes, carrots, melons. This place has given me an opportunity to reach out to these youngsters in a way that I never could when I was a cop. Being a police officer is depressing, because you're always too late. Here, after the time I spend with these kids, most of them straighten up."

It was a warm day. I had told Madeleine I would visit, so I left Sanchez and drove to White Shield, stopping on my way at the Arikara Cultural Center. The building was cool and quiet inside. I wandered the outer edge of the main room and came to an alcove, where a hand-drawn map of Nishu had been tacked to the wall. The houses were marked with the names of their former inhabitants—Clair Everett, Charles Yellow Bird, Nellie Red Fox, Benjamin Young Bird—and noted along the banks of the Missouri were forests Madeleine had told me about: cottonwoods tangled with grape vines; Juneberries, chokecherries, and plum trees; and, closer to the riverbank, diamond willow and sweet clover.

A man appeared beside me. A school group would soon arrive for a language lesson, he said, but he wanted to show me something first. I followed him into a room furnished with a table, a wool blanket, and a shelf draped in a shroud. Beneath the shroud was an Arikara bundle, the man said. The keeper of the bundle had put it there, since he was doing renovations on his house. Now people came all the time to pray. The man had seen tribal police officers in the room, as well as elders, and, in the summertime, the tribe paid thirty local youths to work in their community. The man, who helped run the program, brought his workers to pray as well. "They pray those troubles into the bundle," he said, "and the bundle takes those troubles away."

. . . . .

I ACCOMPANIED LISSA AND CJ to a Yellow Bird reunion one summer. We left Fargo before midnight. Lissa pushed an Evanescence album into the stereo, and for an hour we just listened to the music until she asked if I would drive. By the time I pulled back onto the road, Lissa had fallen asleep.

The highway was empty, the moon set, the stars shining through the halo of our headlights. I wanted to change the music, but I was tired and afraid to take my eyes from the road. Near Garrison, I stopped the car and shook CJ awake, and slept as he drove the rest of the way. I woke when we turned onto the dirt track that led to Madeleine's house. Lissa was still asleep in the passenger seat, the album thrumming on repeat. The windows of the house were dark, as were the windows of campers scattered throughout the yard. "Grandma's man camp," CJ joked. I pitched our tent facing east, but a pole was broken and in the end I gave up, wrapped myself in the mesh, and tried to sleep.

I woke at dawn to the song of cicadas and birds. The air felt heavy, and the wind had picked up, flipping the cottonwood leaves onto their silvery backs. CJ and a cousin were shooting pellet guns from the porch. I went inside and found Lissa rifling through a kitchen cupboard. "Where do you diabetics keep your sugar?" she called into the living room. Madeleine was asleep in a chair, the television volume turned up high, but Cheryl was awake, sewing ribbons onto a pow-wow dress for her great-granddaughter.

"Say, is she dancing already?" Lissa said.

"You can't keep her off the floor," Cheryl replied.

We drank our coffee on the porch as the sun rose high and hot. Lissa's uncles sat with their legs spread, their arms limp at their sides. Michael was talking about climate change, but it was hard to say if anyone was listening, and soon he changed the subject.

He had been reading about a Mandan man named Good Bird who had lived in Like-a-Fishhook, the village the three tribes occupied together before federal agents forced them out. "This man Good Bird talks about the difference between white and Indian policing,"

Michael said. "When he was an eighteen-year-old boy, he tells his father, 'Hey, the white Indian agent wants me to be a policeman.' His dad said, 'What did you say?' 'I said, "I can't be a policeman. I'm way too young."' The difference was, the Mandan didn't hire young people to do the policing. Same thing for the Arikara. The police were older men who had achieved certain things in life. And it wasn't just police. It wasn't just the chief. The chief deferred to spiritual leaders. Men's societies. Women's societies. You had all these systems in place for balance."

"Balance of power," said a cousin.

"Sovereignty," said another.

Lissa had been listening quietly. Now she said, "You know what Tex's new phrase should be?" She was thinking of his marijuana business and paused for effect: "Sovereignty by the kilo."

"Ayyyee," said Michael. "Tex Hall Kush."

In the midafternoon, we gathered beneath an awning. Irene, in tinted glasses and a floral shirt, stood with a microphone. She spoke with dry confidence, listing the family's latest accomplishments, not excluding her daughter's. She liked to tease Lissa while everyone was listening. "Am I missing or am I dead?" she would say. "Because my daughter has finally arrived!"

Irene had been calling Lissa a lot lately, wondering when she would visit next. Now and then, Lissa arrived home to her apartment in Fargo to a package from her mother: Two sticks of lip balm—"One for your purse, one for your car," a note instructed; a sweatshirt that read PRINCESS. While other relatives expressed surprise that Lissa had been "right about all those people," Irene denied ever disbelieving her daughter and seemed to be making a more obvious effort to take her side. Recently, Irene had seen Tex at a funeral. "He came over and gave me a hug and little kiss," she would tell me. "I said, 'You know, if Wayne was alive, you would have never got in all this trouble. He would have been right there saying, 'Don't do that.' He would have protected you.'" Tex had smiled. "I said, 'Now you behave.'"

Others took turns at the microphone. They cursed the oil industry, extolled the virtues of education, told stories that made their relatives laugh. Then a small woman stood. She began in Arikara and turned to English. "I want to pray because there's been a lot of loss in this family," she said. "We all experienced pain. It's going to take some time, because when you go through loss and suffering, you have to allow that time to let go and just let God's spirit and power come in, fix you and make you whole. Do you know that there is no blood in heaven? There's only light. Some of you may have dreams, visions. Some of you may have the experience of encountering that light. And when you come into that light, you begin to get your strength back, your healing, your understanding of your purpose. On this reservation, we have a lot to overcome, and we will overcome it. The atrocities, the injustice, all of the things that we feel that the government has taken from us."

I glanced at Lissa. Her shoulders were bare, turning pink in the sun.

"Creator, God," the small woman prayed. "Through all the trauma, through all the pain, through all the suffering that we experience, the wounding of our spirit, you are the one that can bring healing. I pray right now that you will start with these little babies, touch these children, protect them, keep them, nurture them, help them to grow up to be strong, O God, and not have the effects of the trauma, the things that we had to go through in our lives that caused us, O God, to do things that aren't pleasing in your sight. Forgive us, because we didn't know the damage that caused our spirit to be broken. Lord, I pray that you will heal that emptiness. You blessed us with resources. Let us not be foolish and waste them. And Lord, pray for our leaders. Pray for them, Father. We ask that you give them wisdom and understanding, Lord God. Don't let the enemy mislead and guide them and direct them on a path that's selfish, but like our great leaders, help our people overcome all our addictions and our pains, to bring the healing of our trauma and all of the things that caused the brokenness of our spirit, Lord God. Mend and heal our spirit, O God. Renew and strengthen our mind, body, and soul, so that we can be a blessing to one another and our families."

Her voice rose above the shouts of children on the trampoline, above the singing of girls inside the house, above the pop cans hissing open and forks scraping styrofoam plates, above the cries of babies bouncing on fathers' laps and the whine of dogs at their feet.

Only Madeleine was entirely still. She sat at a table in the middle of it all, her eyes closed, her feet pressed together, her head rested on fisted hands.

I TURNED TO LISSA AGAIN, but she had gone. In the distance, I could see her climbing steps to her grandmother's house. I followed and found her in the kitchen fixing a plate of food. She was going with some cousins to the cemetery to leave offerings on the family graves.

We rode together out the long, dirt drive and south toward the lake.

Lissa was thinking of Chucky again. The night before he died, he had reminded her of the time she had forgiven her mother—before KC disappeared, after Lissa went on the road trip to Idaho with Percy, where they had visited Percy's mother. On her way home from Idaho, Lissa had stopped at the farmhouse in White Shield and found Madeleine, Chucky, and Irene seated in the living room. She forced her mother into a tight hug. *Mom, I want you to know that everything I held against you, I forgive you for that,* she had said, and when she let go, Irene had run into the kitchen—embarrassed, Lissa thought.

But that was not what mattered, Chucky said.

"He told me, 'I watched your mom's face, but more important, I watched your grandma's face. I could see something go over her that was healing for her, too.' He told me, 'Everyone always said I was the smartest Yellow Bird, but it was actually you. You found peace with all that trauma.'"

The lake stretched so far ahead of us that it might have been an ocean.

This was her burden: to bring up their bodies, to let go their spirits, to bury their bones, again.

violence + addiction

navigates two worlds
  — her own tribe
     changed by wealth
     and oilmen

economic recession

systematic violence
  inflicted on a
  tribal nation

extrodinary healing

Author's Note

In the fall of 2010, I left the coalfields of Virginia where I had been living for a little over a year. The county where I lived was in a final phase of extraction. A third of the land had been stripped of trees and topsoil as companies scratched away at what coal remained. Even industry men told me that in twenty years the coal would be gone. I had witnessed the very end of a boom-and-bust cycle, and so, when I arrived on the Fort Berthold Indian Reservation the following spring, I understood immediately what I was seeing: the beginning.

As I returned to the reservation over the years to report for *High Country News* and then for other magazines, it became clear to me that the oil boom within the reservation borders was different from other booms. The MHA Nation is a sovereign entity with rights to govern like those of a state and its own laws and regulations determining how outside interests gain access to its resources. It is also, as federal case law puts it, a "domestic dependent nation." The tribe's dependency on the United States has been manufactured and reinforced by more than a century of federal policies designed to undermine the sovereignty of tribes and assimilate their citizens into European American society. While in recent decades the federal government has given back to tribes some rights it took, it is this legacy of paternalism that left the MHA Nation uniquely vulnerable to exploitation throughout the boom. It is no coincidence, perhaps, that the ways in which the tribe suffered most—the sale of its leases at rates below market value, the surge in crime due to an influx of drugs and perpetrators over whom the tribe had no jurisdiction, and vast ecological devastation—were the province of federal authorities.

For all the ways the reservation was unique, I also saw it as a microcosm of America—a place to which people starved of opportunity would flock, and a place where I could observe the machinations of industry: how it secured access to land; how it sought and fostered insiders; and how it widened divisions within the community between those who had and those who had not.

These were the conditions in which James Henrikson gained access to Fort Berthold, and when I first read of his alleged crimes in February 2014, ten months before I met Lissa, I saw his story—and Kristopher Clarke's story—as inextricable from the story of the reservation.

That October, I returned to Fort Berthold intending to write an article about the tribal election. I was interested in how Clarke's murder and the ensuing revelations about Tex Hall's link to Henrikson had cost Hall his political career and emboldened a growing number of tribal members to speak out against the oil industry. But when I met Lissa the evening of the election, my sense of the story shifted. Here was a woman who had known the story—or at least suspected it—long before others chose to believe it. As with Henrikson's crimes, the revelations regarding Hall had not risen out of nothing. Lissa had spent years trying to convince even her fellow tribal members that Henrikson murdered Clarke. Until Doug Carlile was killed, she said, "nobody believed me."

Even after Henrikson went to trial—when it was irrefutable what he had done—people would remark to Lissa and me how "unbelievable" the story was. It certainly was unusual. None of the prosecutors or investigators I spoke to could think of another

serial-hirer-of-murder who had acted outside a criminal organization. But I wondered if the believability of a story had less to do with
the rarity of its details than with the way a story is told. In the years
that I worked on this book, the murders earned many takes, including on several television crime shows. In each episode, the reservation was a side note—at most, a plot device. But what was the story
of the murders without the story of the reservation? It became sensational, and sensational was not how Lissa saw it. In choosing to
make this book about Lissa, I chose to tell the story of the murders
in the way she first saw them and believed them to be true—that is,
amid their historical context, the valuing of wealth over Indigenous
lives and over life in general. Henrikson's violence, Lissa believed,
was not so uncommon as most would think. His was the violence of
America.

I RELIED MOST HEAVILY ON three types of source material in the making
of *Yellow Bird:* Public records I acquired through databases and
requests, including the video and audio recordings of the interviews
law enforcement conducted while investigating the murders of Clarke
and Carlile; Lissa's extensive email, Facebook, and text message
record, as well as photographs and audio recordings she took to document her search for Clarke; and my interviews with Lissa and more
than two hundred other sources, among them tribal members, case
witnesses, investigators, and prosecutors, as well as acquaintances
from Lissa's past and members of her family. Neither James Henrikson nor Sarah Creveling replied to my interview requests. I did meet
Jill Williams, who was not interested in speaking with me, and so I
relied on the messages she exchanged with Lissa to piece together her
sections. After my interview with Tex Hall in November 2014, he
did not respond to my requests for additional interviews. I also was
unable to interview Darrik Trudell due to a Department of Homeland Security policy that would have required me to show the whole
manuscript to the agency and allow it to issue redactions. Through

interviews with his colleagues in the Department of Justice, FBI, and North Dakota Bureau of Criminal Investigations, and with public records and Lissa's own documentation, I was able to reconstruct his role in the story.

To write about the history and contemporary politics of the Mandan, Hidatsa, and Arikara Nation, I consulted a variety of works whose authors and creators I acknowledge at the end of this note, among them Angela Parker, a member of the MHA Nation whose dissertation helped me immensely in understanding the politics of the reservation. I am deeply indebted to Marilyn Hudson, Ed Hall, and Theodora and Joletta Bird Bear—thorough, careful chroniclers of their tribe's history—whose documents and memories also proved essential to my grasp of tribal politics following the flood. And I was extraordinarily lucky to encounter so much historical knowledge among the Yellow Birds, not only from Madeleine and Irene, but also from Lissa's uncle Loren, a historian for the National Park Service, and her "dad," Michael, a university professor whose writings on decolonization I found tremendously helpful to my own thinking.

All of the dialogue in this book I took directly from interviews, audio and video files, and correspondence Lissa shared with me, which I edited for concision and clarity. Lissa provided audio recordings of several scenes for which I was not present—among them, her visit with KC's grandfather in Oregon—and when I had no audio or video on which to base my reconstruction, I spoke to others who had been present and wrote the scene from their collaborative memories. To re-create Lissa's visit to Judd Parker, for example, I asked them both about the visit separately and found their memories remarkably similar: Lissa told me Judd shared a story about watching a man die in a truck accident; Judd confirmed he told Lissa this story; and then Judd told me the same story in the manner he originally shared it with Lissa. If a person did not remember a scene another shared with me, or the person remembered it differently, I indicated their disagreement in the book. Several times—most notably in scenes with Chucky—the other person present was unavailable or deceased by

Lissa searches for KC in Mandaree, summer 2015. *Photograph by Kalen Goodluck*

the time Lissa told me the story. In those cases, the person's quotes came directly from Lissa or whomever else recalled the scene.

One of the advantages of spending years immersed in another person's life is that you see the patterns of her memory. I have spent enough time with Lissa, now, that I frequently hear her recalling for other people certain events for which I was also present. If my own memory is accurate, then hers rarely has seemed wrong or inventive, but I find it interesting to hear which details rise to the top for her and what meaning she draws from them. Her mind, I have learned, is a trap for visual detail—attuned, in particular, to the absurd. Lissa also has an uncanny knack for dialogue; often she would recall a conversation from years earlier, and later, as I sorted her text messages, I would find this conversation nearly verbatim. Her memory is perhaps most unreliable when it comes to time. Lissa often mixed up the order of events or could not recall the specific year in which something had happened. Thankfully, the records she shared with me were extensive and her digital life so active that I was able to build a detailed timeline. I knew exactly when she and Percy mailed the flyers, for example, or when she went to the sweat lodge.

I spent a lot of time retracing her steps. I saw the Ferris wheel in Seattle; the courthouse in Bend; the property in Sweet Home where Robert Clarke's trailer once stood. I located the priest she had known in prison, as well as the proprietor of the Portland lingerie modeling shop who had not spoken to Lissa in twenty years and still knew her only as Nadia Reinardy. I went to the laundry where she had worked in Fargo, and the welding shop. One weekend, she showed me the places in the Twin Cities where she had lived. She insisted I meet OJ.

She shared far more with me than I put in this book. I was overwhelmed by the quantity of material, by the task of deciding what to leave out. It took years to understand which details, quotes, and anecdotes felt necessary and representative. I listened for clues: What stories made Lissa laugh and cry? What stories made her shake with indignation? What stories did she tell so many times that eventually I could recite them myself? While I had some sense of what the book was about from my own reporting on the reservation, it was during the time I spent with Lissa that the themes naturally emerged. Intergenerational trauma was not something I asked her to discuss. It was something she and her relatives brought up again and again until I realized its place in her story.

BY NOW, I HAVE SPENT eight years returning to North Dakota, more time than I have spent in my adult life returning to anywhere else. It was my familiarity with the place and people there that allowed me to see the potential of this story as it emerged—the threads connecting one person I knew to another, the political and ecological landscape whose patterns of change I had already observed—but I was not without limitations when I wrote this book. My primary limitation was that I am white. I was writing about, and often from the perspective of, a woman who is a citizen of both a tribal nation and the United States, who identifies as Arikara, and whose dual citizenship and cultural and racial identity have been defining features of her life.

A question hovered over me as I wrote: What right did I have to tell Lissa's story? When I brought this question to Lissa, she dismissed it. As you know by now, she does not have much patience for hand-wringing. She lives to cross boundaries, to defy categorization. She had given me permission to write this book, and so she figured I should go ahead and write it.

I did, but still I worried. Could I actually capture the way she thought and felt? Would my biases cloud or falsify her truth? Was I applying my own frame to her story? Had I listened to her closely enough?

I thought about these things every day I sat to write. I spoke about them, too—to friends and colleagues, to Lissa and her relatives. I heard a range of opinions. On one side, I was told not to worry about my whiteness and to go ahead and tell the story exactly how I wanted to tell it. On the other, I was warned it was not my place to be writing this story at all. An uncle of Lissa's admitted to me in an interview that he had no interest in reading a book about Native Americans written by a non-Native person. I thought to myself, *Fair enough*. Certainly, the first writers *I* turn to—whom I trust to tell the truth about Indian Country—are Native, and among them are many of the best American writers to emerge in the past fifty years. But there is also a legacy of white writers defining the way most people think—or don't think—about Indigenous people. I know this legacy has done enormous damage to our country by allowing our governments to justify or conceal acts of genocide and leading so many people to believe that Native Americans no longer exist, rendering modern tribal nations and their citizens invisible.

The danger of writing a book about someone with a cultural and political background that most people know nothing about is that a reader might begin to think they understand everything about that kind of person because they read the book. The book fills a void that should have been filled by public school curriculum. A reader who has never met a Native American might believe that every woman of that identity is like Lissa, when in reality, Lissa, whose experiences indeed are common, is the most iconoclastic person I know.

The question of who has the right to tell whose story became a subject of impassioned conversation among writers and other artists around the time that I was working on this book. In 2017, in an address to the American Academy of Arts and Letters, Joyce Carol Oates argued for "more, not less trespassing." "Perhaps it's a worthier challenge to tell the stories of others," she said, "with as much care as if they were our own." Artists, she added, should not "be surprised when they do provoke hostile reactions. This is the price we pay for our commitment to bearing witness in a turbulent America." Meanwhile, in his column for the *New York Times Magazine*, Teju Cole challenged the argument that "we have a responsibility to tell one another's stories and must be free to do so." This thinking is "seductive but flawed," he wrote. "The responsibility toward other people's stories is real and inescapable, but that doesn't mean that appropriation is the way to satisfy that responsibility. . . . It is not about taking something that belongs to someone else and making it serve you but rather about recognizing that history is brutal and unfinished and finding some way, within that recognition, to serve the dispossessed."

While I admit these discussions gave me considerable anxiety, I am grateful for them in that they led me to have honest conversations with Lissa and her relatives about my role in their lives and in the story I had chosen to tell. From these conversations, I made two decisions. First, I involved Lissa in my process to a degree that some journalists would consider a liability but in my case proved essential. After I wrote several drafts, I brought the book to Lissa, and we read it together from beginning to end. Although we had talked about how I was approaching the story, I believe this was the first time Lissa fully understood my intentions. Not only did she correct my errors, but she helped me see the book's weaknesses and encouraged me to not withhold difficult material but go deeper. I repeated this process with Shauna, Irene, and Madeleine, reading parts aloud to them, and in this way, they all helped me get closer to the truth.

The second decision I made was to put myself in the book. I did this for several reasons. I wanted to be clear who was telling this story—who heard it, interpreted it, chose which details to leave in or out—and convey to readers my limitations as a narrator. Writing from the first person also allowed me to let people talk instead of constantly having to paraphrase their thoughts or fit their quotes into a particular scene. But perhaps most important, it felt honest. Not long after I met Lissa, it occurred to me that she conscripts the people around her into her story, that I could not separate myself from her, and that in the years we would spend together, she would influence my life and I, hers. I wrote *Yellow Bird* at the collision point of two communities— one Native, the other not. As a white writer drawn into the fray, I was a part of that story. "The real fantasy," Zadie Smith has written, "is that we can get out of one another's way, make a clean cut between black and white, a final cathartic separation between us and them. . . . There is no getting out of our intertwined history."

I wrote that "I don't know why Lissa trusted me, and I don't think she knows either." We remember differently how this project began. I remember sitting in her kitchen, my second time visiting Fargo, and asking how she would feel if I made the story about her. She did not answer me then. She remembers walking in the badlands some weeks later when I asked if I could write the book. I was chasing behind her, trying to keep up. She turned and said, "I'll think about it."

What we both remember is how this trust grew over a long period of time. In some ways, our relationship was traditionally journalistic. We signed no contracts, exchanged no money in the course of my reporting besides the gas and meals I bought now and then and the bit of cash I once sent her when she was broke. In the thousands of hours we spent together and the hundreds more on the phone, I either held my notebook or kept my recorder running. But in all this time, it also was inevitable that we drew close—not just as friends, but as something more intimate and specific: a woman who decided to tell another woman everything about herself.

Being white was not my only limitation as I wrote this book. I am a daughter but not yet a mother. I am a woman, but I have not lived as long as Lissa has, nor have I survived as much as she has survived. There were many things I did not understand when I began, but that is the job of a journalist—to ask about what you don't yet know, and then to listen. So I listened to Lissa, to her children, to her mother, grandmother, and uncles, and to everyone else whose stories make up this book. Do I understand their lives in all their complexity? I doubt it. But I understand more than I did eight years ago, and I have done my best to render this story in a way that I hope feels true and meaningful to the people who shared it with me.

May 21, 2019

Works Consulted

BOOKS

Briody, Blaire. *The New Wild West: Black Gold, Fracking, and Life in a North Dakota Boomtown.*

Cash, Joseph, and Gerald Wolff. *The Three Affiliated Tribes, Mandan, Arikara, and Hidatsa.*

Deloria, Jr., Vine. *Custer Died For Your Sins.*

Deloria, Jr., Vine, and David E. Wilkins. *Tribes, Treaties, & Constitutional Tribulations.*

Grann, David. *Killers of the Flower Moon.*

Lawson, Michael. *Dammed Indians: The Pick-Sloan Plan and the Missouri River Sioux.*

Meyer, Roy. *The Village Indians of the Upper Missouri.*

Parks, Douglas. *Myths and Traditions of the Arikara Indians.*

St. Jean, Wendy. *Remaining Chickasaw in Indian Territory, 1830s–1907.*

VanDevelder, Paul. *Coyote Warrior: One Man, Three Tribes, and the Trial That Forged a Nation.*

Waziyatawin and Michael Yellow Bird. *For Indigenous Minds Only: A Decolonization Handbook.*

Wilkins, David E. *Documents of Native American Political Development: 1933 to Present.*

Yarbrough, Fay. *Race and the Cherokee Nation: Sovereignty in the Nineteenth Century.*

ARTICLES, PAPERS, PRESENTATIONS, & THESES

Ahtone, Tristan. "Aiming for a Higher Ground: The American Indian Movement Hopes to Rise Again, but a New Leader Needs to Shake Gang Ties." *Aljazeera America,* January 21, 2015.

Birger, Jon. "EOG's big gamble on shale oil." *Fortune Magazine,* July 29, 2011.

Gilmore, Melvin R. Selected papers, Bentley Historical Library, University of Michigan.

Hill, Kip. "South Hill shooting took place in kitchen." *Spokesman-Review,* December 18, 2013.

———. "Man arrested in South Hill homicide of Douglas Carlile." *Spokesman-Review,* January 14, 2014.

———. "Ruling on false testimony from Henrikson witness won't be admitted, judge rules." *Spokesman-Review,* February 19, 2016.

Holdman, Jessica. "Former tribal chairman joins marijuana company." *Bismarck Tribune,* May 29, 2015.

Horwitz, Sari. "Dark side of the boom." *Washington Post,* September 28, 2014.

Johnson, Michael S. "Story of the Discovery of Parshall Field, North Dakota." *Houston Geological Society Bulletin* 54:5 (2012): 19–27.

Krakoff, Sarah. "Mark the Plumber v. Tribal Empire, or Non-Indian Anxiety v. Tribal Sovereignty?: The Story of Oliphant v. Suquamish Indian Tribe," in *Indian Law Stories,* ed. Carole Goldberg and

Philip Frickey. New York: Thomson Reuters/Foundation Press, 2011.

Parker, Angela. "Taken Lands: Territory and Sovereignty on the Fort Berthold Indian Reservation, 1934–1960." 2011, The University of Michigan, PhD dissertation.

Thompson, Jonathan. "The Ute Paradox: A small Colorado tribe takes control of its energy resources and becomes a billion-dollar corporation—but has it gone too far?" *High Country News,* July 12, 2010.

Yellow Bird, Loren. "'Health Care': Spiritual and Scientific." *Shamanism* 14:1 (2001): 25–27.

Yellow Bird, Loren. "Now I Will Speak (Nawah Ti Waako'): A Sahnish Perspective on What the Lewis and Clark Expedition and Others Missed." *Wicazo Sa Review,* University of Minnesota Press 19:1 (2004): 73–84.

Yellow Bird, Michael. "Neurodecolonization: Applying Mindfulness Research to Decolonizing Social Work," in *Decolonizing Social Work,* ed. Mel Gray, John Coates, Michael Yellow Bird, and Tiani Hetherington. Burlington, VT: Ashgate Publishing, 2013.

Yellow Bird, Michael. "Decolonizing the Mind: Healing Through Neurodecolonization and Mindfulness," Portland State University, Indigenous Nations Studies and School of Social Work, in Portland, Oregon. January 24, 2014.

FILM & MULTIMEDIA

Melby, Todd. "Oil to Die For," in *Black Gold Boom: How Oil Changed North Dakota.*

Peinado, J. Carlos. *Waterbuster.*

Shannon, Jen, and Lex White-Mobley. *My Cry Gets Up to My Throat: Reflections on Reverend Case, the Garrison Dam, and the Oil Boom of North Dakota.*

Acknowledgments

I am extraordinarily lucky to have found an editor as clear-eyed, patient, and passionate about this book as Annie Chagnot. I am equally lucky to have been found by Kent Wolf, who understood my hopes immediately, and who has the miraculous ability to dissolve all my worries with his humor. I am grateful, as well, to Chris Jackson, Julie Grau, and Cindy Spiegel, for believing in this project from the beginning, and to Andy Ward, for shepherding it through at the end. Lucy Carson, Molly Friedrich, and Will Watkins also gave their invaluable support.

Jonathan Thompson offered me the seed of an idea nine years ago. Sarah Gilman trusted me with my first feature, lent me her editing scalpel and then her friendship, and never appeared to tire of hearing about this story. Paul Reyes assigned and edited the essay that made this book possible. Cally Carswell, Kate Julian, Jennie Rothenberg-Gritz, and Anthony Lydgate kindly assigned the stories through which I gained much of my material for this book.

I am thankful to Bill McKibben, for believing in me now for fifteen years and for making so much possible; to Chris Shaw, for believing in me for almost as long and for answering my every email with compassionate reassurance and advice; to John Elder, for his thoughtful interest and generous engagement with the book when I needed it most; to Ted Conover, for inspiring me with his brave, humble approach to reporting and for his support; and to Rob Cohen, for his honest critique back when I *really* had no idea what I was doing, and later for his encouragement.

Tristan Ahtone carefully read the manuscript, offering his critical guidance at a critical time.

This book would not have been possible without the support of the Investigative Reporting Program at the University of California, Berkeley, which funded the majority of my reporting, and, in particular, Tim McGirk, Lowell Bergman, and Janice Hui. I am also grateful to the MacDowell Colony, which endowed me with writing space and dear friends, as well as a Calderwood grant and a Sylvia Canfield Winn Fellowship.

Parker Yesko provided me with crucial research assistance in the early stages of this project. I would be remiss to not acknowledge Mardee Ellis and Michael Snell, the most helpful public records specialists I've ever had the pleasure of working with, and Larry Griffin, who quit journalism years ago but went digging through his hard drive to unearth for me an essential document.

Thank you, Angela Evancie and Kevin Redmon, my "writers without editors," for your intellectual companionship, and for helping me find the right words. And Lauren Markham, our conversations and your keen advice gave this book form. I am lucky to have you as a model, a collaborator, and a friend.

I am indebted to my armada of readers, many of whom I've already mentioned, and also among them Olivette Orme, Meg McClellan, Zoe Sheldon, Brendan Borrell, and Emily Guerin. Chuck Hudson's insights during my reporting and writing proved essential. Marilyn Hudson, one of the first people I met on the reservation, generously gave me a place to stay, which became my home away from home. Kandi Mossett offered me advice in the very beginning. Cheryl Abe made me feel especially welcome. Susan Poisson-Dollar and Beth Baugh made sure I had a place to work, while the Orme family provided countless meals and a comfortable bed after my long days mired in public records. Cody Upton and Francesca Coppola hosted me and inspired me when I came to New York.

I feel a tremendous amount of love for all my friends and relatives who shared in my excitement, bore with me all these years, and gave shape to my own life. Thank you, Corinne, for your steady adventurousness; Maureen, for being my other mom; the Sylvesters, for supporting me in so many ways and celebrating each tiny bit of progress. Mom and Dad, your bottomless love and confidence in me is what brought me here and keeps me going. Win, you may be my little brother, but I learn so much from you. And Terray, thank you for being my patient companion all along, for guiding me, distracting me, and loving me.

I am grateful to the woman who introduced me to Lissa, and to the hundreds of others who spoke with me over the years, many of whom I don't mention. Among them are Loren Whitehorn, RJ Smith, and Dwight Sage; each died not long after I met them, but their honesty, gentleness, and conviction influenced me greatly. I am grateful, also, to Elise Packineau, whose prayer helps close this book.

Most of all, I am thankful to Lissa and her family, the Yellow Birds, for their trust, eloquence, humor, and radical generosity. Nothing has prepared me better for this world than the time I have spent in their wise and loving company.

SIERRA CRANE MURDOCH, a journalist based in the American West, has written for *Harper's*, *This American Life*, *The Atlantic*, *The New Yorker* online, *VQR*, and *High Country News*. She has held fellowships from Middlebury College and from the Investigative Reporting Program at the University of California, Berkeley. She is a MacDowell Fellow.

About the Type

This book was set in Baskerville, a typeface designed by John Baskerville (1706–75), an amateur printer and type-founder, and cut for him by John Handy in 1750. The type became popular again when the Lanston Monotype Corporation of London revived the classic roman face in 1923. The Mergenthaler Linotype Company in England and the United States cut a version of Baskerville in 1931, making it one of the most widely used typefaces today.